THE RELIGIOUS JOURNEY OF DWIGHT D. EISENHOWER

LIBRARY OF RELIGIOUS BIOGRAPHY

Mark A. Noll, Kathryn Gin Lum, and Heath W. Carter, series editors

Long overlooked by historians, religion has emerged in recent years as a key factor in understanding the past. From politics to popular culture, from social struggles to the rhythms of family life, religion shapes every story. Religious biographies open a window to the sometimes surprising influence of religion on the lives of influential people and the worlds they inhabited.

The Library of Religious Biography is a series that brings to life important figures in United States history and beyond. Grounded in careful research, these volumes link the lives of their subjects to the broader cultural contexts and religious issues that surrounded them. The authors are respected historians and recognized authorities in the historical period in which their subject lived and worked.

Marked by careful scholarship yet free of academic jargon, the books in this series are well-written narratives meant to be read and enjoyed as well as studied.

Titles include:

Duty and Destiny: The Life and Faith of **Winston Churchill**
by Gary Scott Smith

God's Cold Warrior: The Life and Faith of **John Foster Dulles**
by John D. Wilsey

One Soul at a Time: The Story of **Billy Graham**
by Grant Wacker

A Christian and a Democrat: A Religious Life of **Franklin D. Roosevelt**
by John F. Woolverton with James D. Bratt

The Religious Life of **Robert E. Lee**
by R. David Cox

For a complete list of published volumes, see the back of this volume.

THE RELIGIOUS JOURNEY
OF DWIGHT D. EISENHOWER

Duty, God, and Country

Jack M. Holl

WILLIAM B. EERDMANS PUBLISHING COMPANY
GRAND RAPIDS, MICHIGAN

Wm. B. Eerdmans Publishing Co.
4035 Park East Court SE, Grand Rapids, Michigan 49546
www.eerdmans.com

27 26 25 24 23 22 21   1 2 3 4 5 6 7

ISBN 978-0-8028-7873-1

Library of Congress Cataloging-in-Publication Data

Names: Holl, Jack M., author.
Title: The religious journey of Dwight D. Eisenhower : duty, God, and country
  / Jack M. Holl.
Description: Grand Rapids, Michigan : William B. Eerdmans Publishing Com-
  pany, 2021. | Series: Library of religious biography | Includes bibliographical
  references and index. | Summary: "A narrative history of Dwight D. Eisen-
  hower's faith that shows the impact of his religious convictions on his public
  life and his legacy of American civil religion"—Provided by publisher.
Identifiers: LCCN 2021003718 | ISBN 9780802878731 (hardcover)
Subjects: LCSH: Eisenhower, Dwight D. (Dwight David), 1890–1969—
  Religion. | Presidents—Religious life—United States.
Classification: LCC E836 .H63 2021 | DDC 973.921092 [B]—dc23
LC record available at https://lccn.loc.gov/2021003718

In memoriam

Dr. Richard G. Hewlett, chief historian of the US Atomic Energy Commission
mentor, 1974–1980

Professor David Brion Davis, Cornell University
PhD advisor, 1961–1969

Professor John J. Nolde, University of Maine
MA advisor, 1959–1961

Professor Walter C. Schnackenberg, Pacific Lutheran University
history major advisor, 1955–1959

Contents

Acknowledgments

First, I want to thank the editors and staff of Wm. B. Eerdmans Publishing Co., who provided insight and creativity that enhanced this project: David Bratt, executive editor, particularly for his work with series editor Heath W. Carter; Jenny Hoffman, senior project editor; Tom Raabe, copyeditor; Meg Schmidt, cover designer; Laura Bardolph Hubers, director of marketing and publicity; and Amy Kent, acquisitions administrator. The editors and staff at Eerdmans have not only been encouraging, but they have also been delightfully engaging throughout the editorial and production process.

In addition, I want to acknowledge the generous assistance of the archivists and staff of the Dwight D. Eisenhower Presidential Library in Abilene, Kansas. James Leyerzapf became my archivist in 1975 and expertly guided me through the library's resources until 2009. David Haight and Thomas Branigar also offered their incredible expertise. Subsequently, Keith Bailey, Christopher Abraham, Valoise Armstrong, Chelsea Millner, Linda Smith, and Mary Burtzloff ably assisted my research.

Dan Holt, former director of the Eisenhower Library, offered me invaluable insights, advice, editorial criticism, and friendship.

With Holt's support and Leyerzapf's and Haight's professional critiques, the Kansas State University Eisenhower Seminar met yearly at the Library to make public presentations of their research papers. Among the students in the seminar whose research contributed to this book were Keith Bates, Alan Bearman, Brian Jones, Glenn Leppert, and Leif Urseth.

Philip Cantelon and Robert Williams, in one way or another, have been involved in every book I have published. How do you thank faithful friends and inspiring colleagues for a half century of their criticism and red ink? Also, I want to acknowledge the excellent advice offered by two professors from Gettysburg College, Michael Birkner and Norman Forness. Several other scholars extended personal assistance in developing themes and analysis. They were Charles A. Appleby Jr., Stephen Ambrose, Jerry Bergman, Carlo D'Este, Charles J. G. Griffin, Merlin Gustufson, Martin Medhurst, David A. Nichols, Martin Ottenheimer, Geoffrey Perret, and William B. Pickett. Carl Skooglund helped me select the title.

Editors are essential to successful writing. In addition to the marvelous editors at Eerdmans, I would like to thank five editors who have played an important role in pushing this project to completion: Mike Briggs, Steven Mintz, Mark Rozell, John Stauffer, and Gleaves Whitney.

Six pastors have also taken special interest in my book by providing theological insight. They are Earl Eliason, Darrel Gilbertson, Julie Kanarr, Jon Lee, Martin Marty, and Keith Swenson.

Finally, this book became something of a family project. For their help and suggestions, I want to acknowledge Len Banaszak, Mark Banaszak Holl, Jack and Thad Gillespie, Darleen Lestrud, Eric Musselman, and David Pifer. Most importantly, Jacqueline, my wife of more than sixty years, has proofread, edited, and commented on more drafts than can be counted. Moreover, she has provided companionship and care through an otherwise lonely endeavor.

In Memoriam acknowledges my indebtedness to the teachers and mentors who helped develop my analytical skills, guided my career, and affirmed my passion to become a historian. I gratefully dedicate this book to them.

The Eisenhower Era

B y all accounts, Dwight Eisenhower was one of the towering figures of twentieth-century American history. His accomplishments were legendary. Prior to his election as the thirty-fourth president of the United States, he was the commanding general of victorious Allied armies in Europe during World War II. Following the war, he served as chairman of the Joint Chiefs of Staff and then as president of Columbia University. President Truman selected him as the first commanding general of the North Atlantic Treaty Organization (NATO) alliance in the early years of the Cold War.

The four Democratic presidents who preceded and succeeded Eisenhower—Franklin D. Roosevelt, Harry S. Truman, John F. Kennedy, and Lyndon Baines Johnson—all characterized their administrations with snappy political slogans: the New Deal, the Fair Deal, the New Frontier, and the Great Society, respectively. No such distinctive slogan defined the Eisenhower years. "I Like Ike" was the best-known slogan of his administration. Yet, the Gallup poll identified him as the most admired American of the second half of the twentieth century, while C-SPAN's 2017 Presidential Historians Survey ranked him fifth among presidents, behind Abraham Lincoln, George Washington, Franklin D. Roosevelt, and Theodore Roosevelt.

Ironically, both as general and as president, he hated the cult of personality that surrounded men such as FDR and Douglas MacArthur; he thought it inimical to the health of the nation. Instead, he favored strong, devoted, perhaps even deeply opinionated men like his mentors Fox Conner and George Marshall, who placed personal ambition below the service of their country. Being faithful to one's duty over private interests was Eisenhower's highest ideal. His model of leadership was oriented toward loyalty to the body he was leading. From his youth in Abilene to the plains of West Point, from Camp Colt at Gettysburg through his service under MacArthur in the Philippines, from high Allied command in Europe during World War II to the presidency of Columbia University and the formation of NATO, Eisenhower strove to be a team builder as well as the team captain. To build group solidarity and "we consciousness," Eisenhower understood that the group, whether it be a football team or a nation, should develop a unique identity based on shared values, history, and purpose. Eisenhower fervently believed that the United States Constitution, American history, and American civil religion served as key sources of national identity.

Although an admirer of Theodore Roosevelt as a youth, Eisenhower revered only Washington and Lincoln among his presidential predecessors (though he thought highly of U. S. Grant as a general and a historian and admired Herbert Hoover as a humanitarian). Democrats would castigate him mercilessly for not using TR's presidential "bully pulpit" to condemn McCarthyism or to promote civil rights. But at times, he preferred to lead quietly, working behind the scenes toward difficult, controversial political goals. This would be particularly true in the areas of civil rights and nuclear arms control.

Today, he is well known among scholars as the "hidden-hand" president who managed his presidency indirectly through his appointed political lieutenants. When Professor Fred Greenstein recognized that Eisenhower had been a hidden-hand president, what surprised him most was that Eisenhower had governed with any hands at all. But governing behind the scenes is not at all unusual for strong presidents—think of Franklin Roosevelt and his oblique political maneuvers, or Thomas Jefferson and his purchase of Louisiana, or Abraham Lincoln, the president Eisenhower most admired.

While Eisenhower has been steadily rising in the estimation of presidential ranking polls, his reputation has been slipping among the base of the modern Republican Party. Ever since Nelson Rockefeller was booed and heckled for sixteen minutes at the 1964 Republican convention in San Francisco, moderate Republicans have been steadily squeezed out of the GOP. There was much about Eisenhower's conservatism that fit with Republican tendencies. His political pals were rich and wellborn. He belonged to exclusive, segregated country clubs. He championed a balanced budget and a reduced national debt. He favored states' rights over an ever-growing federal government. He supported a strong military and had no problem affirming that the United States was "one nation under God."

On the other hand, Eisenhower, an American warrior, was also a self-proclaimed moderate. He openly denounced extremists on the political far right as well as those on the far left. He was a committed internationalist who enthusiastically endorsed the United Nations, NATO, and the International

Atomic Energy Agency. He promoted overseas cultural exchanges and foreign aid. Domestically, he passionately championed public education and encouraged federal support for research in science and medicine. His definition of "American" was inclusive rather than exclusive. Perhaps he is best known for vigorously promoting the use of federal dollars to improve the material infrastructure of post–World War II America. The interstate highway system may be his most significant and lasting legacy.

It is impossible to know, of course, how Eisenhower would line up on the current issues that define postmodern Republicans other than that he would be uncomfortable with denouncing moderates of all stripes. He would not support campaigns for preemptive war, nor would he endorse tax breaks for special interests at the expense of the common welfare of the nation. And he surely would not denounce immigrant populations or support states' rights when they conflicted with the Constitution. Nor would he censure the press as "the enemy of the people." For six of his eight years as president, with some notable frustration, he governed successfully with bipartisan support from a Democratically controlled Congress.

Among the unifying ideals he shared with Republicans and Democrats alike was his fervent civil religion, through which he viewed the history and destiny of nations. Yet, from his father, David, he inherited a worldview that perceived human history as a dialectical struggle between divine and demonic forces. He not only believed that the fundamental difference between the United States and the Soviet Union was religious but also believed that in time the atheistic Communist system would collapse from internal contradictions. In contrast, Western democracy, which relied on the belief in the God-given dignity of all people, could thrive if it escaped both moral and financial bankruptcy during its life-and-death struggle with the Soviet Union and international Communism.

A closely related dilemma was the looming threat of nuclear Armageddon. Eisenhower believed that the management and control of atomic energy were fundamentally a moral problem of directing nuclear science and technology toward peaceful purposes rather than human destruction. Just as God conveyed dignity to all humans, God intended creation to benefit all. But through human misuse, nature itself could be enveloped by a similar divine/demonic tension that corrupted human history.

The importance of religion in Eisenhower's public life cannot be overstated. All biographers note that Eisenhower grew up in a devout religious family. But once they move to the main story of his military life and presidency, Eisenhower's religion is usually left far behind. Although Eisenhower's religion has received some attention from scholars, there are no comprehensive, accurate histories of his religious journey and its legacy for American society, culture, and politics.

The "rags to riches" mythology of Eisenhower's youth in Abilene creates a persistent problem in understanding the complexity of his childhood and the religious tension in which he was raised. As first told by Kenneth Davis in *Dwight D. Eisenhower: Soldier of Democracy* (1945) and promoted by Stephen Ambrose, *Eisenhower: Soldier and President* (1991), the Eisenhower version of the Horatio Alger myth was encouraged by Eisenhower himself. Truly, he was raised in middle America and imbued with values often celebrated there: hard work, perseverance, honesty, frugality, friendliness, informality, and devotion to family, God, and country. But constant emphasis on these sunny attributes obscures the religious declension story that dominated Eisenhower's youth and has masked the influence of the Jehovah's Witnesses religious schooling he received from his parents.

His decision to become a warrior, his "crusade" against fascism and Communism, his belief that he was the only president who could lead America through the Cold War, and his search for nuclear peace were all grounded on the bedrock of his religious beliefs. There is no way to understand the man fully as a warrior or president, or to grasp why Americans responded so eagerly to his leadership, if one glosses over the religious narrative. His River Brethren heritage is widely celebrated, but his parents' Jehovah's Witnesses faith has generally been omitted, ignored, or downplayed.

Eisenhower has often been characterized as cheerful but also as an intellectual lightweight and one of the least religious of American presidents. However, he saw himself as an intensely religious man, and he was profoundly thoughtful and deeply troubled by the challenges of the Cold War and nuclear weaponry. As a warrior, president, and spiritual leader of the American people, he hoped to lead the nation and its allies through the valley of the shadow of death.

Although Eisenhower was no theologian, his faith was not bland and shallow. While his religion may have seemed simple, it was by no means simple-minded. His religious beliefs, thoughts, sentiments, and behavior may lack theological rigor, but they can still be examined through a theological lens— or, to invoke a better metaphor, kaleidoscope. His religious journey includes his River Brethren relatives, the Jehovah's Witnesses beliefs of his parents, the Lutheran tradition of his mother's family, the civil religion of the US Army, the Calvinist principles of Mamie's family, the Episcopalian perspective of his brother Milton, and the Congregational ministry of his White House religious advisor Frederick Fox. His religious beliefs, while dynamic, helped Eisenhower understand his place in history as defined by his "calling"—that is, a warrior's duty to serve God and country. Those beliefs guided his public policy as well as his personal life—dramatically.

Ethically, his faith embraced a conservative, duty-driven covenant to serve God and country, but theologically, it stretched beyond the bounds of his national allegiance toward a radical form of universalism. His faith was pulled in two directions, creating a tension between the religious covenants of the chosen and a radical inclusivity of all God's children. This fundamental tension in the Protestant principle, as described by Paul Tillich (*The Protestant Era*, 1948), not only directed Eisenhower's religious journey from his childhood in Abilene to his death at Walter Reed Hospital, but, as noted by Robert Bellah (*The Broken Covenant*, 1975), has also characterized much of America's religious history, from John Winthrop's "City upon a Hill" to the present.

From his cultural perspective as a warrior and professional soldier, Eisenhower perceived peace as a dialectical variant of war. In Eisenhower's mind, peace and war were divine and demonic manifestations of humankind's existential history. Every step toward peace involved confrontation and resistance, conflict and death. In this respect, Eisenhower's "peace" was not a state of being but rather a verb, or perhaps a dynamic and relative position on a continuum of social and political discourse. In this context, culture is a process of dominance, resistance, conflict, and accommodation, but mostly of power, including the power of political ideals, religious beliefs, and economic self-interest. Consequently, this history wrestles with fundamental moral problems of the twentieth century. His life, like this history, was a fundamental moral enterprise that grappled with the American dilemma as understood by the Puritans and others: How can a moral people live and govern in an immoral world? Eisenhower directly confronted the problem of evil (sin) in a democratic society. Personal ambition, selfishness, and greed were the major sins of individuals and groups in a democracy. In a society that values liberty, freedom, and limited government, how can the centripetal forces of raw individualism be checked and balanced for the greater good of America? As we shall see, Eisenhower's answer to the age-old Protestant dilemma was found in his embracing, and shaping, of America's civil religion.

Inauguration, January 1953

I
nauguration day of the thirty-fourth president, Tuesday, January 20, 1953, dawned cool but quiet. That morning the Eisenhowers' entire official family gathered for preinauguration worship at the National Presbyterian Church, while television crews busied themselves in last-minute preparations for broadcasting the ceremonies across the United States. It had been two decades since a Republican, Herbert Hoover, had occupied the White House, and not since a year before Eisenhower's birth, when Benjamin Harrison moved into the White House in 1889, had a general been elected president. Characteristically, on inauguration morning Eisenhower beamed broadly when the Reverend Edward L. R. Elson greeted him on the church steps. Within twelve days Elson would become pastor to the president. While other presidents had attended worship services prior to their inauguration, as best as anyone could remember, Eisenhower was the first to attend a preinaugural worship service with his entire official family. Eisenhower had also resolved to join Elson's Presbyterian congregation. It was fitting, he believed, for the president of the United States to serve as a spiritual guide of the nation as well as its political leader and commander in chief.

Just after noon, Eisenhower took the constitutional oath of office with his hand resting on two Bibles, George Washington's Bible and the Bible his mother had given him on his graduation from West Point. Both Bibles were opened to Old Testament verses: the Washington Bible to Psalm 127:1, "Except the LORD build the house, they labor in vain that build it: except the LORD keep the city, the watchman waketh but in vain," and Eisenhower's West Point Bible to 2 Chronicles 7:14, the same text chosen by Ronald Reagan and identified by one scholar as the "proof text par excellence of American civil religion": "If my people, which are called by my name, shall humble themselves, and pray, and seek my face, and turn from their wicked ways; then will I hear from heaven, and will forgive their sin, and will heal their land."

The symbolism of Eisenhower's choice of the two Bibles was obvious: with his hand resting on the Washington Bible, Eisenhower acknowledged his belief that the Founding Fathers had established the United States republic on firm religious principles—that democracy in America made no sense without a strong belief in God. Less conspicuously, the presence of the West Point Bible affirmed his mother's dominant role in laying the foundation of his youthful faith that ultimately matured into his call to duty to serve his nation under God.

Following the oath of office administered by Chief Justice Fred Vinson, Eisenhower recited the customary but not constitutional plea, "So help me, God." Then, instead of kissing the Holy Bible, as George Washington and numerous other presidents had done, Eisenhower broke tradition. After shaking hands with President Truman and other dignitaries, kissing Mamie and waving to the cheering crowd, he asked Americans to bow their heads while he read his own inaugural prayer:

> Almighty God, as we stand here at this moment my future associates in the Executive Branch of Government join me in beseeching that Thou will make full and complete our dedication to the service of the people in this throng, and their fellow citizens everywhere.
>
> Give us, we pray, the power to discern clearly right from wrong, and allow all our words and actions to be governed thereby, and by the laws of this land. Especially we pray that our concern shall be for all the people regardless of station, race or calling.
>
> May cooperation be permitted and be the mutual aim of those who, under the concepts of our Constitution, hold to differing political faiths; so that all may work for the good of our beloved country and Thy Glory, Amen.

As in most public prayers, Eisenhower's invocation was addressed as much to his audience, Republican supporters, Democratic critics, and the public at-large, as it was to God. While Eisenhower's unprecedented prayer took the gathering by surprise, few Americans questioned his sincerity or good will. The president's prayer was obviously unpolished, almost extemporaneous, read from notes Eisenhower had made a few hours before at his hotel. To the theologically sophisticated, Eisenhower's language was archaic; his message simple; his sentiments vague. But for those who had ears to hear, this prayer revealed as much about Eisenhower's worldview and his political vision as did his subsequent inaugural address. Eisenhower prayed not only for God's blessing on America but also for wisdom and discernment, strength and resolution to achieve the common good while affirming the glory of God. He had opened a new chapter in the country's long history of civil religion as he self-consciously presumed to lead the nation in prayer.

Although Eisenhower's inaugural prayer was not impromptu, it was authentic and heartfelt, and intentionally calculated to set the tone of the new administration. "It just seemed to me that we had had a little bit too much of the 'personality cult' in the Presidency the past few years," he later explained. "I just thought it might be a rather dramatic way of reminding the United States that a President shouldn't be too proud to humble himself in prayer if he felt like it. Period. And that was that."

Dwight D. Eisenhower is not celebrated as one of the country's deeply religious presidents, although he would have ranked himself high among presidents of religious faith. In 1948, shortly after he was inaugurated president of Columbia University, a reporter, noting his infrequent worship in church, asked about his religious faith. Eisenhower replied impatiently, "I am the most intensely religious man I know."

How could anyone, including Eisenhower, have seriously made such a claim? Did he understand the reporter's question? Was he cynically playing to the press? Who in the world but a sanctimonious fraud would consider himself "the most religious person" he knew? Eisenhower was fifty-eight years old, a World War II hero, and the president of Columbia University. Moreover, he was not naïve about the complexity of religious belief nor unacquainted with deeply religious believers. During the war he had met international religious leaders; he was aware of the deep religious faith of subordinates such as his friend George Patton; he had reminisced about the profound religious faith of his parents, especially his mother, Ida; he was the grandson of the River Brethren patriarch who had led his flock from Pennsylvania to Kansas; and in Abilene he had grown up in a house purchased from his uncle Abraham, another River Brethren minister and itinerant missionary. In other words, Eisenhower was well acquainted with religious fervor and spiritual leadership, and yet he set himself apart when asked about the intensity of his own faith.

Eisenhower's religious beliefs do not play large in traditional Eisenhower biography. Every biographer acknowledges the importance of religion in his upbringing in Abilene, but after Eisenhower left home for West Point in 1911, religion disappears as a major theme in his biography and few emphasize the influence his deeply engrained religious beliefs had on his public life and work.

9

Consequently, historians have largely missed the extent to which Eisenhower's religious values shaped his administration's domestic and foreign policy. This is understandable because Midwestern habits of privacy and the conviction that religion was an intensely personal matter beyond the reach of public concern often masked Eisenhower's most intimate sentiments. Nevertheless, as we shall see, the outward signs of Eisenhower's religious faith were often dramatically evident.

If he had a conversion experience, a time when he accepted Jesus as his personal Savior, he did not talk about it publicly. His personal faith remained mostly cloaked. But after World War II, he talked openly, and often, about God's relationship to the history and destiny of nations. To many, Eisenhower's personal religion remains an enigma, but the legacy of his public or civil religion during his presidency became a major contribution to American cultural and social history of the mid-twentieth century.

Cold War Imperatives

The lawful and peaceful transfer of power as exemplified by the inauguration of a new president is one of the most revered rites of American civil religion. The ceremonies, of course, take place at the national Capitol, not at the Washington Cathedral. Eisenhower's personal prayer was surprising, but his inaugural address was in keeping with the expectations of friends and foes alike. Eisenhower's solemn sermonette alerted the nation, the world beyond, and all posterity that the United States was engaged in a life-and-death struggle that pitted the forces of good against the forces of evil. This great struggle between Communism and freedom defined the twentieth century even more than the Great Depression or the two world wars. As the sun broke through the haze of a cloudless sky, glinting off the horns of the Marine Corps band, Eisenhower saw a dark tempest gathering on the horizon. "How far have we come in man's long pilgrimage from darkness toward the light?" he asked. Were Americans nearing the light—the dawn of freedom and peace for all mankind—or were the shadows of death closing in upon the world? In the presence of God, it was imperative, Eisenhower believed, for those who enjoyed the blessings of freedom, purchased with the blood sacrifice of Americans and their allies who died on the battlefield, to reaffirm their faith in "the abiding creed of our fathers." That American creed, essential to the civil religion, confessed the "deathless dignity of man, governed by eternal moral and natural law," and affirmed that God conveyed inalienable rights to all persons, who were "equal in His sight." Given his rhetoric of "light and darkness," "good and evil," "faith,

Creator, and Divine Providence," no one could miss the overriding religious tension embedded in Eisenhower's inaugural remarks.

The challenge of the age was no less than the survival of the liberal democratic way of life, including American free enterprise, as envisioned by the Founding Fathers. Americans were being called into service under the watchfulness of a divine Providence to bear the responsibility of the free world's leadership. Consequently, two overriding realities should be factored into any interpretation of the Eisenhower presidency. First, in 1952 Eisenhower believed that no other American, neither Republican nor Democrat, had the experience or temperament to successfully guide the United States and the Western alliance through the treacherous landscape of the Cold War— certainly not Harry S. Truman, Adlai Stevenson, Estes Kefauver, Robert A. Taft, Earl Warren, or Douglas MacArthur, who were principal contenders for their party's presidential nomination in 1952. Second, the hour was such that Eisenhower could not ignore the moral imperatives that defined his unconditional duty as an American warrior. Despite the victory over fascism, the nation and Western civilization remained in peril. Spiritually and religiously, Eisenhower believed the United States was under greater threat in the Cold War than it had been during the Great Depression or World War I and II, or at any time since the traumatic Civil War.

Baptized and Confirmed

In the American constitutional system, the United States Senate confirms major presidential appointments to positions in the executive and the judiciary branches of the government. While the Electoral College certifies the election of a candidate, no one confirms the president's fitness to serve except the American voters. Eisenhower never pretended that his election as president of the United States was an act of God. Consistent with his faith, he believed that the American people were literally free from divine interference to make their own choice of leaders. For Eisenhower, on the other hand, his calling to serve—his duty—was grounded both in the Constitution and in the Bible. To swear to uphold and defend the Constitution of the United States, "so help me, God," required that Eisenhower, at long last, make his personal leap of faith into the Christian church.

Eisenhower's affirmation of faith, baptism, and confirmation, just twelve days after his inauguration, have often gone unnoticed by his biographers and were only obliquely mentioned by Eisenhower himself in his White House

memoir, *The White House Years: Mandate for Change, 1953–1956*. Political supporters, including Clare Boothe Luce, had encouraged candidate Eisenhower
to join a church before the 1952 presidential election, but he gruffly refused to
commit such a blatantly partisan act. While Luce believed that Eisenhower's
candidacy was hurt because he did not belong to a church, Eisenhower responded that his religion was a matter strictly between himself and God. This
independence from the institutional church, of course, was in line with Eisenhower's upbringing and evidently persisted to the eve of his baptism.

Religion was one of the matters Eisenhower had been mulling over as he
prepared for his inauguration as president on January 20. He did not intend
to preach that morning; after all, he reminded himself, he was a soldier, not
a man of the cloth. But he believed that the United States was becoming too
secular, and he thought it his duty to let the American public know that he
believed in the beneficence of the Almighty without implying that he would
shirk his responsibilities as president because he trusted in God to make everything right. His "little prayer" became his way of informing Americans
that he intended to become a spiritual as well as a political leader while in the
White House. On inauguration day, when he and his family attended the early
morning communion service at the Reverend Edward L. R. Elson's church,
Eisenhower already considered himself a Presbyterian.

Elson had begun to court both Ike and Mamie for membership in the National Presbyterian Church immediately after the November election. Elson
had served as chaplain of the Twenty-First Army Corps in Europe during
World War II and reminded Eisenhower that he was the only Presbyterian
pastor in Washington who had previously served under Eisenhower. In addition, he had represented Eisenhower at the postwar consistory of the German
Protestant Church that had met to discuss rebuilding the German church. Elson's campaign also included phone calls to the president-elect's staff, encouraging affiliation with the church. Billy Graham, too, encouraged Ike to join
the Presbyterian church. Whether Elson was largely responsible for wooing
Eisenhower to join his church is uncertain, but his friendly encouragement
certainly did not hurt. In addition, the National Presbyterian Church was
convenient to the White House and claimed as members prominent figures
in government and Washington society.

On December 19, Eisenhower announced that he and Mamie would be
attending Elson's church. Elson welcomed Eisenhower to the church with
two promises: he offered to serve as Eisenhower's spiritual advisor and vowed
strict confidentiality regarding their pastor-president relationship.

Four days after the president's inauguration, Eisenhower and Elson met to
discuss the Eisenhowers becoming confirmed members at the National Pres-

byterian Church. Mamie would need only to have her membership transferred from her home congregation in Denver. Eisenhower, however, would have to be baptized and confirmed in the faith to be admitted to full membership in the congregation. He would need no special preparation for the baptismal rite other than willingly to kneel at the font. Confirmation, on the other hand, required that Eisenhower confess his Christian faith and affirm his adherence to Presbyterian doctrines according to the ordinances of the church.

His preparation for confirmation, however, did not require additional study of Scriptures, familiarity with John Calvin's or John Knox's theology, or rote memory of Presbyterian doctrine. Instead, Elson sent Eisenhower a list of the faith questions he would be asked at the confirmation service, accompanied by the answers he was expected to give. Lest this seem unusual, it should be noted that this was common practice for confirmands of all ages among Presbyterians, Episcopalians, and Lutherans during the 1950s. Only elders of the National Presbyterian Church needed to be present for Eisenhower's interrogation and confession of faith (also a common, although not universal, practice for adults). On February 1, 1953, the president and Mamie presented themselves for membership in the National Presbyterian Church: she for transfer of membership, he for baptism and confirmation in the Christian faith. He was sixty-two years old.

Why, then, did Eisenhower do this? Obviously, it was not for votes, but there is no doubt that Eisenhower's decision, in part, was a political act. While he was not naïve about the political importance of being an active member of a church, Eisenhower also wanted to confirm publicly that his calling to become president of the United States was a deeply felt religious obligation as well as a civic duty. But neither Eisenhower nor his pastor ever clearly explained the president's motives. When asked directly, Eisenhower, as was often his way, shrugged the question off by stating that joining a church simply removed an unnecessary irritant to his presidency. But Clare Boothe Luce, brother Milton, and evangelist Billy Graham all reported similarly that Eisenhower believed it was his duty as president to set a religious example and the moral tone for the nation that required not only regular church attendance but also actual membership in a congregation. In sum, his baptism and confirmation assured Americans that their president was a Christian soldier.

Eisenhower's Civil Religion

Superficially, Eisenhower's civil religion may seem to be in concert with his centrist political philosophy. Politically, he represented the mainstream, business-dominated, internationally oriented eastern wing of the Republican Party. As a member of the National Presbyterian Church, he worshiped with prominent leaders of the conservative Washington establishment. Nevertheless, despite his conservative facade, following World War II, Eisenhower routinely highlighted his public service with the fervent rhetoric of crusades. What made Eisenhower difficult to understand then, as now, was that he did not employ the crusade rhetoric simply as literary metaphor. As general and president, he responded to the unconditional call of duty as he understood it. Although his warning about the corrupting political influence of the "military-industrial complex" is his best-remembered prophetic legacy among scholars, among his most important contributions to American political and religious thought was his ardent advocacy of civil religion. More than any other president in modern times, Eisenhower played a principal role in defining civil religion as practiced in twentieth-century America. His Cold War version of civil religion, of course, was born in the struggle against godless international Communism.

From his first month in office, it was clear that Eisenhower gave high priority to religious affairs. Eisenhower would become the first president to be baptized while in office; he wrote his own inaugural prayer and initiated prayer breakfasts at the White House. He was the first president to appoint an official White House liaison for religious affairs. The Eisenhower administration also supported initiatives to use widely the phrase "In God We Trust" and to amend the Pledge of Allegiance to assure Americans that their nation, "under God," would stand united in its fight against satanic Communism. Again and again, Eisenhower defined the fundamental difference between the United States and the Soviet Union not in terms of political and economic systems but in terms of religious belief and commitment.

Unlike many Christians on the right or the left, however, influenced by his army experience, Eisenhower's faith was inclusionary rather than exclusionary. If democracy and capitalism were universally desirable as political and economic systems, then, as we shall see, Eisenhower also believed civil faith would be a prerequisite for lasting, stable, democratic government. In short, his civil religion was a faith in what was then known as "the American way of life." Eisenhower's "middle way" was as much a religious stance as it was a political strategy. As president, he would practice the politics of mediation; meanwhile, his civil faith would embrace all who confessed the American creed: Presbyterians, Methodists, Baptists, Catholics, Jews, Christian Scientists, Unitarians, Bible fundamentalists, Buddhists, Muslims—anyone who could affirm the basic principles of democracy, swear an oath of allegiance, and serve the country. Neither church nor denominational membership was necessary for practicing America's civil religion. He did not care what Americans believed as long as they placed their national trust in God. He was by religious temperament a civil universalist who believed that if the mediating function of democracy failed, then democracy itself failed.

A major theme of this book is that Dwight Eisenhower, an American warrior, was the principal presidential exegete of American civil religion in the twentieth century. "Exegesis" is an obscure, four-bit word used by theologians and biblical scholars that is defined as explanation or interpretation of biblical or religious texts. Sunday morning sermons frequently explore the meaning of sacred texts to religious followers—that is exegesis. An exegete, then, is one who teaches, explains, interprets, or models the meaning of religious writings and symbols to fellow believers. In the midst of the Cold War, Eisenhower assumed the role of America's civil pastor, offering explanation of America's historical mission as leader of the democratic world. The fundamental difference between Americanism and Communism, he insisted, was religious, a difference reflected in the American government and public institutions. As a presidential exegete of civil religion, he was not alone. Presidents before and after Eisenhower, especially Woodrow Wilson, Jimmy Carter, Ronald Reagan, and George W. Bush, also promoted a civil religion reconciling God and country in times of dire threats from foreign countries. Abraham Lincoln's Gettysburg Address, to name one example, became a sacred text of America's civil faith.

American Civil Religion

Just what is the American civil religion? America's civil religion is intensely religious without being deeply theological. First described by sociologist Robert Bellah and theologian Martin Marty during the Cold War, American civil religion includes general belief that God has specially blessed the American people, their country and history. Public recognition of and thanksgiving for God's favor to Americans are usually expressed in holidays and rituals associated with politics, sports, schools, the military, and numerous churches.

Historically, Americans also strongly support the belief in the separation of church and state as outlined in the First Amendment to the Constitution—"There shall be no establishment of religion." Most Americans, however, do not perceive a conflict between separation of church and state and embracing the American civil religion. There is no established, tax-supported state church in the United States, and civil religionists generally do not advocate one. But, while there is no state church, Americans embrace a way of seeing the world that conflates God and country, and they share a broad consensus that religion should play a major role in public life—especially in politics, military, and sports. In 1830, Alexis de Tocqueville observed that "religion in America takes no direct part in the government of society, but it must be regarded as the first of their political institutions. . . . [Americans] hold it to be indispensable to the maintenance of republican institutions." He could have been speaking for Dwight Eisenhower.

Broadly speaking, American civil religion promotes belief in American exceptionalism: the idea that Americans are a chosen people ordained by God with a unique mission and destiny to promote democracy and the "American way of life" to the world and history. This creed is supposedly deeply rooted in America's Judeo-Christian heritage. Exceptionalism was embraced by the Puritans, who believed that they had founded a "city upon a hill," a city that later Americans identified as a beacon of liberty, democracy, and religious tolerance for all the world. Exceptionalism was incorporated in the nineteenth-century doctrine of Manifest Destiny, the conviction that Americans had been ordained by God to settle the North American continent from the Atlantic to the Pacific. Exceptionalism was triumphant in World War II when America celebrated the triumph of their crusade in Europe over the evils of Nazism as a good and just war fought by what journalist Tom Brokaw later called "the greatest generation." In all this, an exceptional America with God's blessing offered the world political, economic, and social salvation.

To support their civil religion, Americans have identified sacred documents, rituals, hymns, saints, and places. The Declaration of Independence, the Constitution, and the Gettysburg Address are probably the most universally acclaimed public documents, each providing a solemn incantation of American vision and destiny. American civil religion rituals include the Pledge of Allegiance at school, the national anthem at sporting events, and the benediction "God bless America" offered at the end of every major political address. Among others, the most popular civil religion hymns are "God Bless America," "America the Beautiful," and "The Battle Hymn of the Republic." Not surprisingly, "Onward, Christian Soldiers" was among Eisenhower's favorite hymns. Because it is unofficial, civil religion's saints have been selected by region, cause, and ethnicity. Among some Americans, Martin Luther King Jr. is revered as a civil religion saint. Among others, Robert E. Lee, even though he tried to destroy the United States, is praised for his American virtues of integrity and loyalty to principle. Almost universally, on the other hand, two of the Mount Rushmore four, Washington and Lincoln, namesakes of the two major monuments on the Washington Mall, stand head and shoulders above all other secular saints. In turn, their birth, death, and burial places define American sacred spaces along with other sacred sites such as the Washington Mall, Arlington National Cemetery, Gettysburg National Battlefield, and Pearl Harbor. There are hundreds of lesser places, such as the Eisenhower home and burial chapel in Abilene, Kansas, where thousands of Americans yearly pay homage to Americans who embodied devotion and sacrifice to the universal ideals and optimism of America's civil faith.

More than any modern president, Dwight Eisenhower embraced, defined, and, most importantly, embodied America's civil religion. His civil faith was simply stated. The United States government was merely a translation in the political field of America's deeply felt civil religion. Among the sacred texts of the American civil religion, he explained to the National Council of Churches, were the Magna Carta, the American Declaration of Independence, and the French Declaration of the Rights of Man. Echoing universalist themes, Eisenhower underscored his belief that the foundations of American civil faith were based both in Anglo-Saxon history and in the European Enlightenment. Together, this Anglo-European heritage had established the principle that government recognized the equality and dignity of man. But this premise, Eisenhower stated repeatedly and consistently, would be completely baseless without the belief in a supreme being, "in front of whom we are all equal."

Theologian Paul Tillich has observed that "religion is the substance of culture [and] culture is the expression of religion." A small amendment of Tillich's definition captures the first principle of Eisenhower's political/religious philosophy: religion is the substance of political culture, and political culture is the expression of religion.

It is within the context of Eisenhower's civil religion that we can best understand his extraordinary claim, "I am the most intensely religious man I know." "Nobody goes through six years of war without faith," he continued. "That doesn't mean that I adhere to any sect. A democracy cannot exist without a religious base. I believe in democracy." Although Eisenhower was a Christian, his faith was not the evangelical Protestant variety, and certainly not like that of his River Brethren forebears, his Jehovah's Witness mother, or, later, his Presbyterian church. Within his circle of acquaintances, no one exceeded Eisenhower in his devotion to duty, which Eisenhower believed was the highest of personal virtues. In his lexicon, a warrior's call to duty was equivalent to a believer's commitment to faithfulness.

Thus, when Eisenhower pledged duty to his country, he had at the same time promised faithfulness to God. In this regard, his was not a bland or shallow faith but a rather muscular faith that sustained him through the trials of World War II and the Cold War. As a supreme military commander, he was entrusted by the nation with the lives of hundreds of thousands of his fellow countrymen to fight a demonic enemy. Believing as he did in the inherent dignity of all men, it was a trust he held on behalf of the Supreme Being. In the aftermath of the barbaric killing of World War II, the dark uncertainty of the atomic age, and the international challenge of atheistic Communism, Eisenhower believed the United States needed spiritual as well as political leadership. Although Eisenhower was not a member of a church, as he evaluated prospects for the presidency, he knew of no other candidate who would bring to the White House a more global perspective or religious intensity than himself.

When Americans voted overwhelmingly for Dwight Eisenhower in 1952, they knew they had elected a World War II hero and a conservative Republican as the thirty-fourth president of the United States. What they didn't realize was that their new president would also see himself as a disciple— an exegete—of the American civil religion. To the delight of most but the discomfiture of some, Eisenhower not only led the nation in prayer at his inauguration, but also, twelve days later, in a brief ceremony, he was publicly welcomed into the fellowship of the National Presbyterian Church. For the first time in American history, the president of the United States had been baptized while in office. At sixty-two, Eisenhower had been elected and inaugurated, baptized and confirmed, and was finally a member of a Christian church. He was poised to lead the nation politically and religiously through some of the darkest days of the Cold War.

The Man from Abilene, 1890–1909

D avid Dwight Eisenhower was born in Denison, Texas, during a thunderstorm on October 14, 1890.* His mother, Ida, who believed that the storm foretold violence in her son's future, named him after his father and a well-known evangelical preacher, Dwight Moody. Because his family moved back to Kansas in 1891, Eisenhower had no recollection of the bitter years lived in Denison on the Red River. His father, David, fled to Denison in 1888 in despair of supporting his family after the failure of his store in Hope, Kansas. In 1891, Grandpa Jacob and their River Brethren relatives rescued David and his family from their Texas exile. Later, young Dwight, as his mother called him, scarcely remembered that he had been born in Texas. Mythology about this strange but brief episode would forever distort Eisenhower family history.

Moving to Kansas

The saga of the Kansas Eisenhowers began in April 1878 when Jacob Eisenhower joined a band of Pennsylvania River Brethren who immigrated to Dickinson County, where they settled southeast of Abilene near the unincorporated hamlet of Hope. Because locusts had recently devastated Kansas, numerous abandoned farmsteads were available for occupancy. Despite challenging conditions, the industrious River Brethren farmers prospered. Jacob's family worked the farm during the week, while on Sunday he conducted worship at home as pastor to the River Brethren, a sect related to Pennsylvania Mennonites. Jacob's was an archetypal tent ministry embracing doctrines of

* How he became Dwight David Eisenhower will be explained later.

Menno Simons, the Reformation Anabaptist who preached that there was no authority outside of the Bible. River Brethren believed in adult baptism, strict moral codes, patriarchal family order, and conservative dress. They were temperate, self-reliant farmers who believed God would provide. They avoided civil entanglement and espoused universal pacifism.

The River Brethren were a tight-knit group. As a matter of faith, they believed they had a duty to care for their family and one another whenever in need. Generous and cheerful care for others became their thanksgiving offering for God's beneficence. Mutual support was central to their discipleship. They not only lived near one another but also became economically entwined. They had migrated west together; they helped one another get settled and established jointly funded enterprises to benefit the whole community.

In 1886, when the village of Hope incorporated, the Brethren built the Belle Springs Creamery near Jacob's farm. Farmers brought their milk to the creamery, where the butterfat was skimmed. Jacob, an entrepreneur as well as a farmer/pastor, invested in the community's creamery, real estate, and a fledgling country bank. After less than a decade of farming and investing in River Brethren enterprises, Jacob and his wife, Rebecca, had accumulated sufficient wealth that they could individually gift their six children 160 acres and $2,000 (equivalent to more than $53,000 in 2018 dollars) when they turned twenty-one.

David Eisenhower

David Eisenhower, Jacob and Rebecca's second-oldest surviving son and Dwight's father, had no interest in plowing the Kansas prairie. He was dreamy, curious, and rebellious. David was also stubborn, self-righteous, and insecure. Because of David's hatred of farming, in 1883 Jacob consented to his attending Lane College, a United Brethren in Christ school enrolling two hundred students located in Lecompton, east of Topeka. David carried one passion away from the farm—he loved tinkering with machinery. Lane's curriculum not only offered liberal arts for ministerial training but also offered engineering and vocational education.

For David, the college provided ideal classes: Greek, mechanics, and mathematics. As a youth, he aspired to become an engineer, and Lane helped prepare for that ambition. Deeply religious, he treasured Greek because it liberated him from unreliable translations of the Bible. Unfortunately, as first in his family to attend college, David had not mastered necessary study habits.

Weary of daily classes, David was sidetracked his sophomore year when he met Ida Stover. Ida was one of the few women at Lane and certainly one of the most attractive. Older than David, she was born in May 1862 in the Shenandoah Valley near Staunton, Virginia. Scarred by the Civil War, Ida's family became deeply religious pacifists. The Stover family was remarkably similar to the Eisenhowers in that they followed a Bible-centered religion that fostered similar piety. As a child, Ida was baptized in the Lutheran church at Mount Sidney, Virginia. As a youth, she memorized 1,365 Bible verses. Using a small inheritance, she moved to Kansas in 1883 to attend Lane College.

Temperamentally, Ida was David's opposite. Where he was dark and morose, she was bright and optimistic; where he was withdrawn and quiet, she was sociable and witty. While he had few friends, she was popular. They shared more similarities than German pietism, however. Both David and Ida were strong willed, independent, and ambitious. He was swept off his feet by this spirited beauty whose passion was music; she was attracted by his devotion and serious aspirations. Besides, both believed they had made a great catch: he would marry the most popular girl at Lane; she would wed the eldest son   ? of one of the most prominent families in Dickinson County. Portentously, father Jacob was not asked to perform the wedding.

David and Ida Wed—Financial Turmoil Follows

After David Eisenhower and Ida Stover married in 1885, neither continued college. Perhaps Lane prohibited married students from enrolling. Although the first six years of David and Ida's marriage have been shrouded in myth and misinformation, as college dropouts, their marriage began happily. As was Jacob's custom, David received a farm and $2,000 when he turned twenty-one. But David had no intention of farming. Instead, according to family lore, David asked his father to finance a mercantile venture in partnership with an experienced merchant, Milton Good. Jacob agreed to mortgage the farm David rejected, using the proceeds to construct a small store with apartments upstairs for David and Ida, and Milton Good and his wife.

Economically, the timing could not have been worse, because Kansas slumped into depression. According to family myth, with no business experience, David quickly lost everything when Good absconded with the cash, forcing him to close the store and mortgage the farm to pay creditors. Bankrupt and humiliated, he blamed his partner, bankers, and lawyers for his failure. With Ida pregnant with their second child, David fled to Texas to find work, temporarily leaving Ida and Arthur, his firstborn, with his brother Abraham in Hope.

Except, according to historian Thomas Branigar, the family's story about David falling into bankruptcy because of his partner's cheating is not true. Branigar has established that there was no bankruptcy and that the store was not sold until 1889, when Jacob's family decided to move to Abilene—sometime after David had bolted for Texas.

In family lore, Jacob Eisenhower's role in his son's business fiasco has been downplayed. Jacob, who was under no obligation to finance David's store with a wedding dowry, assisted, perhaps even encouraged, the commercial investment. It was Jacob who negotiated the financial arrangement with the River Brethren through Chris Musser, who had married David's older sister, Amanda. Because David had no business experience, Jacob was also instrumental in recruiting Good, a respected Abilene storekeeper, to be a partner in the enterprise. There is no record on how David welcomed his father's financial arrangements or his enforced partnership with Milton Good. After a brief honeymoon between David and Milton, however, the partnership soured, and Good sought release from the partnership in November 1886. Again Jacob came to the rescue, loaning David the money to buy out Good, and then promptly forgiving the loan.

David had to pay a price for his emancipation from Milton Good, however. The general store was soon reorganized into a new partnership—the Eisenhower Brothers store. Again, Jacob made the arrangements, and David's ebullient younger brother Abraham, a self-taught veterinarian and River Brethren minister, replaced the departed Good. Circumstances did not improve for David. He clashed with a baker who briefly shared the store's premises.

By October 1888, three years after forsaking his engineering dreams at Lane College, David had had enough. Twenty-five years old, with a second child on the way, inexplicably, he quit the business, abandoned his assets, left his pregnant wife and son with his brother Abraham, and lit out for Texas. To put the best face on his apparent abandonment of his business, young wife, and son, David's family explained that he fled the crushing embarrassment of bankruptcy caused by his unfaithful business partner, Milton Good. Dwight Eisenhower and his brothers apparently believed this family story until they died. Undoubtedly, David was humiliated by his failure in Hope, but in reality, it was his inability to work with the partners Jacob had chosen for him that accentuated his continued despondency over his dependence on his father for financial support.

Within four months of his flight to Denison, Texas, David's parents moved to Abilene. Jacob also faced financial problems. The Hope bank failed, taking with it large sums of Jacob's savings. In addition, Jacob learned that the River Brethren were planning on moving the Belle Springs Creamery to Abilene in 1890. Shortly after Ida delivered her second son, Edgar, Abraham also moved his veterinarian practice to Abilene. With her relatives moving out of Hope, Ida gathered up her new baby and her eldest son and entrained to Texas to join her husband, leaving behind in Abilene her most precious possession, an ebony piano she had purchased with her inheritance.

In his self-imposed Texas exile, David secured a $10-a-week job as an engine wiper with the Missouri-Kansas-Texas Railroad (the Katy line). It was virtually self-scourging. The work was dirty and menial. When Ida arrived, he rented a small house near the railroad tracks and took in a boarder to help pay expenses. No comment was ever made about David's sudden fall from middle-class respectability to common laborer. To her everlasting credit, Ida resumed her place at her husband's side, where she would prove instrumental in facilitating David's reconciliation with his father.

Lonely after the death of his wife and distressed by his son's impoverishment, Jacob encouraged David to return to Kansas. After resisting entreaties from his father and Ida to move back to Kansas, David gave in when his brother-in-law, Chris Musser, now foreman at Belle Springs Creamery, offered him a job as an engineer (or mechanic) to oversee the block-ice refrigeration units in the creamery.

Returning to Kansas

Family dynamics were delicate. Musser unintentionally profited on the mortgage foreclosure when David abandoned his store. But David's talented brother-in-law also knew about his mechanical aptitude. The Belle Springs Creamery offered him a job with a livable wage, with a raise promised when he earned his engineering certificate. When David could not afford the tickets home, Jacob again arranged for Musser to loan David the train fare, to be repaid from his creamery salary. David hesitated, but Ida insisted that they return to Kansas. In the spring of 1892, the Eisenhowers ended their three-and-a-half year exile in Texas.

David and Ida had reached their financial nadir but not their emotional one. They rented a small house just south of the Union Pacific tracks but soon outgrew the rental. In regular succession, Ida gave birth to four more boys: Roy (1892), Paul (1894), Earl (1898), and Milton (1899). Deep tragedy struck in 1895 when sickly Paul died of diphtheria. He was David and Ida's only son to die in infancy. Paul's death proved to be a major turning point in David and Ida's religious life.

Compassionate River Brethren consoled the Eisenhowers that God's ways were mysterious, but that Paul had been called home to heaven, where he rested in the Father's arms. Her Lutheran heritage, on the other hand, could not even assure Ida that her unbaptized baby lived in spirit. Grief-stricken, Ida would not accept the idea that a loving God had taken her son nor believe that her unbaptized baby would be condemned to hell.

Ida's Religious Crisis

During her mourning, Ida was also visited by three local Bible Students, as followers of Charles Taze Russell were called. The three neighbors told Ida that, according to Russellite teaching, Paul was not dead but instead was asleep and awaiting his resurrection in the millennium, when Christ would return. Following unremitting financial distress, loss of social status, two major moves, and the death of Paul, Ida found welcome comfort in her neighbors' ministry. Reportedly, she also purchased Russell's *Studies in Scriptures* and began her subscription to *Zion's Watchtower and Herald of Christ's Presence* (later titled the *Watchtower*), to which she would subscribe for more than fifty years. Without question, Ida not only looked forward to seeing Paul again in the millennium, predicted to happen before 1914, but also anticipated that she would witness the coming Armageddon, during which God would destroy sinners who were not Bible Students. The number of saved, necessarily, would be small—God's elite witnesses.

When they became Bible Students, neither David nor Ida left the River Brethren church, because they had never become baptized members. In the Mennonite tradition, the River Brethren practiced believer's baptism, and neither David, nor Ida, nor the Eisenhower brothers were baptized members of the church. They attended River Brethren services occasionally; Ida even wore the River Brethren habit and cap before her move to Texas. And, as a family, they continued to join David's relatives at River Brethren picnics and socials. The Reverend Ray L. Witter, David's nephew, remembered that for a while the family "helped along," but significantly, David Eisenhower would never join his father's church. Thus, in spring 1895, a decade after their marriage, they established their religious independence from Jacob and the River Brethren flock.

David's Religious Crisis

In 1898, Ida alone was rebaptized by Bible Students. Thereafter, David probably joined the Bible Students fellowship in deference to Ida, but he, too, had been searching for new religious foundations. His father's rigid and doctrinaire sect, while providing invaluable material help, offered little spiritual comfort to David. The River Brethren believed in a sovereign God who provided prosperity, but not without human help. Wealth was a sign of God's blessing the believer's humble initiatives. Failure, on the other hand, was not God's fault but could indicate his displeasure with ambition or pride. David's business failure, therefore, was not only personally humiliating but also, according to River Brethren orthodoxy, may have reflected God's judgment on David's fiscal habits. For a time, he briefly tried Lutheran and Methodist churches. What he needed, of course, was spiritual consolation, strength, and flexibility, which he found in rich abundance with Ida and her friends.

Together, David and Ida began a spiritual journey that would lead them down the road toward Jehovah's Witnesses. In his time of troubles, David found religious escape from the nightmare of the recent past by exploring the millenarian prophecies of Charles Taze Russell. Meditating with his Bible, David decided that God could be known only through faith and not through reason. In this regard, he concluded that organized religion—the church—was not a necessary mediator for true Christianity. A Christian sect like the Bible Students might help spread the gospel, but a church might as easily corrupt Christ's teachings. David drifted toward a mysticism that was strangely alloyed with engineering logic.

Understanding the texture of David Eisenhower's religious faith and its impact on his sons is more problematic. He followed Ida into the Russellite movement and led weekly studies of the Bible and Watchtower literature. Russell's eschatological teachings especially attracted David. Notably, he was fascinated by a "Chart of the Ages," published by the Watchtower in 1898 (see p. 26 for an image of this chart), that depicted God's redemptive history through an interpretative rendering of the Great Pyramid of Giza in Egypt. Presumably, this pyramid chart illustrated a central teaching of the Bible Students that predicted the imminent end of the world. Russell believed that Jehovah had constructed the Great Pyramid of Egypt, whose dimensions confirmed God's divine plan as revealed in biblical prophecy. The pyramid chart summarized biblical history in terms of six great ages divided among three dispensations: (1) from creation to the flood, (2) the present evil world from the flood to Christ's second return, and (3) the reign of Christ in the millennial age. This third dispensation represented the end of history and the earth as prophesied in Ephesians 1:10, "That in the dispensation of the fulness of times he might gather together in one all things in Christ, both which are in heaven, and which are on earth; even in him."

David re-created his own version of the Watchtower pyramid chart, which he kept in the upstairs hallway. This huge, exotic drawing (it may have been as large as five or six feet high by ten feet long) highlighted his skills in mechanical drawing while charting his personal eschatology. David carefully measured and drew the lines and angles of three Egyptian pyramids, plotting their dimensions and extending these measurements into a temporal field where the lines converged to confirm biblical redemptive events. Working independently of church or ministerial authority, David used the pyramid chart to prove for himself the accuracy of the Bible's eschatological prophecies.

Not surprisingly, his sons were intrigued by the chart and their father's millennial predictions. Fascinated by his father's library of ancient history, Dwight spent hours studying his father's pyramid chart. (When he finally visited the Egyptian pyramids following the North African campaign of World War II, his companions were surprised by the extent of his historical and biblical knowledge.)

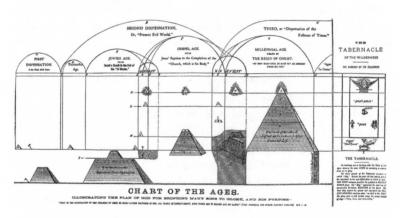

CHART OF THE AGES.

ILLUSTRATING THE PLAN OF GOD FOR BRINGING MANY SONS TO GLORY, AND HIS PURPOSE—

A Home on Fourth Street

As the boys grew, the Eisenhowers' modest rental house and yard became increasingly too small to contain four active children (and a fifth that was on the way). Ida hoped against hope for a girl, and she knew that she couldn't cram a daughter into one of the boys' small bedrooms. Once again, David and Ida's River Brethren relatives came to the rescue. In 1892, at a bankruptcy sale, Jacob had purchased a farmhouse, barn, and three acres on the south edge of town. In turn, Jacob sold the property to Abraham, who established his second veterinary practice in the barn on Southeast Fourth Street. But in time Abraham developed an itch to conduct missionary work among Native Americans. He offered to sell the house to David for $1,000. The house, barn, and land were generously offered in return for providing care for David's aging father, Jacob. Not only did David not have the cash, but he was also dead set against borrowing the money. David balked, not wanting to fall into debt.

Ida, on the other hand, was determined not to squander this opportunity to acquire significantly more living space as well as a huge barn and three acres of good land for a large garden. Again, she stepped forward, this time to negotiate purchase of the house from Abraham, with Jacob serving as the real estate broker. Initially, title to the house was put in Ida's name alone, with Chris Musser or another River Brethren relative financing the deal through gift or loan. Theirs was an unusual real estate arrangement for 1898, and ten years later Ida conveyed the title to David through a quitclaim deed for $1.00.

The Myth of Family Poverty

Every Eisenhower biographer has noted that Dwight Eisenhower grew up in the American heartland. In Eisenhower iconography, turn-of-the-century Abilene was an idyllic, Currier and Ives Midwestern town. Images of Eisenhower's Abilene embodied the frontier ethic, rags-to-riches mythology, and the American Dream. It was here that the Eisenhower brothers learned traditional American values of self-reliance, thrift, hard work, and a cooperative spirit.

Despite repeated encomiums, the Eisenhower boys were not raised on a Kansas farm. As a married couple, David and Ida always lived in small towns (Hope, Denison, Abilene). Traditionally, the Eisenhower family has been described as poor, and certainly they were not as well off financially as many Abilene families. There is no question that the family was financially strapped in Texas and had little spare cash while the boys were growing up. But, while David Eisenhower often brooded over his financial dependency and his fear of debt, the Eisenhowers did not live on Abilene's economic fringe. David was never out of work, and the family was never homeless or hungry. After moving into their uncle's house in 1898 (now enshrined as the Eisenhower boyhood home), they occupied three acres, including fruit trees and a garden, a smokehouse and a chicken house, and one of the largest barns in town, in an era when large barns were themselves a sign of prosperity. When not attending to chores (including cows, chickens, and vegetables), the Eisenhower brothers enjoyed camping, fishing, and athletics, and were leaders among the south-side youth.

Much has been made of the myth that the Eisenhower brothers grew up "on the wrong side of the tracks," the tracks being the supposed dividing line between the rich and the poor in Abilene. Demographically, many of Abilene's blue-collar, skilled workmen lived on the south side, while the "better sort" in Abilene, doctors, lawyers, merchants, and bankers, tended to live on the north side. Also, the Eisenhowers literally lived between the tracks: the Union Pacific and the Santa Fe lines lay just to the north, and Rock Island line ran immediately to the south.

In his colorful biography of Eisenhower, Kenneth Davis dramatizes Eisenhower's "rags to riches" story by emphasizing the stark contrast in wealth and class between Abilene's north and south sides. The effect of this implied separation of social classes was to underscore Dwight Eisenhower's Horatio Alger–like rise from rural poverty to high command during World War II. This notion that the economic classes in Abilene were sharply divided by the railroad tracks was firmly believed by Dwight's brother Edgar, who was sensitive about his economic and social standing.

But neither Dwight nor Milton shared Edgar's perspective on their family's second-class status among Abilene's elite. Though the differences between the south side and the north side were real, Eisenhower himself thought that class conflict between the sides of town was greatly overblown. "Exaggerated," he noted, concerning Ken Davis's dramatic contrast between north and south Abilene. While the boys were in grade school, they experienced a lively rivalry with schoolchildren their own age who lived in north Abilene. But, by the time they reached high school, that childish rivalry had largely dissipated. Some of Ike's closest friends, such as the gifted athlete John "Six" MacDonald, were poor and Catholic in a predominately Protestant town, but Six lived about ten blocks away, in the north end.

After high school, Ike befriended north-ender Everett "Swede" Hazlett, the son of a physician who played a major role in encouraging him to apply for West Point. In retrospect, Hazlett thought that Dwight's brother Edgar's dichotomy between the haves and the have-nots in Abilene was just a bunch of "hooey." Without question, the tracks were a major physical presence in this Midwestern railroad town, but young Eisenhower never regarded them as an economic or a social barrier he had to overcome.

While these extraordinary boys lived a rather ordinary childhood, all the Eisenhower brothers (except the oldest, Arthur) graduated from high school at a time when that accomplishment itself was exceptional among Kansas youth—a fact of which Eisenhower himself was fully aware. When president of Columbia University, Eisenhower reminisced that Abilene's most precious legacy was the gift of boundless opportunity:

> I was of a big family of boys, six of us. And we were very poor, but the point is we didn't know we were poor. . . . The mere fact that we didn't do all the things that others in cities may have done made no impression upon us whatsoever because there was constantly held out in front of us, by every-one around us, until it was deeply embedded in our consciousness, that opportunity was on every side.

David's wounded pride over his financial failure in Hope never entirely healed. Almost alone among their relatives, David and Ida had attended college. He had had high aspirations of becoming a scholar, or an engineer, or a business-man. To his great credit, in 1904 David earned a diploma in refrigeration engi-neering through a correspondence school. But his return to Abilene to work for Chris Musser at the creamery signaled the defeat of David's independent ambi-tions. If their sons looked forward confidently toward unlimited opportunities, David was forced to accept the economic reality that his semiskilled labor at the Belle Springs Creamery defined his destiny. Their poverty is best described as the loss of self-respect and the confidence that they could make it on their own without the support of David's father and family. In the Holy Bible, the poor are not only identified as those without wealth, but, more importantly, as widows, orphans, the sick, and ne'er-do-wells who are dependent upon others for their care and nurturing. Dependency—that was the real meaning of being "poor" for David Eisenhower and his family. While Abilene and the creamery had become their sanctuary, they also underscored David and Ida's continued dependence on River Brethren relatives for a job and housing.

While Ida reflected hope and encouragement and provided her family its driving energy and spiritual vision, David presented a darker presence. The failure of his store in Hope had changed him. From his perspective, he had been virtually stripped to his name, the only thing surviving of any real value besides his wife (and her precious piano) and their children being his personal integrity. David had expected to be the family's breadwinner, but in his own mind, his dependency on his River Brethren relatives for a job marked him as a failure. He did succeed, however, in maintaining his grip on the tradi-tional patriarchal structure of the German immigrant family. On their return to Abilene, David worked ten and a half hours a day at the creamery, six days a week, but he established firm control of his family's daily routine. "Family life revolved about him," Dwight recalled. "School, chores, meals, and all other activities—winter and summer—had to be adjusted to meet his requirements." He was the "Supreme Court and Lord High Executioner," the "czar" who did not spare the rod. "Father had quick judicial instincts," Eisenhower remembered. His mother, on the other hand, had "insight into the fact that each son was a unique personality and she adapted her methods to each." Ida was the parent who talked of "standards, aspirations and opportunities." His father believed in training and discipline. "He was not to be trifled with unless you were prepared to take the consequences."

Limits of Pacifism

David and Ida may have been devout pacifists, but they tolerated fighting among their boys and ignored the violent "war" games the brothers often played. The Reverend Ray Witter recalled that during the Spanish-American War, the cousins would gather on the Witter farm to build forts, battle the Spaniards, and play war like other young boys. More often than not, Ida would turn a benign eye toward her boys wrestling in the yard or roughhousing in the kitchen. David expected his sons to stand up for themselves or to stand together, if necessary. Once when a bully chased Ike home, David demanded to know why his son allowed himself to be persecuted. "Because if I fight him, you'll give me a whipping, win or lose," Eisenhower replied with exasperation. "Chase that boy out of here," was David's simple reply. With a hoop, Eisenhower turned on his heels, ran the boy down, threw him to the ground and threatened to beat him if he were ever harassed again. The lesson was indelible. A swift, fearless response to aggression, accompanied by a credible bluff to beat the tar out of your tormentor, quelled personal fear and bought lasting peace of mind.

David's pacifist beliefs did not preclude corporal punishment for his boys, and Dwight discovered he had reason to be wary of his father's whippings. David had a passion for education and was disappointed when his eldest son, Arthur, quit high school to work at a Kansas City bank. Secretly, Edgar became a truant from high school in order to work for a local physician. When David discovered Edgar's deception, he became furious. Catching Edgar and Ike in the barn, he grabbed a leather strap and, without a word, began to thrash his son. Eisenhower was shocked and, although only twelve years old, cried out loudly for his father to stop.

Perhaps Dwight hoped that his commotion would summon Ida. When no help arrived, he desperately grabbed his father from behind, trying to pin David's arms to his sides. Turning on Ike, David growled, "Oh, do you want some of the same? What's the matter with you, anyway?" In turn, Eisenhower sobbed, "I don't think anyone ought to be whipped like that, not even a dog." Although Edgar returned to school and eventually graduated from the University of Michigan, Eisenhower never forgot his father's uncontrolled rage, nor the lasting fear it instilled in his sons.

Dwight also had a fearsome "Dutch" temper of his own to master. When Arthur and Edgar were given permission to go trick-or-treating on Halloween, his parents decided that Ike was too young to join his brothers. Enraged that he was grounded at home with the babies, Dwight threw a massive temper tantrum. Beside himself with anger, he beat his fists bloody against an apple tree. David tried to shake some sense into the boy, and when that failed, he switched Ike with a hickory stick and sent him to bed. For an hour he lay sobbing, until Ida came into the room to console her son. She sat patiently in a rocking chair while Ike composed himself. Then, treating his battered fists with salve, she talked quietly about his terrible temper and his need to control it. "He that conquereth his own soul is greater than he who taketh a city," she said, paraphrasing Proverbs. Hatred was a horrible thing, Ida counseled her third son. The object of his hate probably did not care, possibly did not even know—the only person hurt was Dwight himself. As she lovingly bandaged his hands, Ida told him, of all her boys, he had the most to learn about self-control.

The Brothers' Religious Education

While David Eisenhower ruled the roost in matters of family discipline, together David and Ida established their independence from the River Brethren community by providing religious and moral education for their boys. The question about the religious instruction of young Eisenhower and his brothers has never really been an issue of "whether or who," but rather an uncertainty about "what and how." Contrary to what has often been written, their religious education did not take place in the traditional Sunday school or church setting. They did not belong to, and did not regularly attend, the River Brethren church, nor were they schooled in River Brethren catechism. The Reverend Ray L. Witter, David's nephew, remembered that the Eisenhowers occasionally attended the Brethren service, and for a brief time one summer the boys visited the River Brethren Sunday school. According to Witter, both David and Ida occasionally attended church socials but did not join the church. Although Dwight remembered attending church picnics, neither of his parents became members of the Abilene congregation.

Ida and David were their children's principal religious instructors. The boys all remembered daily prayers and Bible reading and a pietistic and morally rigorous household regime. David typically read from the Bible before asking the blessing at mealtime. After dinner, the family usually gathered for Bible study, the boys being encouraged to read passages aloud until they made a mistake.

Already at age twelve, Dwight had read the entire Bible, encouraged by Ida's promise of a gold watch when he finished. He also memorized the Ten Commandments, the Beatitudes, and several Bible passages. By the time he left for West Point, Eisenhower had read the Bible again and had discussed it "chapter by chapter" with his mother. As reported in the *Christian Century* (March 1975), in 1954 the Bible was the Eisenhower family's "one authoritative guide, read every morning at family prayers, quoted again and again when family decisions were in the making. Both father and mother could quote the Bible for any occasion and almost from beginning to end. . . . They owned a concordance, but the sons remembered that on the rare occasion when reference to it became necessary both parents were almost furtive in seeking its aid." Eisenhower later recalled that his mother "was never happier than when reading the Bible."

Wary of modern Bible translations, David also favored his Greek Bible obtained at Lane College. Was David proficient in Greek? Perhaps not, but according to Dwight, his father "balanced his career as a mechanical engineer with the study of Scriptures in the original Greek." The core of David's faith could be summed up in one religious axiom that he stressed over and over again: "religion, placed in man by God, is most natural to him." By his own confession, repeatedly over the years, both in war and peace, Eisenhower was to "rediscover this changeless truth" taught to him by his father. He did not realize it at the time, but this singular belief of David's would one day also stand at the center of Eisenhower's own civil religion.

The house on Southeast Fourth, after the Eisenhowers moved into it, became a center for the Russellite movement in central Kansas. Ida became especially active and was instrumental in bringing David along. In addition to maintaining a Bible-centered household, David and Ida neither drank, smoked, played cards, gambled, nor swore—common virtues among small-town, Midwestern Protestants at the turn of the twentieth century (although Ida loved playing solitaire).

From 1896 until 1915, the Bible Students, as the Russellites were called, met on Sunday afternoons in the Eisenhowers' parlor, where Ida played her piano and led the singing. For two decades, David was an "elder" conducting the weekly Bible study until growth, or disagreement, required them to rent a hall for their weekly gatherings. Generally, the Eisenhower boys were not involved in these small weekly meetings—some accounts affirm their participation, others state that the boys were excused from these Sunday activities. Involved or not in the weekly Bible study, Dwight was fully aware that the group was not from the River Brethren community but rather were Bible Students, or Russellites, not yet known as Jehovah's Witnesses. In an extended memoir associated with his father's death in 1942, Eisenhower affirmed Ida's involvement with the Jehovah's Witnesses:

> My mother, as I have shown, was deeply religious. The Bible provided her favorite reading, but she did not just repeat it by rote; she strove, always, to understand it. A woman as individualistic as she was not able to accept the dogma of any specific sect or denomination. Gradually, over the years, she had gravitated toward a local group known as The Bible Class. In this group, which had no church or minister, she was happy. Sunday meetings were always held in the afternoons at the homes of the members, including ours.
>
> The usual program of worship included hymns, for which Mother played the piano, and prayers, with the rest of the time devoted to group discussion of a selected chapter of the Bible. The meeting was for serious study and for adults only. There was, eventually, a kind of loose association with similar groups throughout the country but, so far as I know, this was chiefly through subscription to a religious periodical, *The Watchtower*. After I left home for the Army, these groups were drawn closer together and finally adopted the name of Jehovah's Witnesses. A principal tenet in their beliefs was the rejection of force of any kind in human relations. They were true conscientious objectors to war. Though none of her sons could accept her convictions in this matter, she refused to try to push her beliefs on us just as she refused to modify her own.

Eisenhower's reflections on his mother's religious affiliation are important in several respects. First, he confirmed that his mother developed a deep skepticism about organized religion, denominational dogma, and the ordained ministry. There is no question that Ida abandoned her Lutheran roots and no evidence that she embraced the River Brethren community. Next, although his Abilene home had served as a regular meeting place for the Bible Students, Eisenhower implied that neither he nor his brothers became involved with the sect. It appears that while the Eisenhower boys were rigorously home-schooled in Bible studies and moral values, they remained unchurched during their childhood.

Finally, Eisenhower confirmed that his mother accepted a "principal tenet" of the belief system of Jehovah's Witnesses—that the state had no moral right to wage war. Thus, at the very time her warrior son led the Allies to victory in World War II, she continued to support conscientious objectors against the war. For his part, whether publicly or privately, Eisenhower never expressed anything but sympathy and support for his mother's religious convictions. During World War II, when the press carried a story about Ida's "pacifism" and her Jehovah's Witnesses faith, Eisenhower wrote his brother Arthur that his mother's religious happiness "means more to me than any damn wise crack that a newspaper man can get published."

Time of Troubles

The River Brethren had been wary of the Bible Students since 1891. In 1913, tensions between the River Brethren and the Bible Students became public when a Brethren publication, the *Evangelical Visitor*, endorsed an anti-Russellite pamphlet, *The Blasphemous Religion Which Teaches the Annihilation of Jesus Christ*. River Brethren ministers were encouraged to alert their congregations to the dangers presented by the Russellites.

Then, sometime between 1915 and 1919, David's religious foundations were shaken again. In 1915, the same year that Dwight graduated from the US Military Academy at West Point, the Bible Students stopped meeting at the Eisenhower home, ostensibly because the Eisenhowers' parlor had become too small to accommodate the growing congregation. Was there tension within the group as well? Because 1914 was also the year in which the world was supposed to end, Bible Students must have experienced high anxiety and expectation, probably followed by disappointment, and in David's case, disillusionment, when the millennium did not arrive. The moment of Christ's second coming—that fullness of time—had proven empty.

With the end of the world not in sight, in 1916 Russell died and was succeeded as Watchtower president by Joseph F. Rutherford. Under Rutherford's leadership, the Bible Students eventually adopted the name Jehovah's Witnesses and developed some of their most controversial practices, including opposition to the flag salute and avoidance of medicine, vaccines, and blood transfusions. Rutherford also attacked his predecessor by condemning Russell's pyramidal teaching.

Most extremely, declaring that all other religions were Satan's "snare and racket," Rutherford encouraged Witnesses to disassociate themselves from other Christians. In Abilene, tensions between the Bible Students and the River Brethren intensified. From the outside, the Brethren and the Bible Students seemed to share similar beliefs. Both emphasized biblical fundamentalism and shared a common interest in eschatology. Both were conservatively pietistic, stressing plain living and condemning worldly vices. Both distanced themselves from government and opposed war, although for somewhat different reasons.

No doubt, their similarities made them bitter rivals as well. Rutherford not only declared all other religions false but also accused priests and ministers, such as David's father and brothers, of being the devil's agents leading their flocks into eternal damnation. Not unexpectedly, the River Brethren responded with equally strong denunciation of their own. Dwight's favorite uncle, Abraham (David's brother), called the Watchtower "fool-hearted nonsense" and an "infamous lie" that covered up the realities of "a hell fire judgment." For David, the declension had gone too far. Profoundly disenchanted when Russell's prophecies proved false, and perhaps distraught with Rutherford's authoritarianism, David withdrew from the Watchtower. Although he would never reconcile himself religiously with his River Brethren relatives, neither would he shun them—nor, for that matter, would he or Ida shun their sons.

Was Dwight Eisenhower aware of the intensity of the religious conflict and declension among Abilene's Christians? Did he know that his family's home sat in the center of the religious storm? If so, he and his brothers, and time, have obscured the family's religious divisions and controversy. In 1946, after Ida died, the youngest son, Milton, removed his father's pyramid chart and all evidence of Ida's affiliation with the Jehovah's Witnesses from the Eisenhower home. His older brothers apparently made no objection. Subsequently, the boys did not actually deny their parents' religious heterodoxy, but neither did they object, or attempt to correct the record, when well-meaning biographers got the story wrong. For example, in 1945, Ken Davis, writer of Dwight's authorized biography (*Soldier of Democracy*), recorded that "on Sundays the whole family went to Sunday school in the River Brethren meeting house," where Chris Musser (the boy's uncle and David's boss) was Sunday school superintendent. Thereafter, the family returned home, where the boys did all the cooking and housework because "Sunday was the parents' day off."

Davis's narrative was seriously misleading not only because he incorrectly implied that the Eisenhower family remained faithful members of the River Brethren church, but also because he ignored mention of the parents' principal Sunday afternoon activity—the weekly meeting of the Bible Students. In his review of Davis's book, Dwight was content to allow these inaccuracies to pass, at least until he wrote his own memoir twenty years later. Having missed the mark of church affiliation, however, Davis accurately captured the essence of the Eisenhower brothers' religious heritage:

> The rather strict religious training which the boys received did not, perhaps, produce the precise effect which the parents desired. None of the boys was converted to any strict orthodoxy. None became particularly "religious" in the ordinary meaning of that term. Indeed, all of the boys would seem later to react against religious dogma . . . , but retain all [their lives] a profound respect for the moral tenets which the parents derived, or thought they derived from their religion. The boys might say that around the core of mystical nonsense was a good solid husk of common sense.

Surely this last point should never be lost.

Jacob Eisenhower, David's father, died in 1906 at age eighty. His grandson, Dwight, had scant memories of his grandfather. Although fifteen years old when Jacob died, Dwight only remembered his dark, sober clothing, his patriarchal beard, and his horse and buggy that undoubtedly carried Jacob to River Brethren services each Sunday. Eisenhower remembered his grandfather moving into their home but nothing else of note that he cared to share. For nearly a decade, however, Jacob had lived in the Eisenhower household during a crucial period of religious formation for both the parents and their boys. Undoubtedly, he witnessed, perhaps even participated in, family daily devotions, but he probably had nothing to do with the weekly meetings of the Bible Students. Eight years is a significant time in the life of any family with young children, yet there is no record of their interaction with Jacob, religious, financial, or otherwise, during this entire time. Within two years of Jacob's death, in 1908, Ida transferred title to the house to David. Fortunately, the religious dust-up between the Jehovah's Witnesses and the River Brethren did not take place until after Jacob was gone.

After Jacob's death, the Eisenhowers' River Brethren network of relatives and friends continued to provide substantial family linkage and occasional financial support for the Eisenhower brothers. The Eisenhowers belonged to a large, prominent, extended Abilene family that somewhat mitigated the fact that they were south-siders. To some extent, his many relatives and their friends in the River Brethren community may have influenced Eisenhower's religious development. Although numerous Eisenhower biographers have incorrectly declared that the Eisenhowers belonged to the River Brethren church, the brothers unquestionably enjoyed a significant River Brethren heritage.

Taming the Goose-Stepping Tyrant

Ida's family also deeply influenced Dwight. One of Eisenhower's earliest recollections—an event occurring just before his fifth birthday in 1895—was of a tough and prolonged war fought at his uncle's farm near Topeka. On one visit, Eisenhower ventured to play in the barnyard, only to be chased back into the farmhouse by an aggressive, territorial gander. Every attempt Eisenhower made to explore the barnyard was repulsed by the goose, which drove the crying boy away. Eventually, Uncle Luther came to Eisenhower's rescue. Stripping a worn-out broom to a short, hard knob, Uncle Luther placed the weapon in Eisenhower's hand and sent him out to do battle with the gander. In short order, Ike confronted the barnyard tyrant, smacked the bird on the fanny with Uncle Luther's broomstick, and established himself as the proud boss of the back yard.

Eisenhower's lifelong lesson from his earliest memory is illuminating: "I never [made] the mistake of being caught without the weapon . . . [and] quickly learned never to negotiate with an adversary except from a position of strength." But the symbolism in this simple story is also revealing of Eisenhower's adult sense of civic and religious duty. The story immediately follows the first chapter of *At Ease: Stories I Tell to Friends* (1967), about his years at West Point. The confrontation with Uncle Luther's goose introduces his Abilene years. The barnyard battle was, in fact, Eisenhower's first war to liberate the oppressed, and himself, from goose-stepping despotism. When he told this story near the end of his life, the old warrior may not have been aware of Martin Luther's doctrine of the left and right hand of God. But consistent with Luther, Eisenhower was comfortable with the duty of carrying the broomstick of justice in his left hand even if that meant leaving to others the calling of extending the right hand of grace.

The Skinned Knee

The most significant religious event of Eisenhower's youth was associated with a skinned knee that became morbidly infected. On the way home from school one day, he tripped on a wooden platform and scraped his knee. At first the injury seemed minor, but within two days he fell into delirium from "blood poisoning." Examining the infected wound with his scalpel, Dr. Conklin predicted that amputation above the knee might be required to save Eisenhower's life. The fourteen-year-old boy, horrified at the prospect of no longer playing baseball or football, asked Edgar to stand guard to prevent amputation under any circumstances. "I would rather be dead than crippled, and not be able to play ball," he told his parents and physicians, including the specialist called in from Topeka.

The doctors were frustrated, but his parents understood. Although they were religiously opposed to their son playing violent football, their personal faith also counseled them that Dwight should make his own decisions on how to live. No amputation was allowed, and eventually the pain and infection in his knee began to ebb. Although he recovered fully, he was so weakened that he dropped out of school that spring and had to repeat the grade.

The struggle to save his leg, he wrote in an early draft of the incident, marked "a turning point" in his life. He called it "[one] of the many instances when faith and Christian prayer have sustained me in life." Grandfather Jacob was still alive, and he undoubtedly spent time praying at Dwight's bedside. Dwight later speculated that his parents established a vigil in deference to Jacob's River Brethren beliefs in miraculous cures through prayer. His father and mother took turns in leading prayer, perhaps with Jacob also participating. During the second night, Edgar joined the prayer vigil, and before it ended, all the Eisenhower brothers knelt at Dwight's bedside.

Later, when he constructed this famous story, Eisenhower had difficulty defining the purpose of prayer and God's response. In his first version, he described in rather conventional Protestant terms his family's supplicating prayer vigil, implying that God had answered their prayers positively. Subsequently, he became extremely sensitive to stories that his parents, as faith healers, conducted a two-week marathon prayer vigil to save his life. In his second version, he wrote that his deeply religious parents had included petitions on his behalf in their daily prayers, "never doubting that the Almighty would hear their prayers, no matter what the Divine judgment would be." In his last version, Eisenhower simply stated that David and Ida included in their daily prayers petitions for his recovery, "never doubting the Almighty would hear." In his storytelling, he ultimately tiptoed around affirming the efficacy of his parents' prayers and refused to speculate on God's response. To the end of his days, Eisenhower avoided any talk of a "miraculous" cure, and he was anxious to set the record straight, at least in his own mind, as to how this incident mirrored his parents' religious faith.

Although Bible Students, his parents obviously had not hesitated to enlist the best medical care available. They prayed for their son's recovery, of course, but only during regular daily family devotions, and not night and day for two weeks, as some stories had it. Disassociating David and Ida from the Jehovah's Witnesses' suspicions of modern medicine, Eisenhower said his parents did not believe in "faith healing." What they did believe in, Eisenhower asserted, was comforting their children in an hour of profound darkness. What is strikingly absent from Eisenhower's account of this "marked turning point" in his life is what impact, if any, the family's prayers had on his own religious life. Obviously, he was moved emotionally when he teetered on the edge of losing both his leg and his life, but if this experience was "one of the many instances when religious faith sustained [him] in life," he was mute about how it affected his belief in prayer or his faith in God. Characteristically, Eisenhower did not reveal his innermost religious beliefs publicly.

An Extraordinary Family

Ultimately, the Eisenhower brothers may have wished for a more mainline religious heritage. Nevertheless, David and Ida Eisenhower raised one of the most remarkable family of boys in the history of Kansas, or anywhere else. The unique Midwestern small-town values that supposedly explained their success no doubt contributed significantly to their distinction. More important was their parents' sense of divine election softened by pragmatic values and practical ambition. Even as each boy rejected his parents' religion and moved from Abilene, he carried with him a special feeling of destiny modulated by common sense.

To be sure, Abilene itself played a major role in shaping Eisenhower's character, morals, and worldview. For his part, Dwight Eisenhower embraced the mythic American saga by frequently attributing his success to being raised in small-town Kansas. While he was growing up between 1900 and 1910, Abilene increased in population from 3,507 to 4,118. By twenty-first-century American standards, the Eisenhower brothers were incredibly autonomous. David Eisenhower was a strict disciplinarian who did not hesitate to whack his boys with a leather strap when he believed the punishment was warranted. Among the boys' daily chores was carrying their father's lunch to the creamery at noon. Nor were Scripture lessons or prayers optional. Public school attendance, at a time when high school was not a universal expectation, was also required. But beyond the family's and school's daily routine, the boys were free to play, roam, and associate as they pleased. David interacted little with his sons (and said less) outside of household and spiritual matters. They did not play catch or games with their father. In turn-of-the-twentieth-century Abilene, there were no Boy Scouts, no Little League, and few youth activities outside of church that were supervised by adults. Consequently, the boys were pretty much left to their own initiative and imagination to organize their outings and sports with friends of their own choosing.

North versus South: A Schoolboy Fight

Schooling, then as now, was always more individualized than play. Eisenhower might study with a friend, but after school he generally ran with the gang. Eisenhower's first grade school, Lincoln School, was located just across the street from his home. Garfield School, for the upper elementary grades, lay north of the tracks, and south-siders were sometimes hassled by north-end boys. Arthur, Edgar, and Dwight in turn fought as champions for the south-side boys in neighborhood standoffs. The schoolboy fights were real enough, but according to Eisenhower, their importance has been greatly exaggerated by biographers eager to dramatize his hardscrabble youth. Still, other boys regarded Eisenhower as a south-side leader. He was known among his peers as someone who would stand up for his rights as well as those of his brothers and others who were wronged. According to the boys' silent code, he was accorded a position of respect among the pack and was left alone, "almost the highest tribute he could obtain," Eisenhower recalled.

His most celebrated schoolboy fight was against Wes Merrifield, a champion of the north side. Merrifield was short and squat but fast and powerful. At thirteen, Dwight was smaller than Edgar, and not particularly athletic or fast. Merrifield was renowned for his strength and endurance; Eisenhower was known for his courage and determination. On an October afternoon, the two boys squared off in a vacant lot across from the Abilene city hall. A crowd of boys, who had been eagerly anticipating the fight between the champion of the north side and the champion of the south side, formed an impromptu ring around Wes and Ike. From the start, Eisenhower bore the brunt of the legendary fight. By all accounts, Eisenhower was beaten early in the fight, but although his face and eyes were bloodied and swollen, he refused to quit. The fight wore on for more than two hours; the crowd of boys was awed by the spectacle, yet the fighters continued slugging it out until both were utterly spent. Biographer Ken

Davis rhapsodized: "When the physique is exhausted and skill no longer counts, when the sharp pain gives way to an aching ordeal which has no apparent end, one must draw his fighting stamina from the spirit. Determination, fortitude, the very essence of self-control are then measured. The contest becomes one of character; its continuance becomes a spiritual achievement."

In the end, the boys called the fight a draw. Merrifield panted, "Ike, I can't lick you," to which Eisenhower allegedly replied, "Well, Wes, I haven't licked you." The fight over, the ring parted and Eisenhower walked slowly home, snuck into the house, and went upstairs to bed. At dinnertime, when his parents saw his black eye, they strongly reprimanded him for brawling in town, but they also apparently took pity on their battered son when they allowed him to stay home from school for the next three days. The story of Eisenhower's fight with Wes Merrifield has been told and retold because it revealed the warrior spirit of this unusual boy who in World War II would lead the Allies to victory in Europe. But it revealed something else: win, lose, or draw, when possible Eisenhower characteristically treated his opponents with respect.

Schooling

Throughout his schooling in Abilene, Eisenhower was a good to excellent student. In grammar school he demonstrated relatively high reading proficiency, no doubt obtained by reciting the Bible out loud in family devotions. Grade school primers were much more easily mastered than the vocabulary and syntax of his family Bible. He also learned arithmetic quickly, in part because the mathematical problems were logical and their solutions were either right or wrong. In high school, however, he disliked algebra because its problems seemed abstract or unrelated to practical application. Geometry, on the other hand, proved to be an entrancing intellectual venture. He did so well in plane geometry that the principal and his mathematics teacher decided to take away his textbook (after promising him an A+ in the course), leaving Eisenhower to solve the daily class problems without benefit of the math text.

In addition to his high school studies, Eisenhower read widely in his parents' library. For the first decade of the twentieth century, the Eisenhowers maintained a decidedly literary household. In addition to religious books and devotional journals, David and Ida collected a sizable library of several hundred books, including wholesome novels and histories. Dwight was especially captivated by ancient history that complemented his fascination for the large pyramid chart. Although he lived in a pacifist household, the books that interested him most were histories of ancient Egyptian, Assyrian, Persian, Greek, and Roman battles and warriors. His greatest ancient hero was neither Greek nor Roman, however, but the Carthaginian Hannibal, whose leadership dazzled young Eisenhower. He marveled that Hannibal's greatness shone through in history written by his enemy. Just as Robert E. Lee was one of his military heroes, he admired Hannibal because he was an underdog who brilliantly led his army despite overwhelming handicaps due to lack of support from Carthage. He liked the romance associated with Lee and Hannibal, although he realized that Western civilization and his life in Abilene would have been much different had either general been successful in winning wars.

Besides his proficiency in mathematics, his high school teachers recognized Eisenhower's interest in history. Appropriately, Abilene High School helped create his foundation in American history, especially the history of the colonial and revolutionary eras. The Civil War, only forty years before, was almost a current event among Kansans. Dwight studied the great battles at Vicksburg and Gettysburg, but his greatest American hero was George Washington. He never tired of reading heroic accounts about Washington's campaigns at Princeton and Trenton, or about the fortitude of Washington and the Continental troops at Valley Forge. We do not know what Eisenhower the boy thought about Washington, but the retired general and president admired him for his stamina and patience in adversity and his indomitable courage and capacity for self-sacrifice.

Eisenhower recalled that he read history because he loved it and not because it offered lessons from the past. Nevertheless, his high school history studies not only stimulated his patriotic love of country but also implanted in Eisenhower a mustard seed that would grow into one of his most basic personal values: a lifelong commitment to do his duty as he understood it. So much did his love of history identify him at high school that when he graduated in 1909, the yearbook, the *Helianthus* (Latin for sunflower), predicted that his brother Edgar would someday be president of the United States while Dwight would become a professor of history at Yale.

A World of Work

Religion and schooling played a large role in the formation of Eisenhower's character and values, but so did work and sports. Like all the Eisenhower boys, Dwight performed daily chores around home, worked in the garden, and cared for whatever animals were housed in the barn. So that his sons had pocket change, David dedicated plots outside the main garden where the boys could grow anything they wanted to sell to Abilene neighbors. Edgar hated the idea, but Dwight enthusiastically raised sweet corn and cucumbers that he knew would sell well in the north end. He liked having his own plot and liked even more having his own hard-earned money to spend as he wished. While living in Texas, Ida had learned how to make Mexican tamales. Eisenhower badgered his mother into teaching him to make tamales that he could sell to neighbors around town.

The tamale business combined well his love of cooking and his entre-preneurial instincts. It was fun to make the tamales, fun to sell them three for five cents around town, and fun to share the leftovers with his brothers and friends. Furthermore, the extra money allowed him to purchase shot-gun shells, fund his camping trips, and buy sports equipment for his baseball and football team. While Edgar felt socially denigrated peddling vegetables in town, Dwight, better humored and positive, maintained his perspective and dignity.

Work was literally part of the local religion. Eisenhower recalled that in horse-and-buggy Abilene, all able-bodied men worked hard physically. As Eisenhower shrewdly observed, almost all men had horses to be curried and rubbed down, buggy and wheel axles that needed greasing, and coal burners for heat and hot water that needed stoking. The class differences between the prosperous north end and the poor south end were exaggerated in a so-ciety where there was very little social stratification because of a man's job. Eisenhower recalled that two of the most admired men in town were barbers, and that skilled workmen such as his father, whose on-the-job training and correspondence course had secured for himself a position as a refrigeration engineer, were well respected in the community. In addition, before the pas-sage of child labor laws in the 1920s, work for male youths outside the home was natural and expected throughout the community. Although their parents did not help them find work, the Eisenhower boys had no trouble securing part-time jobs.

Under the supervision of various farmers and tradesmen, Eisenhower learned the basics of the Midwestern Protestant work ethic demanded by the Abilene economy. Daily reliability, an ability to learn skills, and a willingness to work hard were essentials to building a reputation for being a good worker. Stick-to-itiveness was also important, but for Eisenhower that did not mean hanging on to the same job from season to season, or even from month to month. As his sense of duty grew, sticking to it meant completing the job at hand to the best of his ability. His first jobs were menial farmwork suited for young boys. One year he spent the month of September picking apples and, after the harvest, made extra money (twenty-five cents a day) carrying drops to the cider mill. Another summer, the manager of a small company making galvanized steel storage bins enticed him to work at the local factory for more money than he was earning on the farm. Within a short time, Eisenhower remembered, he became "a sort of straw boss" at the factory.

When Edgar left for college in the fall of 1909, Dwight moved into his open position at the Belle Springs Creamery. Initially, he worked in the creamery's icehouse, added when creamery management expanded into the ice and ice-cream business. His first task was to move three-hundred-pound cakes of ice in the storage area, a task, he moaned, that built up his body but not his mind. When not stacking ice cakes, he helped load ice onto delivery trucks destined for town or into boxcars for shipment down the line. From iceman he was promoted to fireman, a harder but higher-paying job, to help stoke the coal-fired boilers in the furnace room. Finally, in his last year in Abilene, Eisenhower was promoted to second engineer in the ice room, in effect a one-man foreman of the 6:00 p.m. to 6:00 a.m. night shift. The job paid $90 a month, $40 more than his father had received when he had started work at the creamery seventeen years earlier.

A Passion for Sports

Sports, not work, were Eisenhower's passion during his high school years. All agreed that older brother Edgar was the better athlete, but Dwight was a natural leader of his high school teams. Sporting facilities in Abilene were primitive at best. Adults were largely uninvolved with the high school teams. Their football coach, a football star already graduated from high school, was an unpaid volunteer with no training. For the most part, the boys made or purchased their own equipment. There was no high school athletic league; no school bus (or wagon) for transportation to games. The high school supported neither the baseball nor the football team, and there was no regular schedule. Games were scheduled from year to year, and there were no letters or championships to win. The boys played only for the love of the game.

To provide some organizational stability and to generate income to finance the purchase of uniforms, balls, bats, and transportation, Eisenhower and his teammates organized the Abilene High School Athletic Association, whose dues were twenty-five cents a month. Team players were required to join the association, while girls, parents, and others interested in supporting high school athletics were encouraged to become association members. The boys also charged admission to their baseball games, but because of their poor won-loss record, gate receipts were low.

His planning skills, his attention to administrative detail, and his selfless devotion to his teams' and players' betterment elevated him to president of the association his senior year. In addition to scheduling the games, the association's president interfaced with the high school administration. Initially, the athletic association was not recognized by the school and almost fell apart when some of the best athletes were not elected to leadership positions. Eisenhower appealed to the school authorities, who agreed to include the association among the school's official organizations. Among his proudest achievements as a high school student was drafting the Abilene High School Athletic Association's constitution, which survived for decades after he left school.

Eisenhower made both the football and baseball team his junior year. In baseball, he played centerfield, while in football he played both offensive and defensive end or tackle, as needed. The 1908 Abilene High School football team had a perfect 7-0 record, outscoring opponents 129–9. The drawback of becoming a local football powerhouse was that Eisenhower, as the athletic association's president, was able to persuade only four teams to play Abilene in 1909.

He enjoyed baseball, but he loved rough-and-tumble football more. For Eisenhower, the football field became a field of honor. Football may have shaped his competitive drive; it certainly provided an ideal outlet for his leadership skills and his finely tuned sense of fair play. He had a reputation for being a tough lineman who could intensify his own hard-hitting play if he felt opposing players were unfairly rough on his own team. Yet, football legend also records that he was not loath to admonish Abilene players if they crossed Eisenhower's boundary of fair play.

Perhaps the best-known incident reflecting Eisenhower's sense of fair play, sportsmanship, and respect involved a black player. Blacks did not constitute a large segment of Abilene's population—according to the 1890 census, they made up about 4 percent of the county's population. In a game with Chapman, the opposing team showed up with a black center. No one on the Abilene team was willing to play opposite the black athlete. What happened next is lost in myth; some accounts claim Eisenhower lectured the team and threatened to return home and not play again that season if Abilene did not take the field. Eisenhower's own account played down the dramatic confrontation with his team and the racist implications of the incident. There was no speech to the team, Eisenhower insisted. Because no one else would play against the Chapman lineman, Eisenhower played center that day, although he never played the position before. All accounts agree that he shook hands with the black athlete both before and after the game. Eisenhower did not feature this story in his memoir *At Ease*, but referring to the incident after the war in 1946, he observed that after the game the rest of the team was somewhat ashamed of themselves.

Bob Davis and Joe Howe

Growing up in Abilene, Dwight Eisenhower also formed close friendships with adults who ended up playing a major role in developing his character. His closest adult friends were not uncles or aunts, official youth leaders, local schoolteachers, church or Sunday school leaders, or friends of his parents. Ida certainly knew the men around town who had befriended her son, and, at a minimum, she gave her tacit approval to his association with them. Still, these very important friends had little or no association with his family, school, work, or sports.

One of the most influential mentors of the young Eisenhower aged eight to sixteen was his hero, Bob Davis. An illiterate bachelor in his fifties, Davis was a handyman who excelled at trapping, fishing, and hunting. At six feet tall, he towered over the boy, but he was gentle and welcoming to Dwight, the antithesis of his father, David. Davis, perhaps lonely, enjoyed tramping along the Smoky Hill River with his young protégé. For Eisenhower, Davis was a glamorous figure who embodied the frontier ethic and "mountain man" skills. From Davis he learned to fish with nets along the river, trap muskrats and mink, skin and cure hides, shoot ducks with a double-barreled gun, and navigate a flat-bottom boat with a single oar.

On weekend campouts sanctioned by Ida, Davis taught Eisenhower woodland lore: for example, how to determine which direction was north from moss growing on trees, how to identify and follow animal tracks, how to build a campfire and prepare a camp dinner. Davis also taught the young boy the rudiments of poker. Ida would have been aghast had she known that Dwight was receiving lessons in gambling that would prove invaluable at West Point and beyond. Davis was a conservative poker player who taught Eisenhower to play the odds and calculate the percentages. Given his mathematical aptitude,

Dwight was a natural at poker and, thanks to Davis, developed into a sharp poker player who rarely lost at the table. Eisenhower fondly remembered Davis as a philosopher and great teacher who provided him a perspective on life and living that was unavailable elsewhere in Abilene.

Joseph W. Howe, the editor of the *Dickinson County News*, hired needy students for after-school work and set aside a back room in his newspaper office as a gathering place for high school boys to talk, study, or enjoy fellowship. Because one of Eisenhower's teammates, Six McDonnell, worked for Howe, Dwight became a regular visitor to the office. But Joe Howe and Bob Davis could not have been any more different. Davis was illiterate and lived on the social and economic margins of Abilene; Howe was the editor of a local newspaper and served on the local school board, was a state senator, and chaired the local Democratic Party. Davis gave Eisenhower an intimate education of the fauna and flora of the Smoky Hill River watershed; Howe expanded his world in time and space through newspapers and books while encouraging him to pursue his education at the best college he could find. At Howe's office Eisenhower gained regular access to daily papers from cities like Kansas City, New York, Cleveland, and St. Louis. And in Howe's private library he discovered numerous histories unavailable at his school or home.

It was in Howe's library, not his parents', that he discovered a biography of a man who would become one of his historical heroes: *The Life of Hannibal*. Because Abilene had no public library while Eisenhower was in high school (whose own library was meager), he relied on Howe's comparatively large collection for term papers and essays. Howe helped broaden Eisenhower's horizon not only by inspiring his interest in history but also by whetting his curiosity about the world beyond Kansas. Howe also recruited Eisenhower to participate in local Democratic politics and would feel betrayed some forty years later when Eisenhower ran for president as a Republican. Something derailed their friendship, probably the passage of time and Eisenhower's commitment to the Republican Party. Despite his great debt to Howe, Eisenhower omitted him from his memoir *At Ease*, while offering Bob Davis generous praise for his devotion to the boy from Abilene.

If politics in a democratic society is the relatively peaceful process that distributes scarce community resources by determining who gets what, when, why, and how, then Eisenhower obtained a solid elementary civic education in Abilene through his work and athletic activities. He developed a keen sense of fair play. He worked and played hard, and while on the job or on the playfield, he emerged as a leader who could accept a subordinate position for the greater good of the company or the team. He had a hot temper but rarely held a grudge. In conflict, he often disarmed an adversary with his quick, warming smile. He developed a deep respect for men who represented a broad spectrum of Abilene society: David, his father, who was largely self-educated; his generous and supportive grandfather Jacob and uncle Abraham; Bob Davis, a natural man who taught him poker; Joe Howe, editor and civic servant, who helped needy boys; Dickinson County farmers, who willingly hired town boys; small-time businessmen struggling in a local manufacturing plant who nevertheless gave him considerable responsibility; the local telegrapher, who connected Abilene to the world; and two town barbers, who were among the most-respected and best-liked men in Abilene.

His hometown meant many things to Eisenhower; it was the place that provided him a good home, a satisfactory public education, and the usual Midwestern values. Eisenhower was not deeply reflective or philosophical as a boy, yet growing up in Abilene, he perceived that he had opportunities for work and improvement provided by adults helpful to him and his friends. Although he did not regard himself as poor, neither did he see himself as a favored nephew of Belle Springs Creamery management. He believed that all Kansans, Bob Davis as well as Joe Howe, were free to pursue their individual economic destiny. As president of the Abilene High School Athletic Association, however, he also learned that mutual cooperation and compromise were necessary to achieve community goals.

Finally, despite the religious tension within his family and community, Abilene instilled in Eisenhower deep grounding in his fundamental belief in the immutable human dignity of all people. Ultimately, he decided that this was what his father had meant when he taught that "religion, placed in man by God, is most natural to him." He had grown up in a family and community that affirmed the basic worth of every person before God. At home, at school, and on the job, Eisenhower had been given economic and social opportunities that were his to seize. In addition, David and Ida instilled in their sons the belief that they were exceptional children of God, each called to his own vocation. Finally, the most important legacy Eisenhower took from Abilene was his parents' affirmation that his life and destiny, under God, were his alone to chart.

CHAPTER THREE

Duty, Honor, Country, 1909–1920

W
hen Dwight Eisenhower graduated from Abilene High School in June 1909, he had little idea of what he was going to do with his life. As a high school graduate, Eisenhower enjoyed an elite status at the beginning of America's Progressive Era. He was one of only 9 percent of eighteen-year-olds in the United States who held a high school diploma. The high school yearbook prophesied that he would become a history professor at Yale University—a good joke, almost as funny as the idea of Edgar becoming president of the United States. As siblings, Edgar and Dwight had been intense rivals. Yet, after they graduated from high school together, the brothers formed an unusual pact to jointly finance their college educations. Neither boy wanted to attend the agricultural and engineering college in Manhattan. Edgar already knew he wanted to study law at the University of Michigan in Ann Arbor. Dwight, uncertain about what to study in college, agreed to sit out the first year to work and to save money for tuition for both of them. Their plan was to alternate work and study and put themselves through school with some help from their father, David.

The brothers' grand plan for their college education did not work out, but the results of their efforts were more than satisfactory. David was decidedly sour on the idea of Edgar studying law. Already, his oldest son, Arthur, had challenged his father's deepest prejudices when he moved to Kansas City to become a banker. Instead of law, David encouraged Edgar to attend the University of Kansas to study medicine. But Edgar, like his father, chose his own vocational path. As a holdover from his business failure in Hope, David hated lawyers as well as bankers, and consequently at first refused to aid Edgar. With no help from David, Chris Musser, the family's financial angel, stepped forward with financial assistance. Supposedly, David never learned of Musser's generosity, or, at least, no one ever talked about it. Ultimately, Dwight was able to send his brother $200 (about $5,000 in today's dollars) to help pay Edgar's college expenses, and, eventually, David also chipped in to assist his son.

Upon Edgar's departure for Michigan, Dwight moved smoothly into his brother's position at the Belle Springs Creamery. By all accounts he enjoyed his two-year sabbatical from school. The Belle Springs management knew the Eisenhowers well, and soon Dwight was promoted to second engineer, becoming the night foreman. This shift provided him lots of free time, especially during the long Kansas winter nights. After he completed his work, Eisenhower's friends were free to visit with him during slow night hours.

"The Student in Politics"

In November 1909, Eisenhower's friend Joe Howe, editor of the *Dickinson County News*, invited him to address the annual banquet of the Dickinson County Young Men's Democratic Club. In his speech, "The Student in Politics," Eisenhower denounced Republicans as "the party of privilege" while praising Democrats as "the party of the people." Professing admiration for the Republican Square Dealers and the Bull Moose insurgents, Eisenhower declared that he would nevertheless vote for bona fide Democratic Party reform against the Republican Party establishment of Joseph Cannon, Nelson Aldrich, and other "hide bound party men" who supported the high Payne-Aldrich Tariff of 1909.

His was a Progressive-like stance against eastern banking and industrial interests protected by excessively high tariffs, to the detriment of common, working men like his father, local farmers, and Abilene small businessmen, all struggling under the yoke of the "gold bugs." It was a bold political statement for a recent Abilene High School graduate.

Also buried in the speech was an open message for his father, David. As a young man starting out in politics, Eisenhower declared that he would not vote for the party of his father but would independently make his own political choices. What could this mean? Although David was a registered Democrat—probably another sign of his independence in Republican-dominated Abilene—given his Jehovah's Witnesses beliefs, he had not been active in local politics. The doctrine of Jehovah's Witnesses forbade involvement in secular politics not only because politics were corrupting but also because they were pointless, with the end of the world near. Politically, Dwight Eisenhower's statement made no sense except in the most abstract context. Was there double meaning in young Eisenhower's speech? He had intoned the old proverb, "As the twig is bent, so will the tree be inclined." Although declaring himself a young Democrat, by participating in the political banquet Dwight had taken pains to proclaim publicly that he was not simply following in his father's footsteps, either politically, vocationally, or, for that matter, religiously. Despite this remarkable political harangue that Joe Howe printed verbatim in his newspaper, Eisenhower was not noticeably active in local Abilene politics. As we shall see, however, his "Student in Politics" speech endorsing the Democratic Party very soon came back to haunt him.

"Swede" Hazlett and the Road to West Point

When Everett "Swede" Hazlett returned to Abilene from military school in Wisconsin in June 1910, Eisenhower and Hazlett struck up a warm friendship that included nightly rendezvous in the creamery boiler room. Talk naturally included discussions about their future schooling. Hazlett had already received an appointment to Annapolis but had failed the mathematics entrance examination. Because of Dwight's mathematical aptitude, he was able to help his friend bone up to retake the exam. Hazlett, in turn, encouraged Eisenhower to consider the Naval Academy or West Point rather than to follow Edgar to the University of Michigan.

Although Eisenhower liked the idea of striking out on his own, he was even more attracted by the prospect of receiving an expense-paid college education courtesy of the United States government. An appointment to Annapolis or West Point would not only immediately emancipate him from the drudgery at the Belle Springs Creamery but would also free him from dependence on his father for a college education. Given Eisenhower's interest in military history, his passion for athletics, and his proficiency with firearms, it is not surprising that he caught the dream of attending one of the United States' military academies. Making inquiries, Eisenhower learned that only the junior Republican senator from Kansas, Joseph Bristow, still had openings for appointments to Annapolis and West Point. As luck would have it, Bristow, a newspaper publisher and editor, was a Progressive Republican from Salina. Obviously and unexpectedly, the young Abilene Democrat faced a serious challenge in securing Senator Bristow's support.

Still, not only was Eisenhower popular in high school but he was also well known around town. In what might be regarded as his first campaign to secure a political appointment, his diplomacy, persuasiveness, and determination were impressive. First he canvassed local Abilene business and community leaders, ostensibly seeking their advice concerning attending either West Point or Annapolis and, of course, obtaining their enthusiastic support. Next, he asked his good friend Joe Howe (an editor, like Bristow) to write to the senator on his behalf. Howe also told him he needed to mend fences with top Republicans in town, namely, Charlie Harger, editor of Abilene's conservative paper, the *Reflector*.

Harger, a Harvard graduate, had supported Theodore Roosevelt but was a political rival and critic of the Progressive Republican Bristow. Not only did Harger promise his endorsement, but he insisted that Eisenhower obtain the sponsorship of Phil Heath, editor of the *Abilene Chronicle*, a Progressive Republican newspaper. Heath had also been Bristow's campaign manager in Dickinson County. All in all, Eisenhower assembled an impressive dossier with strong letters of recommendation from Abilene's business community to forward to the senator. And all this from a young man who, when he ran for president of the United States years later, was accused by certain editors of lacking political skills or determination.

Eisenhower wrote Senator Bristow to introduce himself; he forwarded his letters of recommendation and requested Bristow's appointment to either Annapolis or West Point. Impressed by Eisenhower's local support as well as his solid high school record, Bristow gave Eisenhower permission to take the senator's qualifying exam given in Topeka. Fortunately, in anticipation of taking the competitive entrance exams for either Annapolis or West Point, Eisenhower had reenrolled in Abilene High School in the fall of 1910 to take refresher courses in mathematics, chemistry, and physics (and, because there were no eligibility rules at that time, once again to play football for Abilene High). In addition, he and Swede Hazlett studied together nightly, establishing team-studying techniques that would benefit Eisenhower for years to come.

At Bristow's exam in Topeka, Eisenhower placed second out of eight, receiving his highest scores in grammar, algebra, and arithmetic. Because he had stated he was willing to attend either Annapolis or West Point, Bristow could appoint him to either school. Mindful of the political sensitivity of his appointments, however, Bristow forwarded the examination results to his friend and political ally Phil Heath in Abilene. Heath advised Bristow to nominate Eisenhower to West Point for the class of 1915, enrolling in June of 1911. Although Bristow informed him of his nomination to West Point, Eisenhower still needed to pass West Point's grueling four-day entrance examination given at the Jefferson Barracks in St. Louis, Missouri.

While waiting for the West Point examination date, he continued his studies, including borrowing books from Joe Howe's library. On March 25, 1911,

Eisenhower wrote Bristow in Salina, thanking the senator for his support and informing him that he had passed the examination and would report to West Point on June 14. Years later, Eisenhower generally dismissed questions concerning his motivation to attend West Point, stating what to him seemed obvious and acceptable—that he was a poor boy, without prospects, inheritance, or influence, who had jumped at the opportunity to receive a free education at the expense of Uncle Sam. He gave Swede Hazlett sole credit for encouraging him to attend West Point, although other accounts state that Joe Howe, among others, had alerted Eisenhower to the possibility of enrolling in one of the country's service academies. What Eisenhower never acknowledged was that receiving his appointment to West Point was not akin to collecting dropped apples for the cider mill. Behind Eisenhower's good fortune there is also a story of influence, connections, mentoring, ambition, merit, and luck.

Heartbroken Parents

Across America in 1910, Dwight Eisenhower's decision to attend the United States Military Academy at West Point would hardly be considered an act of rebellion, let alone a declaration of independence. But in Abilene, Kansas, Eisenhower's decision to enroll at West Point was a blow to his devoutly pacifist parents. Already, his older brothers had challenged their father's deepest prejudices against bankers and lawyers when Arthur moved to Kansas City to become a banker and Edgar defied his father to study law. Now, with his decision to become a soldier, Eisenhower had to deal with his parents' deeply ingrained pacifism. Being a young Democrat proved a relatively minor handicap in securing an appointment to West Point when compared to quieting his parents' profound religious disappointment. Their son's chosen career in the military—to become a warrior—could not have clashed more directly with their core pacifist religious beliefs.

They were heartbroken, but impassive, when they learned of Dwight's appointment to the academy. Characteristically, while disapproving, David and Ida's religious beliefs dictated that Dwight must make his own decision about his life's work, just as David had made his own decisions. Unwarranted intrusion into their son's life would constitute an act of great violence abhorred by his pacifist parents. They believed that fundamental life decisions, such as Ike's choice of career, or his refusal to allow his leg to be amputated, were moral decisions made between their son and God. And only God, not them, could judge his choice of calling. To insist otherwise would not only violate their relationship with their son but also reflect their lack of trust in God. The Eisenhowers embraced the Protestant belief that no one required a mediator between themselves and God. No church, no priest, no parent could decide how best to serve God. "It is your choice," his mother simply confirmed.

A Lonely Train Ride

On the June morning that Eisenhower left Abilene for West Point, his father was at work. His brothers were either at work, at school, or out of town. Only Ida, Milton, and his dog Flip were on hand when the early morning train for Kansas City arrived. Ida hated displays of emotion, especially when a family member left home. As was her custom, she said good-bye to her son on their side porch. Feigning cheerfulness, Ida instead broke down in tears. Ike tried to reassure his mother with a hug and asked Milton to take care of her. That was too much for Milton, who also began to cry. Hearing the train's whistle across the prairie, a flustered Ike kissed Ida good-bye, told his dog to stay, and hurried up the street alone to the station while Ida retired to her room. Later, Milton reported that for the first time in his life he had heard his mother sob.

There is a second version of his departure that also reflects the tension of his decision to attend West Point. Ida had shed no tears when Arthur left for Kansas City to work at the bank nor when Edgar left for Ann Arbor to study law at the University of Michigan. But when Dwight left, she wept almost as if in mourning. She cried, she later said, because Eisenhower's decision to attend West Point had challenged her faith; but she would not, could not, believe that her soldier son, contrary to Watchtower doctrine, would be condemned to hell. In this version taken from oral history, Eisenhower, unable to calm his mother, departed home abruptly about midnight and almost ran to the creamery, where he waited in the boiler room with a friend until the train arrived about 3:00 a.m.

Now, it cannot be determined whether Eisenhower caught the 3:00 a.m. train from Denver to Kansas City or if he caught a later train sometime around 6:00 a.m. It is not important, except that no matter which train he caught, one must wonder where his father, David, was. Was he in bed when Eisenhower left home around midnight to catch the night-owl train, or was he at work later in the early morning when Eisenhower caught the train at Union Station about 6:00 a.m.? Either way, in bed or at work, it seems extraordinary that David did not see his son off to New York. The creamery was located along the main line, just a few blocks from the railroad station. Given the sterling work record of both David and

Dwight at the creamery, it seems improbable that their River Brethren relatives who ran the creamery would not have allowed David at least a half hour leave to say good-bye to his son boarding the train just blocks away. The River Brethren, also pacifists, could not have been happy about Eisenhower's choice of a military career, but would they have been so hard-hearted as to deny father and son their farewells? Eisenhower family tradition kindly agrees that David was occupied at work the morning Eisenhower left for West Point. David's absence was probably not simply stubbornness and pride; David, like Ida, was undoubtedly profoundly hurt that his son was leaving for the United States Military Academy and simply couldn't reveal his religious and personal fears to his wife and family.

His son Dwight shared David's emotional reticence. Years later, in March 1942, Brigadier General Eisenhower, then deputy to General George Marshall for Operations of the United States Army, sat alone in his Washington office meditating on his father's death. According to Eisenhower lore, because of the press of war duties, there was no possibility for him to return to Abilene for his father's funeral. The irony that he was too caught up in the war to attend David's funeral may have escaped him. "I closed the door of my office and sat thinking about the life we had all had together," he later wrote. He noted:

March 11, 1942

My father was buried today. I've shut off all business and visitors for thirty minutes—to have that much time, by myself, to think of him. He had a full life. . . . He was a just man, well liked, a thinker. He was undemonstrative, quiet, modest and of exemplary habits. . . . His word has been his bond and accepted as such. . . . Because of it, all central Kansas helped me secure an appointment to West Point in 1911. . . . My only regret is that it was always so difficult to let him know the great depth of my affection for him.

One wonders whether David also sat silently and alone thinking about his son on that June morning in 1911, all the while listening as the train bearing Dwight eastward toward his military destiny picked up speed while passing the Belle Springs Creamery.

West Point

If Eisenhower had any misgivings about attending West Point, all doubts were swept away his first day at the academy. As intended, the day began with calculated chaos, as self-important upperclassman barked incomprehensible orders and forced the new cadets to run double time around campus. All changed that evening, however, when, dressed in his new uniform, Eisenhower and the other plebes assembled on the Plain, the West Point parade ground, to watch the Corps of Cadets, the famed "Long Gray Line," pass smartly in review. As designed, the military band, the flags, the pomp, and parade quickened Eisenhower's pulse and refreshed his tired body. He was fully alert when the assembled plebes raised their right hands to pledge allegiance to the Constitution and to the government of the United States. Now, he was not only a cadet at West Point but also, by act of Congress, a member of the US Army. For Eisenhower, it was a transforming moment not unlike a believer's baptism practiced among his relatives back in Kansas. Suddenly the Stars and Stripes took on concrete meaning for Eisenhower. "From here on it would be the nation I would be serving, not myself," he resolved.

Ida believed that West Point would transform her son. He had been born David Dwight Eisenhower, but had been called Dwight by his mother while growing up in Abilene so that there were not two Davids in the house. When he signed the adjutant's register at West Point, he initiated the transformation by formally changing his name. Without doubt, Dwight D. Eisenhower's West Point years were remarkably beneficial. The class of 1915 would become the "class that the stars fell on," as more than half of the class that served in World War II became generals, while Eisenhower and his good friend Omar Bradley rose to the five-star rank of General of the Armies.

Eisenhower and his cohorts had enrolled at West Point at a propitious time for young, upwardly mobile military officers. During his four years at West Point, Eisenhower, like students everywhere, made little immediate impact on the institution itself. On the other hand, while three of Eisenhower's major biographers provide insightful analysis of his West Point years, they offer widely differing interpretations of what impact, if any, West Point made on Eisenhower.

The most agnostic of the biographers, Ken Davis (also a prize-winning biographer of his political hero, Franklin Delano Roosevelt), believed that Eisenhower's fundamental personality and values were largely untouched by West Point. "His basic attitudes and beliefs were already set," Davis wrote. "Four years on the dedicated Plain could do nothing to change them. The metal was hard enough to take a high surface polish, under extreme pressures, without cracking—and it was polish which West Point gave him—polish and the basic mental tools of his trade." In his annotation of Davis's biography,

Eisenhower verbally snorted but did not disagree with Davis's assessment. "A Solomon sits in judgment," he noted laconically.

In dramatic contrast to Davis, Geoffrey Perret, in *Eisenhower*, observed that West Point was the central, lasting institution that shaped Eisenhower's identity and established purpose in his life. Davis's biography lingered in Abilene before moving Eisenhower to West Point. Perret shrewdly noted that Eisenhower's personal memoir *At Ease* began at West Point, which was Eisenhower's way of saying that *here* was where his life really began—not in Abilene but at the academy. Understandably, Perret does not use evangelical language to argue that Eisenhower was "born again" when he took the oath at West Point. Neither Eisenhower nor his biographer would describe that moment on the Plain when he accepted his new destiny as a religious experience.

But Perret's implication is clear. At West Point, Eisenhower began to hear themes of the "calling" his mother had talked about so much in his youth. The school's motto—Duty, Honor, Country—evoked something considerably larger than what he had known in Abilene: a personal commitment not only to the nation as a whole but also to values of self-sacrifice, community, loyalty, friendship, and brotherhood that transcended Kansas, his family, and his private ambitions.

Eisenhower's was a cultural transformation at West Point that not only involved learning the US Army's way of warfare but also included assuming another identity based on adopting a new "we consciousness," a typical product of all rites of passage. College fraternities, through their rituals and secrets, accomplish similar transformations. The stronger a group's "we consciousness," the stronger and more clearly defined are the boundaries between who belongs within the culture and who is an outsider. All social groups with a strong sense of "we" share an equally intense negative reference, as in Army versus Navy. At West Point, "we consciousness" was built upon shared experience (hazing and being hazed), propinquity (drill, close quarters, and shared meals), isolation (from former family, associates, and civilian life in general), shared values (Duty, Honor, Country), common language (West Point and army argot), and, most importantly, a sense of common history and destiny as officers and gentlemen in the United States Army that was inculcated by the West Point program and staff.

Regimes such as West Point also tend to promote a phenomenon known as "convergent thinking," that is, an intense rite of passage tends to weed out those who cannot or will not embrace the mores and culture of the initiating institution; conversely, those who successfully navigate the initiation passage generally emerge believing that the process was not so bad but that it appropriately, in the case of West Point, separated the men from the boys.

Of course, West Point was not unique among American institutions in developing distinctive rites of passage. Traveling east through Illinois, Eisenhower remembered seeing the grim walls of the penitentiary at Joliet, Illinois. While speeding northward from New York City on the West Shore Railroad, he likewise may have noticed America's most infamous prison, Sing Sing, looming gray and foreboding on the opposite bank of the Hudson River at Ossining. Almost thirty miles due south of West Point as the crow flies, Sing Sing was linked to West Point by both the Hudson River and American institutional history. Military schools and American prisons share several social and cultural assumptions. Both are responsible for molding young men, primarily, into loyal soldiers or productive citizens in an institutional setting isolated from the society into which each must return. Both West Point and Sing Sing have been compared to monasteries, a curious institutional model in a democratic society where anti-Catholic prejudice ran high. At Sing Sing, the tiny gray cells and massive cell blocks aped monastic architecture, while silence and regimentation copied monastic discipline. Perched atop a river bluff, its gray granite walls housing the "Long Gray Line," West Point inspired awe and reverence in like measure.

While the prison's objective was to punish convicts, its principal goal was to purge the souls of criminals through a prison discipline of isolation and silence. Hopefully, Bible reading and hours of solitary contemplation would promote penitence from sin among the prisoners. Although a secular penal institution, Sing Sing Penitentiary sought religious conversion and reform of its inmates in what might be regarded as a utopian or dystopian setting, depending on one's point of view. Not surprisingly, some of Sing Sing's most notable wardens were former military officers.

Similarly, West Point employed techniques of isolation, military regimentation, and humiliation to mold army officers. The United States Military Academy initially adopted the Greek ideal of education and training in a remote sanctuary on a hill, a sacred place of wisdom and skill. But in *Eisenhower: A Soldier's Life*, biographer Carlo D'Este observed that "West Point has been aptly described as a military monastery whose occupants were isolated from the outside diseases of commercialism and money grubbing," a description that was also apt for Sing Sing. D'Este noted that Douglas MacArthur once compared West Point to a "provincial reformatory" where fear dominated four years of penal servitude. Like Sing Sing's foreboding architecture, the West Point setting was intentionally austere to encourage cadets, like the convicts downriver, to look inward, examining their self-worth and self-reliance. Importantly, while West Point strove to mold Eisenhower into a United States Army officer, Eisenhower also self-consciously pondered his own identity and destiny. He might have been shocked had he known that convicts at Sing Sing wrestled with the same question he often asked himself about West Point, "What am I doing here?"—a question that led to reflections about where he had come from, by what route, and why?

Dwight Eisenhower fit easily into the West Point routine, where, by his own account, he was more interested in athletics than in his studies. Although he attended the required chapel services, contrary to his pietistic upbringing, he resumed card playing and took up smoking cigarettes, the latter against the rules for cadets. Although the rules were clear and enforced with punishment tours, he continued to smoke. This small rebellion was not surprising, but it was also evident that young Eisenhower was not merely rebelling against army discipline. Like many youths who have unresolved issues with their fathers, Eisenhower struggled with issues of authority. It has been said that the oldest child generally follows the rules while the youngest child doesn't give a damn about the rules. Middle children, like Eisenhower, it has been observed, often probe and poke at authority to find out what the rules really are.

Issues with Authority

Given the marked freedom that young boys enjoyed in Abilene, Dwight's issues with authority were not pronounced while he was in high school. Occasionally he skipped classes, on occasion his famous temper flared, from time to time he seemed indifferent to school rules. By all accounts, he did not share a close bond with his father, who never camped, fished, or hunted with his sons. But he loved Bob Davis, who, in contrast to his father, mentored Eisenhower but did not attempt to raise him. Joe Howe, on the other hand, had tried to provide needed structure and direction in his life and, consequently, had earned for his efforts some resentment and ingratitude from Eisenhower.

Lack of parental supervision or adult guidance in his life is evident during Eisenhower's slow transition from high school to West Point. In crucial steps during the application process to West Point, he falsified his age to be a year younger than he actually was and either forgot or did not know that his birthplace was Denison, Texas, rather than Tyler, as he represented. These were strange errors for the twenty-year-old Eisenhower, for even if he thought there was some temporary advantage gained by his misinformation (the age limit for Annapolis was nineteen), surely he knew the truth would eventually come out.

More problematical and inexplicable was his high adventure in St. Louis when he was at the Jefferson Barracks taking the West Point entrance examination. Having had free rein around Abilene and having been accustomed to working all night, Eisenhower, along with another candidate, decided to explore St. Louis one night during their four-day examination rather than turning into their bunks at taps. One thing led to another, and after midnight they found themselves stranded in East St. Louis, Illinois, on the east bank of the Mississippi River, too late to catch a streetcar back to the barracks. A bartender kindly told them how to walk back across the railroad bridge to catch a 1:00 a.m. streetcar to their quarters. Arriving well past curfew, the aspiring cadets circumvented the guard at the main gate, climbed over the wall in inky darkness, found their dormitory, and snuck undetected into bed. Later, even Eisenhower admitted that his midnight ramble in St. Louis had been foolish, but it certainly reflected his devil-may-care indifference to the possible consequences of a would-be West Point cadet being caught sneaking into the US Army's Jefferson Barracks in the wee hours of the morning.

His indifference, or insensitivity, at being caught in questionable behavior at this time has never been assessed. Undoubtedly, Eisenhower loved high adventure, especially if it flirted with danger. Although described as "adrift" by one biographer, after high school he was probably plagued by ennui and inflated self-confidence. Either in the summer of 1910 or late spring of 1911, before entering West Point, he joined the Junction City Soldiers, a semiprofessional baseball team, to play center field under the assumed name of Wilson. He later explained that his motive for playing semipro baseball was that he needed the money to help pay college expenses, a reason that rings true only if his sights were not yet fixed firmly on attending West Point. But the fact that he played under an alias indicates that he knew full well he needed to protect his amateur status if he wanted to play college sports anywhere.

But Eisenhower protected his subterfuge well. Had he been discovered, he may have been refused entrance to or graduation from West Point; certainly the coveted letter (the Army *A*) he earned playing football his sophomore year would have been denied or revoked. As it turned out, Eisenhower badly wrenched his knee during his first season playing varsity at West Point in 1912. One can only wonder why he took the risk to play semipro baseball for a couple of weeks in May while packing his bags for West Point. The answer may be as simple as the fact that he needed ready cash to pay his train fare and expenses to Chicago and points east. But his boldness at playing for the Junction City Soldiers is as breathtaking as it is puzzling.

Eisenhower would prove to be a good student, but he did not excel academically. Generally, the classes were not difficult for him. His easygoing approach to school, his good humor and leadership skills, and his love of sports were complemented by his lackadaisical concern for West Point's strict discipline. He resented rigid, arbitrary authority and soon racked up a remarkable number of demerits. Much of Eisenhower's flagrant rule breaking could be considered late-adolescent mischief, yet there is something odd in the behavior of this young man who reached his majority in his plebe year. Although well trained in housekeeping by his mother, Eisenhower received regular demerits for his unmade bed, dusty shelves, dirty shoes, and generally messy quarters. When he did not skip chapel and classes, he was often late in attendance or late in submitting his work. He was sometimes sloppy in uniform and careless on duty, and even reported himself once for not staying at his post as Officer of the Guard. More seriously, perhaps, he smoked cigarettes and gambled at poker, both clearly forbidden by West Point rules. Although occasionally caught smoking in his room, he was never officially reprimanded for gambling.

Hazing

Freshman hazing was commonplace among American colleges until the 1960s, especially at schools with fraternities or at military schools where plebes were subjected to intense initiation rites. Hazing plebes at West Point was customary when Eisenhower arrived in June 1911. Eisenhower loved a good time and reveled in verbal and physical give-and-take with his peers. He was popular for his unfailing good spirits as well as his mischievous temperament. But despite his ultimate commitment to the army, Eisenhower frequently held institutional culture at arm's length, whether it be church, political parties, or, as at West Point, hazing tradition. Although he participated in hazing as both a plebe and an upperclassman, Eisenhower was uncomfortable with this institutionalized form of bullying. He did not complain about West Point's hazing tradition publicly but settled his personal ambivalence with it privately.

As a plebe, he daringly challenged the system through an exaggerated, passively aggressive response to harassment by a corporal in his division. Having figured out that the punishments dealt out by overzealous upperclassmen carried no serious bite, Eisenhower schemed about ways to torment his tormentors. After a minor infraction, the corporal ordered Eisenhower and a friend to present themselves in his room in "full-dress coats." Obeying the corporal literally, the two plebes reported wearing only their cutaway coats and nothing else. Completely losing his temper, the corporal roared his disapproval of the plebes' outrageous military deportment, and in doing so, roused numerous upperclassmen within earshot. Upon investigating the commotion, some cadets were as shocked as the corporal, but others thought the scene was hilarious. Reprimanded amid cries of righteous indignation and gales of horse laughter, Eisenhower and his friend were sent back to their rooms but ordered to return "in complete uniform including rifles and cross belts." Thereafter, the two misfits were forced to stand at attention until the wall behind them was outlined by their sweat. In the long run, however, Eisenhower counted complete victory over the corporal. Not only did the plebes now have something to snicker about whenever they encountered the mortified cadet, but also Eisenhower himself was never again subjected to hazing at West Point.

When the tables were turned during his second year at West Point, Eisenhower did engage in some hazing of the plebes; that is, until the day that he literally ran into a cadet from Kansas. The collision knocked the plebe down. With proper upperclass mock indignation, Eisenhower asked the plebe, with all the sarcasm and scorn he could muster, what his previous condition of servitude was. Then he blurted out, "You look like a barber!"

"I was a barber, Sir," the dishonored plebe replied. With neither a word, nor a joke, nor an apology, Eisenhower spun on his heels and, mortified, returned to his quarters, where he confessed to his roommate that he had just done something terribly stupid and unforgivable.

"I have managed to make a man ashamed of the work he did to earn a living." He must have been flooded with thoughts from home—of his dad, Bob Davis, former colleagues at the creamery, farmers and field hands with whom he had sweated, and a host of others, especially the town barbers whom he fondly admired. The incident troubled Eisenhower the remainder of his life, and never again did he hassle a plebe at West Point.

West Point Football

In the fall of 1912 Eisenhower suffered his greatest setback and calamity at West Point. During his plebe year he had worked hard to gain weight, increase his speed, and build up muscle. To his delight, his hard work paid off when he made the varsity football team the following season. Slowly he worked himself into the lineup, playing both ways, as was common in 1912: running the ball on offense and playing linebacker on defense. Regarded by his coach and the press as one of West Point's most promising football players, he severely injured his knee playing Tufts, just a week before the climactic Army-Navy game. Despite his injury, he had played enough to win his coveted Army *A*.

The knee injury, however, not only ended his season but also ended his Army football career and almost cost him his commission. He would remain as active in sports as he was able, but mostly he was confined to the sidelines as cheerleader and coach of the junior varsity team. In a sense, his finest hours at West Point were over before the end of his third semester at the academy. Years later Eisenhower did not contradict Ken Davis's assertion that his football injury resulted in his most bitter disappointment at West Point. There would be no gridiron glory for Ike.

Eisenhower worked hard at staying positive, but when he returned to Abilene on furlough the summer of 1913, he arrived with a chip on his shoulder and something to prove. He arrived in Abilene unannounced in the dead of night. He would rather tell no one he was coming home than be disappointed when no one, especially his father, met him at the station. Flip, his dog, was the first one to recognize his familiar gait as he approached the house. Ida was overjoyed to see her son, and Eisenhower had to struggle to control his emotions. His father, as usual, was cordial but taciturn.

Abilene's Great White Hope

After two years of West Point conditioning and toughening under his belt, Eisenhower apparently returned home with something to prove, but for the moment he had to content himself with youthful vanity. He was welcomed in Abilene as a minor hero by adults and children alike. He reveled in their attention and strutted around town in his form-fitting West Point gray uniform, to the admiration of his friends and the appreciation of at least one pretty girl, Gladys Harding, whom he now had the courage to ask out on a date.

In 1913 boxing was popular in Abilene and at West Point. His knee injury in football had forced Eisenhower to forgo boxing as well, but his interest in the sport remained high. Boxing was one of Abilene's most popular spectator sports, and impromptu boxing matches between men or boys were not uncommon in the basements of the Tip-Top Restaurant and Sterl's Department Store. Boxing fans in Abilene were also very much aware that Jack Johnson, from Galveston, Texas, was the first black boxer to win the world's heavyweight title in 1908. Overnight, Johnson became the most famous African American in the world. And just as immediately, the boxing establishment searched for a "Great White Hope" to dethrone Johnson. Former undefeated heavyweight James J. Jeffries, who had not fought in six years, was cajoled to come out of retirement to reclaim his title from the black champion.

On July 4, 1910, almost a year before Eisenhower left for West Point, Johnson defeated Jeffries, then America's Great White Hope, in the "Fight of the Century" in Reno, Nevada. Following Johnson's victory, rioting broke out across the United States in nearly twenty-five states and fifty cities, in many cases sparked when local police forces, aided by white ruffians, tried to quell black celebrations. More viewers watched the film of the Johnson/Jeffries fight than any other movie until the showing of *The Birth of a Nation* in 1915. Johnson exacerbated racial tensions by his flamboyant lifestyle and open contempt for racial taboos involving the black prizefighter's sexual relations with white women. Whites saw Johnson as pompous and arrogant, in short, an "uppity" black who did not keep his proper place in American society.

When he stepped off the train from Kansas City in June 1913, Eisenhower stepped into the middle of rising racial tensions in Abilene. Dirk Tyler, a burly black porter and town roustabout, had established himself as the unofficial fisticuffs champion of the town. Emulating his idol, Jack Johnson, Tyler purportedly swaggered about town, to the deep resentment of Eisenhower's friends. Worse, the white boys felt bullied by the big black fighter, who they believed had threatened to beat anyone who stood in his way. "You ought to take him, Ike," a friend urged. Otherwise, Dirk Tyler was likely to run into serious trouble.

Whatever thoughts Eisenhower might have entertained about becoming Abilene's Great White Hope against Dirk Tyler, inexorably the matter seemed to resolve itself. While Eisenhower sat in the barber chair getting his hair cut, Dirk came into the shop, where he worked. It is not certain whether the two men were goaded into a fight by whites or whether Dirk directly challenged Eisenhower. Apparently, Eisenhower was also put off by Dirk's swagger, which he thought teetered between condescension and contempt. Given Eisenhower's deep embarrassment over the hazing incident at West Point, Dirk could not have picked a more symbolic place than the town barbershop to challenge Eisenhower to a fight. There is no doubt that West Point's honor was at stake, but Eisenhower also thrived on personal risk and physical challenge.

Eisenhower replied calmly that he would fight Dirk as soon as his barber finished cutting his hair. Word quickly spread: there would be a fight between black Dirk Tyler and Abilene's homegrown cadet from West Point in Sterl's basement. Soon a crowd gathered and formed a makeshift ring, a referee was selected, and the men agreed to fight two-minute rounds, with a minute breather between rounds.

Stripped to the waist and sweating, the heavily muscled Dirk seemed to loom before the crowd even more threateningly. Characteristically, Eisenhower hurriedly devised a plan. An experienced amateur boxer, he knew that Dirk was strong but probably not fit, and thus vulnerable to body blows. His best option against Dirk's size, strength, and weight was to counterpunch and, if possible, to launch a surprise attack on his foe's midsection.

There was a worry. Jack Johnson, Dirk's hero, always started slowly, feeling out his opponent for several rounds, probing for weaknesses and vulnerability. Johnson's white critics had brayed that his boxing tactics belied cowardliness. Eisenhower knew that with his weakened knee, if Dirk employed Johnson-like tactics, he could falter. But to Eisenhower's great advantage, Dirk turned out to be more of a barroom brawler than a professional boxer. At the signal to box, Dirk rushed to the middle of the ring, his ham fists flailing the air. Eisenhower, despite his gimpy knee, easily parried and sidestepped Dirk's rush. What happened next occurred so fast—a virtual blur of action—that no one is certain how Eisenhower ended the fight in less than a minute. Some believe that Eisenhower countered Dirk's rush with a series of right and left uppercuts to the jaw that flattened Dirk on the spot; others say he hit the black porter with a single, hard punch to the solar plexus that instantly paralyzed him. Whatever, the fight ended quickly, with Eisenhower the hero of the moment among his friends in Abilene.

There is a striking similarity between the story about Eisenhower defeating Dirk and his childhood conquest of the tyrant goose in Uncle Luther's farmyard. In both stories, Eisenhower is ostensibly outmatched by the speed and brawn of a demonic foe: Dirk and the goose. In both instances, he is called upon to reestablish peace and order in the town or on the farm: in the first by his friends, in the second by Uncle Luther. And in both instances, fortified by moral courage, equipped with superior skills, and sustained by a calm analysis of his tormentor's weaknesses, Eisenhower triumphed not only in his civic duty but also in his calling to restore peace. It is unimportant whether or not the goose provided Christmas dinner. What is different about these stories is the fact that Eisenhower supposedly provided redemption to Dirk Tyler. Following the fight, the champion's friends teased Dirk so unmercifully that Eisenhower felt compelled to intervene to protect Dirk from Abilene hazing. In local legend, oozing white superiority, the story ends happily when Dirk, properly chastened, once again becomes a nice, friendly guy. On reflection, however, Eisenhower knew that his thrashing of Dirk Tyler was not something about which he could be proud.

Demerits at West Point

One might think that, after his 1913 furlough in Abilene, Eisenhower returned to West Point refreshed and raring to go. But because there would be no football for him that fall, Eisenhower felt lassitude and discouragement that he tried to sublimate through feckless behavior. For his remaining years at West Point, Eisenhower continued to collect conduct demerits at an astonishing rate, accompanied by an ever-accelerating smoking habit and a passion for winning poker. Because cigar and pipe smoking were allowed in dormitory rooms, Eisenhower coyly accounted for his supply of cigarette tobacco by explaining that he purchased bags of Bull Durham tobacco at the cadet store. He simply rolled his own cigarettes, a common practice among young college smokers. What he didn't explain, however, was the source of his rolling paper, which was not available at the cadet store. Cigarettes and poker playing, of course, became early partners, especially when cigarettes became commodity currency in cash-strapped institutions such as Sing Sing and perhaps West Point. Where Eisenhower obtained his contraband cigarette paper has never been explained.

Eisenhower's most daring and reckless exploits at West Point involved going AWOL (absent without leave) from campus on larks to Newburg, New York. Reminiscent of his escapade from the Jefferson Barracks during his West Point entrance examinations, Eisenhower and others would escape their dormitory through lavatory windows, creep by the sentry post, and take off up the Hudson River in a rented boat to Newburg, fifteen miles from West Point. According to one version, once in Newburg, the cadets drank "coffee" and ate sandwiches. No mention is made of their buying cigarette papers or purchasing other contraband for their return to school. For this alone, Eisenhower and his comrades could have been expelled. In addition to their toots into Newburg, during summer camp Eisenhower and his friends reportedly paid a local grocer from nearby Highland Falls to leave a cache of food at the base of the steep cliff rising from the Hudson River, where it could be retrieved at high risk of disciplinary penalty. Perhaps the cache contained only candy bars, crackers, and other innocuous food items; perhaps it also contained libations and other black-market goods smuggled year-round via Eisenhower's "underground railroad" into the Point via the barrack's latrine. It is Carlo D'Este's opinion that Eisenhower was almost certainly in the middle of most mischief at the academy.

Were West Point officials clueless about the off-campus shenanigans of Eisenhower and his friends? Or did they covertly admire the initiative and daring exhibited by these prospective army officers? In later years, when Ei-senhower learned that one of his classmates had been promoted to general, he scoffed, "How did *he* ever make general? He never broke a regulation in his life!"

Obviously, fellow cadets knew of his misdeeds, but the vaunted West Point honor system apparently applied only to academic sins. Eisenhower had actu-ally reported himself for comparatively minor infractions of cadet regulations, but he saw no need to be forthcoming about behavior that might have resulted in his expulsion from the academy. While all this was quite understandable, it is also fascinating how Eisenhower and his fellow cadets could compartmen-talize high standards of military conduct required by duty and honor from behavior that was clearly against the rules but acceptable as long you were not caught. The West Point honor system evidently did not require cadets to rat on their compatriots for academy infractions not related to classroom performance.

West Point Graduation

When he graduated in the spring of 1915, he ranked 125th in discipline out of a class of 162 (he finished 61st, or in the thirty-eighth percentile, academically). Over a hundred plebes from the entering class of 1911 did not graduate with him. He had been promoted twice, and twice he was busted back to private for behavior unbecoming of a West Point cadet (which included inappropri-ate dancing at a school social). In his senior year, however, he was selected to be a color sergeant, an honor that included carrying the academy colors during dress parades. While Eisenhower embraced West Point's values: "Duty, Honor, Country," upon graduation he did not appear to be an outstanding prospect for high command in the US Army. One evaluation noted his leader-ship potential as a commander of troops, but another thought he would serve the army in much the same manner as his sojourn at West Point—he would enjoy army life, giving to duty and play equal measure. Evidence that West Point administrators knew something of Eisenhower's clandestine adventures was reflected in the placement recommendation that he should be assigned to a post with a strict commanding officer.

Despite his wrecked knee, questionable disciplinary record, average grades, and lingering melancholy, Eisenhower graduated from West Point well liked by cadets, faculty, and administrators. He had arrived at West Point alone with a smoldering anger toward rigid, arbitrary authority and a high sensitivity toward institutional unfairness toward himself and others. During his some-what bumpy years at West Point, he took major steps at resolving his conflict with authority and controlling his ferocious temper. He had proven to himself that he could thumb his nose at petty regulations and get away with it. As a cadet, he was most interested in playing varsity athletics, at which he did not excel, and making lasting friendships, for which he was best remembered.

In concert with most of his class, he internalized the academy's motto— Duty, Honor, Country—and made it his own. And yet, he kept emotional distance from his alma mater, and when given the opportunity to become West Point's commandant, he demurred. His college transcript, however, was not indicative of what he had learned about becoming an American warrior. At West Point, Eisenhower learned and practiced leadership skills that won him friendships and esteem from cadets and faculty alike. He not only learned how to take the measure of a man, but he also discovered that to gain the respectful confidence of men, he had to give them respect and affection in return.

In addition to duty, honor, and country, Eisenhower would come to cher-ish a fourth ideal that was most evident in his behavior as a young man. Not yet fully developed but originally inspired by Ida and David and nurtured by West Point, Eisenhower self-consciously worked at developing humility—by not acting or believing that he was better than others. His internal struggle to restrain his latent anger, his large ego, and his driving ambition may have accounted, in part, for his middle-of-the-pack academic accomplishments. He was ashamed by his hazing of the plebe that had been a barber. He felt uneasy about dominating fellow cadets at poker. His thrashing of Dirk Tyler, while troubling, could be justified in his own mind as long as he rationalized that, while he respected Dirk, the beating had been for Tyler's benefit. He fought always to contain his hot temper. And he wanted to earn his way in life through merit and not favoritism but was embarrassed that too often he had advanced through influence fueled by his charm and infectious grin. He learned that his practiced humility would not appear phony if clothed in genuine respect and caring for others. In this way, respect and friendship for all became the foun-dation stone of his belief in the inherent dignity of man, a belief that helped him transcend his personal demons.

Graduations are festive occasions; they are a time for the graduate, his family, and his friends to celebrate years of study and accomplishment and to look forward to a future blessed by the fulfillment of youthful dreams and ambition. Like baptisms, confirmation, and weddings, a graduation can be a time of decision filled with potential and life-defining meaning; a pregnant moment in which the self can receive a new birth of identity. Culturally, each of these events marks a significant transition in personal history in which the celebrant emigrates from one historical group to another . . . before and after groups that define who the celebrant was and has become.

On June 11, they gathered on the Plain at West Point: the graduates, the corps of cadets, faculty, officers, the secretary of war, and most importantly, parents, brothers and sisters, girlfriends, and adoring relatives, to applaud the commissioning of the cadets who would become collectively the storied class of 1915. Who could know what lay ahead for these young men? As he walked quickly through the graduation ceremony, Eisenhower had no need to look right or left, or to try to identify his mother's voice in the crowd. Ida was not there. Nor were his father or his brothers. Four years before, he had left Abilene alone to seek his destiny. And now, for the moment, he was alone again, but this time he knew he would soon be assimilated by one of the oldest fraternities in the country—the United States Army.

Transformation

In addition to donning an army uniform, perhaps the greatest change in Eisenhower's life when he left Abilene was that he no longer lived in a religious community. Although his parents were not members of the River Brethren congregation, David and Ida maintained a Bible-centered household. For more than thirty years, the army became Dwight Eisenhower's surrogate church. Although Dwight and Mamie Doud were married in a home wedding by a visiting English pastor in Denver in 1916, they did not join a church until 1953 when they moved into the White House. In effect, the army became Eisenhower's church, if not his religion, with his devotion to duty and his developing belief in the dignity of man serving as the cornerstones of his personal faith.

From the time he graduated from West Point until he became president of the United States, there is scant record that Dwight and Mamie attended chapel or church while Eisenhower was on active duty in the army. On the contrary, there is evidence that his attendance at worship services was spotty at best. When he served under General Douglas MacArthur in the Philippines, he was scolded by MacArthur for not attending church. Eisenhower allegedly shot back that he had "gone to the West Point Chapel so god damned often" that he was never going to church again.

Later, during World War II, Eisenhower's naval aide, Captain Harry C. Butcher, kept a diary of his three years with the commanding general from

1942 to 1945. Strikingly, during that entire stressful time, Butcher recorded only one occasion when Eisenhower attended church: on September 2, 1942, when Eisenhower had "to live up to his own proclamation of National Day of Prayer." Butcher saw the apparent hypocrisy of Eisenhower declaring a day of prayer for the troops and yet avoiding public prayer in chapel himself. Years later, his Gettysburg pastor, Robert MacAskill, explained that Ike and Mamie moved so often while in the army that they did not have an opportunity to sink deep religious roots. Perhaps so. But countless others in the armed services found time and opportunity to attend public worship despite their frequent military moves. Undoubtedly, Eisenhower had been attracted by the ecumenical orientation of the military chaplaincy. Although MacAskill believed the army had liberated Eisenhower from sectarianism and denominationalism, Eisenhower's aversion to institutional religious affiliations can in fact be traced back to his family history in Abilene. From his youth, Eisenhower had never embraced denominationalism, and, despite his baptism in the Presbyterian church, he never would.

Fort Sam Houston

In mid-September 1915, Eisenhower reported for his first duty assignment in the US Army as a second lieutenant in the Nineteenth Infantry Regiment stationed at Fort Sam Houston in San Antonio, Texas. The peacetime duty was not arduous, and the second lieutenants at Fort Sam Houston enjoyed considerable free time. Almost twenty-five years old, Eisenhower was nonetheless the most junior second lieutenant on the post.

Within a few weeks of his arrival at Fort Sam Houston, Dwight Eisenhower met Mamie Doud. Their introduction was casually informal. On a Sunday afternoon in October 1915, Officer of the Day Eisenhower, passing by the married officers' quarters on his way to inspect the guard posts, was interrupted when Lulu Harris, wife of Major Harris, invited Ike to meet her friends. As he hesitated to stop because he was on duty, Lulu Harris explained to her guests with a stage whisper that Eisenhower was "the woman-hater of the post." Harris's tease focused Eisenhower's attention on her friend, an attractive young girl who was looking at the handsome second lieutenant with great interest. Satirically, Harris jibed that he was not being invited to stay but merely to greet her guests.

Presently, Eisenhower was introduced to the Douds from Denver, who were wintering nearby in San Antonio. Their daughter, Mamie, to whom Eisenhower took an immediate interest, had recently made her debut in San Antonio. He was intrigued by her fashionable appearance: she was small but vivacious and attractive, "saucy in the look about her face and in her whole attitude." Spontaneously, he invited her to join him on his inspection rounds, and just as eagerly, with her mother's permission, she agreed to accompany him. They were an incongruous pair as they strolled the grounds of Fort Sam Houston; he dressed in olive drab uniform, his campaign hat squared on his head, his service pistol holstered at his side; she wearing her Sunday dress accented with fashionable laced boots she had purchased in New York. When their courtship began, she was eighteen and he was twenty-five.

If theirs was not love at first sight, it was close. After meeting Mamie, Ike's interest in other girls quickly waned. On the other hand, she lived near an army post, where eligible women were in short supply. For the next four months, despite his meager pay, Eisenhower dated Mamie whenever he could, favoring an inexpensive Mexican restaurant in San Antonio and the equally cheap Orpheum vaudeville house. Eisenhower otherwise walked two miles to the Doud residence to visit Mamie at her home, and when Mamie was occupied with another date, he might wait patiently on the Douds' veranda, chatting with Mamie's parents, John (Pupah) and Elivera (Nana).

The Douds offered adult friendship such as Eisenhower had not known in Abilene, and he warmed to the affection they showed him. John Doud was not certain that a soldier would make a proper husband for his debutante daughter, but he nevertheless chastised Mamie for apparently being overly coy with Eisenhower, advising his daughter to stop her flighty nonsense lest Eisenhower give up in disgust.

When Mamie stopped dating others, the couple simply assumed that they would marry, although Eisenhower had made no formal proposal. According to their granddaughter Susan, "Ike was captured by the utter femininity of 'Miss Doud,' a creature who embodied all the mystery of another world. . . . And Mamie was overwhelmed by Ike's sex appeal and masculinity." On February 14, 1916, they became engaged when Eisenhower presented Mamie his West Point class ring.

Pupah Doud gave his consent to the marriage on the condition that the couple wait until November when Mamie turned twenty, and that Eisenhower give up his ambition to become an army aviator. His daughter might marry a soldier, but Doud, believing that flying was a dangerous experiment, would not give his consent to Mamie's becoming the wife of an aviator. It was a bitter choice for Eisenhower, who had been on cloud nine after his acceptance for flight training. He chose Mamie, of course, and, not incidentally, her warm and loving family. But his resolve to marry while giving up his dreams of fly-ing also prompted a lifelong professional decision that he never regretted. "The decision," he later wrote, "was to perform every duty given me in the Army to the best of my ability and to do the best I could to make a creditable record, no matter what the nature of the duty." This vow, privately taken, set the boundaries between his duty to his country and his love of his wife.

Wedding Bells

In the spring of 1916, the United States Army edged toward a war footing. When Mamie agreed to get married as soon as possible, Eisenhower applied for a twenty-day leave. His colonel was unsympathetic but forwarded the leave request to General Funston, the department commander, who granted the request. He received ten days leave, barely enough time to travel to Denver, make arrangements, get married, honeymoon, and return to his duty station. The Douds were stunned by this sudden development but nevertheless gave their blessing to Mamie's determination to become Ike's bride. Plans for a big formal church wedding were scrapped, which did not disappoint Eisenhower, and instead, on July 1, 1916, Ike and Mamie were married in the Douds' music room, followed by a formal luncheon in the dining room.

After a brief honeymoon in the Colorado Rockies, they returned to Denver to thank the Douds once again and then boarded the late afternoon train for Abilene to pay their respects to David and Ida, who had not been able to at-tend their wedding. Ironically, Eisenhower may have returned to Abilene with his bride on the very same Union Pacific train that had carried him alone east-ward toward West Point five years earlier. This time, when the train arrived in Abilene around 4:00 a.m., David was waiting at the station to welcome home his son with his new bride. Incongruously, Mamie called the Eisenhowers "Grandpa" and "Grandma," but despite the great contrast between the Doud and the Eisenhower households, she was instantly embraced by Eisenhower's family, especially his brothers, Earl and Milton, who had never had a sister, which complemented Mamie's never having had brothers.

Because they had to leave for Texas the same day, instead of breakfast, Ida fixed the newlyweds a fried-chicken dinner with all the fixings. At 11:00 a.m., less than eight hours after their arrival in Abilene, Ike and Mamie boarded the train for Kansas City, where they transferred to the Missouri-Kansas-Texas Railroad (Katy railroad, the same railroad for which David had worked when Eisenhower was born) for their return to San Antonio as husband and wife.

War Clouds

Life became hectic and uncertain for the Eisenhowers on their return to Fort Sam Houston when American involvement in World War I upset any possibility of establishing a normal domestic routine. Too soon, Eisenhower was detailed as supply officer at a camp twenty miles from San Antonio. Thereafter, he transferred to Camp Oglethorpe, Georgia, to train officer candidates in trench warfare. Then he moved to Fort Leavenworth, Kansas, to train second lieutenants. In the meantime, Mamie, who had become pregnant, returned to Denver, where in September she gave birth to a son, Doud Dwight, quickly nicknamed Little Ike, shortened to Ikey and finally to Icky. Mamie's repeated separations from Ike were particularly difficult for the young mother. She had cried over her loneliness when Eisenhower left her. Trying his best to console Mamie, Eisenhower nevertheless reminded her that his duty would always come first. In time, she accepted this immutable fact, and it strengthened her.

Concurrently with receiving emergency leave to visit his wife and baby in Denver, Eisenhower sought assignment to a combat unit in France. When his requests were repeatedly denied, he despaired that he might end up sitting out the entire war assigned to Stateside training. At West Point, all traditions nourishing "élan and esprit" emphasized commanding troops bravely under fire. The hallmark of a successful officer was his ability to lead men in combat. Somewhat desperately, Eisenhower envisioned himself standing glumly, hands in his pockets, at West Point reunions while former classmates reminisced about their exploits in battle. That would be intolerable punishment for missing out on the war, and Eisenhower wondered whether he could stay in the army if he were denied the opportunity to fight.

Trouble in Abilene

Simultaneously in Abilene, Ida joined forces with fellow Jehovah's Witnesses to protest the war in Europe. In 1916, Woodrow Wilson campaigned for reelection with the slogan "He Kept Us Out of War." But following the declaration of war against Germany on April 6, 1917, the pacifistic Jehovah's Witnesses felt betrayed by presidential duplicity. Congress reacted to bitter antiwar opposition by passing the Espionage Act of 1917 and the Sedition Act of 1918, making it a federal crime to discourage recruitment or to make disloyal statements against the United States and its war aims. Before the end of the war, outspoken critics like Kate Richards O'Hare of Girard, Kansas, editor of the socialist publication the *National Ripsaw*, were arrested, convicted, and sentenced to prison along with Socialist Party leader Eugene V. Debs and anarchist Emma Goldman. Jehovah's Witnesses were also targets of war hysteria, especially after publication of *The Finished Mystery*, an alleged antiwar tract. On May 7, 1918, the Justice Department indicted twenty members of the Watch Tower Board of Trustees, eventually securing twenty-year prison sentences for the Watch Tower staff.

In Abilene, anti-German feeling ran high, perhaps because of the large minority of townsmen with German ancestry. Strongly linked to the anti-German bias, however, was religious intolerance. When Ida Eisenhower appeared on the street one Saturday selling the *Watch Tower* (the magazine's name was changed to the *Watchtower* in the 1930s), she stirred up deep hostility because of her apparent sympathy for the German cause. Despite the fact that Ida was asked not to make more trouble, she continued to sell the *Watch Tower* until one of Dwight's friends warned David that Ida risked arrest as antiwar and pro-German. Faced with this harsh assessment, David convinced Ida to suspend selling the *Watch Tower* for the duration of the war. If Dwight was aware of his mother's public opposition to the war, he remained silent and uncritical of her religious activities. The larger question is, did the army and the Justice Department know of Ida's antiwar activities?

With participation of the United States in the European war accelerating, Eisenhower was saddled with increasing responsibilities for training and supplying troops. In the winter of 1917, he was sent to Camp Meade, Maryland, to help the 301st Tank Battalion prepare for deployment to France. Men in the tank battalion were volunteers who considered themselves an elite corps whose tanks, juggernauts of combat, would play a decisive role in winning the war. Captain Eisenhower's morale was especially high because he had been told he would command the battalion in Europe. His euphoria did not last long, however, when at the last minute his commanding officer decided that Eisenhower was too valuable as a trainer of raw troops to be sent off to war. Instead, he was dispatched to Camp Colt at Gettysburg, Pennsylvania, to establish the army's first training and marshaling center for its new Tank Corps.

Camp Colt

Under Eisenhower's command, Camp Colt ballooned from a minor post of one thousand soldiers to a major tank-training center of just under eleven thousand men. The assignment was bittersweet. Although he had been denied his chance to lead troops in battle, Mamie and Icky were able to join him in Gettysburg, where for the first time they enjoyed comfortable family housing. His superior officer also tried to soften Eisenhower's disappointment by recommending him for promotion to major (temporary) and then to lieutenant colonel (temporary), making him one of the youngest lieutenant colonels in the army. Ultimately, in 1922, Eisenhower was awarded the Distinguished Service Medal for his work at Camp Colt, the army's highest peacetime decoration, usually given to generals and colonels but not to lieutenant colonels.

As commander of the tank-training corps, Eisenhower was responsible for the spiritual well-being of his men. At a ceremony dedicating an American flag, perhaps for the first time as an army officer, Eisenhower invoked America's civil religion. Reminding his men that in France they would be fighting under a flag whose principles stand "for justice, freedom and the right," he prayed that the ideals embodied in Old Glory would sustain them. "May you, when the work is done, return to your native land, but if God wills that you should stay, then let your comrades say that every man of the 330th showed in his every act all that America could ask of a Loyal son." This was a common prayer of hope and comfort in which Eisenhower implied that a provident God was somehow watching over the US Army and its men while participating in the outcome of what had become a holy war.

Spanish Flu Strikes

Besides preparing the Tank Corps for war, his most difficult challenge was fighting the Spanish flu pandemic that hit Camp Colt in 1918. Hundreds of soldiers became ill, and before the epidemic had run its course, 175 men died. Eisenhower met this emergency with characteristic firmness and innovation, going all-out to fight the flu virus. First, he did not meddle with the medical staff but put his full confidence in his chief physician, urging employment of all known remedies to curtail the epidemic. He ordered all available tents to be set up and limited his men to four in a tent. Troopers known to be exposed were isolated. In addition to quarantine, Eisenhower directed that all personnel receive inoculations for smallpox and typhoid fever and authorized use of experimental disinfectants in the camp. Finally, he initiated an enlightened strategy authorizing the military doctors to treat civilians in Gettysburg as well as to cooperate with hospitals and churches in town. Because there were few coffins, the dead were removed to a morgue tent as quickly as possible.

The influenza scare was over in a week, leaving in its wake a shaken Eisenhower. Before it ran its course, the 1918 Spanish flu pandemic had killed more people worldwide than had died in World War I, and more American soldiers (about forty-five thousand) than were killed in any single battle of the conflict. In contrast to Eisenhower's sentiments that a providential God would look over the men on the battlefield, no one in the tank command suggested that a beneficent God had sent this scourge on the American army. Eisenhower had been desperately worried that Mamie or Icky might be stricken with the flu. Fortunately, most of his headquarters staff were spared, in part because of the diligent sanitation efforts of the camp doctors. In fact, the efforts of Eisenhower and his medical staff to contain contagion were so successful that, after the crisis passed, the War Department transferred thirty doctors from Camp Colt to provide instruction on how Eisenhower's command had coped with the epidemic. Although noticeably successful in fighting the Spanish flu, Eisenhower would never again lose as many men under his direct command as he did that horrible fall.

Peace in Europe

The Spanish flu behind him, Eisenhower worked feverishly to get his men ready for their November departure for the battlefields of France. As fate would have it, Germany surrendered before Eisenhower's unit could embark for Europe. Suddenly, he was faced with an entirely different problem— demobilization, for which he had received no preparation at West Point. Anticipating that Eisenhower would be leaving for France, Mamie and Icky had already left Gettysburg for Denver. Because the War Department did not believe that the tent encampment at Camp Colt was suitable for another winter, Eisenhower relocated his corps, six thousand strong, to Camp Dix in New Jersey. There he directed the deflation of his command in as orderly a manner as possible, until he was in charge of about three hundred men, who constituted the small nucleus of the US Tank Corps. Ultimately, the Tank Corps was moved to Fort Meade to await the War Department's decision whether or not to continue it.

It had been less than a year since Eisenhower had left Fort Meade for Camp Colt. He had missed the war he was told was the "war to end all wars." He believed that a soldier's place was in the fight. He had not quite accepted the reality that in the military his place was where his superiors ordered him to be. He would soon be returned to his permanent rank of captain, with a reduced income and an uncertain future. He was old compared to his classmates, his knee bothered him from time to time, and he often envisioned himself in the years ahead shuffling papers behind a desk. Mostly, he was mad and disappointed, and he resented the fact that, for some reason, the war had passed him by.

Yet, though he was tempted to quit the army to accept a better-paying position in private industry, since graduating from West Point he had become a warrior. Although he had missed combat, he was proud of his service during the war and, in his own way, he knew that he had made important contributions to the war effort. He had succeeded in turning American civilians into first-rate soldiers and officers, not by the textbook, because there wasn't one, but through his own leadership skills and experience. He had learned valuable lessons during the war that he did not want to squander in civilian life.

Eisenhower, Patton, and Tanks

After his furlough in 1919, Eisenhower returned to an uncertain future at Fort Meade. On the bright side, at long last he had actual tanks in his command, British, French, and German tanks, as well as a few American-made machines. On the downside for Eisenhower, with the end of the war, Tank Corps officers who had seen action in France returned to camp, among them Colonel George Patton. At Fort Meade, Eisenhower lost the independence he had known at Camp Colt. Now, he was exasperated when the new Tank Corps commander, a veteran of Pershing's staff in France, ordered him to coach the Fort Meade football team. Eisenhower accepted the coaching assignment and successfully produced a winning team, but tanks, not football, had become the focus of his career. Eisenhower loved motorized machines, and if he could not fly airplanes in combat, the tank provided an excellent alternative.

Eisenhower and Patton, who moved in next door, quickly became best friends. Despite the large differences in their backgrounds—Patton was the scion of a wealthy California family and a devout Episcopalian—they had much in common. Both loved horseback riding and shooting; they both played cards and swore profusely; and they shared a passion for tanks. They talked "tanks" incessantly: tank tactics, tank armament, firepower, maneuverability, and vulnerability, and teamed up to test their theories in the field. They even completely disassembled a tank bolt-by-bolt, including the engine, and then put it back together in running order. Finally, using tactical problems developed at the Army's Command and General Staff College in Leavenworth, Kansas, they added tanks to support troops in the solutions approved by the

Leavenworth faculty and observed that, in every scenario, troops supported by armor always won.

Boldly, they submitted their tactical theories to cavalry (Patton) and infantry (Eisenhower) military journals. Subsequently, the chief of infantry ordered Eisenhower to cease publishing his theories of tank warfare. He was warned that his ideas were both contrary to army doctrine and dangerous to the service and the men. If he did not stop publication, he could face a court-martial. Unlike their contemporary Colonel Billy Mitchell, whose air power theories also ran afoul of established military doctrine, Eisenhower and Patton chose not to defy their superiors. He was angered by the army's intransigence concerning tank warfare, but Eisenhower did not fall on his sword over his censorship. Just as he had not sacrificed his marriage over John Doud's refusal to support his ambition to fly, so he did not resign from the army in the face of its blindness toward his theories on tank tactics. He was beginning to find his footing along a middle way that avoided the pitfalls of extremism.

Despite his dustup with the army over tank warfare, Eisenhower and Mamie settled into a happy, satisfying life at Fort Meade. The army assigned them spacious, albeit rustic quarters. They could entertain again and enjoy the post social life as an army couple. One Sunday afternoon the Pattons invited the Eisenhowers to lunch with General Fox Conner and his wife; it was an afternoon that would prove fateful for Eisenhower's military career. And after their long separation, like newlyweds, Ike and Mamie became reacquainted, now held tightly together by the bond of parenthood. They were especially pleased when their son Icky became the mascot of the Fort Meade tank corps. Eisenhower's men presented Icky with a tiny uniform in which the three-year-old proudly paraded around the base. When the tank crew went out on drill, they would ask to borrow Icky, who rode along with them in a tank, just like one of the boys. Best of all, with the weight of war off his shoulders, Eisenhower spent precious time devoted to Icky, in turn roughhousing and cuddling with his little boy. But their idyllic summer and fall of 1920 was far too brief.

Icky's Death

Just before Christmas 1920, Icky apparently came down with the flu. Having just escaped the Spanish flu epidemic, his parents became apprehensive on Christmas Day when the child worsened. Two days later they rushed him to the post hospital, but the military doctors, not well versed in pediatric medicine, missed that Icky had contracted scarlet fever. A specialist called in from

Johns Hopkins confirmed the belated diagnosis with little hope of treatment other than waiting it out. After Icky was placed in quarantine, Eisenhower and Mamie were forbidden direct contact with their son. He recorded the pathos of the final days with his son:

> We did everything possible to save him. The camp doctor brought in specialists from the nearby Johns Hopkins Medical School in Baltimore. During his illness the doctor did not allow me into his room. But there was a porch on which I was allowed to sit and I could look into the room and wave to him. Occasionally, they would let me come to the door just to speak to Icky. I haunted the halls of the hospital. Hour after hour, Mamie and I could only hope and pray. In those days, before modern medicine eliminated scarlet fever as a childhood scourge, hope and prayer were the only possibility for parents. At the turn of the year, we lost our firstborn son.

From Mamie:

> The night he died, I was home with such a heavy cold they thought I might be getting pneumonia. Ike had gone to the hospital and later, near morning, Icky died in his arms. We never talked about it. I did not ask him because it was something that hurt him so badly.

The loss was devastating for Ike and Mamie. They decided to bury their son in the Doud family plot in Fairmount Cemetery. When they left for Denver, devastated tankers turned out to provide an honor guard for Icky's casket from the fort to the train. "This was the greatest disappointment and disaster in my life," Eisenhower wrote a few years before his death, "the one I have never been able to forget completely." Was he reminded that his mother Ida suffered a similar disaster when her son Paul died at ten months of diphtheria in 1895? Perhaps not, because, like Eisenhower, his parents had kept their grief private, sparing their boys deep trauma over losing a brother.

The Douds did their best to comfort their grieving children over the loss of Icky, but if David and Ida reached out to Dwight and Mamie, their consolation is lost in history. At the dedication of the American flag at Camp Colt two years before, Eisenhower had assured his men that if God willed that they not return from battle alive, Americans all would remember them as loyal sons. Now that his own beloved son was gone, Eisenhower whispered no hint that Icky's death was the will of a providential, beneficent God. In this regard, neither Ike nor Ida believed that God had taken their boys from them.

Icky's death marked a turning point in Ike and Mamie's married life. To-gether, they did not share a faith that offered solace or hope concerning their son's passing. Consequently, they could not offer consoling ministry to each other. They appreciated, of course, the sympathy cards and flowers received from well-wishers, but by and large, they worked through their grief alone. Eisenhower buried himself in his job, but Mamie had no work to lessen her sorrow. Not surprisingly, observers noticed that innocence had been lost along with their exuberance for life. Painfully, after they returned from Icky's funeral in Denver, Ike and Mamie resumed life in their diminished officers' quarters.

Fox Conner's Premonitions, 1921–1939

In the two decades between the great wars, Eisenhower's religious sentiments flowed deeply underground, silently hidden from public view.
Yet, the twenty years from 1921 to 1940 were the formative years in Eisenhower's life that produced the five-star General of the Armies and the president of the United States. Highlights of his career in these years included his
tutorial with General Fox Conner in Panama; his graduating first in his class
at the Command and General Staff School in Leavenworth; his service with
General Douglas MacArthur in Washington, DC, and the Philippines; and
his brilliant staff work that brought him to the attention of General George C.
Marshall prior to Pearl Harbor. He matured as a professional army officer and
enjoyed close working relationships with the army's top leaders, but because
he served in the peacetime army, he remained a major for sixteen years, from
1920 to 1936.

These were also the years when the outward signs of Eisenhower's religious life all but disappeared. After he left Abilene, Eisenhower avoided formal
religious commitment. He had developed a dislike for formalized religion,
including creeds, doctrine, liturgy, worship, prayer books, sermons, clergy,
and most public religious trappings.

Indeed, during these years he developed an equal disdain for organized religion, political parties, and labor unions, all of which he believed were selfish
in their objectives and socially divisive in their exclusiveness. Ultimately, he
developed suspicion of most public interest groups whose motives seemed to
him self-interested. He had been stung by religious declension in Abilene—
the bitter conflict between the Jehovah's Witnesses and the River Brethren.
Consequently, he came to hate extremism based on religious, political, economic, or class strife. In addition to religious uproar in his hometown, the
legacy of Bleeding Kansas and the Civil War, "Sockless" Jerry Simpson's prairie

populism and Carrie Nation's hatchet-wielding temperance reform, the Republican gold bugs and Bull Moose insurgency caused Eisenhower to embrace religious, political, and social moderation—what he would call "the middle way" when he became president of the United States.

Eisenhower's moderate conservatism was shaped during these crucial years when he rose slowly through the ranks of the United States Army. He was no intellectual, but he was a deeply thoughtful man who left behind a legacy of remarkably consistent ideas, reflections, and images of his life and times. His middle way would become his personal gyroscope not only for the decisions concerning the American economy and politics but also for his practice of American civil religion. Eisenhower's public reaction to events during these years and after was rarely overtly religious, but four deaths—the death of his first son, "Icky," in 1921; the death of Mamie's best friend, Katie Gerow, in 1935; the death of his best friend, Jimmy Ord, in 1938; and the death of his father, David, in 1942—were to have profound personal religious consequences.

Fox Conner's Protégé

Although he was discouraged that he had missed the war and heartsick over Icky's death, Eisenhower's dogged devotion to duty during these trying years and his outstanding talent for organization brought him to the attention of the army's high command. General Fox Conner, his Sunday lunch partner at the Pattons, had already mentioned Eisenhower to General John J. Pershing, the commander of the American Expeditionary Force in World War I. After the war, through his personnel connections, Conner secured command of an infantry brigade at Camp Gaillard in the Panama Canal Zone. Eisenhower, too, was looking for another billet. With no future in the Tank Corps, and unwilling to be stereotyped as the army's best football coach, he was delighted that Conner wanted him for a position on his staff. Conner was looking for a bright, promising young officer like Eisenhower to serve as his aide in Panama, and with George Patton's enthusiastic endorsement, Conner maneuvered to have Eisenhower assigned as his executive assistant.

Reputedly, Conner had been the brains of "Black Jack" Pershing's staff during World War I. Mississippi-born, he entered West Point in 1894, and, although an average student, through hard work he graduated high in his class. But also, like Eisenhower, he accumulated a conspicuous record of demerits, mostly for tardiness and smoking. In addition to his proficiency as an artilleryman, Conner had developed a reputation of being a military intellectual, broadly read in military history and theory.

Conner believed he and Eisenhower shared similar personalities. Although Conner grew up in a comparatively wealthy family, both men had been raised in small-town settings far from eastern urban sophistication. Both loved to ride and fish, and Conner discovered to his delight that Eisenhower enjoyed reading and discussing great books. Eisenhower quickly discovered Conner's extensive library, a room stacked to the ceiling with tomes on military history and strategy. His interest in military history had been crushed at West Point, where tedious classes required memorization of battlefield minutiae, with little analysis of great engagements such as the Battle of Gettysburg.

Initially, Conner encouraged Eisenhower to read books of military fiction, which whetted Eisenhower's appetite for historical accounts that corresponded to the novels' settings in the Revolutionary War, the Napoleonic Wars, and the American Civil War. Gradually, Conner introduced him to weighty volumes on military history and theory, all of which they discussed. Eisenhower's prowl through Conner's library was reminiscent of his fascination with his parents' and Joe Howe's modest collections, but in Panama, Conner's library was not only richer and more stimulating than those Abilene collections but Eisenhower also profited from Conner's private tutoring. Conner did not limit his assignments to military topics, however, but encouraged his student to read a wide range of Western writers such as Plato, Tacitus, Nietzsche, and Shakespeare.

The meat of their impromptu seminar included the memoirs of U. S. Grant and William Tecumseh Sherman and detailed accounts of the American Civil War. Sometimes on horseback while making rounds, sometimes around campfires, frequently in his library, Conner led meticulous discussions of each book, always raising probing questions concerning complex military campaigns: Under what circumstances were decisions made? What would have happened had decisions been different? Were there viable alternatives for decision makers? Conner wanted Eisenhower to explore the significance of major battles—why they were fought, what the commanding generals hoped to accomplish—and to assess the generals' real reasons for action as compared to their public explanations. According to Eisenhower, Conner instilled life and vitality into the previously dead subject of military history.

As his readings with Conner intensified, Eisenhower clarified his own identity as a military officer. His sense of duty was firmly rooted, but Conner awakened in him a new vision of mission and destiny as a military officer. Indicative of the seriousness with which he took these studies, Eisenhower built himself a study on the second floor of his Panama quarters. In it he set up bookshelves, hung maps, and organized his reading notes. Conner was pleased with Eisenhower's dedication to his studies as well as the efficiency of his work in Panama. Their discussions were wide-ranging and included homespun, commonsense counseling that a son might receive from his father. Conner offered Eisenhower two aphorisms that forever anchored his leadership and work ethic: "Always take your job seriously, but never yourself," and "All generalizations are false, including this one." The advice well suited Eisenhower, who, under Conner's tutoring, sorted out a lifelong distinction between intensity and extremism in belief and action.

The capstone to his studies with Fox Conner was their exploration of military theory and strategy on the broadest scale. Eisenhower had already read Carl von Clausewitz's 1832 work *On War* with George Patton while in the Tank Corps. Now, under the tutelage of Conner, he read this nineteenth-century classic in military theory yet again. In all, he read Clausewitz from cover to cover three times, as often as he read the Holy Bible. With Conner, he engaged in discussion of Clausewitz's ideas about military strategy on a level normally only possible in advanced seminars in graduate schools or at the army's Command and General Staff School. His studies, however, were not one-dimensional. In concert with Clausewitz, he read Napoleon's memoirs, Jomini's treatise on Napoleonic warfare, and Foch's *Principles of War*, all in translation. The theorist Eisenhower was most influenced by was Denis Hart Mahan, the father of Arthur Thayer Mahan, the great advocate of sea power. D. H. Mahan de-emphasized the European emphasis on military science with its *a priori* "laws of warfare" while adopting a pragmatically American approach of flexible, *a posteriori* analysis of battlefield problems. Planning was essential, but a planned battle, in Mahan's opinion, was impossible to orchestrate because a military commander was always at the mercy of weather, unknown forces, and unpredictable opposing commanders. Or, as Eisenhower later wrote, "planning is everything, plans are nothing."

Mahan's flexible pragmatism appealed to Eisenhower's moderate, analytical temperament. The lessons of warfare were difficult to teach because almost every tactical and strategic problem was unique to time, place, available technology, participants, and their perceived objectives. Certain small-scale tactics may appear universal in application, but on the larger scale, little was predictable in battle. Indeed, the success of commanders might depend upon luck, that is, on factors outside the soldier's control. Theology, however, was not pertinent. In general, a providential God might guide the fortunes of great nations, but interpreting his purpose did not factor into military theory in the early twentieth century. Also left unexplored was the question of whether a loving, personal God, while preventing some casualties but not others, in any way affected the outcome of battle.

Some generalizations, however, were possible. Speed, not God, was a common factor in most strategic victories, according to Mahan. He referenced the Romans, but he might have been writing about the German blitzkrieg in Poland in 1939 or the battle for France in 1944. Without the benefit of hindsight on World War II, Eisenhower reflected that Mahan could have been forecasting the military disaster of stalemated trench warfare in World War I. "No great success can be hoped for in war in which rapid movements do not enter as an element," Mahan observed. "Even the very elements of Nature seem to array themselves against a slow and overly prudent general," he warned. To Eisenhower's credit, his rapid response to the German offensive in the Ardennes during the Battle of the Bulge might well have been inspired by his reading of D. H. Mahan in the Panamanian jungles in 1922.

Ironically, Conner and Eisenhower discussed modern warfare while riding horses along the canal, assessing the preparedness and weaknesses of America's vital waterway. Not yet a disciple of Fox Conner, Eisenhower profited from Conner's strategic vision that was both global in scope and expansive in time. In turn, Conner was excited to have "discovered" Eisenhower, whom he compared favorably to George C. Marshall. Conferring his highest praise on Eisenhower, Conner observed that Eisenhower and Marshall were a lot alike in that they attacked problems in the same way.

There has been a persistent myth that Eisenhower languished in the army unnoticed and unappreciated until the verge of World War II, but that was simply not so. In fact, in the 1920s and '30s, Eisenhower received strong incentives to remain in the army as a well-regarded, promising officer who received a succession of choice assignments. In the fall of 1922, when Eisenhower received his Distinguished Service Medal (DSM), Conner was especially proud to be the commanding officer who pinned the medal on Eisenhower's chest. During World War I, Eisenhower not only achieved the highest rank of any 1915 West Point graduate (lieutenant colonel), but he was also the only member of his class to receive the DSM for his services, even though he had seen no combat.

After three years in Panama, Ike and Mamie were glad to move along. With Conner's encouragement, he had applied to attend the army's Command and General Staff School at Fort Leavenworth, Kansas, prerequisite to promotion and higher command. Again, Conner pulled strings to secure Eisenhower's appointment, and Eisenhower received his orders to report in August 1925. He was thrilled and later recalled, "I was ready to fly—and needed no airplane!"

The realities behind his good fortune did not escape Eisenhower. He knew hard work and devotion to duty had helped him earn a spot at the army's most prestigious advanced school. At the same time, he knew he would not have received his early boost to the Command and General Staff School without Conner's patronage. He was an embodiment of a powerful truth: "It's not what you know but who you know." Without Conner as his godfather, Eisenhower knew that his military career would have been very different. It is arguable whether the years spent in Panama topped by his study at the Command and General Staff School were more important for his career than his four years at West Point. He certainly understood that his friendship with Conner was a turning point—"a watershed in my life," as he recalled in his memoir. Young men are often reluctant to curry the favor of their superiors because they do not want to be perceived as sycophants. Eisenhower had no such inhibition. "Don't be afraid to reach upward," he advised pastorally; not only might one find a friend, one could be graced with unexpected blessings.

The Command and General Staff School

Excited as he was, Eisenhower was also filled with trepidation over attending the Command and General Staff School. He had not attended the Infantry School at Fort Benning, the normal prerequisite for the Command and General Staff School. Eisenhower likened his enrollment at Leavenworth to attending college without having graduated from high school. He knew that the stakes were high, and the expectations of Fox Conner were higher still. Success at this school would be a "passport" to the best assignments in the army; outstanding performance marked an officer for promotion to high command. Mediocrity, on the other hand, might relegate him to coaching army football until he retired from the service.

An apprehensive Eisenhower sought advice from his mentor. Conner reassured Eisenhower that his three-year tutorial in Panama made him more prepared for Leavenworth than anyone he knew. A major part of the Leavenworth training involved drafting orders using the army's precise format. Every day, Conner had required Eisenhower to write a field order for the operation of Fort Gaillard, which rendered the "technics and routine" of formulating clear logistic plans and preparing operational orders second nature to Eisenhower. His pal George Patton lent him notes from the 1923–1924 course, from which Patton graduated twenty-fifth. Eisenhower also obtained copies of former Leavenworth problems and spent his free time solving the problems and checking his answers against the solutions approved by the Leavenworth faculty. His studying was a joy because Eisenhower loved solving puzzles, and he discovered that the Leavenworth problems, while challenging, were not impossible to resolve correctly if one used common sense.

The Command and General Staff School curriculum turned out to be Eisenhower's métier. Leavenworth's problems were similar to the "war gaming" that Eisenhower and Conner had devised in planning their defenses of the Canal Zone. In addition, many of the problems were derived from the Battle of Gettysburg, terrain and history that Eisenhower had explored exhaustively during his days at Camp Colt and his studies with Conner.

Eisenhower also quickly perceived that success at the school would be achieved only through self-discipline and careful pacing of one's study hours. He noted that several of his eager colleagues were studying so long and hard through the evening that, by morning, they were exhausted, foggy minded, and discouraged. To keep himself fresh and alert, he limited his nightly homework to two and a half hours. On Friday and Saturdays, however, Ike and Mamie partied at the officers' club or relaxed with friends.

In addition, several officers formed study groups with as many as eight members. Although he recognized the advantage of studying with a partner, Eisenhower did not want to waste time in large-group bull sessions. Instead, with his friend Leonard "Gee" Gerow, he established a study room on the third floor of his quarters, where he and Gee could study in absolute privacy. As in Panama, he assembled his library, covered the walls with maps, and studied around a large worktable. According to Eisenhower, the room became his command post, off limits to everyone but Gerow and himself.

He graduated first in the 1926 class of 245 at the Command and General Staff School, an accomplishment that confirmed all the expectations of Fox Conner. Although he never dreamed he might be first in his class, understandably his performance at the school also strengthened Eisenhower's confidence that he had made the right decision to stay in the army after World War I. He was now marked for favored assignments, and he knew it.

To celebrate their triumph, Eisenhower and Gerow threw a small but lively party for themselves and a few friends at the exclusive Muehlbach Hotel in downtown Kansas City, Missouri. Brother Arthur, now vice president of the Commerce Trust Company, underwrote the bash and arranged for a generous supply of bootleg liquor to lubricate the nine merrymakers. Eisenhower was a moderate drinker. Nonetheless, on this night he cut loose with loud, and off-key, renditions of his favorite songs, including "Abdul Abulbul Ameer." Their small company partied privately well past midnight—a rare exuberant display by Eisenhower of raw joy and relief.

Abilene Family Reunion

Thereafter, Ike and Mamie traveled to Abilene to attend a rare family reunion with David, Ida, and his five brothers. At least two reunion pictures survive: one, taken by Ike and Mamie's son John, shows the brothers lined up by age, with Arthur, the eldest, at the far left while David and Ida are seated in front of the line. The second, perhaps the most famous of the Eisenhower family photos, taken by Jeffcoat, Abilene's leading professional photographer, depicts the six brothers and their parents on the family porch. (This photograph is included in the photo section following p. 310.) But the grouping is far from natural or relaxed. All are sober-faced, with the possible exception of Ike, who at least looks pleasant. Off center but commanding the photograph, Dwight sits on the steps in front of his parents. He is dressed in his army uniform, his Distinguished Service Medal evident on his coat. His jet-black boots, reaching nearly to his knees, sparkle in the afternoon sun. Predictably, Milton, the baby, stands between his seated mother and father. Perhaps most interesting, David is neatly framed by his three most successful sons, Dwight, Milton, and Edgar, while the other brothers, Earl, Arthur, and Roy, divide the left half of the frame among them, with Roy sitting almost alone at the end of the porch. Of course, this 1926 family portrait depicts Jeffcoat's representation of the Eisenhower family and not that of David or Ida, but it faithfully reflects the enigmatic nature of this unusual reunion.

In many ways, the reunion was an extension of Eisenhower's celebration party in Kansas City. Because their house could not accommodate their large extended family, most of the Eisenhower daughters-in-law and grandchildren stayed home, with the exception of Mamie and John, and Roy's wife, Edna, who drove over from Junction City to help Ida with the cooking. According to most reports, David was his usual taciturn self, while Ida, much more outgoing and delighted to have her boys all together for the first time in twenty years, gaily commanded kitchen preparations.

The 1926 Eisenhower reunion climaxed with the famous "Big Parade" through downtown Abilene. Linking arm in arm, forming a line that stretched across the street, the six brothers marched uptown through the business district. They said they were looking for the chief of police, Henry Engle, but actually they were having abundant fun showing off Eisenhower family solidarity and pride. Presumably, the chief had hassled some of them as children, and now they wanted to show Engle the solid men they had become. But there was nothing mean in their purpose or demeanor, and bystanders smiled and wanted to shake their hands. Ken Davis wrote, "Their progress through the town became a kind of triumphal procession . . . marked by such an exuberant vitality, such a gay defiance of all hostile fate, that those who witnessed it never forgot it." Abilene remembered the Big Parade decades later for what it was—the joyful public celebration of the Eisenhower brothers announcing to their neighbors and Abilene's business elite that this was just the beginning of a new Eisenhower era for the town.

American Battle Monuments Commission and Army War College

At the end of World War I, General of the Armies John J. "Black Jack" Pershing did not retire but instead became head of the American Battle Monuments Commission, an independent army unit outside the normal chain of command charged with preparing a documented history of the United States' participation in World War I, including guides to American battlefields and cemeteries in Europe. His former mentor Fox Conner, now deputy chief of staff, easily arranged for Eisenhower's appointment to Pershing's staff.

Assignment to the commission turned out to be ideal for the officer who would become commander in chief of Allied forces in Europe during World War II. His principal task was to prepare a comprehensive history of American participation in World War I, using unit histories and army records as his primary sources. In addition, he compiled a compendium of all battle monuments and military cemeteries in Europe, including the location and description of each site. Writing in the clear, straightforward English that had won him honors at the Command and General Staff School, Eisenhower's two-hundred-page narrative of American combat in World War I remains one of the most concise and readable histories to this day. If Eisenhower's prose lacked eloquence, nonetheless, like his later history of American forces in Europe during World War II, *Crusade in Europe*, he proved a military historian of unusual skill.

Assisted at times by his brother Milton, who lent journalistic talents, he was especially attentive to the logistics of fighting in France and the European continent. Could there have been better preparation for his leadership of Allied armies after Normandy than this assignment? As Jean Edward Smith, in *Eisenhower in War and Peace*, noted, "It is difficult to imagine a more useful assignment for a future supreme commander than to write a history of the analogous American effort in World War I." With the exception of Pershing and Fox Conner, who had directed the operations of American forces in Europe, Eisenhower, because of his assignment with the Battle Monuments

Commission, understood the American strategy and battlefield tactics used in World War I better than all his contemporaries.

At the conclusion of his assignment with the Battle Monuments Commission, Eisenhower enrolled in the army's War College at Fort McNair in Washington, DC. Much more relaxed than the intensive curriculum at the Command and General Staff School, the War College required no examinations, gave no grades, and did not numerically rank its graduates. While the Leavenworth school featured applied lessons in approved army doctrine, the War College more creatively explored what the approved doctrine should be. Amplifying its relaxed air, the school sometimes served as a "thank you" last assignment for aging colonels about to be retired. In contrast, at thirty-seven, Major Eisenhower was one of the youngest students ever enrolled in the school.

In 1927, America was nearing the end of the Roaring Twenties. Since 1921, fiscally conservative Republicans had controlled both houses of Congress and the presidency. While avoiding balance-of-power diplomacy in Europe (often wrongly characterized as "isolationism"), the government slashed both domestic and military spending. Eisenhower was part of that small but dedicated corps of underpaid officers with few prospects of advancement who held the US Army together during the lean years of one of America's most prosperous decades.

At the War College, Eisenhower was required to write an original paper on a topic of his own choice. Given the political and financial climate of the Coolidge administration, he chose a controversial topic. At the end of World War I, the army discharged more than four million men with no further obligation to the United States. The regular army had been reduced to a skeleton force. In the event of a national military crisis, Eisenhower reasoned, the United States Army could not field sufficient trained forces to meet a serious military challenge such as that anticipated by his mentor Fox Conner.

Eisenhower's War College essay proposed to amend the National Defense Act to create a Regular Army Reserve. Rather than squander the training of enlisted volunteers, Eisenhower desired to extend their commitment to five years; two years on active duty followed by three years in the army reserve. The essay, of course, had no standing as an official proposal to the secretary of war. On the other hand, the commandant of the War College realized that Eisenhower's criticism of American military preparedness could cause some trouble. Nonetheless, he said the essay had "exceptional merit" and forwarded it to the chief of staff for circulation in the War Department. In addition, Eisenhower received superior ratings for his performance at the War College. Those ratings, and General Pershing's high praise for his draft of the American

Battle Monuments guide, ensured Eisenhower another choice assignment after leaving the War College.

Assignment: Paris, France

Not surprisingly, in the spring of 1928 Eisenhower was offered a position on the army's general staff. Pershing, however, wanted him to return to the Battle Monuments Commission to revise and expand his original report, which would require relocation in France. The prospect of joining Ike in France, with their headquarters in Paris, was too alluring for Mamie to pass up. For once, she prevailed by insisting that Eisenhower accept the European assignment rather than join the general staff. Their year together in Paris, which included family exploration of cathedrals and battlefields and tours of France, Belgium, Germany, Switzerland, and Italy, was one of the sunniest of their married life. Mamie especially loved Paris's theaters, nightclubs, and shopping, while Ike enthusiastically tromped the battlefields with John, who once found three helmets on a Canadian battlefield.

Mamie communicated to her parents the beauty of the French countryside and cathedrals and the lingering horror of the Great War. Ten years after the war, they still found barbed wire, open trenches, helmets, broken rifles, and other detritus of war scattered in ravaged fields. Before an alert driver stopped him, John thought about punting a pineapple-shaped ball he discovered in a meadow. Mamie somberly noted the carnage they encountered in countless military cemeteries, including sixty-five thousand unknown dead in the British cemetery at Ypres. Obscene death was everywhere. They visited the Trench of Bayonets, where French soldiers "going over the top" had been bombarded by German artillery, collapsing the trench that buried men dead and alive with their bayonets vainly protruding toward the sky. The French government had designated the site a war memorial. Despite these ugly reminders of war, the Eisenhowers returned to the United States refreshed and reinvigorated, their family bonded more closely by shared adventure and experience in Europe.

Back in Washington, DC

Back in Washington, DC, the Eisenhowers moved into the Wyoming Apartments near Dupont Circle. If not as glamorous as Paris, the Wyoming was comfortable and convenient, and housed numerous well-placed government and military personnel. While their budget was tight, Mamie's father generously helped them meet Washington expenses by paying for a maid and sending along checks that the Eisenhowers used for entertaining purposes. They enjoyed Washington social life and did not shy from inviting high-ranking army officers and politicians to dine with them. The Eisenhowers' reentry into Washington society was aided by the fact that Milton, Eisenhower's youngest brother, was an up-and-coming official at the Department of Agriculture. Indeed, before World War II, Milton was undoubtedly better known in Washington circles than his brother Dwight. On the other hand, among Dwight's friends and close associates, the apartment at the Wyoming became known as Club Eisenhower, renowned for its hospitality and generous parties, repeating the reputation they had enjoyed previously in Texas and in Paris.

Eisenhower reported for duty with the assistant secretary of war on November 8, 1929, just eight working days after the stock market crash of "Black Tuesday," October 29, that marked the beginning of the Great Depression of the 1930s. Despite the grim economic news, Eisenhower was pleased with his assignment to General Moseley. His good friends Gerow and Wade Hampton "Ham" Haislip were also assigned to this office, and he knew from the outset that he would be writing studies related to industrial mobilization. Eisenhower welcomed the opportunity to study in depth the economic and industrial institutions that would be mobilized in the next major war predicted by Conner.

In the War Department, Eisenhower received an intense education on the interrelationships among the government, the military, American industry, and politics. During this time, Eisenhower became the army's expert on all phases of military and industrial mobilization. He drafted two key reports on mobilization: "Fundamentals of Industrial Mobilization," June 16, 1930, and "Brief History of Planning for Procurement and Industrial Mobilization," October 2, 1931, which he wrote as a student at the Army Industrial College. As recognized by historians, these and other reports on mobilization represent some of Eisenhower's most distinguished analytical writing.

In his travels around the United States, which began his lifelong cultivation of major business leaders, he met some of America's leading industrialists and financiers, including Bernard Baruch. He discovered, however, that industrialists were not interested in military contracts unless they could be guaranteed hefty profits; and almost universally, they were wary of government oversight and even more nervous about the consequences of government strategic planning. It was his first encounter with what he would later characterize as the "military-industrial complex." All in all, he labored at a frustrating task of planning mobilization for a major war in the midst of deep economic depression. Everywhere he turned he encountered self-righteous antimilitarism among the American public and elected officials, fanatical distrust of World War I industrial profiteers, determined isolationism regarding the growth of fascism in Germany and Italy, and widespread distrust of government management of industrial production.

Lest one think Eisenhower labored at a thankless task, those who counted in his opinion—Pershing, Conner, Marshall, MacArthur—were well aware of his remarkable ability to write studies that presented clear analysis of facts and argued cogently for enhanced preparedness. He not only wrote papers and speeches for his superiors but also was called upon to testify before congressional committees. In this regard, Eisenhower earned a deserved reputation for being able to handle himself well on Capitol Hill.

General Douglas MacArthur, who became army chief of staff in November 1930, moved to employ Eisenhower's talents while Ike was still officially working for the War Department. In November 1931, after Eisenhower drafted the chief of staff's annual report, MacArthur commended him on his "outstanding talents" and his ability to perform on highly important missions. Mamie framed the MacArthur letter, just as she had framed a similar letter from Pershing. And, like Pershing and Fox Conner, MacArthur recruited Eisenhower to serve on his personal staff. One of his first assignments as MacArthur's unofficial aide was to prepare a report for the secretary of war on the status of the Philippine Islands. For the foreseeable future, MacArthur (as drafted by Eisenhower) recommended maintenance of the status quo, with the caveat that the Philippines would not be ready for self-government "until they have reached a substantially higher cultural plane."

The Bonus Marchers

By far the most controversial event in which Eisenhower participated under General MacArthur in Washington, DC, was the army's suppression of the World War I veterans' Bonus March and the burning of their makeshift camp on Anacostia Flats. As the Great Depression deepened in 1932, a ragtag company of veterans from the American Expeditionary Force formed a Bonus Expeditionary Force (the Bonus Army) that descended on Washington to demand that Congress make early payment of their war bonuses. The veterans' bonus was scheduled to be paid in 1945, but destitute veterans felt they could not wait that long.

While Congress debated whether to pay the bonus early, nearly twenty thousand Bonus Marchers, including a few suspected Communists, gathered in the capital to demonstrate for payment of their bonuses. The veterans marched during the day, and at night they camped around town wherever they could find space and tolerance, including in a shanty "Hooverville" in Anacostia.

The demonstrations were largely peaceful; in June the House passed a bonus bill, but the Senate rejected it. Thousands of Bonus Marchers drifted away, but others, including some late arrivals with nowhere to go, settled in abandoned buildings near the Capitol that were scheduled for demolition. Before adjournment, Congress appropriated funds to help the marchers return home. Their nesting in the city's vacant buildings provoked the police to evict the squatters. Veterans resisted by throwing bricks at the police, seriously injuring the chief of police, among others. Responding, police shot and killed one Bonus Marcher and wounded another. With the confrontation spiraling out of control, the DC commissioners asked President Hoover to restore order. In turn, aware of the political sensitivity of using the United States Army to suppress civilian unrest, Hoover ordered MacArthur to assume personal command of the troops sent in to quell the disorder and remove the remaining Bonus Marchers from Washington.

Eisenhower accompanied MacArthur's entourage but apparently did not take part in chasing down the remaining Bonus Marchers. Nor did Eisenhower record whether he armed himself with a loaded pistol. His friend George Patton also commanded tanks and a cavalry squadron and may have been saved public embarrassment when all five tanks broke down before they engaged the protestors. As the troops and cavalry swung into action, they were met with more petulance than physical resistance from the demonstrators. A few brickbats, rocks, and sticks were thrown, which the army met with tear gas, while the streets and camps were steadily cleared. Within a few hours, the troops were poised to cross the Anacostia Bridge to clear the largest camp.

Hoover, having been warned that women and children remained in the camp, nervously sent an order to MacArthur not to cross the river. On his own, MacArthur met with the leader of the campers, who asked for time for the remaining demonstrators to gather their belongings before clearing out. MacArthur paused to feed the troops. Then, assuming the camp was vacant, he directed his troops forward and was surprised to encounter a few stragglers. As the army rounded up the last of the demonstrators, fire broke out among the shanties in the Hooverville. Soon the Anacostia encampment was ablaze.

The subsequent image of federal troops evicting bedraggled veterans from Anacostia with tear gas and fire proved a public relations disaster not only for the army but also for MacArthur, who appeared both ungrateful for their sacrifices in war and insensitive to their economic misfortune. Afterward, Eisenhower believed that the Anacostia fire was started by the Bonus Marchers themselves, but other accounts contend that the police, anxious to remove the camp once and for all, actually set fire to the shanties. Years later, Eisenhower recalled this moment: "The whole scene was pitiful. The veterans, whether or not they were mistaken in marching on Washington, were ragged, ill-fed, and felt themselves badly abused. To suddenly see the whole encampment going up in flames just added to the pity one had to feel for them."

This shameful incident had neither long-term impact on the US Army nor negative consequences for the careers of participants such as MacArthur, Eisenhower, and Patton. The depression was grinding the army down, and the negative press, while not welcome, could have hardly made matters worse than the parsimonious US Congress with its draconian budget and personnel cuts. While MacArthur's image suffered both contemporaneously and historically, the sorrowful story of the Bonus Marchers has been all but lost to history, their memory submerged under the lingering effects of the Great Depression, blotted out by the hoopla and controversy of FDR and the New Deal, and erased by the glorification of the "greatest generation" and their triumph in World War II. Among lessons learned, perhaps Major Eisenhower profited most from the Bonus March debacle.

Lessons of the Bonus March

In general, Eisenhower did not believe federal troops should be used to quell civil domestic disturbances except under the most extraordinary circumstances. Eisenhower believed the lessons of the Bonus March were fourfold. First, when the assignment was fraught with political implications, a military commander, even a four-star general, should make certain that his civilian bosses (the president, Congress, and even the press) are all supportive of his plans. MacArthur's greatest mistake, then and later, was that he did not keep civilian authorities fully and currently informed, especially in matters transcending military affairs. As a middle-of-the-road military manager, Eisenhower would never forget the necessity of building a leadership coalition that included the most influential civilians to deal with government's most difficult problems.

Second, Eisenhower believed that the Bonus March not only reinforced caution in the use of federal troops to quell civilian disturbance but also confirmed the need to use overwhelming force when confronting rioters. The large number of troops MacArthur mobilized for this operation dismayed some critics, but Eisenhower offered no apology for the size of the force. The objective was to deploy overwhelming numbers, slowly, patiently, giving rioters every opportunity to disengage and withdraw. "Adequate force minimizes casualties," Eisenhower concluded. "Suspected weakness on the side of law and order encourages riotous elements to resist, usually resulting in open conflict, while obvious strength gains a *moral* ascendancy that is normally all-sufficient." This rule of thumb would hereafter guide Eisenhower's use of military power, especially in his presidential years. He believed that the exercise of military power is best achieved by the concentration of force whose apparent power was as manifest as its real power. In general, overwhelming numbers, properly equipped, well led, and strongly disciplined, would present a moral force as compelling as its actual destructive ability.

Third, and most practical, Eisenhower had observed the effective use of intimidation to limit casualties. Ever the apostle for tanks, he especially lauded Patton's squadron as "particularly valuable in quelling civil disorder." The Renault tanks, however unreliable, created the impression of irresistible and inexorable power. Because they could be seen and heard from some distance, they created fear throughout the mob, not only among the front ranks. If those in the rear were not pushing their compatriots forward, an important dynamic in crowd behavior would be neutralized. The cavalry, in addition to its mobility, was also a useful deterrence for similar reasons.

But most effective in riot control was the judicious use of tear-gas bombs by well-trained infantry advancing with steady determination. Because the gas cloud could be seen from a distance, "this harmless instrument," as Eisenhower described it, quickly sapped the will of leaderless crowds to resist. Thus the moral suasion of tear gas transcended its immediate effectiveness and extended to those in the mob not directly stricken by it. He concluded, repeating his mantra: "The greater the real and apparent strength of the force on the side of law and order, the smaller will be the casualties among the disaffected elements."

Fourth, Eisenhower anticipated important lessons in resolving asymmetrical conflict, the classic dilemma of David versus Goliath in which an underdog combats an apparently superior force. According to some modern theorists, the outcome of most asymmetric conflicts depends on which side establishes and maintains legitimacy. The stronger side will win if it can convince the weaker side that it cannot prevail against the strong side's legitimate authority. Conversely, the weak side will likely win if it can maintain, while convincing additional supporters, a belief in the illegitimacy of the dominant force.

In the asymmetrical conflict between the army and the Bonus Marchers, the demonstrators significantly outnumbered the soldiers; but the army held an overwhelming advantage in training, leadership, and armament. To establish its legitimacy, or moral authority, as Eisenhower called it, the army had not only to display its strength but also to indicate dramatically that it was prepared to use its full force to quell the mob. To maintain legitimacy, on the other hand, the army had to avoid combat and establish communication with the mob if at all possible. If fighting ensued, it was crucial that the demonstrators become the illegitimate aggressors. For a poker player like Eisenhower, mastering the dynamics of such high-stakes games of bluff and bluster became his greatest strength in dealing with asymmetrical conflict.

Importantly, Eisenhower's justification of the use of overwhelming force against the Bonus Marchers revealed the seed of his civil religion faith. Foremost among the objectives of the army had been to reestablish moral authority over the demonstrators. The collapse of moral authority, in this instance, was fundamentally a spiritual problem. Moral authority, as conceived by Eisenhower, connected the governing authorities to the governed with mutual respect and confidence. Moral authority conveyed legitimacy to the government and the army while requiring deference from the governed and the veterans. To maintain law and order, leaders cannot ignore disrespect, insult, or degradation of civility among the governed. The army's task in restoring order was to reestablish civil righteousness, wherein governors and governed enjoyed again a right, if not perfect, relationship based on civil and moral law. In the United States, restoration of civil righteousness meant mutual recognition of the moral authority, or legitimacy, of America's constitutional system.

The Left and Right Hand of God

By 1932, Eisenhower had moved far from his mother's religious pacifism but not far from her Lutheran roots. Four hundred years earlier, Martin Luther's political theology had professed that God works in and through two kingdoms: God governed spiritual life with his right hand through the church's proclamation of law and gospel; he governed secular life with his left hand through civil law and temporal institutions. Believers readily perceive God's presence in his church, but it is more difficult to detect the workings of the Holy Spirit in secular realms. Luther emphasized that the Spirit is often heavily veiled in worldly affairs. Of armies, whether comprised of Christians or not, engaged in warfare, Luther wrote, in his 1526 treatise *Whether Soldiers, Too, Can Be Saved*: "When I think of a soldier fulfilling his office by punishing the wicked, killing the wicked, and creating so much misery, it seems an un-Christian work completely contrary to Christian love. But when I think of how it protects the good and keeps and preserves wife and child, house and farm, property, and honor and peace, then I see how precious and godly the work is."

Unhappy about using federal troops to quell the veterans' demonstration, Eisenhower did not regard his participation in dispersing the Bonus Marchers as "precious and godly work." Nor, to use Luther's sixteenth-century rhetoric, did he believe it was the army's task to "punish the wicked" demonstrators because of their civil disobedience. Nonetheless, it was righteous duty for the army to use tanks and cavalry, and especially tear gas, to disperse the mob, because these weapons had significantly helped to reestablish moral authority between the Bonus Marchers and their government, or the right civil order between the veterans and the army.

Years before, he had accomplished a similar task in the farmyard with the help of his uncle Luther. Then, the tyrant goose had neither been seriously injured nor permanently displaced but had yielded to young Eisenhower's determination to establish harmony among the farm animals. According to Martin Luther's political theology, in both instances, one trivial and the other importantly political, Eisenhower served as an agent of God's left hand in sustaining civil peace. It would not be until after World War II that Eisenhower would adopt a version of this Lutheran theology to describe his calling as a military officer to the National Council of Churches.

When his tour of duty ended at the office of the assistant secretary of war, Eisenhower hoped to secure a command of troops, always his aspiring dream. But he could hardly decline MacArthur's insistent offer to join his staff, especially when the general promised a troop command on Eisenhower's next assignment. In his diary Eisenhower confessed that he was flattered by MacArthur's attention. "Gen MacA was very nice to me—and after all I know of no greater compliment the bosses can give you than I want you hanging around." Prior to the Bonus Marcher demonstrations, Eisenhower confided to his diary that he greatly respected MacArthur, although he occasionally found the general difficult, and always complicated, "reserved," "impulsive," "brilliant," "tenacious," and "extremely self-confident."

MacArthur inspired great loyalty yet could be disconcertingly "reactionary and almost bigoted." His great intellect was only exceeded by his enormous ego.

But he was an astute judge of military talent, and he assured Eisenhower that until he retired Ike would be "one of the people earmarked for his 'gang.'" Everyone wants to be wanted. In January 1933, receiving the title of senior aide, Eisenhower noted that his work with MacArthur would be "little different from what I have been performing for him for two years but he alone will be my boss."

Political Changes

In 1909, as a young Democrat, Eisenhower criticized the business-dominated Republican Party for launching an excessively protectionist tariff in favor of the eastern manufacturers at the expense of the economic health of the rest of the nation. In denouncing the Payne-Aldrich Tariff of 1909, he charged that rapacious Republicans had established a system of legalized robbery. But after he left for West Point, Eisenhower steadily drifted from his Abilene political roots toward becoming nonpartisan as a soldier. Army officers frequently did not vote in partisan elections. Two of the main rituals defining good citizenship in Abilene had disappeared from Eisenhower's structured life by the 1930s: regular attendance at a community church and faithful voting at local polls. Instead, as America entered the New Deal era, devotion to the army principally defined Eisenhower's United States citizenship. Many of his long-term duty stations, including Panama, France, Washington, DC, and the Philippines, were not within the forty-eight United States.

As the Great Depression intensified, Eisenhower witnessed firsthand the inevitable shift in political power as Republicans, for the first time since the Civil War, slid helplessly into the role of a minority party, while the Democrats, who had elected only two presidents since James Buchanan in 1856, were swept into office by the landslide elections of 1932. Eisenhower had long since abandoned his loyalty to the Democratic Party, but he believed it was a good thing that Franklin D. Roosevelt had overwhelmingly won the presidency and would be supported by large majorities in Congress.

Army friends called him "Dictator Ike" because he argued repeatedly that the only way for Americans to dig themselves out of the depression was to concede strong executive authority to the president. When FDR declared a national bank holiday, Eisenhower cheered, "More power to him!" Additionally, Eisenhower hoped that Congress would grant Roosevelt more authority to manage the American economy. But he revealed something of a Republican bent when he argued that America should get its own economic house in order and worry less about promoting international economic cooperation.

Unlike shrill criticism of FDR from panicked Republicans, Eisenhower did not worry that Americans were vulnerable to German fascism. America was protected, he believed, by its Constitution. But he also realized that Roosevelt had accumulated far greater power than the average American recognized. Holding true to old values and economic theory learned in Abilene, Eisenhower lamented the curtailment of economic competition by New Deal programs. Yet he conceded that certain treasured economic ideals had to be sacrificed during the immediate emergency. Regarding the New Deal's economic program, which, as a presidential candidate he would loudly denounce, he confided to his diary in October 1933: "I believe that unity of action is essential to success in the current struggle. I believe that individual right must be subordinate to public good, and that the public good can be served only by unanimous adherence to an authoritative plan. We *must* conform to the President's program regardless of the consequences. Otherwise, dissension, confusion and partisan politics will ruin us."

There was little love between the flamboyant New Dealers brought to Washington, DC, by the Roosevelt administration and the tradition-bound officer corps of the US Army. Among the army's top brass, perhaps George Marshall was singular in his understanding that Roosevelt's reforms promoted modernization of the armed services. Eisenhower, more progressive than many of his colleagues, developed neither enthusiasm nor optimism for the American political process while assigned to the War Department in Washington, DC. Across the political spectrum, from radical populists to archconservatives, many Americans, like Eisenhower, revered the political principles outlined by the Declaration of Independence and the United States Constitution but distrusted the political and economic goals and ethics of political parties and the politicians who led them.

Just as he held organized religion at arm's length while holding dear the childhood lessons his mother taught from the Bible, so Eisenhower embraced American democratic ideals while distancing himself from the hurly-burly of the political process. In part, he believed it was his soldier's duty to stay out of the partisan fray; in part, he was dismayed that political extremism and religious bigotry often walked arm in arm. Although he was not enthusiastic about the New Deal, Eisenhower was unsettled by bitter attacks against Roosevelt that carried no thought but that the New Deal was all wrong. Such mindless opposition, Eisenhower believed, threatened public support of FDR's initiatives, which, he said, "*alone* can bring us out of current troubles."

Apolitical and Unchurched

While free of politics, Dwight and Mamie also remained uninvolved in church. Apologists for their absence from church during these days often explain that constant moving from post to post forced the family to rely on base chapels for their religious worship. More likely, Ike and Mamie had little interest in church attendance during the first three decades of their marriage. Their six-year sojourn in Washington, DC, provided ample opportunity to attend any church they chose, including an army chapel. The Presbyterian Church of the Pilgrims was close to the Wyoming Apartments. But even if southern Presbyterians were unattractive to the Eisenhowers, there were other Presbyterian and Christian churches nearby.

Dan Holt, former director of the Eisenhower Presidential Library, has repeatedly noted that the army worked Eisenhower mercilessly during the interwar years, and especially during his assignments in Washington, DC, at times pushing him close to physical and emotional collapse. Although Eisenhower looked robust and fit, he complained of backaches, headaches, and other ailments, all no doubt brought on by unrelenting stress. In 1934 he was hospitalized for a month with severe pain mostly brought on by the stress of his job. With no promotions in sight, in the depth of the Great Depression, his pay was cut twice. They were saved from penury by John Doud's generous monetary gifts and by the Wyoming Apartments cutting rents to maintain full tenancy during the depression.

With many Americans in church on that day, Sunday provided the one morning of the week the Eisenhowers could relax and loaf. Their son John recalled that Ike and Mamie often spent all morning in bed reading the paper. On occasion, John tried to talk his parents into attending a church. After Mamie explained that his father needed his rest, on occasion John would walk alone to a nearby church attended by his friends. For Ike and Mamie, hymns, prayers, and sermons were not yet part of their Sunday routine.

MacArthur's term as chief of staff finally came to an end in 1935. For President Roosevelt, the decision of where to assign MacArthur next was easy. Although he welcomed MacArthur's help implementing the Civilian Conservation Corps, FDR gladly approved the request of the Philippine president Manuel Quezon to have MacArthur serve as an advisor for establishing a Philippine army. Officially, MacArthur and his mission were to identify the military needs of the Philippine government, which was due to be granted independence within ten years, under the terms of the Philippine Independence Act of 1934.

MacArthur and his father, General Arthur MacArthur, had long, personal histories in the Philippines; in fact, Douglas regarded the islands as his "home." Serving as military advisor to President Quezon also meant that MacArthur would continue to be his own military boss. In addition, the Philippine assignment provided MacArthur an excellent springboard into retirement, with attractive prospects for public service or private business. Most importantly, MacArthur's military mission to the Philippines offered the strong-willed general great latitude of independence in developing the Philippine army. From Roosevelt's perspective, it did not hurt that the assignment exiled MacArthur far from the centers of power in Washington, DC.

Anxiety about an Assignment

MacArthur insisted that Eisenhower accompany him to the Philippines, a high compliment that MacArthur enhanced with the promise of a significant raise in salary. As always, Eisenhower professed that "duty with troops" was his first desire. But he accepted MacArthur's offer, in part because he had been fascinated with the idea of serving in the Philippines since his graduation from West Point. But mostly, he was not inclined to disobey what amounted to a direct order from MacArthur to join the Philippine military mission. He was not naïve, however, about the challenges of raising and organizing a Philippine army, as his 1932 draft report for MacArthur had indicated.

Before departure for the Far East, Eisenhower discussed Philippine matters with his trusted friend Leonard Gerow, who had returned to Washington, DC, after duty with American troops in the Philippines. Clouding their reunion was the serious illness of Gerow's wife, Katherine—indeed, it was her illness that brought them back to Washington for treatment at Walter Reed Hospital. The Eisenhowers rallied to support Gee and Katie, Mamie's best friend. Despite major surgery, however, Katie died in June 1935, just before Eisenhower received his orders to report to Manila.

Mamie was devastated and scared after Katie's death, and soon she informed Ike that she would not accompany him to Manila. Despite the national economic depression, their stay at the Wyoming Apartments had been secure and satisfying, marking some of the best years of their marriage. In the summer of 1935, Mamie was not willing to abandon her comfortable nest in Washington for an uncertain future in Manila. As she confided to her parents, her reasons for staying in Washington were manifold. Ostensibly, she believed it was important for John to finish the eighth grade at his school.

But, filled with unhappy memories of Panama, this *mess*, as she repeatedly called it, overwhelmed her with uncertainties. MacArthur had not set any time limit on Eisenhower's Philippine appointment. What if Ike didn't like his job? What if his health failed him while in Manila? Could she manage so far away from her parents in Denver? Her dearest friend had just returned from the Philippines to die . . . and she confessed to her parents, "After Katie's experience I am *scared*."

Eisenhower tried unsuccessfully to convince Mamie to join him in the Philippines, but, respecting his mother's ethics, he did not demand it. He knew she was frightened. Katie had probably died of cancer, but Mamie could not shake the thought that she may have died from a mysterious tropical disease. She was probably using John's schooling as an excuse, a shield to protect herself from the uncertainties of a move to Manila. Eisenhower understood Mamie's fears and her desire to hang on to the security represented by the Wyoming, but he was deeply disappointed in her decision to remain in Washington.

MacArthur asked Eisenhower to designate another officer to share executive duties in the Philippines. Eisenhower suggested Jimmy Ord, a close friend and classmate from West Point. At this time, Ord was on the staff of the Command and General Staff College; he was also proficient in Spanish, an official language of the islands. Using resources at the school, Ord and Eisenhower developed a skeletal plan for island defenses based on minimal funding. Their fictional army had one strategic objective—to create local defense forces that might hold out against an invasion until outside assistance from Philippine allies could arrive to roll back the aggressors. Their defense plan did not envision a navy, which would be too expensive. But, similar to Fox Conner's and Eisenhower's plans for Panama, their vision did include a small air force, which was essential, Eisenhower believed, to help tie together far-flung island defenses and to scout and harass enemy naval forces.

Embarking for Manila

MacArthur's company departed Washington, DC, on September 29, 1935, bound for San Francisco, where they would board the SS *Herbert Hoover* for the Philippines. Before sailing, MacArthur received news that the president had appointed a new chief of staff, reducing MacArthur to his permanent rank of major general. MacArthur was furious. He believed Roosevelt would appoint the successor chief of staff after he arrived in the Philippines, which would have allowed him to disembark in Manila with four stars on his shoulder. Now he felt betrayed by Roosevelt and, in an explosive denunciation, fulminated against "broken promises, arrogance, unconstitutionality, insensitivity, and the way the world had gone to hell."

MacArthur's tantrum, in which he blamed FDR personally for his public humiliation, startled Eisenhower and showed him a side of the general he had not seen before. For Major Eisenhower, now joining MacArthur in virtual exile, the future, at best, was uncertain. Sailing alone from depression-racked America on the liner *Herbert Hoover* must not have seemed propitious for an ambitious but aging Eisenhower. But with Fox Conner's prediction of another world war looming ever more certain, Eisenhower shrugged off personal doubts and loneliness while throwing himself single-mindedly into his work. MacArthur's entourage arrived in Manila on October 26, and, without the distraction of his family, Eisenhower settled into a two-room apartment in the Manila Hotel, where MacArthur occupied the hotel's penthouse, with air-conditioning.

Forming a Philippine Army

There is no evidence that Eisenhower ever questioned the appropriateness of the US Army's mission to help raise, train, and arm the Philippine army in the 1930s. But Eisenhower soon discovered that the task of building anything but a paper legion was impossible because the Philippine government could not afford to raise an adequate army. Because of Japanese military aggression in the Far East, the War Department was reluctant to allocate the necessary armaments to the Philippines. Fearful that America's unprepared and under-manned armed forces might soon be challenged in the Pacific, the War Department kept a tight rein on American arms. Eisenhower haggled to obtain obsolete Enfield rifles for the Philippine troops, but even these old weapons proved difficult to obtain.

A major source of Eisenhower's frustration was MacArthur himself. MacArthur talked grandly of establishing a Philippine army of thirty divisions, supported by an air force of 250 planes and an offshore patrol of sixty PT boats. But to Eisenhower, MacArthur's was all vainglorious talk. The Philippine Military Mission would do well, in his opinion, to equip one regular division supported by twenty reserve divisions, an air force of 80 planes, and an offshore patrol of thirty PT boats. Eisenhower's projections were brutally realistic and based on the rock-bottom budget provided by the Philippine government and reluctant contributions from Washington.

Eisenhower assumed that MacArthur touted the thirty-division Philippine army to justify his lofty rank. On July 1, 1936, Eisenhower noted in his diary that the Philippine National Assembly and President Quezon named MacArthur a field marshal in the Philippine army, less than a year after he had been reduced to major general. According to Eisenhower, MacArthur was "tickled pink, and feels that he's made a lot of 'face' locally." Coincidentally, on that same day, Eisenhower was promoted to lieutenant colonel in the US Army.

Ike and Mamie Apart

Back in Washington, Mamie, determined not to let Ike's absence depress her, refused to let any grass grow under her feet. She maintained an active social life and continued to party and dine with their old friends. During the Christmas and New Year's season of 1935, when loneliness became most acute, Mamie dutifully sent Ike letters and cards and made certain that his Christmas package arrived in Manila on time. Nevertheless, she also went out almost every night during the holiday season, including New Year's Eve, which she spent with Captain Horace Smith and his mother. She got home at 3:45 a.m. after stopping to visit with Milton and Helen Eisenhower. Her granddaughter Susan Eisenhower reports, in her reminiscence of Mamie entitled *Mrs. Ike*, that "throughout the winter and spring, Mamie had no shortage of activities to occupy her, and no lack of friends to see or escorts to lend their arms."

For his part, Eisenhower did not mope around Manila. Although his job was frustrating and his relationship with MacArthur difficult, the workday itself was not long. He departed the hotel at 6:00 a.m. for flying lessons, reported into the office at 8:00, would usually see MacArthur, who reported for work even later, and then ended the workday about 1:00 p.m. After lunch and a nap, he would rendezvous with his regular bridge group at 3:00. Eisenhower was an excellent bridge player and generally won at the high-stakes game played in Manila. But he did not play bridge every afternoon. Not infrequently he also golfed with friends or relaxed at the Army-Navy Club across the green from the Manila Hotel. There were also numerous social engagements with high-level American officials and Philippine officials, including President Quezon, where Eisenhower was often a stand-in for MacArthur. Just as Mamie had found suitable escorts for social occasions back in Washington, Ike sought to fill the void made by her absence from Manila.

He found welcome companionship with Marian Huff, the wife of a naval officer who also served on MacArthur's staff. Marian became one of Eisenhower's favorite golfing partners and, because she was excellent at bridge, often sat as Eisenhower's partner at the bridge table. Her husband did not seem to mind his wife's socializing with Ike, while son John, although perhaps both young and naïve, saw nothing amiss in his father's friendship with Marian. Eisenhower was frequently attracted to vital women, which, of course, included Mamie first and foremost.

Almost certainly, word drifted back and forth across the Pacific Ocean of Mamie's and Ike's loneliness and unhappiness. Eisenhower's letters became increasingly infrequent and perfunctory; he even failed to write the Douds. The lack of Ike's normal good cheer and optimism was striking to Mamie, and she worried that her husband was falling out of love with her. She knew that she had made a big mistake in not following him to the Philippines. She realized that he had not shared even basic information about working for MacArthur—she knew neither his rank nor his salary. On the other hand, surely he knew of her lively social life, and she of his friendship with Marian Huff. By spring 1936, it was evident to Mamie that Eisenhower was not returning early from the Philippines. She had one choice if she wanted to save her marriage—she would have to join her husband in Manila.

Mamie and John landed in Manila on October 30, 1936, almost a year after the MacArthur mission arrived. When Eisenhower met them at the pier, Mamie discovered to her astonishment that he had shaved his head almost bald. He flashed his usual big grin, but their reunion was tense. Walking toward the Manila Hotel, Eisenhower quipped, "I gather I have reason for divorce, if I want one." Perhaps Ike was joking, but it was one of those serious double-edged jests that carries with it both playfulness and threat. And his was the kind of remark that is etched in family lore, marking a significant milestone in the Eisenhower marriage. According to the family, Eisenhower's jest did not imply that Mamie had been unfaithful but rather that he failed to share the excitement of her whirlwind social life while he was away.

A Family Settles In

In a sense, they would have to begin their marriage anew. Behind them were the halcyon days of Washington, DC, and the Wyoming Apartments, where father, mother, and son had all shared a life together; ahead were difficult years of constant moving, separation, and war. They would be exciting years for Ike, as his career blossomed, but trying times for Mamie, as she adjusted to the demands that increasing fame made on her husband.

Once in Manila, Mamie was determined to rescue her marriage as best she could. Friends who knew of their troubles advised Mamie once again to "vamp" Eisenhower, as she had done in Panama. Also as in Panama, Mamie disliked the oppressive heat in Manila, and she hated the mosquitoes and lizards with whom she shared her bedroom. It gave her the creeps that hotel staff sprayed her sleeping quarters every night before she crawled into a bed encased in mosquito netting. She was fearful of the frequent earthquakes that shook Manila and despised the paternalistic Philippine culture. Most of all, she was deeply unhappy about Ike's friendship with Marian Huff, his favorite bridge and golfing partner. She confided to her parents in Denver, "You know I am pretty level-headed about what I know is right. I made a terrible mistake in not coming out here with Ike. It's up to me to rectify lots of things."

While she could not recover the warmth of their interlude in Washington, Mamie quickly erased Eisenhower's bitter loneliness. She threw herself into Manila's vibrant social life with as much gusto as she could muster. She accompanied Eisenhower on arduous excursions around the islands, and, most importantly, she took up golf, working diligently to master the basics of the game. Although she was never proficient at golf, she did claim to enjoy getting out to hit the ball around. "That makes me feel better," she admitted. Eisenhower showed how pleased he was at her efforts by inviting her to play with him and his friends. Not wanting to slow the foursome, Mamie declined, but she accepted Ike's offer to give her personal lessons, from which she profited during private, nine-hole outings.

Perhaps the best medicine for their marriage was the fact that they were united again as a family with their son John. While John stayed in Manila long enough to follow the results of the 1936 presidential race with his father at the Army-Navy Club, in November Eisenhower drove John 150 miles north on Luzon to attend Brent School, an Episcopal high school in Baguio. Although Eisenhower and Mamie did not see him frequently, John was close enough for them to visit in Baguio during school vacations.

Although family life in Manila greatly improved, all their trials were not over. Shortly after Mamie arrived at dockside, to her consternation, she had learned that Ike was taking flying lessons. Who would be surprised that he had taken advantage of her absence to pursue a twenty-year-old dream? She was, of course, deeply apprehensive about this new adventure. It did not help that Eisenhower reported some near disasters. With his instructor, he delighted in taking John for airplane rides. Once on their return from Baguio, they had miscalculated their takeoff, could not gain altitude, shuttered into a stall, and just missed crashing into the ridge that marked the end of the airport. It was a close call with death that emphasized the inexperience of both the instructor and his student.

Not ironically, it was adversity that drew Eisenhower and Mamie closer together. One incident virtually washed away the resentment between them. Shortly after the new year of 1937, Mamie decided on her own to visit John at Brent School. With a friend she set out on a trek through mountainous Luzon in a car driven by a sergeant from Eisenhower's office. Following a minor accident and a small altercation in a local village, Mamie, now terrified, arrived in Baguio coughing up blood from a ruptured blood vessel in her stomach. Rushed to the local hospital, she slipped into a coma and lingered near death. Alarmed, Eisenhower flew to her bedside, staying with her until the crisis passed.

It was Mamie's worst nightmare come true, confirming all that she had feared in coming to the Philippines. Memories of Katie Gerow's suffering must have crossed her mind as she lay recuperating in the hospital for more than a month, trapped by tropical heat and rain. Yet, when the tempest passed, she emerged stronger and more resolute than before in saving her marriage. She had encountered her greatest fear and, with her family's help, had overcome it. In her hour of extreme need, Eisenhower flew to her bedside while her son John borrowed the Brent station wagon, with driver, to comfort her at the hospital.

The Death of Jimmy Ord

The great risk of flying was tragically confirmed in January 1938 when Eisenhower lost his best friend in the Philippines, Jimmy Ord. Although Eisenhower made only brief reference in his memoir to Ord's death, this tragedy was his greatest personal loss since the death of Icky. Just after the new year, Eisenhower was hospitalized with severe gastric pains, a prelude to his ileitis attacks during his presidency. Stopping by the hospital to cheer Ike, Ord told Eisenhower he was flying to Baguio that afternoon in a plane piloted by one of the Filipino students. Eisenhower urged Ord to fly with a regular army officer, but Ord wanted to express confidence in the new air corps. On their approach to Baguio, Ord decided to alert his hosts by dropping a message in their yard. Flying low and too slow, the student pilot stalled the airplane and crashed into a tree. Neither the plane nor the pilot were seriously hurt, but Ord, who was leaning out of the cockpit to toss his message, crushed his chest against the fuselage in the crack-up. He died shortly thereafter.

It was Mamie's sad task to relay the tragic news of Ord's death to her husband. January was always a difficult month for Ike and Mamie, who annually grieved the anniversary of Icky's death. Now, from his hospital bed, Eisenhower had the mournful duty of arranging Ord's funeral, establishing the requisite board of inquiry, and consoling Emily Ord, his friend's widow.

The day following Ord's death, he wrote Emily, who was at Fort Monroe in the United States. Suppressing his personal feelings of bewilderment, loss, and grief so that he could provide Emily a dispassionate report of her husband's fatal accident, he assured Emily that Ord would be given a military funeral with full honors and asked at which church the service should be conducted. Other than that, he offered no traditional religious consolation but affirmed that his and Mamie's hearts were with her along with their deepest love and sympathy. The memorial service held for Ord at Manila's cathedral was crowded with dignitaries, including President Quezon. Eisenhower and Mamie attended the service, of course, but not General MacArthur, who always avoided funerals, which was remarkably ironic because MacArthur reportedly had once scolded Eisenhower for not attending church.

With Ord gone, the planning for the military mission fell on Eisenhower's shoulders, but without his friend, he lost his enthusiasm for building a Philippine army. Not since Icky's death had Eisenhower felt so personally abandoned: "Many people have lost a close personal companion and an intimate friend. I've lost this, also my right hand, and my partner on a tough job, who furnished most of the inspiration needed to keep my plugging away. With him gone much of the zest has departed from a job that we always tackled as a team, never as two individuals."

In effect, Ord's death was a major turning point in his life and may have altered the course of history. Although MacArthur's attitude toward Eisenhower appreciably softened after this tragedy, Ord's passing also removed the buffer that had made tolerating MacArthur's megalomania possible. Because both MacArthur and Quezon insisted that Eisenhower extend his assignment in the Philippines, he dithered somewhat during the spring of 1938. Despite the loss of his closest friend and the impossible task of building a Philippine army, one thing was clear to him. He would stay in the army.

Furlough

It was apparent to all—especially to MacArthur and Eisenhower—that he needed time off. Because he had had no vacation in three years, in his discussions with MacArthur about extending his Philippine appointment he insisted on a furlough as a condition for staying on in Manila. MacArthur readily agreed to grant him four months' leave, provided Eisenhower would use part of his furlough to petition the War Department for more resources for the Philippine army.

The Eisenhowers escaped Manila on June 26, landing in San Francisco on July 18. After a few days visiting the Douds in Denver and his parents in Abilene, his vacation included visits to the Beech Aircraft plant in Wichita and the Winchester plant in New Haven, among others. Finally, and most importantly, he reconnected with the War Department in Washington, lobbying on behalf of the Philippine army with General George Marshall, chief of war plans. Although he did not solve MacArthur's shortage of arms and ammunition, Eisenhower did reassure his boss that he had received a sympathetic ear from the War Department. He also had an opportunity to visit with his old friend Gee Gerow, who was now executive officer of the War Plans Division. Undoubtedly, given what waited for him when he returned to Manila, his stop in Washington, and especially his brief conversation with Marshall, was fortuitously timed to place him back on the main track of his army career. On November 10, 1938, just five days after returning to Manila, Eisenhower decided to resign from MacArthur's service as soon as possible. He believed his usefulness had ended, but he vowed not to give MacArthur satisfaction over his unhappiness. On the surface, all would appear "lovely."

A Valedictory Address

With his plans to leave the Philippines well launched, Eisenhower was invited to present the commencement address to the Reserve Officers' Training Corps at the University of the Philippines in March 1939. The invitation enabled him to deliver his valedictory address to the army of the Philippines. As appropriate for the occasion, the selected text for his farewell was from Luke 11:21 in the King James Bible: "When a strong man armed keepeth his palace, his goods are in peace." Ignoring conventional exegesis of this parable, which has always identified Satan as the "strong man" and Jesus as the only victor who could vanquish Beelzebub, Eisenhower held up this wisdom of the "greatest of all men" (he rarely mentioned Jesus by name) as divine justification for the Philippine people to build defenses as strong as possible "when coveted by a more powerful neighbor." This lesson, of course, many Filipinos had already learned from decades of occupation by the Spaniards and the Americans. Framed by Jesus's parable of the strong man, Eisenhower delivered a thinly veiled secular sermon on the necessity of the army to clothe itself in duty and selflessness in the defense of the nation.

Speaking directly to the scions of the Philippine upper classes, Eisenhower lectured that even a weak nation with a ragged, poorly equipped citizen army could defend itself against a determined aggressor if it were led by dedicated professional officers who put self-interest aside for the good of the nation. He did not preach that they served at the left hand of God assuring justice and peace for the country, but he did urge them to consider themselves "the crusaders for and shining examples of" unity and cooperation in their land. America could not have been far from his mind when his peroration ended as follows: "Let your actions prove to the country that the ROTC places pride of service above personal convenience, duty above immediate economic gain."

His address to the ROTC cadets summarized the core principles of Eisenhower's religion without confessing personal faith. Commitment to duty, his primary self-commandment, helped him keep his anger in check when frustrated with MacArthur. Through duty he mastered self-discipline and tried to control his "Dutch" temper. Duty, for Eisenhower, was comparable to the devotion required of a pastor. Both military officers and religious officiates were required to give their oath of service to authority higher than themselves; their duty included discipline, allegiance, and selfless devotion to that authority. An army could not be led to victory unless officered by such men. Eisenhower encouraged the newly commissioned ROTC officers to be as committed to the Philippines' progress and welfare as he was devoted to the American way of life, a truth that he revered above all others.

September 3, 1939: World War II

On September 3, 1939, two days after Hitler's blitzkrieg against Poland, Eisenhower, Mamie, and John hunkered down in front of a short-wave radio to listen to Neville Chamberlain's announcement that Great Britain had declared war on Germany. The year before, Eisenhower had told John that he supported Chamberlain's Munich agreement only because an unprepared Great Britain had no other choice. Now, the war that Fox Conner had long predicted and for which Eisenhower had prepared himself was beginning. He predicted that it would be a long, devastating war, "as bloody and as costly as was the so-called World War." Communism, anarchy, poverty, crime, and general disorder would likely be the winners. He chafed to get back to America, which he believed would be pulled into the conflict sooner or later. More than anything, he wanted to return to his own army to help prepare the United States for war.

His final departure from the Philippines proceeded without rancor. To the end, Quezon wanted him to reconsider, offering Eisenhower a blank check if he would accept a new contract. To the end, MacArthur kept him busy writing policy statements and speeches. Although there seemed to be a hundred odd jobs to complete, MacArthur was surprisingly pleasant. Ultimately, Quezon hosted a beautiful farewell luncheon for Ike and Mamie. And in the end, on December 12, when the Eisenhowers boarded the ship for the United States, MacArthur showed up at the pier hatless, with a smile on his face and a bottle of fine scotch in his hand as a going-away present. The gesture confused John, who did not understand MacArthur's complex character. It was the last pleasantry that Eisenhower would enjoy with the general.

Although Eisenhower's four-year stint in the Philippines could have isolated him from the main circles of the army during crucial years immediately preceding World War II, as Holt and Leyerzapf have observed, Eisenhower's Philippine experience proved invaluable in preparing him to meet the challenges of the world war long foreseen by Fox Conner. "In the Philippines," they wrote, "[Eisenhower] learned to build and train an army from practically nothing while being as politically and diplomatically sensitive as possible, negotiating difficult logistical circumstances, and working with hair-trigger personalities."

They landed in San Francisco in time to celebrate New Year's Eve. Crowds pushed them along Market Street. They rode jam-packed cable cars and enjoyed the evening of lights, horns, and cheering celebrants. All the noise and glitter marked the end of a decade of peaceful family life. As Eisenhower ruefully noted in his memoirs, too soon John would leave the family nest for West Point. Mamie would be caught in years of anxiety and loneliness for her husband and son while Eisenhower was thrust upon the world stage during one of America's bloodiest wars.

Crusade in Europe, 1940–1946

E isenhower titled his World War II memoir *Crusade in Europe*. As the war progressed, he explained, "there grew within me the conviction that as never before in a war between many nations the forces that stood for human good and men's rights were this time confronted by a completely evil conspiracy with which no compromise could be tolerated. Because only by the utter destruction of the Axis was a decent world possible, the war became for me a crusade in the traditional sense of that often-misused word." From Eisenhower's perspective, while World War I had been fought to make the world safe for democracy, World War II was fought to save Western civilization.

As a son of pacifists, who is surprised that Eisenhower developed strong justification for fighting World War II? Eisenhower's mother followed Jehovah's Witnesses teachings and was a "conditional pacifist," meaning that she only supported war ordained by God. But, as evidenced by her public protests, Ida approved neither World War I nor World War II. Differing from Ida, Eisenhower countered that both world wars were just wars. There was tension between their opposing views about warfare, but because of respect and affection, neither mother nor son discussed nor publicly condemned the other's religious beliefs.

Eisenhower gradually embraced the idea that World War II was a justifiable crusade. Religiously, World War II was a just war that called him to protect America's national interests and to defend law and justice ordained by God. While in the Philippines, Eisenhower perceived Hitler as a power-drunk egocentric who was criminally insane. He was baffled why intelligent Germans accepted Hitler's leadership. "Hundreds of millions will suffer privations and starvation, millions will be killed and wounded because one man so wills it." Hitler's persecution of the Jews and his subjugation of Austria, Czechoslovakia, and Poland were "as black as that of any barbarian of the Dark Ages." The only possible outcome, he believed, was Hitler's total victory or Germany's destruction. In religiously apocalyptic rhetoric, the crusade in Europe became a struggle to the death between champions of freedom and hoodlums who threatened to destroy modern civilization.

Eisenhower's perception of human nature shaped his ideology, philosophy of life, and religious, political, and economic beliefs. David and Ida instilled in their sons the conventional Christian doctrine that mankind was forever torn between self-interest and passion (original sin) and faithful commitment to God and his children. If human nature were unchecked, chaos (Satan) would prevail, at least temporarily. For Eisenhower, this divine/demonic dynamic—an eternal tension between the common good and self-interest—pervaded the family, Abilene, the army, the nation, and the world. Unregulated self-interest constantly threatened community and civilization. Only voluntary restraint countered chaos bred by rapacious self-conceit. Hitler was especially dangerous because unrestrained self-interest had gained control of the powerful German state. After Hitler destroyed civil self-discipline, there was no countervailing force to protect the dignity and freedom of people who fell under the heel of German boots.

If an army officer's greatest virtue was devotion to duty, his lowest vice was selfish advancement of his career. Sentimentality concerning Eisenhower's Kansas roots aside, his dialectical worldview was the strongest legacy of his upbringing in Abilene. As he cinched his belt in preparation for war, Eisenhower increasingly revealed that his civil ideology rested on religious beliefs learned from David and Ida in their Bible Students' home. Eisenhower lived in a world under constant tension from forces of order and disorder, both internal and external. As his father, David, had predicted, the world was relentlessly threatened by an apocalyptic clash between the children of light and the devils of darkness. Only vigilance could stave off catastrophes of slavery and anarchy from sweeping over the United States.

Similar to his mother, who dutifully peddled the *Watchtower* along Abilene's streets, Eisenhower called Americans to awaken to the dark threat of Nazi aggression. Given his parents' religious influence, it is not ironic that Eisenhower became a watchman on his return from the Philippines. He would have been horrified at the suggestion that he preached repentance, but had he consulted his father's Bible, he would have learned that the Greek word for repent, *metanoia*, can be translated "turn around." And a "turning around" by the American people and the US Army was exactly what he advocated. Posted in the woods of the far Pacific Northwest, at Fort Lewis, Washington, upon his return from the Philippines, Eisenhower's was a voice crying in the wilderness when he campaigned for American preparedness in 1940. This "minor prophet" was only a lieutenant colonel, but he rallied the troops under his command as best he could. Fortunately, he was not alone. The new chief of staff, George Marshall, was on guard as well.

In 1940, Eisenhower was more alarmed by complacency in America's military establishment than he was about the threat from fascists in Europe or Japan. America's greatest military weakness, Eisenhower believed, was that the army had grown soft in pursuit of self-interest. American officers, of course, reflected the attitudes of ordinary Americans and Congress. In *Crusade in Europe*, Eisenhower recalled that he encountered no "sense of urgency" at Fort Lewis. Athletics often took precedence over rigorous training. Too many officers had sheltered themselves from disconcerting change. Others had been stripped of ambition by a numbing career with no promotions or the belief that the infantry was forgotten and passé.

Countering lassitude, Eisenhower continually preached on the importance of morale. Morale, Eisenhower believed, is closely tied to self-respect and devotion to duty. An army that coddles personnel does not produce high morale but rather encourages sloth, inefficiency, and, worst of all, self-pity. To maintain high morale, an army must constantly demand, individually and collectively, unswerving devotion to duty, professional efficiency, and the highest standards of discipline and loyalty. To his friend Everett Hughes, he advised that the best way to build morale in 1940 was to weed out the weaklings in the officer corps. The sooner ineffective officers fall out and disappear, the better, in Eisenhower's opinion.

Fort Lewis

In professional terms, Eisenhower's posting as a battalion commander in the far reaches of the Pacific Northwest might seem a demotion from his position in Manila, where he was MacArthur's chief of staff creating the Philippine army, an appointment that included access to President Quezon. At Fort Lewis, he was just another lieutenant colonel with command of a half-strength battalion composed of regular army and recent recruits. But Eisenhower claimed he was in his glory commanding troops. To his friend Gee Gerow, he graphically described his battalion's maneuvers in the cutover stump barrens of the Pacific Northwest. Through four days and nights, Eisenhower and his men crawled in "Hades—stumps, slashing, fallen logs, tangled brush, holes, hummocks and hills!" He reveled in it, not only because he knew that the historical measure of a military officer was his ability to command troops, but also because this opportunity to lead enlisted men was the reason why, he told himself repeatedly, he had endured years of suffocating desk work under MacArthur.

Professionally, Eisenhower told everyone that he couldn't have been happier in the summer and fall of 1940. His dream of commanding troops fulfilled, on the eve of a war, his prospects for further advancement were bright. Eisenhower was delighted when Colonel George S. Patton Jr., expecting to be promoted to command the Second Armored Division, recruited him to serve either as chief of staff or as a regimental commander. Eisenhower savored the prospect of serving in Patton's tank corps, but he made it clear that his preference was to command troops. "I'm at long last doing 'command' duty," he replied to Patton. "It's not only that, like yourself, I like to work with soldiers, but I am weary of desk duty. I suppose it's too much to hope that I could have a regiment in your division, because I'm still three years away from my colonelcy. But I *think* I could do a damn good job commanding a regiment . . . if there's a chance of that kind of assignment, I'd be for it 100%."

Because Patton and Eisenhower believed that war was imminent, they drove their troops and officers with an intensity they shared with George Marshall. While Eisenhower was having the time of his life in soggy Puget Sound country, in April the "phony war" in Europe ended when Nazi Germany launched its blitzkrieg against western Europe. Norway and Denmark fell. On May 10, 1940, Hitler invaded the Netherlands, Luxembourg, Belgium, and France. Soon Paris fell and the British beat a retreat to Dunkirk, where they executed a heroic evacuation of over three hundred thousand troops to Great Britain. When France surrendered on June 22, Nazi Germany had conquered most of western Europe, from the Atlantic and the North Sea to Poland, Czechoslovakia, and Austria. In the United States, President Roosevelt responded with a declaration of nonbelligerency. In September Congress established the first peacetime draft in American history.

The threat from Hitler became simply too great to ignore. Eisenhower was confident that once Americans got their dander up, the forces of hell could not hold them back. He predicted, "The American population, once it gets truly irritated, is a self-confident, reckless, fast-moving avalanche." At the moment, his only important task was to get his troops ready so that America could fight a winning war. But he was dismayed by the indifference to the German threat shown by many regular army officers, who chafed at longer hours and personal inconvenience. "Jesus wept," he lamented to Everett Hughes. "If ever we are to prove that we're worth the salaries the government has been paying us all these years—now is the time!"

During the spring and summer of 1940, Eisenhower developed a local reputation of being "Alarmist Ike." The officers and men at Fort Lewis, annoyed by his constant harping about the coming war, tagged him with this sarcastic nickname. But they did not know the son of Ida Eisenhower very well, because "Watchman Ike" took quiet satisfaction in their insolence. Their indifference to the nation's peril only stimulated him to greater action. "Alarmist Ike" became his irreverent badge of honor. It was as if "Watchman Ike" glimpsed the Armageddon prophesied by the Jehovah's Witnesses just on the horizon— only the onrushing beast was Hitler's goose-stepping Nazi SS storm troopers. As the hapless French had discovered, only a prepared, self-disciplined nation could save itself from this evil onslaught. No one at Fort Lewis but "Alarmist Ike" talked as urgently about the coming war, or of the inevitable judgment awaiting an unprepared America. Above all, Eisenhower could not tolerate carrying on business as usual. To create a new army, he had to weed out the old order, just as the New Deal had done politically. Eisenhower confessed to Gerow, "It is a hard thing to do, and in many cases too hard for some of the people in charge. But it is a job that has got to be done."

Actually, Eisenhower's first crusade was at home in America, not in Europe. For Americans who have become accustomed to venerating World War II veterans as "the greatest generation," it is difficult to appreciate just how pathetically the American army had deteriorated by 1940. Years later, Eisenhower commented wryly, "In the summer of 1941, with the Germans racing across Russia and their Japanese ally unmistakably preparing for the conquest of the far Pacific, the Army could only feebly reinforce overseas garrisons."

As the United States Army ramped up for war, Eisenhower knew that more staff assignments likely awaited him. He knew that the army was critically short of talented administrators and that his planning talents had come to the attention of the top army brass. Exasperated, he confided to his friend Leonard Gerow, "The job of staying with a regiment is a damn near hopeless one." Among his many virtues, George Marshall was an outstanding talent scout. Marshall's roster of promising officers read like a Who's Who of American World War II generals: Bradley, Stilwell, Ridgway, Patton, Collins, "Beetle" Smith, Allen, and Major Dwight Eisenhower.

Everywhere, commanders were scrambling to find experienced staff officers such as Eisenhower. Within months, Lieutenant General Walter Krueger, commander of the Third Army, stationed at Fort Sam Houston near San Antonio, asked George Marshall to assign Eisenhower to the Third Army as chief of staff, a position normally filled by a brigadier general. Krueger wanted a chief of staff who possessed broad vision, had progressive ideas, grasped the magnitude of commanding an army, and had "lots of initiative and resourcefulness." Marshall concurred that Eisenhower was his man.

The Louisiana Maneuvers

It was during his time on Krueger's staff that Eisenhower catapulted into national prominence. He arrived at Third Army headquarters just in time to help plan and execute the largest peacetime war games in history. Called the Louisiana Maneuvers, the war games spilled over into Texas. Almost half of all US Army combat troops were involved. Krueger's Blue Army excelled both on defense and offense, and Eisenhower, as chief of staff and principal press officer, basked in his commander's success. Eisenhower, who held daily press briefings, especially impressed reporters Hanson Baldwin of the *New York Times*, Richard Hottelet of United Press, and Eric Sevareid of CBS. Colonel Eisenhower proved a natural with newsmen, who were captured by his grin and appreciated his candor and accessibility.

Because Eisenhower was the public face of the Blue Army, he received disproportionate coverage, and accolades, for Krueger's success against the opposing Red Army. Historical myth credits Eisenhower's brilliant performance in the Louisiana Maneuvers for his rapid rise to command in World War II. In truth, Eisenhower was already known as one of the most talented young officers in the army. When Marshall inspected the maneuvers that fall, he quietly asked Krueger to recommend the best officer to head the War Plans Division in Washington. Without reservation, Krueger named Eisenhower.

As intended by Marshall, the Louisiana Maneuvers helped weed out incompetent and aging officers unfit to command troops in modern, mechanized warfare. For Marshall, the maneuvers provided a "combat college for troop leading." Eisenhower proved not only an outstanding planner but also an astute evaluator of leadership. In the end, the purge was ruthless. Hundreds of officers were dismissed from service or assigned dead-end jobs. Three-quarters of corps and division commanders were replaced; and only eleven of forty-two senior officers survived to form the backbone of the new United States Army. Of course, the maneuvers also highlighted rising stars, including Patton, Mark Clark, and Eisenhower.

The Louisiana Maneuvers taught Eisenhower to make no distinction among regular army, reserve, and national guard officers. What counted was how well an officer inspired and led his troops—and, as chief of staff, he had to identify those who could do the job and those who could not. He discovered that at every level—from second lieutenants to generals—the army was short of officers who had the requisite moral courage, military efficiency, and self-sacrifice.

Just three days prior to Pearl Harbor, Eisenhower was invited to address the commissioning of second lieutenants at Kelly Field, Texas. Although he was unable to attend the graduation because of the outbreak of war, drafts of his remarks have survived. Appropriately, Eisenhower reflected on the essentials of military leadership. Armaments and supply were important. But the primary essentials of military leadership were "a spiritual unity," the "devotion of self to a common cause," and the development of a common sense of duty. Echoing his own hunger to lead troops, Eisenhower emphasized that of all commissioned officers, the lieutenant is closest to the enlisted men.

> It is the lieutenant's privilege to live close to his men, to be their example in conduct, courage, and in devotion to duty. He is in position to learn about them intimately, to help them when in trouble, often to keep them out of trouble. No matter how young he may be nor how old and hard boiled his men he must become their counselor, their leader, their friend, their old man. . . . To gain the respect, the esteem, the affection, the readiness to follow into danger, the unswerving and undying loyalty of the enlisted man—that is the privilege and the opportunity of the lieutenant, and it is his high and almost divine duty. It is the challenge to his talents, his patriotism, his very soul!

"Their counselor," "their friend," he emphasized. Eisenhower might have added "their shepherd," "their father," but that would have been too unmilitary—too unsettling—so instead he slipped into barracks jargon: "their old man," who inspired respect and affection.

Although he did not use religious language to depict military leadership, there was no question that Eisenhower viewed the commissioning of officers as a secular ordination and call to duty that was almost divine. By the end of World War II, Eisenhower would no longer distinguish his military calling from the performance of his divine duty. Parenthetically, as a marvelously successful army football coach, Eisenhower might have selected a different leadership paradigm: that of the coach. But rather than stressing the importance of teamwork in successful military leadership, he consistently emphasized paternal/spiritual values. Just as he had lectured the Philippine ROTC graduates, Eisenhower highlighted devotion to duty along with self-denial of personal ambition. Before Pearl Harbor, however, he seems to have viewed leadership as an individual quality rather than a communal responsibility, indicating that building interservice and international teamwork was not yet on his professional agenda.

Brigadier General

At the completion of the Louisiana Maneuvers, Eisenhower was promoted to brigadier general, the normal grade for the chief of staff of the Third Army. He had been expecting the promotion, but during the promotion announcements, his good friend Mark Clark intentionally left out Eisenhower's name. Threading his way among the celebrating officers, a dejected Eisenhower worked his way toward the door. Dramatically, Clark again called everyone to order and confessed that he had forgotten a name, "Dwight D. Eisenhower!" Everyone laughed, including Ike, who shot back at Clark, "I'll get you for this, you sonofabitch."

Of course, he was pleased to have been promoted to brigadier general. After General Krueger pinned on his shiny new star, Eisenhower was thrilled when a battalion of the Second Division, Third Army honored him with a congratulatory review. Ruefully, he knew that his step upward was also a rung away from his command of troops, his dream of serving under his friend George Patton inexorably slipping away.

Eisenhower's promotion to brigadier general was a major watershed in his career. As General Eisenhower, his identity—his life's purpose—had fully matured. Behind him were the years of education and internship in the arts of military leadership. He stood at the threshold of fame and history; confident and well prepared to perform the warrior's duty that awaited him. Yet, he remained unbaptized by fire; he had not experienced the horrific devastation and unimaginable brutality of modern warfare. Intellectually he knew the deadly power of the army he was building, but in the fall of 1941, he did not think of the United States Army as the savior of Western civilization. That would come later. Germany and Japan presented dire threats that the US Army would surely be called upon to parry, but he had not yet envisioned the global mission, the crusade, on which the United States would soon embark.

In keeping with the Kansas upbringing, his moral and spiritual world was personal and internalized—isolationist, one might say, not global. As the world tumbled into war, if Eisenhower wondered where God was in all the tumult, he apparently never asked aloud. In his unused graduation address to the Kelly Field cadets, Eisenhower exegetically outlined his personal faith. Above all, he believed that every man should faithfully follow where his duty called, without complaint. In turn, duty required that he respect the God-given dignity of others. As he emphasized for the new lieutenants, respect was among Eisenhower's highest virtues; affection was one of God's greatest gifts; loyalty was among life's greatest rewards. Ultimately, the officer's duty challenged "his very soul." Eisenhower's religious awakening would be gradual; he had no religious experience like Paul on the road to Damascus. But the spiritual seeds planted by his mother and father in Abilene began to take root as World War II engulfed him.

Pearl Harbor

On Sunday afternoon, December 7, 1941, an exhausted Eisenhower napped at home when the Japanese shattered his peaceful world. Five days after Pearl Harbor, he received an urgent call from Washington, ordering him to report immediately to George Marshall at the War Department. He knew what was coming—his chances for troop command blasted—Eisenhower reported to Marshall a week later on Sunday morning, December 14.

Marshall was waiting for him with a summary of the military disasters in the Far East, from Hawaii to the Philippines and China and beyond. Without sufficient planes, ships, or troops, the United States and its allies were taking a beating. But Marshall was determined to try to save as much of the Pacific as possible, and more importantly, to win the war. "How are we going to do it?" he bluntly asked Eisenhower.

Momentarily stunned, Eisenhower asked for a few hours to reply. While Marshall's challenge was undoubtedly a test of his new brigadier general, Eisenhower understood more about the Far East than any general officer at Marshall's disposal. He knew that reports to Marshall must be succinct, factual, and without bias. Within three hours Eisenhower briefed Marshall with his assessment: to continue the fight against the Japanese, the United States should establish a strong base in Australia from which to counterattack; although the Philippines were lost, the army should do its best to delay collapse; finally, despite setbacks, it was important that the United States not appear to abandon its allies in the Far East. Marshall agreed and gave Eisenhower responsibility for managing the war in the Pacific. "Do what you can to save them," Marshall simply ordered.

Thereafter, Marshall offered Eisenhower a homily on management. There were a lot of bright men under his command, Marshall observed, but too many of them relied on Marshall to make their decisions. Marshall expected his officers to solve the problems under their jurisdiction. Otherwise, they were of no use to him. Also, when in trouble, Marshall would cut men short if they ventured, "Well, sir, I assumed . . ." "You are paid to anticipate, not to assume," Marshall shot back, and that was that. Not long thereafter, Marshall appointed Eisenhower chief of the War Plans Division.

By all accounts, Marshall was inscrutable. Possessing keen intelligence and an almost infallible judge of character, Marshall was nonetheless an exceedingly private man. He valued initiative among his officers and demanded results. But there was little *bon amie* from the general. He could be gracious but was ruthless in culling out the unfit. Eisenhower found him remote and austere. Although almost everyone else in the army called him "Ike," Marshall only slipped once, otherwise always addressing him as "Eisenhower." Nonetheless, in addition to great respect, he also inspired affection in Eisenhower. In Eisenhower's opinion, Marshall's highest leadership qualities included accepting responsibility for his own decisions, delegating authority, and resolutely backing the judgment of his subordinates.

Advising Roosevelt and Churchill on the conduct of the war, Marshall insisted that there be a supreme commander for each theater of war so that the Allies would fight under a unified command. Marshall's idea was new and untested. On Christmas Day, he asked Eisenhower to prepare a mission statement for the supreme commander, including selection procedures, authorities, and safeguards to national sovereignty. With little amendment, Roosevelt and Churchill approved Eisenhower's plan. Unwittingly, Eisenhower had established the guidelines under which he would later serve as supreme commander of Allied forces in Europe. For the time being, he became Marshall's de facto deputy commander for all army operations.

The Death of His Father

His father's death on March 10, 1942, not the war, rekindled Eisenhower's religious concerns. When David died, his son was trapped in Washington, struggling with the ever-worsening situation in the Pacific and increasing responsibilities for Europe. Unable to return home to bury his father or to comfort his mother, he felt terrible that there was no time to grieve with his family. "War is not soft," he wrote. "It has no time to indulge even the deepest and most sacred emotions." In his diary he simply noted, "Father died this morning. Nothing I can do but send a wire." No doubt memories of Icky flooded his thoughts, because Eisenhower never recovered from the loss of his first son. He may have also thought of his old friend Jimmy Ord, whose death four years before had disheartened him.

As busy and important as he was to Marshall that spring, it is surprising that Eisenhower could not arrange some emergency leave to attend his father's funeral. He may have been absolutely indispensable to Marshall at this time. Or he may have shied away from his father's burial because Naomi Engle, Ida's close friend and a strong Jehovah's Witness, had taken charge of arranging David's funeral. Two elders of the Jehovah's Witnesses would conduct the funeral service, which included readings from Watchtower publications. Eisenhower could have worn a civilian suit at graveside, of course, but the dynamics of the general's presence at a funeral service of the Jehovah's Witnesses would have been awkward.

Instead, on March 12 Eisenhower stole thirty minutes to meditate in private, first thinking of his father and then about his mother, who would now be living alone in Abilene. That evening he credited his father's integrity for helping to secure both his and his son John's appointment to West Point. Although proud of his father, he lamented, "My only regret is that it was always so difficult to let him know the great depth of my affection for him." From Eisenhower's perspective, love between a father and a son was a given, but affection could be difficult to gain. Eisenhower made a significant distinction between familial love and mutual affection. For himself, on that day he had chosen duty to his country over filial obligation. With the exception of attending funerals, this prayerful interlude was his first acknowledged personal religious activity since leaving West Point.

Dustup with Marshall

Unintentionally, on Friday, March 20, Marshall brutally angered an exhausted and grieving Eisenhower by implying that his aide would not receive additional promotions during the war. While discussing other promotions, Marshall explained that he was not going to repeat the errors of World War I by promoting staff officers over field officers who were actually fighting the war. "Take your case," Marshall continued. "I know that you were recommended by one general for division command and by another for corps command. That's all very well. I'm glad that they have a high opinion of you, but you're going to stay right here and fill your position, and that's that. While this may seem a sacrifice to you, that's the way it must be."

Eisenhower's pent-up emotions boiled over. He had missed the war in 1918 and was confined to a training command at Camp Colt, Gettysburg. After the war, he had languished sixteen years as a major until promoted to lieutenant colonel in 1936 with the rest of his West Point class. When he finally secured command of a battalion with the Fifteenth Infantry, he served less than a year before being rudely shoved into another staff position. Now he took personally Marshall's insinuation that he would be chained to a desk throughout the war.

"General, I'm interested in what you say, but I want you to know that I don't give a damn about your promotion plans as far as I am concerned. I came into this office from the field and I am trying to do my duty. I expect to do so as long as you want me here. If that locks me to a desk for the rest of the war, so be it!" Burning with resentment, Eisenhower stalked toward the exit, cooling slightly when he reached the door. Turning, Eisenhower saw Marshall staring at him intently, and realizing the ludicrousness of his behavior, he flashed his characteristic grin. In return, Eisenhower thought "a tiny smile quirked the corner of his face."

But his "Dutch" temper, as MacArthur called it, did not cool quickly. Returning to his desk, Eisenhower poured out his anger into his diary. The more he devoted himself to faithful performance of his duty, the further he seemed to drift from his heart's desire to lead troops. Had he wanted to be a paper-pushing bureaucrat, there were numerous opportunities for him to join private corporations for a handsome salary. It was not so much that Eisenhower thought he deserved higher rank, but he seemed trapped between his ambition and his duty. What he wanted most, and couldn't seem to secure, was a firm grip on combat command. As a perceptive historian has observed, "It seems like he had a personal or career devil perched on one shoulder and a duty, honor, country angel clinging to the other."

The following morning, he purged his diary of his temper tantrum. "Yesterday I got angry and filled a page with language that this morning I've 'expurgated,'" he wrote on March 21. Remembering his mother's admonition, he wrote, "Anger cannot win, it cannot even think clearly. In this respect Marshall puzzles me a bit." Eisenhower had witnessed Marshall explode in anger over small matters. But Marshall quickly subsided, almost as if nothing had happened, leaving Eisenhower to wonder if his display of temper had been for effect. But not so, Eisenhower. Four decades before he had raged against injustice and beaten his fists bloody against a tree stump when his father told him he was not old enough to go trick-or-treating on Halloween. David's response was to whip his son and send him to bed. But Ida came to the room to nurse and soothe her angry son. "He that conquers his soul is greater than he who conquers a city," she reportedly counseled him—advice that he had always tried to follow. "I blaze for an hour!" he wrote in his self-censored diary. "So, for many years I've made it a religion never to indulge myself, but yesterday I failed."

Three days later, Eisenhower was stunned to learn that Marshall had recommended to the president that he be promoted to major general. Obviously, Eisenhower's promotion was already in the works when he blew up in Marshall's office. Marshall could be inscrutable and sometimes insensitive. Had he been toying with Eisenhower the previous week? Had he been unaware that Eisenhower was still mourning the death of his father? Was it possible that Marshall did not know that David had died? Perhaps Eisenhower had so suppressed his grief that Marshall noticed no difference in his demeanor until Eisenhower's temper exploded. Eisenhower's famous grin, well practiced since his childhood, probably reassured Marshall that Eisenhower, like himself, was a master of self-control. In his justification to Roosevelt, Marshall explained that Eisenhower was not really a staff officer but was actually an operations officer, second in command to Marshall himself.

Emissary to London

Not surprisingly, Eisenhower was delighted by his promotion to major general. Just one week after his outburst in Marshall's office, he knew he had received Marshall's stamp of approval. Besides, Eisenhower fantasized, "When I finally get back to troops, I'll get a division."

Marshall's timing of the promotion was exquisite. Two months later, on May 23, Marshall dispatched Eisenhower and Mark Clark to London to assess America's military mission, but more importantly to enable Churchill and British officers to evaluate Eisenhower.

Marshall had already decided that change had to be made in the army's London office, but he wanted Eisenhower's opinion as well. Eisenhower spent much of his time in England with British officers, emphasizing Marshall's doctrine that the war could only be won under a single, unified command. Eisenhower himself, who worked fourteen or more hours a day, was also disquieted by the lack of urgency among American officers in England.

On his return to Washington on June 2, Eisenhower recommended that the American commander in England be replaced with someone who conveyed urgency as well as the reassurance of America's commitment to the British alliance. "Our own people are able but do not quite understand what we want done. It is necessary to get a punch behind the job or we'll never be ready by spring, 1943, to attack. We must get going," Eisenhower wrote in the diary. In keeping with Marshall's expectations, Eisenhower provided a list of recommended changes. Marshall welcomed, but did not need, Eisenhower's assessment of the London command.

Commander of the European Theater of Operations

Within days of reporting to Marshall, Eisenhower packed his kit to return to London, this time as American commander of the European Theater of Operations (ETO). Reportedly, he informed Mamie that he was going to command "the whole shebang." His job was to organize and train, but perhaps not lead into battle, all American armed forces assigned to the European front. He faced two formidable challenges: first, he had to mold a united American command in Europe, including the army, navy, and air force, and second, he had to build an effective partnership with the British, already badly bloodied in the war and not yet confident of American leadership.

Eisenhower understood the importance of the gigantic task before him. "It is a big job," he wrote in his diary. Building the Anglo-American alliance in preparation for an invasion of Europe would be "the biggest job of the war" outside of Marshall's. His assignment did not include command of the invasion forces, but watchman that he was, he believed that successful planning made all the difference between victory and defeat against the German army.

One of his first tasks was to assemble a team that not only integrated American armed services within headquarters but also incorporated British allies into meaningful command positions. Here, Eisenhower was at his best. He had already lobbied Marshall to appoint his close friends, George Patton and Mark Clark, to top command positions. For his chief of staff, Eisenhower chose Walter Bedell "Beetle" Smith, an irascible, profane, bulldog of a man. Eisenhower knew that this Prussian-like officer was just the man to put "punch" into training men to fight Hitler. Eisenhower found this bumptious officer surprisingly shy, yet selfless, with a remarkable mastery of detail, a passionate devotion to duty, and a clear comprehension of main issues. Smith, who remained with Eisenhower throughout the war, became indispensable as Eisenhower's administrative officer. He cursed, yelled, bullied, insulted, argued, and terrified with abandon. Beetle Smith was not lovable, but because he was loyal and could be suavely diplomatic if required, he became a "crackerjack" as Eisenhower's chief of staff.

Kay Summersby

Students of Eisenhower's religion and leadership must eventually confront his alleged affair with Kay Summersby, his driver throughout most of the war. Eisenhower first met Summersby in May 1942 during his assessment of the American command structure in Britain. A volunteer ambulance driver during the Blitz, Summersby, a winsome Irish beauty, was assigned to help the Americans. When he returned to England in June to command United States forces in Europe, Eisenhower remembered the lively driver who seemed familiar with London's every nook and cranny. She soon became his personal chauffeur. Eisenhower was fifty-one; she was thirty-four.

For her part, Summersby quickly fit into Eisenhower's official family. Her father had been a lieutenant colonel in an illustrious Irish regiment. Like Eisenhower, she loved to ride horses and play bridge. Perhaps most importantly, she knew her way around English society and proved an important mentor to Yanks unschooled in British society and manners.

There is no question that Eisenhower was lonely, missed Mamie, and longed for female companionship, which he had enjoyed throughout his life. While in England, Africa, and Europe, Mamie was always on his mind, and he flooded her with letters, notes, and cards, 319 in all, during the war. Yet from North Africa, he confided to Mamie's sister, "I think I have learned more about the value of feminine companionship in the last month than I ever knew in my life."

Since leaving for England, he enjoyed the company of few women and felt their absence keenly. He did not feel he could share these thoughts with Mamie, however. Earlier he confided that he might get a dog. "You can't talk war to a dog," he wrote before leaving to invade Morocco, "and I'd like to have someone or something to talk to occasionally that does not know what the word war means! A dog is my only hope."

When Eisenhower and Summersby met in the spring of 1942, she was involved in an affair with a married American military engineer, Major Richard Arnold. At that time, she was married to Gordon Summersby, a British officer serving in India. After both Richard and Kay obtained divorces, they pledged to marry, hopefully in June 1943. Thereafter, Summersby's fiancé was shipped to North Africa to participate in Operation Torch, the Allied invasion commanded by her boss.

To be near her American lover, Summersby requested a transfer to North Africa when Eisenhower's headquarters moved with the invasion force. But already there was talk around London about Ike and Kay, who now accompanied Eisenhower to social occasions as well as to official functions. When the ship carrying WAC (Women's Army Corps) officers, including Summersby, was torpedoed off Gibraltar, Eisenhower suffered anxious hours until he learned that they had safely reached Algeria. Complicating his life even more, in a November 1942 issue, *Life* magazine featured Eisenhower and his staff. Photographed for the entire world to see was General Ike and his pretty driver Kay.

That Kay Summersby was not Eisenhower's only driver did not comfort Mamie. While fighting German field marshal Erwin Rommel, the "Desert Fox," in northern Africa, on his domestic front he still had to soothe tensions with Mamie, who was left alone in Washington. His letters to Mamie repeatedly affirmed his love. Writing home just after Christmas, Eisenhower reassured her:

> Sometimes I get to missing you so that I simply don't know what to do. As pressure mounts and strain increases, everyone begins to show the weaknesses of his makeup. It is up to the Commander to conceal his.... No one else in the world could ever fill your place with me—and that is the reason I need you. Maybe a simpler explanation is merely that I LOVE YOU!! which I do, always. Never forget that, because, except for my duty, which I try to perform creditably, it [his love for her] is the only thing to which I can cling with confidence.

In a reprise of his New Year's letter written shortly after the debacle at Kasserine Pass, an exhausted Eisenhower confessed the following: "Sometimes I get so homesick for you I don't know what to do. But I always know this—for me there is only one woman and only one ambition with respect to a woman— that is to come a-running to you and hold onto you firmly, forever." It was February 14, 1943, their twenty-seventh anniversary. He begged her to ignore the "stories, gossip, lies, etc. [that] get started without the slightest foundation in fact." He went on, "I'm trying to do my duty, and my only hope is that this war will be over quickly." That would allow him to return to her side.

Mamie knew that Eisenhower's duty always came first. But was his devotion to duty the reason he could not, or would not, be forthcoming to Mamie about his relationship with Kay? Ike never wrote that Summersby was also his personal secretary and social companion. Two days after his "homesick" letter, he snorted, "So *Life* says my old London driver came down! So she did—but the big reason . . . is that she is terribly in love with a young American Colonel and is to be married to him come June." Then he hedged, "And anyway, *my own* driver is Sergeant Drye [*sic*]!"

Eisenhower was not alone in trying to ease Mamie's loneliness and anxieties. George Marshall regularly wrote personal notes to the wives of his top commanders. Although he never fueled rumors about their husbands, Marshall left the distinct impression that he was personally keeping watch over them while they were away at war. Mamie also received weekly letters from Sergeant Mickey McKeogh, Eisenhower's loyal valet, keeping her up to date as best he could about his boss's daily activities.

On June 6, 1943, Eisenhower received word that Colonel Richard Arnold, Kay's fiancé, had been killed by a land mine just two weeks before their wedding. Eisenhower knew Colonel Arnold well and liked him, and he counted Arnold's death among those that had saddened him the most. Eisenhower waited until he could be alone with Kay that evening to break the news about Arnold's death. Devastated, Summersby collapsed sobbing on the couch while Eisenhower, his arm around her shoulders, passed her hanky after hanky to dry her tears. Only fifteen months before, Eisenhower had sat alone in his office silently grieving the death of his father. Almost three months later, he was jolted by the death of his brother Roy. He had consoled others grieving the death of a loved one, including Mamie when Icky died in 1921, and Gee Gerow when Katie died in 1935, and Jimmy Ord's family after his colleague was killed in the Philippines in 1938. He could also recite the names of lost officers in a grim roll call: "Andrews—Dykes—Duncan—Stewart—Vogel and others; all senior officers and good friends of mine that are no more. War is often sad." The terrible losses at Kasserine Pass still troubled him. As ever, the pain of Icky's death welled up in him. "Activity helps," he comforted Kay. "I've learned that myself."

As comrades in arms, Eisenhower and Summersby shared the bond of soldiers at war tempered by grief and bereavement. Without question he had developed a deep affection for his beautiful driver that intensified after the tragic loss of her lover. Instinctively, he wanted to protect her as he would have protected a sister. When his orderly Micky McKeogh complained that Summersby had tried to boss him around, Eisenhower gently counseled, "Bear with her, she is not a very well person."

Eisenhower's solicitousness for Kay's health and welfare was not unusual. When McKeogh fell ill, Eisenhower visited him every other day in the hospital and made certain that the army cooks provided adequate food. In fact, it was his habit to visit army hospitals regularly, including visits to Summersby's roommate, Sue Sarafian, after an automobile accident, and Walter Bedell Smith when he fell ill in England.

Although he did not use paternalistic metaphors in his graduation speech to the Kelly Field graduates in 1941, Eisenhower tended to view his personal staff as family, and they reciprocated his loyalty and affection. When McKeogh and Pearlie Hargrave, another WAC on the staff, married, Eisenhower hosted their wedding reception. Had Kay Summersby and Colonel Arnold married as planned that June, surely Eisenhower would have hosted another wedding reception whose gala party would have mitigated the rumors about his relationship to Kay.

There is no question that Eisenhower treasured Summersby because she offered him much-needed feminine company. She was someone with whom he could vent frustrations, who would not stifle his barracks profanity and would offer him humor and affection. Eisenhower struggled not only with his prolonged absence from Mamie but also with the loneliness of command. Throughout his life he usually had a close buddy by his side: his brothers, Bob Davis, Swede Hazlett, George Patton, Jimmy Ord, "the gang," and so on. But as the supreme theater commander, it was impossible to have an army buddy, whether a favored officer or an enlisted man.

Eisenhower seemed almost oblivious to the rumors and potential scandal of his relationship with his comely driver. He made no attempt to hide Summersby or to conceal his affection for her. She was his companion at lunches and dinners with Roosevelt and Churchill. After the war they attended the theater together in London with Eisenhower's son John and his date, who was introduced to him by Kay, and went out for dinner and dancing on occasion.

He could be inexplicably reckless in his personal behavior, even though it might have dire consequences for his career. His stint with professional baseball just before entering West Point, his midnight escapade into East St. Louis from the Jefferson Barracks during West Point entrance exams, and his AWOL larks from the military academy are cases in point. Was he clueless, stubborn, infatuated, or just plain careless in his relationship with Kay Summersby?

John Eisenhower has observed, "Dad would have made a lousy philanderer because he was so damned Victorian and moral. Sure he was attracted to vital women ... but these were friendship, not torrid affairs." Although John misses the mark concerning Victorians, he may be correct that Eisenhower's moral compass was strong enough to keep him from crossing the line sexually in his relationships with other women. Was his relationship with Kay materially different from his friendship with Marian Huff, Ike's bridge and golfing partner in Manila? David Eisenhower, his historian grandson, is the most cryptic family member about the alleged affair with Kay Summersby. "However far it went, the two were attached," David has written. "Eisenhower [his grandfather] was under tremendous pressure and in need of company. Beyond this, the truth was known only by them, and both are gone."

Eisenhower's valet, Mickey McKeogh, and Summersby's roommate and close friend, Captain Sue Sarafian Jehl, both dismiss the idea that the two had an affair. Summersby's executor and friend Anthea Gordan Saxe also doubted that the two had been lovers. Saxe believed that Kay's love for Richard Arnold was genuine and deep—she kept all his letters and pictures until the day she died. On the other hand, she left no letters from Eisenhower or any other direct evidence of an affair other than her posthumously published memoir, *Past Forgetting*.

Was there a love affair between Eisenhower and Summersby between 1942 and 1945? First of all, there is no question that the lonely general found Summersby attractive and comforting, just as he had previously enjoyed the company of Marian Huff. He obviously enjoyed Summersby's companionship and felt no reluctance in showing her off among the top brass and English society.

She was, perhaps, one of the four most important women in his life, alongside his mother, Mamie, and Anne Whitman, his presidential secretary. But while Ida and Mamie had a lifelong influence over Eisenhower, Summersby's importance in his life lasted only through the war. Because his staff was constantly at his side and he was surrounded by tight security, historians Geoffrey Perret and Carlo D'Este doubt that it was physically possible for Eisenhower and Summersby to find the necessary privacy to carry on an affair. Other biographers believe that where there is a will there is generally a way in wartime romantic relationships. Michael Korda, reviewing the evidence in 2007 and noting that where there is romantic smoke there is often sexual fire, reaches a conclusion similar to David Eisenhower's: nobody can really know the truth of the matter, and historical speculation is out of order. "The only sensible verdict," Korda writes, "is the old fashioned one of the Scottish courts which lies somewhere between guilty and not guilty—not proven." Finally, William Pickett, in his definitive study of Ike and Kay during the Second World War, offers what may be the last judgment concerning the alleged affair between these two wartime associates who became the closest of friends: "but no credible evidence emerges to support the talk of an affair."

Ida

His mother was very much on Eisenhower's mind as American troops pushed through North Africa on their way to invading the European continent via

Italy. While preparing for the assault on Malta and the invasion of Sicily, he received disquieting reports from Kansas. Jehovah's Witnesses were exploiting the news that Ida, a pacifist in this, as in all, wars, was the mother of the American commanding general. For the most part, Ida Stover Eisenhower bore her personal cross stoically, silently. She had hoped her son would fail the West Point entrance exams and then wept bitter tears when Dwight left for the US Military Academy in 1911.

Reportedly, her faith shaken by her son's decision to become a soldier, she experienced a brief period of "mourning." Privately, she hid her "weakened faith" from her sons and perhaps her husband. But Ida and David did not shun Dwight for his decision to attend West Point, as other members of their Watchtower group might have done. When Ike graduated from the Military Academy in 1915, his mother gave him a copy of the American Standard edition of the Holy Bible, a version favored by the Bible Students because it consistently used the word "Jehovah" in reference to God.

Shortly after Eisenhower's graduation from West Point, however, Ida's religious foundation began to crumble around her. After twenty years of David often serving the group as the Bible-study conductor or "elder," in 1915 the Russellites moved their meeting from the Eisenhower home to Kingdom Hall, purportedly because they needed more room for their services. The following year, in 1916, the founder of the Bible Students, Charles Taze Russell, died, to be replaced by Joseph F. Rutherford. Rutherford, who adopted the name Jehovah's Witnesses, proved divisive, not only lashing out at other religions but also condemning many of Russell's beliefs, especially pyramid teachings, which were represented by David's large chart that hung upstairs just outside the boys' bedroom. Rutherford also encouraged Witnesses' teachings that opposed the Pledge of Allegiance to the flag, involvement in politics, service in the armed forces, vaccinations, fluoridation of water, and use of aluminum cooking utensils. Especially sensitive were allegations that Witnesses were faith healers.

By 1919, disillusioned by the failure of the Watchtower prophecy about the end of the world in 1914 and by the change of leadership following Russell's death, and Rutherford's extreme and rigid doctrines, David had drifted away from the Jehovah's Witnesses. After her sons left home and David and Roy died in quick succession in 1942, Ida was essentially alone.

David's death unsettled her memory and left her physically frail. She was aware that her memory had failed; she explained that after David died, something went out of her. Following their father's death, the Eisenhower brothers tried to maintain Ida in her Abilene home. With Eisenhower's approval, they hired Naomi Engle, a lifelong friend and devout Witness, to live with Ida. As Ida's health declined, she became increasingly dependent on Engle for care. There is no evidence that Engle substantially modified Ida's daily routine. Except for her public opposition to World War I, Ida's public witnessing for her faith had not upset the family. Inevitably, Eisenhower's swift rise to international fame focused publicity on Abilene and everything associated with the town's best-known citizen.

Was Naomi Engle simply clueless about Eisenhower family dynamics, or did she just not care about the consequences of exposing Ida to publicity while witnessing for Watchtower? In April 1943, while the Allies attacked Rommel's Afrika Korps, Ida and Naomi attended a Jehovah's Witnesses assembly in Wichita. Predictably, she attracted attention from the Witnesses and the press. According to the *Wichita Beacon*, "The 82-year-old mother of America's famous military leader . . . was the center of attraction at the meeting Sunday, and her name was heard in just about every conversation, speech and discussion. The program's subject was 'how to become a good Jehovah's Witness.'"

Ironically, while Ida was "Witnessing" in Wichita, Eisenhower resolved that the war had become a personal crusade against the evils of the Third Reich. Consequently, he decided not to dignify Hitler's regime by meeting personally with captured German generals.

When he received a clipping about the Witnesses assembly, he grumbled to Arthur that "some reporter made a point that our dear old Mother likes to go to conventions of her beloved Jehovah's Witnesses." As far as he was concerned, his mother's religious happiness was more important than "any damn wisecrack" published in the newspapers. He believed in his heart that she loved her country. On the other hand, he held contempt for Jehovah's Witnesses, who exploited her in the name of pacifism and yet jumped on the publicity bandwagon like any politician taking advantage of the war to promote his sect. Although Jehovah's Witnesses preached a "dogmatic hatred of war," Eisenhower doubted that they detested war any more than he did.

> They probably have not seen bodies rotting on the ground and smelled the stench of decaying human flesh. They have not visited a field hospital crowded with the desperately wounded. But far above my hatred of war is the determination to smash every enemy of my country, especially Hitler and the Japs—or to put it more simply, my hatred of war will never equal my conviction that it is the duty of every one of us, civilian and soldier alike, to carry out the orders of our government when a war emergency arises.

In a nutshell, he adeptly contrasted his mother's religious faith concerning war with his own. Perhaps it was coincidental, but understandable, that Eisenhower's religious views concerning war crystallized at the very moment he learned about his mother's antiwar involvement with the Jehovah's Witnesses. It was as if his mother's pacifism compelled him to work out in his own mind a justification for the fighting, the destruction, and the killing for which he was responsible before God.

Why Americans Fight

World War II pushed to the surface Eisenhower's latent religiosity, including its emphasis on prayer. Like thousands of servicemen, Eisenhower wrote to a pen pal during the war, whom he encouraged to pray for the troops. In a rare display of religiosity, Eisenhower held a little service for a small group of his staff as he watched the Allied armada depart Malta to invade Sicily in July 1943. Unpredictably high winds threatened to upset careful planning and timing. Eisenhower feared that the fleet of towed gliders might be blown off course at the cost of the entire command. Scanning the scene from a high hilltop, he suddenly snapped to attention, reverently saluted the airplanes above him, and then bowed his head in silent prayer. Later, Eisenhower admitted that the Allies probably suffered more losses than they would have had the wind remained calm, but the attack was far from a disaster. He confided to an aide: "There comes a time when you have done all that you can possibly do, when you have used your brains, training, and your technical skill, when the die is cast, and events are in the hands of God—and there you have to leave them." As he noted in *Crusade in Europe*, "There was nothing we could do but pray, desperately." Significantly, this comment echoed advice his mother had given him as a boy: "Do the best you can, and leave the rest to God."

In their own way, both Ida and her son faced death on separate long journeys. As mentioned, among his most serious worries during the Battle of Sicily was the fate of airborne troops in gliders. Eisenhower, who had longed to command combat troops, now felt the burden of responsibility for the lives of men who had died fruitlessly because of the vagaries of the weather or because he had failed to anticipate the dangers they would face or because he decided that troops were more expendable than machines. While Ida had protested the killing in the name of Jehovah, he had to justify their dying before God and country not only for himself but also for his men and their mothers.

By what moral right did his country draft men to send them into harm's way? It is widely believed that in the heat of battle, soldiers generally do not fight for transcendent reasons but rather as a "band of brothers" beside their comrades. However much Eisenhower may have understood this dynamic, comradeship was not a suitable justification for war. Fittingly, in the tradition of his parents' faith, Eisenhower ultimately believed that the answer to the question "why do we fight?" was essentially religious, and every soldier had to find it for himself. He confessed to the National Council of Churches:

> I believe that every soldier—every American soldier, at least—seeking to find within his own soul some reason for being on the battlefield, for enduring the things that he has to endure there, has in the long run got to fix this relationship [with God and country] in his own mind if he is to be really a soldier who can carry forward the terrible load that devolves upon him in those circumstances.

And what was that relationship between God and country that each American soldier should understand? Eisenhower believed that God was the principal author of human freedom—a freedom nurtured by community and based upon trust and respect. Free government (that is, government that affirmed that God conveyed dignity on all persons) in theory helped individuals solve problems they could not solve acting alone. Cooperation, in contrast to regimentation, promoted individual freedom while governing selfish ambitions. Of course, watchmen like Eisenhower stood at God's left hand to defend the community both internally and externally against those who would deny freedom and human dignity in the name of parochial self-interest. For Eisenhower, the Father's gift of freedom was analogous to the grace of self-determination granted him by his father and mother when he decided to attend West Point in 1911—autonomy that Ida had tearfully accepted.

During the battle for North Africa, Eisenhower sent a note to American soldiers that summarized his rationale for war against the Nazis. In North Africa, Anglo-American forces had launched "a crusade to eliminate ruthless aggression from the earth" and to protect themselves and their children from arrogant despotism. He saluted the memories of lost comrades and prayed that "All Mighty God" would comfort the soldiers' loved ones. Of course, the great crusade had just begun. With the help of their allies, including the Russians and Chinese, Eisenhower assured his men that victory was certain. Onward the crusade into the heart of Europe! "Our Allies march forward with us. The God of Justice fights on our side."

The Sicily campaign lasted thirty-eight days, followed by the American/ British invasion of Italy and tough fighting up the Italian peninsula. With their southern Mediterranean flank secure, the Allies began serious planning for the invasion of Normandy in France, already code-named Overlord. However, one of the biggest decisions was yet to be made—who would be the Allied commanding general? Prior to the Teheran Conference, where Roosevelt and Churchill met Soviet premier Joseph Stalin, Eisenhower conferred with Roosevelt and Chief of Staff Marshall in Cairo.

After their meeting, Marshall ordered Eisenhower to take a few days off—rest and relaxation for his exhausted Mediterranean commander. Gratefully, Eisenhower took a short trip up the Nile Valley and then flew to Jerusalem for a brief visit. When they toured the pyramids at Luxor, he surprised his traveling companions with his detailed knowledge of the pyramids and their history. On the eve of the greatest amphibian invasion in history, he recalled silently how his father's pyramid wall chart had predicted the final Battle of Armageddon. He did not record his impressions of Bethlehem, Jerusalem, or Calvary, but on return to Cairo he learned that he would be the commander in chief of Overlord.

The Patton Incident

His vacation over, Eisenhower now had to deal with fallout from the Patton incident. In August 1943, his friend General George Patton, visiting wounded in field hospitals, encountered two enlisted men, neither of them physically injured. Patton lost his temper, accused the soldiers of being cowards, ordered one from the hospital and slapped the other. It turned out later that one had a high fever and the other had been taken from the front lines against his will. Although Patton received a reprimand, the army tried to hush up the incident by asking reporters to overlook the matter because Patton was one of America's most effective combat generals.

The story was too good to keep quiet, however, and in November Patton's outrageous behavior hit the headlines. Fortunately, in August, Eisenhower had informed George Marshall about the slapping incident, lamenting that while Patton was an outstanding combat commander, he was "a one-sided individual" who, particularly in his handling of individual subordinates, was "apt at times to display exceedingly poor judgment and unjustified anger." Eventually the Patton incident blew over, and while Marshall was not happy with the terrible publicity, he accepted both Eisenhower's explanation of Patton's character and Eisenhower's belief that Patton was irreplaceable as a leader of the tank corps.

But Eisenhower was answerable not only to Marshall but also to American mothers, one of whom wrote him expressing fear that her boys might end up in Patton's command. Unwittingly, Mrs. June Booth poked Eisenhower where he was most sensitive. She would "die of worry," Mrs. Booth wrote, if her sons had to serve under "such a cruel, profane and impatient" commander instead of under "a fine Christian person like our grand General MacArthur."

Anyone who knew him might have expected Eisenhower to blow like Mount Etna. Instead, he steadied himself and wrote Mrs. Booth one of his most compassionate and insightful epistles on military leadership. Reflecting that his own son was destined for the battlefield, he shared the anguish of every parent whose child was sent to war. "War is a sad, a desperate and a tragic business," he counseled Mrs. Booth, a business that bore heavily on all involved.

As supreme commander of the Mediterranean theater, he balanced military objectives against the loss of lives. Even with the finest leadership, the heavy cost in lives was difficult to bear, both as a nation and as a parent. But deaths of American troops caused by blundering leadership were even more unbearable. The greatest gaffe in war, Eisenhower asserted, is "indecisiveness, slowness and hesitation." Generals who acted decisively saved lives; all others, however kind and sympathetic, wasted men. Mrs. Booth was correct in deploring Patton's abusive behavior in the field hospitals. But in Sicily General Patton saved thousands of American lives. "By his boldness, his speed, his drive, he won his part of the campaign by marching, more than he did by fighting. . . . Had he weakened for one second he would have given the enemy time to organize—and we would have paid for that mistake in American lives."

Expediency would have relieved Patton of his command, Eisenhower continued. But duty required him to inform Mrs. Booth that Patton "should not be lost to us in the job of winning the war." He assured Mrs. Booth that he had made his decision as both a "God-fearing American" and a soldier, and he prayed for her support.

A Providential God

As the burden of leadership increased in December 1943, so did the inherent tension in Eisenhower's religious beliefs. There was always, of course, tension between his driving ambition and his call to duty. More problematical was his balancing America's belief in a just and providential God (Jehovah) with his personal conviction that a generous, loving God (Father) was the font of individual dignity and freedom. How could a just but loving God both manage history and foster human freedom? The Jehovah's Witnesses believed that God was the Lord of History; all human history was played out according to God's divine plan. But Eisenhower didn't believe that God willed Icky's death any more than Ida believed that God had called his brother Paul to his heavenly home.

After experiencing war, he modified his belief in a providential God. He decided that God did not stalk the battlefield, sparing some soldiers while summoning others home. Yet God seemed to call forth extraordinary leaders during America's greatest crises, for example, Washington during the Revolutionary War and Lincoln during the Civil War. But Eisenhower amended his belief in American exceptionalism; to be sure, God had blessed America, but that did not mean that the United States was a divinely favored nation above all other nations. Although American democracy provided a shining example for the world, a "city upon a hill," he believed that other people bore a similar historic mission, and this included America's principal ally in the war, Great Britain. Occasionally, Eisenhower rhetorically spoke of a providential God, but he came increasingly to believe that God played no decisive role in determining human history, including war.

He prayed to God, but not for the Almighty's interference in history. For example, prior to the D-Day invasion of Normandy in June 1944, Eisenhower asked for "the blessing of Almighty God upon this great and noble undertaking." Faced with uncertain weather that could spell disaster for the invasion forces, Eisenhower knew that the decision to launch Operation Overlord was his alone. At this defining moment, he did not pray for God's intervention with the weather or even for victory on the French beaches. In the early morning of June 5, with the rain still falling, his chief weather officer forecast that the storm would abate, enabling the invasion to proceed. "Okay, we'll go," Eisenhower said simply.

Afterward, as Geoffrey Perret has reported, "On D-Day, he could only smoke and worry, hope and pray." But pray about what? If Eisenhower prayed at this time, his prayers were undoubtedly private meditations for wisdom, strength, and blessing. There was subsequent mythology that, like Washington at Valley Forge, Ike spent hours on his knees in prayer before the invasion of Normandy. Instead, in a sentiment reflecting his River Brethren heritage, or at least Ida's influence, Eisenhower wrote about the hours before D-Day:

> If there is nothing else in my life to prove the existence of an almighty and merciful God, the events of the next twenty-four hours did it. This is what I found out about religion. It gives you courage to make the decisions you must make in a crisis, and then the confidence to leave the result to higher power. Only by trust in one's self and trust in God can a man carrying responsibility find repose.

But trust in what? Why did Eisenhower want God's blessing of the Normandy invasion? His seeking God's blessing on the eve of D-Day was akin to his asking for his father's blessing when he went away to West Point. While David wanted his son to become a doctor, he faithfully allowed Dwight to make his own life decisions without his father's recrimination. In his Normandy prayers, Eisenhower was not asking God to be on America's side during the invasion. He knew that Germans across the channel were offering similar prayers, with similar trust in God. Rather, by asking for blessing he hoped to affirm that his call to duty was in line with God's will. Whether asking for God's blessing or his father's blessing, the motive was the same.

But knowing God's will was always a problem. Eisenhower believed that his calling to be God's agent for peace with justice was not dissimilar to that of Abraham Lincoln. At times during the war, Eisenhower reflected on Stephen Vincent Benét's account in "John Brown's Body" of Lincoln's wrestling with the problem of discerning God's will:

> They come to me and talk about God's will . . .
> Day after day
> . . . all of them are sure they know God's will.
> I am the only man who does not know it.
> And yet, if it is probable that God
> Should, so very clearly, state His will
> To others, on a point of my duty,
> It might be thought He would reveal it to me
> Directly, more especially as I
> So earnestly desire to know His will.

In the final analysis, Lincoln had to follow his own convictions, Eisenhower observed. "I was in the same fix." The best one could do was to try to discern the will of God through prayer or, more effectively, as Lincoln, through prayerful consultation with one's advisors. After doing that, and with what some have called a leap of faith, Eisenhower made his decision alone, trusting in himself and trusting, like his father, that God would bless the faithful and just.

In a measure of his character, and his faith, Eisenhower assumed full responsibility for the D-Day decision. Even with God's blessing, he knew that victory was not foreordained and that failure on the Normandy beaches was possible. As was his custom before amphibious landings, on the afternoon of June 5, Eisenhower scribbled a contingent press release: "Our landings at the Cherbourg–Le Havre area have failed to gain a satisfactory foothold and I have withdrawn the troops. My decision to attack at this time and place was based on the best information available. The troops, the air and the navy did all that bravery and devotion to duty could do. If any blame or fault attaches to the attempt, it is mine alone."

On the eve of D-Day, Eisenhower's most visible prayerful act was his visits with the troops. On Malta, he had said a small prayer as they flew overhead on their way to Sicily; a month before the Normandy invasion, he had talked with British general Bernard Montgomery's men; now, on June 5, he personally visited the 101st Airborne. He needed to be with the troops—his troops that he was sending into battle that night. He had visited scores of units during the days leading up to D-Day, but finally he wanted to be with the troops he believed were most at risk.

Most of the men in the 101st Airborne had never jumped into battle, and few of them had seen their supreme commander. The men, of course, were dressed for battle, with blackened faces, khaki fatigues, jump boots, packs, ammo belts, and helmets covered with camouflage mesh. Dressed in his snappy "Eisenhower jacket" and an unadorned officer's hat, Ike did not pretend to be anything more than he was—a rear-echelon commander. He moved easily among the men, inquiring if they were ready, asking where they were from—"anyone here from Kansas?"—assuring them that they would receive air cover during their assault. Although tense like the men, he was at ease giving his blessing to their endeavor. Then, on the roof of division head-quarters, he watched the C-47s take off for France one after the other. When they turned to leave, Kay noticed tears in his eyes.

The Monuments Men

During the hectic days prior to Overlord, Eisenhower remembered his obliga-tions under the Roberts Commission. Established in June 1943, the American Commission for the Protection and Salvage of Artistic and Historic Monu-ments in War Areas, chaired by Supreme Court Justice Owen J. Roberts, tried to shield historical and cultural treasures, including cathedrals, universities, museums, ancient and medieval architecture, as well as associated works of arts and statuary.

In this war to save Western civilization, Eisenhower had already dealt with similar issues in North Africa and Italy. On their advance up the Italian pen-insula, Allies sought to save historical treasures from destruction, especially in and around Rome. At Cassino, the Germans had exploited the Americans' reluctance to destroy historical treasures by establishing defensive positions among cultural artifacts.

Prior to World War II, few armies tried to spare national monuments. With encouragement from FDR and the Roberts Commission, however, Eisenhower required commanders, if militarily possible, to protect historical monuments and cultural centers they encountered on their march across Europe. Modern warfare would not allow them to spare all historical treasures, but in most cases, Eisenhower believed, destruction of cultural sites was neither necessary nor justified.

His order was succinct: wherever possible, "commanders will preserve centers and objects of historical and cultural significance." The Museum, Fine Arts and Archives (MFAA) programs under the Civil Affairs staff provided Allied commanders with lists and reports of historical treasures both in enemy territory and in occupied areas. Preservation of historical monuments included after-action damage assessment, temporary repairs, and plans for restoration by a small cadre of "Monuments Men" who accompanied combat troops throughout the European campaign.

After D-Day

Following D-Day on June 6, 1944, the Allied armies rolled across western Europe in eleven months, receiving the unconditional surrender of German troops on May 7–9, 1945. The Allies' march from Normandy to the Elbe River was no parade, but rather was a bloody campaign against the doggedly desperate German Wehrmacht. Breaking out of the Normandy beachhead took longer than planned, but on July 25, 1944, a month after capturing Cherbourg, the Allies surged forward while the American right wing swung wide, forming a pincer movement that almost encircled the Germans at Falaise.

Caught between the Americans to the south and Canadian and Polish troops to the north, the Germans frantically tried to escape the Falaise entrapment. While thousands managed to escape, the Allies captured ten German divisions. Two days after the massive surrender, Eisenhower visited the scene of his greatest military victory to date, and wrote:

> The battlefield at Falaise was unquestionably one of the greatest "killing grounds" of any of the war areas. Roads, highways, and fields were so choked with destroyed equipment and with dead men and animals that

passage through the area was extremely difficult. Forty-eight hours after the closing of the gap I was conducted through it on foot, to encounter scenes that could be described only by Dante. It was literally possible to walk for hundreds of yards at a time, stepping on nothing but dead and decaying flesh.

Eisenhower's broad-front strategy that stretched the Allies from the Alps to the North Sea was challenged in December 1944 when German panzer and SS units spearheaded a counteroffensive through a weak spot in the Ardennes Forest. But the Battle of the Bulge proved to be Hitler's last-gasp effort to smash Eisenhower's strategy and halt the Allied invasion of Germany. As Eisenhower immediately realized, the Germans' offensive was doomed, and while the Allies' cost in men and material was high, the failure of the Ardennes offensive marked the beginning of the end of Hitler's regime. In January 1945, the Russians launched a major offensive in the east; by the end of February, with Allied strength near its maximum, Montgomery and Bradley were poised to invade Germany across the Rhine River.

With the end of the war in sight, Eisenhower became vexed by German tenacity and brutality. The Battle of the Bulge had been a nightmare of bitter cold, driving snow, and overcast skies that all but grounded the American air force. But more than the surprise attack or the variant weather, Eisenhower had been stunned by reports of German *Kriegspiel* that included German units operating behind the lines disguised as American soldiers and SS officers who ordered the summary execution of scores of American prisoners of war.

His mounting hatred for the Germans was barely concealed in his Christmas exhortation to his troops: the Germans' savage attack in which they used "every treacherous trick to deceive and kill" was their last, desperate gamble to win back their losses of the summer and fall and to forestall the collapse of the Nazi regime. But by rushing out of his fixed defense, Hitler had offered the Allies an opportunity to inflict a crushing defeat on the "Thousand Year Reich." Allied soldiers should be of one mind: "to destroy the enemy on the ground, in the air, everywhere—destroy him! United in this determination and with unshakable faith in the cause for which we fight, we will, with God's help, go forward to our greatest victory."

Eisenhower embraced the doctrine of unconditional surrender. There was no moral way to accept an armistice with or extend amnesty to the Nazi regime. As biographer Jean Edward Smith noted in *Eisenhower in War and Peace*, "In many respects, Germany's total defeat resembled the total defeat of the Confederacy in the American Civil War," with Eisenhower playing an analogous role to that of Union general Ulysses S. Grant. Both wars had been long and brutal because, in both instances, not only did the opposing army need to be destroyed but also the political structure of the enemy regime had to be thoroughly crushed. No peace was possible with either the Third Reich or the Confederacy.

The Drive to Berlin

With the Battle of the Bulge behind him, Eisenhower gathered his forces along the Rhine to launch a war-ending assault into the heart of Germany. Eisenhower commanded nearly four million American, British, and Canadian troops in seventy-three divisions. Meanwhile, Soviet troops, led by Marshall Georgy Zhukov, pressed relentlessly toward Germany and Berlin from the east.

As supreme Allied commander, Eisenhower knew of the semi-independent strategic bombing campaign against German industrial centers by British and American air forces. Allied and Soviet bombers repeatedly hammered Hamburg, Cologne, Munich, Leipzig, and Berlin, among other cities. German industry, transportation, and civilians came under daily attack with great loss among Allied airplanes. With Americans poised on the Rhine, almost 1,200 British and American bombers struck Dresden, Germany, targeting the railroad marshaling yards while plastering the central city with high explosives and incendiary bombs. Probably twenty-five thousand Germans died in the firestorm that leveled the city. Within three months the war in Europe would be over, but enormous horrors lay on the horizon.

After capturing the Ludendorf railroad bridge on March 7, General Omar Bradley, with Eisenhower's concurrence, pushed his troops across the Rhine to establish a toehold on the east bank. Thereafter, Patton in the south and Montgomery in the north crossed the Rhine. Once the Rhine was breached, advancing Allied armies could be slowed but not stopped. In April, Patton's Third Army captured a German salt mine into which the Third Reich had stashed over $50 million in gold bars and millions in Reich currency. Also discovered by the Monuments Men were hundreds of stolen paintings, scores of art objects, and piles of eyeglasses and gold and silver fillings from victims of Hitler's genocide. After Eisenhower personally inspected the mine, with Patton and Bradley he visited the Ohrdruf-Nord concentration camp, where SS guards had murdered almost everyone in an attempt to silence direct testimony of German cruelty. Bodies were strewn everywhere, some piled in heaps, others partially cremated, some starved to death. The stench of decaying flesh was so overpowering that the stink of Patton's vomit was scarcely noticed.

Buchenwald

The next day, Eisenhower visited the Buchenwald concentration camp, where he encountered living skeletons, some of whom were professional soldiers who pathetically did their best to salute. The evil he encountered in the concentration camps appalled him. Although he had personally inspected the carnage in the Falaise Pocket and was aware of the devastation of Dresden, the depravity discovered after the liberation of the German death camps was beyond comprehension. "The other day I visited a German internment camp," he wrote Mamie. "I never dreamed that such cruelty, bestiality, and savagery could really exist in this world! It was horrible." To George Marshall he reported, "The things I saw beggar description. . . . I made the visit deliberately, in order to be in a position to give firsthand evidence of these things if ever, in the future, there develops a tendency to charge these allegations merely to 'propaganda.'" To Mamie he confessed that the end of the war was so soul wrenching that "a man gets to the point he thinks the whole world must be nuts—completely—including himself."

Lest American troops think the war was anything less than a crusade against abject tyranny and demonic selfishness, a tour through the concentration camps was arranged for men who could be spared temporarily. "We are told that the American soldier does not know what he is fighting for," Eisenhower observed. "Now, at least, he will know what he is fighting against." Likewise, German civilians were taken to the camps not only to view the Nazi atrocities but also to assist in disposing of the corpses and removing the filth and rot. Any thought of extending personal respect and professional courtesy to defeated German generals was forever abandoned in the death camps. In this regard, Eisenhower's stern demand of Nazi unconditional surrender from General Jodl at Reims on May 7 contrasted sharply with General Ulysses S. Grant's gentlemanly acceptance of Robert E. Lee's surrender at Appomattox Court House in 1865.

With the end of the war only days away, Eisenhower's thoughts turned to home and Mamie. He longed for her to be at his side. But it seemed doubtful that arrangements for her to join him in Europe could be made. "The country is devastated," he wrote. "Whole cities are obliterated; and the German population, to say nothing of former slave laborers, is largely homeless. There is certain to be unrest, privation and undoubtedly some starvation next winter. It is a bleak picture. Why the Germans ever let the thing go as far as they did is completely beyond me."

His letters to Mamie in May 1945 were filled with longing, love, and reassurance. Sending her "loads of love," he wrote, "How I miss you—and it gets worse every day. Don't worry, for Lord's sake, about 'decisions' about our future life. Let's just try to keep a bit of tolerance for fixed habits and a sense of humor and then try to have some fun together. I love you." He cautioned her, however, that "with destruction, disorder and disease all rampant in Germany," the prospects of her joining him in Europe were not bright. Unfortunately, it proved impossible to cut through the red tape required in Washington to make the arrangements.

Guildhall Address

On June 12, 1945, at Churchill's invitation, Eisenhower flew to England to speak at London's historic Guildhall. In the Guildhall Address, Eisenhower summarized his religious justification for fighting and winning unconditionally the "just war." His themes were not original, but they were heartfelt. Eisenhower believed that World War II had been a titanic struggle between divine and demonic forces reminiscent of the mythic battles of ancient history. The great honor of being named a free citizen of London was countered by the "feelings of profound sadness" at the very moment of victory. He was proud to have served as Allied commander in chief but was mindful that his extraordinary achievement was paid for by the blood sacrifice of countless millions. The war had fostered international brotherhood and battlefield camaraderie and had brought out the best in Anglo-American partnership. He was certain that World War II would "glow forever in the pages of military history."

But the price in suffering and death had been staggeringly high. He acknowledged the incomparable heroism of the Londoners in weathering the Battle of Britain, which he characterized as Hitler's unprecedented war of terror. There had been a feeling of wonderment among Americans who witnessed the British travail firsthand. "Our eyes rounded as we saw your women, serving quietly and efficiently in almost every kind of war effort, even with flak batteries." At stake were freedom of worship, equality before the law, and freedom of speech—all essential to life, liberty, and happiness. Perhaps the best that had emerged from the war was a sacred Anglo-American partnership to secure peace and justice in the postwar world. The great lesson of World War II was that the United States and Britain could not afford to stand alone against the hosts of hell who attacked Western civilization.

Although Eisenhower emphasized familiar redemptive themes in his Guildhall Address, there was no hint that the Allies had paid in blood for the collective sins of the West. Not only was the atonement theme inappropriate for his victory speech, but it was also unthinkable that the Allies' triumphal alliance shared any responsibility for the rise of Hitler or the demonic terror unleashed on the world.

On the other hand, concerning America, Eisenhower wrestled with the idea of national sin. In the abstract, he believed sin was humankind's disobedience of God, best defined as human selfishness—the singular pursuit of one's self-interest in disregard for the needs of others. Civilized society, conversely, depended upon self-restraint of its citizens, who voluntarily respected the rights of others. Beyond that he struggled. Once when he was desperately missing Mamie, he wrote that he was befuddled as to "why we have to have wars to separate families and cause all the anguish."

> I think that all these trials and tribulations must come upon the world because of some great wickedness; yet one would feel that man's mere intelligence to say nothing of his spiritual perceptions would find some way of eliminating war. But man has been trying to do so for many hundreds of years, and his failure just adds more reason for pessimism when a guy gets really low.

Unaware of the deep roots of his thoughts, Eisenhower had developed a worldview in which children of the earthly city were forever torn between divine and demonic forces in history. World War II had convinced him that peoples or nations could sin (he never systematically developed this idea), and that the rise of Nazism represented a collective spiritual/religious failure of the German people.

Like most Americans, Eisenhower believed in human progress guided by the benign hand of Providence. Human history recorded the gradual, steady expansion of Western civilization from the Greeks and Romans, through the Dark Ages, into the Reformation, the Renaissance, and the Enlightenment. Carried westward by the age of discovery, progress, embodied by the New England Puritans, had established a "city upon a hill" beckoning the Old World to join the triumphal march of civilization across the new continent where America achieved its manifest destiny. Although a citizen of Abilene, Kansas,

Eisenhower shared few of his fellow Midwesterners' suspicions of eastern cities or decadent Europe and thus could genuinely express his pride in being named a free citizen of London. The Anglo-American bond that grew out of the war was a crusader's alliance against those who would debase the Atlantic community's heritage of God-given freedom.

As a believer in the idea of progress, Eisenhower had no easy explanation for the devolution of German culture in the twentieth century. How could the nation that had served as the cradle of the Protestant Reformation; the home of Bach, Beethoven, and Brahms; and the native land of Lessing, Goethe, and Schiller have fallen into barbarism to become the demonic scourge of all that was divine in the human soul? And how could a defeated Germany become cleansed through denazification? He had no ready answer to these vexing questions. Somehow following World War I, the German people had suffered a massive spiritual and economic collapse under the Weimar Republic, which paved the way for the ascendancy of the Nazi paganism. Privately, he speculated that men like Pastor Martin Niemöller, the dissident Lutheran pastor who had been imprisoned by the Nazis in Dachau for his support of the Confessing Church, might play an important role in the redemption of the German people.

The situation in Germany was desperate. The economy had collapsed. Five and a half million displaced persons, liberated Jews, homeless civilians, former prisoners of war, uprooted Germans from outer provinces, disarmed soldiers, and wounded and sick needed food, shelter, and clothing to survive the winter of 1945. Eisenhower was well aware of the seriousness of the human crisis. "This morning I returned from three days in Berlin and Warsaw," he wrote Mamie. "The latter is the worst picture of complete ruin I've seen. . . . As winter approaches the conditions here seem to promise a bleaker and bleaker situation! God knows what will be the outcome. But there will be lots of suffering—among friends and foe alike. . . . Europe, as a whole, is in an awful mess."

In the midst of the hunger, sickness, death, and postwar misery, a lonely Eisenhower wrote Mamie about Icky on the anniversary of their son's death. Without a brush or paints, he sketched a nostalgic scene of a world full of life, hope, and love as he wished it to be without war and suffering. "It's difficult to realize that if Icky had lived he would have been 28 today. We could easily have been grandparents—and I'd have loved it! It would be especially nice to be with you today."

At last, in June 1945, Eisenhower was liberated from the war and suffering of Europe when the army granted him his first furlough in almost two years. The heroic general returned to the United States to be feted by Congress and to enjoy a victory parade in New York City, a visit to West Point, and a sentimental journey to Kansas to rendezvous with his mother and brothers. Mamie rejoiced to have her husband home. Upon Eisenhower's triumphal return to Abilene, a reporter asked Ida how she liked having her famous son return home. "Which one?" she cleverly replied, to the delight of the newsman, allowing her gently to sidestep praising her warrior son publicly.

Ida's Death

A year later, in September 1946, Ida died peacefully in her sleep with almost a smile on her face. Grief-stricken, Eisenhower excused himself from honoring Field Marshall Montgomery in Washington. When the family gathered for her burial in Abilene, Eisenhower arranged for a military chaplain to conduct the service in the family home. There would be no repeat of David's funeral, at which the Jehovah's Witnesses hijacked the service. In addition to the chaplain, members of the American Legion and the Veterans of Foreign Wars served as pallbearers, which was at best incongruous with and at worst disrespectful of Ida's Jehovah's Witnesses beliefs.

Following the funeral, Milton purged the family residence of all traces that Ida had been a witness for Watchtower. David's pyramid chart disappeared from the upstairs hallway, to be lost in the dustbin of history. Milton also removed some fifty years of Ida's *Watchtower* magazines, but in keeping with his respect of the printed page, he found a sanctuary for them with one of her faithful friends. Although the Eisenhower Library and Museum has restored the Eisenhower house to a remarkable facsimile of the family home, the most important artifacts of Ida and David's authentic religious life are gone. Of all the Eisenhower family, only Dwight acknowledged forthrightly Ida's long affiliation with the Jehovah's Witnesses. Of her serene death, he penned an enigmatic benediction: "Ida Stover Eisenhower deserved such a peaceful start for the long journey."

The Most Intensely Religious Man, 1946–1952

Although best remembered among Americans as the commander in chief of the Normandy invasion, Eisenhower's most important legacy to American political and religious thought was as a presidential believer in the civil religion. Just as the horror of World War II awakened his religious sentiments, so the danger of the Cold War intensified his religious commitments. More than any other president in modern times, including Jimmy Carter, Eisenhower played a major role in shaping and defining American civil religion as practiced after World War II.

Along with other Cold Warriors, Eisenhower repeatedly stated that the fundamental difference between the United States and the Soviet Union was religious, not political or economic. There were, of course, major political and economic rivalries with the Russians. The major economic nemesis of the United States, however, was not the Soviet Union but rather the New Deal and, as we shall see, the military-industrial complex. As president, Eisenhower's "middle way" between Communism and fascism and between the New Deal's welfare state and libertarian isolationism was as much a religious stance as it was a political strategy.

"I Am the Most Intensely Religious Man I Know"

In May 1948, Dwight D. Eisenhower stated, "I am the most intensely religious man I know." This extraordinary confession was not made by a zealous teenager but by the fifty-eight-year-old president of Columbia University. What did Eisenhower mean? It was Eisenhower's commitment to duty that molded the core of his civil religion. Duty was not simply an obligation he owed the United States government. Duty was more than a moral commitment to lead an upright life. Eisenhower was a called servant of God's left hand of justice, and duty defined his unconditional commitment to serve the beneficent Supreme Being. It was in this sense that he knew no person more intensely religious than he. His close associates—George Patton, Fox Conner, and Douglas MacArthur—all shared a sense of duty. But none of them exceeded the intensity of Eisenhower's belief that his duty, like his human dignity, was God's supreme commission.

All Eisenhower biographers emphasize the role of religion in his youth, but few emphasize the importance of his deeply ingrained religious beliefs in his public life. Yet, if Eisenhower authentically perceived himself as a profoundly religious man, one would expect to encounter his religious values shaping his administration's domestic and foreign policy. And they did, except that his Midwestern habits of privacy and his demand of confidentiality from his pastors often masked Eisenhower's sentiments. It is not odd that the "hidden-hand" president also hid his religious affections, but this does not make Eisenhower's religion any less essential for understanding the man and his legacy.

Revisionist historians have succeeded in rehabilitating one aspect of the Eisenhower presidency. Historians now generally concede that Dwight Eisenhower governed in firm control of the White House. Historians have not been as generous in acknowledging the importance of his political leadership. Although he ended the Korean War, launched Atoms for Peace, balanced the budget and presided over general prosperity, presented the first civil rights legislation since Reconstruction, brought scientists into the White House, promoted People to People and Food for Peace programs, built the interstate highway system, and appointed Earl Warren to the Supreme Court, Eisenhower is not remembered as an effective, thoughtful, or creative president. In part, this was because in the first decade of the Cold War, he was perceived as a grandfatherly president rather than as a shrewd politician.

As the Cold War president, his public role called not for a dynamic chieftain but for a calm, reassuring parson. Thus, for many, this World War II hero was not only a Cincinnatus who stood above party politics but also, like George Washington, a selfless hero motivated by a transcendent call to duty. Most negatively, Eisenhower has been described as a passive president who presided over the drift and confusion of the 1950s. As a passive president, Eisenhower has been portrayed as an ineffectual, uninformed, and disinterested leader. In recent years, somewhat kindlier but not more positively, he has been defined as a consolidation president who continued the achievements of Franklin D. Roosevelt and Harry S. Truman but offered no innovations of his own.

In contrast, the argument presented here is that Eisenhower, as the nation's president/pastor, played a seminal role in fostering America's civil religion revival in the first decades of the Cold War. His vision was not generally prophetic; he preached no debilitating jeremiads—not even his "Military-Industrial Complex" speech could be categorized as such. His role was exegetical—defining, explaining, and encouraging. But, as we shall see, his leadership was neither consolidating, nor passive, nor negative when it came to promoting civil religion, civil rights, or peaceful uses of atomic energy.

Years of Preparation

The seven and a half years between the German surrender in May 1945 and Eisenhower's election to the presidency in November 1952 were years of preparation for Eisenhower. During these interim years, he served as chief of staff of the United States Army (1945–1948), president of Columbia University (1948–1953, with a leave of absence from 1950 to 1953), and supreme Allied commander of NATO (1950–1952). In addition, while president of Columbia, he was appointed acting chairman of the Joint Chiefs of Staff by Truman in 1949. In 1946 Congress made his wartime rank of General of the Armies permanent, and in 1948 he published his World War II memoirs, *Crusade in Europe*, written with the help of his son, John Eisenhower. Doubleday had sold about a million and a half copies by the turn of the century. As a military memoir, *Crusade in Europe* has rivaled U. S. Grant's admired classic.

In 1946, Eisenhower made forty-six major speeches and testified before Congress thirteen times; the following year he made thirty speeches and testified before Congress twelve times—a pace of almost one major presentation a week for two consecutive years. Despite giving over one hundred talks, he rejected almost four thousand invitations. The pressure from civic and professional organizations, churches, charitable groups, colleges and universities, veterans, and the government did not let up when he became president of Columbia University. In December 1948 he received 146 speaking requests; in July 1949, 70 invitations; in October 1949, another 142.

Epideictic Oratory

Rector Charles Griffin of Kansas State University has suggested an insightful key for interpreting Eisenhower's prepresidential speeches; this interpretive discernment applies to many of his presidential speeches as well. In a paper from 2003 entitled "Imaging Peace," Griffin contends that Eisenhower was primarily an epideictic speaker, that is, an inspirational speaker who was not argumentative but rather sought to create a bond between himself and his audience. Funeral oratory, victory speeches, and commemorative addresses are characteristic epideictic speeches. Because inspirational oratory is frequently celebratory, Eisenhower's often seemed to lack substance. Sometimes scorned as mere rhetoric, many of his postwar speeches and political talks have been ignored as nonserious public statements. Even Abraham Lincoln's Gettysburg Address and Martin Luther King's "I Have a Dream" speech are often remembered more for their rhetorical eloquence than for the substance of their ideas.

In contrast to argumentative speeches heard in courts of law or legislative halls, inspirational speeches, like sermons and prayer, are essential for building community identity and values, especially when the future is uncertain or threatening. When the recent past needs interpretation or the future is murky, the epideictic speaker interprets and evaluates events in terms of the audience's historical and cultural paradigm and employs vocabulary, values, and historical lessons to which listeners can relate both rationally and emotionally. In this regard, Eisenhower bathed his listeners with broad, inclusive language so as to relate as intimately as possible with the greatest number of people. Consequently, his speeches were generally comforting, not controversial, with affirmation of broad, universal values common to the gathering. In summary, Eisenhower's quintessential speeches were educational or, in religious terms, exegetical.

Prior to his election as president, Eisenhower promoted middle-of-the-road consensus among his eager listeners. He projected the aura of speaking for Americans, rather than for himself, by burnishing broadly shared values—universal values that he believed defined Americans but were also inclusive of all humankind. It is hardly surprising that millions of Americans viewed him not only as a president in the making but also as a natural leader of the "free world."

Between 1946 and 1950, when he assumed command of the NATO forces, Eisenhower's speeches rehearsed the themes that would characterize his conservative presidency. To newly commissioned military officers, he usually talked about the importance of leadership—individual leadership first, but above all national leadership. While courage and loyalty were invaluable virtues for a soldier, personal leadership always required integrity, intelligence, and common sense. Answering the call to duty with the mastery of emotions and ambitions not only was leadership's highest virtue but was also the essential requisite for any successful leadership role. The larger implication of Eisenhower's motivational messages to officers was that the United States had a God-given duty to serve the world.

On the other hand, when talking to a chamber of commerce or a bar association, Eisenhower emphasized that education was the cornerstone of American democracy. Slightly amending Frederick Jackson Turner's frontier thesis concerning the westward expansion of American democracy, Eisenhower believed that "in America, the schoolmarm always followed the explorer." If democracy was the political expression of a deeply held faith, as Eisenhower professed, then education was the foundation stone in the American system. Remarkably, he informed the Houston Chamber of Commerce that the landmarks of advancing civilization were the schools and libraries of the pioneers, *not* factories and stores.

If the businessmen were disconcerted to hear that educational institutions, not commercial establishments, were the hallmark of American democracy, they were mollified when Eisenhower attacked the New Deal. In the litany of anti–New Deal conservatives, America's freedom under God, the nation's most precious possession, was under attack by the antibusiness collectivism of the New Deal. Eisenhower pleased his audience by affirming that an attack on any one of America's freedoms—personal, economic, social, or political— was an attack upon the whole. National security could be maintained only when the freedoms of all citizens were protected. Business freedom and free markets, of course, as examples of free enterprise, came under daily assault by New Deal programs.

When speaking to the chamber of commerce in Galveston, Eisenhower denigrated the New Deal by lambasting federal employees. In Galveston, he was careful not to criticize elected officials, but it was open season on the civil service, "the bureaucrats," as he dismissively tagged them. He scoffed at the New Deal bureaucrat parked in a "nice cushioned chair in some lush office" deciding the fate of American agriculture, business, education, or health care, and solving "all our problems for us." Lest Gulf Coast Texas Republicans missed his point, Eisenhower concluded that the New Deal's "morass of paternalism and regimentation" robbed Americans of their God-given abilities to do their best for their families, themselves, and their country. The faithful in oilman Sid Richardson's Texas were delighted.

Who knows what his brother Milton thought of Eisenhower's blistering attack on civil servants, such as himself, who had served faithfully in the Department of Agriculture through the depths of the Great Depression? It should be noted that Eisenhower's screed against government employees was an uncharacteristic jibe from the soldier who believed deeply in the God-given dignity of all men at work, including those who served as barbers. To the American Bar Association in St. Louis, he repeated his mantra concerning America's God-given freedoms but, in this instance, instead of excoriating New Deal bureaucrats he attacked Karl Marx's *Communist Manifesto.*

As president of Columbia University, Eisenhower learned what other religious and political leaders in the United States also understood. It was politically safer, but just as effective, to attack atheistic Communism as it was to denounce the godless New Deal. By focusing on the spiritual horrors of the Communist system, he could extol the free enterprise system—capitalism—without passing withering judgment on his fellow Americans. By implication, the Democrats did not escape criticism, but to the American Bar Association he could emphasize the genius of American public education and thank those teachers who daily taught their students about the equality of opportunity through democracy in economic action. Again in St. Louis, he praised the "middle way," the middle ground between left-wing atheistic Communism and right-wing satanic fascism. But as Americans pondered this potential president, he proposed a middle way defined as the middle of the road between New Deal paternalism that crushed free enterprise and reactionary isolationism that quarantined America from international commerce. The middle way was the only way to mediate sharp political differences in American politics.

"We Are Not Isolationists"

Most often, he talked about national security. As chief of staff of the army, he could not criticize national security policy with the same vehemence with which he attacked New Deal domestic policy. In his June 1945 homecoming to Abilene, he emphasized Europe's need for immediate food relief. "We are not isolationists," he preached to his fellow citizens, because Abilene and America were part of a great world civilization. Relentlessly, he carried this same message to whoever would listen, including the American Legion, the Daughters of the American Revolution (DAR), the Economic Club of New York, and International Business Machines, among others. His message, with variations, was always the same: "We have come to this. We dwell in a world in which the possibilities of destruction are so great as to terrify peoples everywhere. Yet we must still acknowledge human weaknesses within ourselves and others. It is with this world that we must now concern ourselves, even as we reach toward and strive for a better one."

To maintain United States leadership of the free world in the nuclear age,

Eisenhower believed that Americans would have to broaden democracy at home and abroad. He reminded the DAR that American democracy was founded on three pillars: the unshakable belief in the dignity of man as guaranteed by God, the system of free enterprise, and the nationwide principle of cooperation in which government protected the collective interests of all. It was the American wellspring of cooperation that Eisenhower believed had to be extended to the entire free world to ensure the security of all. Only through cooperation was success possible in the pursuit of peace. If the free world did not cooperate for the good of the whole, he predicted there would be no prosperity, no happiness, and most importantly, no freedom for anyone.

His opinions were not just glittering generalities. While some conservative Christians railed against the United Nations, Eisenhower put less stock in personal salvation than he did in collective security. To a conference of mayors, he strongly supported the United Nations. "I believe that we must have faith that [the] United Nations and world order will finally prevail," he confessed. "If they do not, we are facing a very sorry future." Thereafter, he rallied cadets at West Point with the entreaty that the true American soldier "is a leader in world cooperation."

He promised army and navy chaplains in Washington, DC, that he was not going to lecture them on the Bible, but he stated bluntly that without "moral regeneration throughout the world," there was no hope for mankind. "We are all going to disappear one day in the dust of an atomic explosion," he prophesied, if we did not collectively pray for and work toward disarmament. There was a great hunger in the world, he told veterans in Little Rock, Arkansas, for food and material goods, for political and social stability, and for security and freedom from fear. Each of these worldwide hungers threatened human freedom everywhere. But it would take something more than generous foreign aid and cooperation among international agencies to calm the world's angst. Despite the rising tide of anti-Communist hysteria, Eisenhower counseled the chaplains that material progress and moral regeneration must walk hand in hand with "mutual tolerance and understanding, a sympathy for the other fellow's point of view." This comment, which presumably included the Soviet Union, was in marked contrast to his contempt for Nazi Germany.

Developing a Mature Political Philosophy

By 1948, Eisenhower had developed a mature political philosophy. At the dedication of IBM's facilities in Poughkeepsie, New York, attended by Thomas J.

Watson and Eleanor Roosevelt, Eisenhower outlined his belief that the success of American democracy depended upon citizenry who believed that God conveyed basic human rights to every individual. While America's Founding Fathers acknowledged this doctrine, Eisenhower traced the religious origins of the belief that God bestowed dignity on all citizens to the signing of the Magna Carta in 1215.

Thereafter, speaking at the Jewish Theological Seminary in September 1948, Eisenhower traced the origins of American political freedoms to ancient Jewish history. Atheistic dictators (Communist leaders) treat human beings no better than animals, Eisenhower began, but freedom-loving peoples believe that because all people are born with a God-given soul, all enjoy inalienable rights that cannot be destroyed. This belief, he acknowledged, came from ancient Jewish rabbis who taught that "although man is made of the dust of the earth, having had the breath of life breathed into him, he is a living soul." In this sense, Eisenhower stated, "All of the free world is the seed of Abraham, Moses and the ancient kings." It was on the basis of this universal religious doctrine, he believed, that the American army had fought during World War II. Finally, Eisenhower expressed his hope that someday religion would not divide the nation and that a time would come when no American would need to be defined with "a qualitative adjective of any kind."

In a practical sense, Eisenhower told a group of national advertisers, promoting the dignity of others meant monitoring one's self-interest while shunning selfishness. Eisenhower noted that everyone belonged to subgroups smaller than the nation. Family, business, profession, church, associations, education, and all manner of other differences segregated citizens into multiple groups. Each group had an identity, history, values, and experiences more or less unique to itself. Given the diversity of American life, Eisenhower believed that through their churches, civic organizations and clubs, unions, schools, and even politics, Americans could seek cooperative ways to advance the collective good while promoting a common American identity.

Hard Choices

Although his public appearances served their immediate purpose, the problem with Eisenhower's postwar inspirational speeches is that they never dealt with the hard choices of American politics. To skeptics, they read like pie-in-the-sky platitudes of a well-meaning but intellectually shallow soldier whose calls for spiritual renewal and brotherly cooperation overlooked stark realities of American political culture. For example, the general was silent on the influence of power and money in American government. He never mentioned racism, oppression, or domestic terror, which were rampant in the United States. He ignored segregation, discrimination, and injustice. He did not evaluate intractable choices of the political process: distribution of scarce resources, regulation of predatory economics, redistribution of concentrated wealth, or ecological degradation. He overlooked that Americans aligned by capital or labor, race or gender, religion or region were pitted against each other in perpetual conflict. Nor did Eisenhower affirm that the political process itself, with its system of representation and checks and balances, while messy and often dirty, was the democratic alternative to recurring civil war and revolution. But few successful American politicians address these issues. For Eisenhower to do so almost certainly would have wrecked any prospect of his running for president in 1952.

On the other hand, regarding foreign affairs, he spoke with great authority. In June 1950, to the Nassau County Bar Association, Eisenhower began his talk, as he had in the Philippines, with a reading from the Holy Bible. Rarely did he speak of Jesus in public, but on this night he quoted "Our Savior's" words in Luke 11:21: "When a strong man armed keepeth his palace, his goods are in peace." Luke 11:21 was Eisenhower's prooftext that, with trust in God, Americans were responsible for providing for their own military security. It had been the same on the Normandy beaches. The nation's goods were not only America's territory and its people, but they also included a strong public education system, a distinguished scientific community, and a vibrant national economy.

Then, surprisingly, Eisenhower asked the New York lawyers what initiatives, big and small, America should direct toward international Communism. Concerning small responses, he asked what the United States should do regarding Yugoslavia. Most Americans did not know where Yugoslavia was, let alone know anything about its history, its culture, its geography, or its leader, Marshall Tito. What are the national aspirations of the Yugoslavs as compared to those of the Americans? he inquired. Would it be appropriate for the United States to insist that Yugoslavs adopt American political and economic institutions before it says, "You are our friends"? Of course not. But Eisenhower went even further. Unless Americans developed understanding of what the Yugoslavs wanted as a people and a nation, world peace could never be attained.

Regarding the big question, the possibility of war with the Soviet Union, his thoughts may have been even more unsettling to the Long Islanders. Eisenhower urged his audience not to pay attention to the prophets of war. A war with the Soviet Union was possible but not likely, Eisenhower thought. He believed increased defense spending was necessary because that was the price of securing peace. But, having visited the Soviet Union and having witnessed the utter devastation suffered by the Russians in World War II, he did not believe the Soviets wanted to fight another war any time soon. He disliked the term "Cold War," he told the lawyers. It was too negative—too suggestive that, at any moment, the "Cold War" might turn "hot." Rather than being obsessed about fighting the Cold War, Eisenhower believed America should focus on efforts to inch peace closer to reality.

Then he startled the audience by ridiculing the idea that the United States should launch a preemptive strike on the Soviet Union before it could mount a sneak attack against the United States. What war aim would justify a "preventive" strike on the Soviet Union? he questioned. Putting aside the ghastly consequences of nuclear obliteration—the human sacrifices, the blood and death, the squandered national treasure, and the crushing debt of the war—let's say the United States won the war. Then what? Would the United States leave the vast Soviet Union to ruin or attempt to democratize the Russians through prolonged occupation? Who wants the job of occupying Russia? he asked rhetorically. How long would it take to make democrats out of the Communists? Furthermore, Eisenhower did not believe that Americans would be willing to make the long-term sacrifices in men and money necessary to finish the job once the fighting stopped. Whatever the outcome, the so-called preventive war would neither prevent horrific suffering nor secure a lasting American peace.

International Cooperation

When addressing the North Atlantic Council, the principal political decision-making body within NATO, in November 1951, he again quoted the Prince of Peace as recorded in Luke 11:21. But in this instance, the "strong man's palace" was the twelve nations that constituted NATO. But to be effective, he believed that members of NATO would have to concede a measure of national sovereignty in the interests of establishing European security. He enthusiastically endorsed European union. In Eisenhower's opinion, a Western Europe unified against Communist expansion needed to develop a common European economy and army. Eisenhower endorsed a plan for a European Coal and Steel Community proposed by Robert Schuman. Problematically for some NATO members, Eisenhower's European army would include troops from

West Germany. He did not propose forgiveness or atonement for the Germans but offered something just as effective: a military and economic partnership that would allow Germany to retrieve international self-respect.

Just as he had shared with the Nassau County Bar Association, he told the NATO ministers that he did not believe the Soviets wanted war. Military preparedness and economic stability were essential to achieve containment of Communist expansion in Europe, but even more important, in Eisenhower's opinion, was the unwavering confidence that the European community could "build a unity that will win the peace." NATO's most important task was to forge a European commitment to protect the precious "goods" in their common house. To maintain their freedom, European nations must understand that "the concept of collective security by co-operation must be successful or there is no acceptable alternative for any of us."

Although his talk to the NATO council was basically inspirational in purpose, it was also candid and prophetic. He was understandably vague in defining the "common goods" that each NATO ally committed to defend. Consequently, the principle he emphasized most strongly was cooperation; he hoped the experience of building NATO would itself provide the shared experiences and develop common values necessary to promote a historical "we consciousness" that was requisite to forming European identity. But he sagely warned that in the defense of their way of life, Europeans should carefully respect mutual values so that they did not violate each other's culture nor "destroy from within what [they] are trying to defend from without." In this regard, he proved an astute student of history and government.

The Gabriel Silver Lecture

Of all his speeches at this time, perhaps the Gabriel Silver Lecture was Eisenhower's most important. Of his hundreds of talks, the Silver Lecture best summarized Eisenhower's mature thoughts about peace and the role of the United States in the Cold War. Rhetorically, the speech was long and challenging. But it provided those who had heard his many speeches a comprehensive summary of Eisenhower's views on peace, the Communist threat, military cooperation, and world government.

In honor of his father, Leo Silver, a wealthy Columbia University alum, endowed the Gabriel Silver Lecture on Peace on the condition that Dwight Eisenhower present the first lecture. Grateful for Silver's generosity, Eisenhower was enthusiastic about giving a thoughtful lecture on the topic of war and peace to the Columbia University community. He and his assistant Kevin McCann worked diligently on his most serious and scholarly presentation as president of Columbia. He was pleased with the initial reaction to the lecture when the *New York Times* gave front-page coverage to his talk the following morning.

He began the Silver Lecture with a straightforward affirmation of his belief in the primacy of public education in a democracy, a theme he had been preaching since 1945. In the American system of democracy, he believed, government policy expressed the will of the people as formed from the knowledge, idealism, and public purposes fostered in the nation's schools. "What you teach," Eisenhower categorically declared, "is what the country does." He had experienced this truth in his own public education; he had witnessed the diabolical twist of this truism in Nazi Germany.

The war amplified Eisenhower's belief in the eternal conflict between divine and demonic forces in human history. In war and its aftermath, Eisenhower had observed the interplay between utter human depravity and sweet holy consecration. Despite its unspeakable horrors, its crippling human and material cost, and the irreplaceable destruction of civilization's treasures, Eisenhower had led a crusade of allied nations on a sacred mission. Similarly, through the reconstruction of Europe under the Marshall Plan, despite nasty rivalries, the suppression of freedom in some sectors, and disheartening cynicism from many quarters, the Allies had been able to establish a fragile, teetering economic and political balance in Europe. During the war Eisenhower had witnessed firsthand human behavior "in personal and social life that is creative and destructive at the same time."

Europe's postwar uncertainly brought Eisenhower quickly to the main theme of his lecture: What is peace? For what can the world reasonably hope? Eisenhower did not define peace abstractly as the absence of strife or sin among human societies. Peace, in Eisenhower's opinion, was not the heavenly city of God on earth. It was not possible, he told the Columbians, to paint war black and peace white. You've heard it said, he remarked, that "there never was a good war, or a bad peace." But that was nonsense. He did not romanticize war or glorify honor, valor, and duty. But in the darkest hours, he had experienced heartwarming sacrifice, transcendent comradeship, and greatness of human spirit. During the war he had seen drawings and paintings by soldiers that lifted the spirit and fed the soul. On the other hand, a false peace could become a viper's den of "chicanery, treachery and . . . expediency." Although he had opposed the atomic bombing of Japan and had been depressed by the destruction of Hiroshima, he believed that Chamberlain's capitulation to

Hitler at Munich "was a more fell blow to humanity than the atomic bomb at Hiroshima." "Willing hands can rebuild a better city," Eisenhower observed, obviously referring not only to Hiroshima and Nagasaki but also to Tokyo, Dresden, Cologne, London, and Berlin; but freedom lost is often paid for by generations of hate and brutal oppression. Echoing Franklin D. Roosevelt, Eisenhower warned that fear that caused men to sacrifice their liberties was a greater threat to peace than war itself.

Consequently, until war was outlawed, being unprepared for armed conflict was "well-nigh as criminal as war itself." Earthly peace was not heavenly. Rather, peace on earth was "*something* of an armed truce." Envisioning peace, Eisenhower was true to his dialectical worldview of human liberty caught in a historical struggle between the conflicting principles of autonomy and heteronomy. No person, no nation could obtain peace alone. Ironically, fear played a significant role in keeping war at bay. The specter of nuclear war, the possibility of total destruction of civilization, could serve as an effective deterrent in forestalling nuclear holocaust. "There is no prod so effective as a common dread; there is no binder so unifying."

But a stable, satisfactory, and long-lasting peace required a great deal more than a common dread. Eisenhower's formula for world peace was not utopian, but in his opinion it was achievable, if perhaps imperfectly.

Continuing with a variation of FDR's "Four Freedoms" (freedom of speech and worship, freedom from want and fear), Eisenhower outlined four principles for achieving peace with freedom. First, peace demanded that justice and opportunity become universal goals for all nations. "Starvation and hardship, ignorance and its evils, oppression and discrimination" were the raw materials of strife and war. Peace was possible only if normal human hungers were fed, and these included not only the physical hunger for food and shelter but also the universal human hunger for education and opportunity. Regarding "freedom from want," Eisenhower highlighted the great disparity of the distribution of wealth in the world. Ostentatious wealth concentrated in prosperous nations, unless redistributed, would create dangerous bitterness and envy among less fortunate peoples. The way out of this dilemma, Eisenhower believed, was not for the standard of living among the wealthy nations to be lowered but rather for the favored nations to promote freedom of opportunity through education, technology, and economic development among the poor. This was not a matter of altruism, he explained, but rather an issue of urgent self-interest and preservation for wealthy nations.

Enlightened self-interest, however, should not lose sight of the fact that "man's spiritual side is still the dominant one." Without a strong spiritual base that energizes national optimism, nothing much can be accomplished other than meeting the needs of the day. Freedom of religion inspired hope in God's goodness that spurred "humans everywhere to work harder, to endure more now that the future may be better; but despair is the climate of war and death." For this reason, Eisenhower foresaw the eventual collapse of the Soviet Union. Not all the people within the Soviet Union accepted the Marxist mantra "There is no God, and religion is an opiate." For that reason, "some day they will educate their rulers—or change them," Eisenhower predicted. Eisenhower's faith in improvement, even for the Communists, was almost unbounded.

He asked the Columbians to compare the world of 1950 to that of 1850. In Eisenhower's opinion, "the world of 1950 [was] a far brighter and better place than the world of 1850," even in the Soviet Union. This was a stunning assessment from Columbia's president, who was only two years from becoming president of the United States: "even Russia, despite its all-powerful police and purges, is for the average Russian a vast improvement compared to the Russia of 1850."

Eisenhower's second requirement for an enduring peace followed from his first. The freedom-loving democracies had a special responsibility, a calling, to promote international understanding, friendship, and cooperation. Astoundingly, he concluded that, with the possible exception of the Soviet Union, "there is no need to remake the world . . . in the likeness of the United States." No nation had a monopoly on virtue or truth, and none was without problems or need of improvement. Since the beginning of World War II, he had preached the need for international cooperation among the free nations of the world to combat demonic enemies of peace.

Fundamentally for Eisenhower, peace was a verb—a process. In the long run, the best way to combat the spread of Communism and to promote peace was to negotiate bilateral and multilateral treaties of friendship, to foster regional consortia to promote economic development, and to support international efforts to combat disease and encourage education. Because the Soviets also gave lip service to these actions, Eisenhower thought limited (and watchful) cooperation with the Communists was possible. Certainly, cultural and scientific exchanges could prove profitable. This general principle may seem unremarkable until one recalls that Eisenhower was deeply worried that the strong anti-Roosevelt isolationist sentiment in the Republican Party led by Ohio senator Robert A. Taft might undo his efforts at building multinational partnerships sponsored by the United States.

Eisenhower did not neglect issues of military preparedness, disarmament, and collective security in his Silver Lecture. Necessarily, he believed that peace could only be secured from a position of both military and economic strength, but when all camps equally bristled with arms, motives became suspect and trust evaporated. The atomic bomb might serve as an uncertain deterrent to war for a few years. But a nuclear arms race would eventually lead to disaster. As clearly as possible, he warned his audience, who were gathered at ground zero in a prospective nuclear war:

> When even one major power, surreptitiously or flagrantly, builds and maintains a military machine beyond the recognized needs of reasonable security, a war of aggression is a constant threat to peaceful nations. At the very least, these armaments become the gangster's gun—a notice that might and might alone shall serve as judge, jury and sheriff in settling international dispute. That is the only realistic interpretation, since no government otherwise would squander its revenue or exhaust its economy on so sterile an enterprise.

For Eisenhower, it was self-evident that international disarmament was essential to a stable, enduring peace. If the threat of nuclear war was constant, fear would erode peaceful efforts. Disarmament under the supervision of a strong United Nations constituted his third and fourth prerequisites for achieving peace. Even though he did not actually refer to the 1946 Baruch Plan for the international control of atomic energy, it would have been obvious to his audience that he was endorsing this plan or something very like it. By advocating disarmament negotiations, of course, Eisenhower was making a tacit promise that he, for one, not only was willing to negotiate arms control with the Soviets but also was confident that, with appropriate inspections, such negotiations could be fruitful. The United States and the Soviet Union, plus their allies, would be required to respect United Nations authority to verify all disarmament agreements.

He insisted that neither the United States nor any other nation would be required to sacrifice sovereignty, because the United Nations would have no power to intervene in the internal affairs of any state. On the other hand, no nation should arrogate to itself the responsibility for policing the world. For Eisenhower, disarmament and appropriate United Nations policing authority were necessary corollaries to establishing "justice, freedom . . . and a climate of mutual understanding and cooperation among nations"—the substance of a lasting, equitable peace.

To forestall cynicism or despair, he closed his Silver Lecture with a call for action on the part of Columbia University and the United States. The time was ripe, he believed, for new ideas, new initiatives for world peace. At midcentury, the United States and the world stood at a turning point in history. The future was bright. Columbia University could provide world leadership in nutrition, medicine, nuclear energy, conservation, international affairs, and peace studies, to name a few areas. The United States, with its vast resources of energy and material prosperity, but especially with its deep reserves of intellectual and moral strength, remained a hopeful beacon for free people everywhere. He looked for no quick victories, no sudden conversions. Progress was achieved one step at a time by a patient, persistent people. America's best foreign policy, he concluded, was "to live our daily lives in honesty, decency and integrity; at home, making our own land a more fitting habitation for free men; and abroad, joining with those of like mind and heart, to make of the world a place where all can dwell in peace."

The Silver Lecture was important not only because it faithfully summarized key ideas that he had developed in his several postwar speeches but also because it formalized his political and moral rationale for running for president of the United States. As the university's president, and as America's preeminent warrior, he echoed with authority America's longing for a just peace. What is most important to note in the Silver Lecture is that Eisenhower did not envision peace as a distant utopian dream or heavenly award after death. Peace-as-action existed here and now, even in the midst of war. As a verb, peace was an incremental process that step-by-step strove toward international justice. Freedom was not merely prerequisite to peace, but rather peace and freedom were inextricably linked in Eisenhower's mind. Without progress toward freedom, peace existed only as an ideal.

In many respects, Eisenhower's concept of freedom reflected his Kansas heritage. The allegory about the tyrannical gander upsetting Uncle Luther's peaceful farmyard captures his belief that freedom included fair play, justice, cooperation, and a live-and-let-live community free of intimidating bullies. Of course, given human nature, the peaceable kingdom required policing by peace officers such as himself. The implication of the Silver Lecture was that societies, such as Nazi Germany or the Soviet Union, that deny basic freedoms exist apart from the free, peaceful world. Some, like Nazi Germany, needed to be crushed; others, like the Soviet Union, would collapse because of their internal contradictions.

Eisenhower's remarkable Silver Lecture not only summarized his numerous postwar speeches but also foretold most of the major foreign policy and defense initiatives of his future administration. At Columbia University, he rehearsed distinctive themes that shape his "Chance for Peace," "Atoms for Peace," and "Military-Industrial Complex" speeches that highlighted his presidency. By the spring of 1950, when he was fifty-nine years old, Eisenhower's thinking on all manner of subjects—that is, war and peace, government and society, diplomacy and foreign aid, religion and the state, the national economy and international partnerships, science and education—had fully matured.

President in Waiting

The half decade between 1945 and 1950, and especially his brief tenure as president of Columbia University, served as an enriching sabbatical for Dwight Eisenhower. Concurrent with the growth of his religious sensibilities, Eisenhower became politically more confident and reflective. After the enormous sacrifices of blood and treasure in World War II, he was dismayed by the pell-mell demobilization of the United States following the Japanese surrender. Understandably, almost everyone pushed not only to bring the "boys" home but also to slash military spending and limit international commitments. Increasingly, he believed no one else had the necessary experience or temperament to lead postwar America.

With hindsight, Eisenhower's presidency seems almost inevitable, like that of George Washington or U. S. Grant. With the possible exception of MacArthur, no hero of comparable stature to Eisenhower emerged from World War II. Talk of a presidency for Ike began as early as the North Africa campaign. During the war he consistently brushed aside any ambition of becoming president. At this juncture, he thought the presidential speculation was silly, but even to deny such ambition would make him appear to be ridiculous.

More importantly, political ambition on his part would constitute a fundamental betrayal of his duty. "For a soldier to turn from his war duty for any reason is to be guilty of treachery to his country and disloyalty to his superiors," he wrote his brother Arthur. "The President is my Commander-in-Chief. Nothing could sway me from my purpose of carrying out faithfully his orders in whatever post he may assign me." If Arthur did not get his point, Ike concluded with this: "I will not tolerate the use of my name in connection with any political activity of any kind."

In the immediate postwar years, however, he was alternately adamant that he was uninterested in politics and coy about the possibility of running for president. Immediately after the war, both Democrats and Republicans courted Eisenhower to run on their party's ticket. Nevertheless, he wrote to Swede Hazlett that he could conceive of no circumstance under which he would consider accepting a political position, from "Dog Catcher to 'Grand High Supreme King of the Universe.'" But while he frequently said no, he never shouted, "Hell, no!" And to some, his biography *Soldier of Democracy*, published in 1945, looked very much like a campaign biography.

In truth, presidential talk flattered Ike, whose "little engine of ambition" was fueled by the enthusiasm of his admirers. Of course, he could not let personal ambition (selfishness) direct his life. But it might be a different matter if he were drafted to be president. The trouble was, this quintessential planner was not yet prepared to enter the hurly-burly of American politics. He had neither political staff nor regular political advisors. He had no well-defined constituency or organized support from political leaders. He had no campaign plans, no war chest or fund-raising apparatus. As a potential presidential candidate, he had neither a political base from which to run nor a platform on which to stand. But all this was about to change rapidly.

While Eisenhower effectively removed himself from the 1948 presidential campaign, interest continued to build for a possible run for the White House in 1952. For the first time in sixteen years, Truman's surprising defeat of Thomas E. Dewey in 1948 swung the door wide open for a stronger Republican bid in 1952 should Truman decide not to run for reelection. Eisenhower remained publicly uncommitted concerning his political ambitions, if any, but privately he told friends who could be of material help in a presidential campaign that, like Washington, he might be open to a "draft" if duty called him to serve as president. At least that was the way Eisenhower wanted to be perceived. Not surprisingly, informal Eisenhower-for-president groups, mostly Republican, sprouted here and there like volunteer spring wheat on the Kansas prairie.

President of Columbia University

Eisenhower was unsettled in his own mind regarding his immediate future. In November 1945, he wrote Hazlett that there was nothing he wanted more than to retire. He did not have the heart to demobilize the army that he had worked so hard to build. His job was nothing more than "straight duty," he complained. He fantasized about becoming president of a small college when the war ended, but no small college came calling. He was not enthusiastic about moving to New York City, but when IBM's Tom Watson, on behalf of the Board of Trustees, offered him the presidency of Columbia University, with Milton's encouragement, he could not resist the attraction of heading a major Ivy League university, where he might make a significant contribution to the education of students who were about the age of the troops he had commanded.

Eisenhower's installation on October 12, 1948, as the thirteenth president of Columbia, proved a festive occasion, attracting twenty thousand persons to witness the pomp and splendor of a medieval pageant featuring unprecedented tribute from American college and university leaders. Thereafter, he enjoyed a brief honeymoon at Columbia. Even before his arrival on campus, he personally convinced Columbia's legendary football coach, Lou Little, not to accept Yale's offer to move to New Haven. Their misgivings aside, the Columbia University community welcomed Eisenhower with optimism generated by the general's charisma and the promise of better days to come. Prior to his inauguration as university president, he announced an ambitious development plan to celebrate Columbia University's bicentennial in 1954.

With Milton's assistance, his inaugural address stressed the importance for free institutions such as Columbia to promote "democratic citizenship." He assured faculty, students, and alumni that academic freedom would be respected at Columbia and that "the facts" about Communism, fascism, and other repressive political systems would be openly taught and freely discussed. Already stung by accusations that the university harbored Communists, the faculty welcomed his forthright defense of free discussion. Famed reporter Edward R. Murrow commended Eisenhower for his affirmation of academic freedom during the intensifying Cold War, while *Newsweek* found him a strong successor to the "irreplaceable" Nicholas Murray Butler.

Residency at Columbia's presidential mansion at 60 Morningside Drive proved bittersweet for the Eisenhowers. Successor of Columbia's beloved President Butler, Eisenhower was mistrusted by many faculty and students who thought him unqualified, aloof, and clueless concerning academic leadership of a major research university. In addition to his lack of the traditional academic credentials held by an Ivy League president, his successful World War II memoir did not compare favorably to the independent scholarly research and publication of the faculty. Although America's military hero, he was not an object of pride for those at Columbia who expected their president to be a world-renowned intellectual/administrator. Furthermore, he disdained the major task for which most trustees thought he was hired—fund-raising. Unfortunately, Eisenhower's management style also proved inappropriate on the university campus, where collegiality was among the highest of virtues.

For all his administrative talent, Eisenhower, unlike his brother Milton, did not have an academic temperament.

And, like Milton, he also proved to be peripatetic. Eisenhower continued his crushing schedule of public speaking and consulting with the defense officials in Washington, often skipping staff and faculty meetings on Morningside Heights. When appointed informal chair of the Joint Chiefs of Staff, he attempted to commute between Washington and New York, spending his long weekends at Columbia catching up on his presidential duties. Eisenhower's frenetic schedule was too much even for the energetic president/general. In March, he collapsed from an acute attack of ileitis, an inflammation of the small intestine. Following recuperation at Truman's "Winter White House" in Key West and the Augusta National Golf Club, Eisenhower returned to Columbia in mid-May, but he left again in mid-July for a two-month vacation.

When he returned to Columbia in September 1949 from his prolonged illness/recuperation/vacation, he discovered that the buoyant enthusiasm that characterized the fall of 1948 had evaporated. There had been serious miscommunication between Eisenhower and the trustees concerning his fundraising role as president. For his part, Eisenhower repeatedly tried to make it clear what he was willing to do—and not do—but frank conversations during the hiring process about mutual expectations became lost in the anxious fog of embarrassing failure should his recruitment as president fall through.

Eisenhower was not completely innocent of the misunderstanding, however. He ought to have known—from Milton, if from no other—that the management of an elite university would challenge the leadership skills at which he excelled: strategic planning, group process, personnel evaluation, team building, crisis management, morale building, and political sensitivity. Instead, rather than elevating Columbia to his first priority, Eisenhower continued to believe that his ultimate concern, his defining duty, was to assist the United States Army in maintaining international peace. His long absences in Washington underscored his unconditional commitment to his duty to the government rather than to the university.

Given Eisenhower's priorities, Columbia's faculty was markedly unenthusiastic about his idea that Columbia's principal mission was to produce educated American citizens. Wise enough not to advocate citizenship development through the arts and sciences curriculum, he supported initiatives, all of which he laid out in his Gabriel Silver Lecture, that did not conflict with Columbia's academic and research agenda. In the business school he proposed studying the lessons of manpower allocation learned during World War II. In addition, he encouraged the establishment of a nutrition center in the school of public health, a center for citizenship education in the teachers college, and a chair for peace studies in an Institute for War and Peace Studies. Finally, and closest to his heart, Eisenhower established the American Assembly, where government, business, professional, and academic leaders could meet from time to time to discuss the pressing social, political, economic, and international issues facing the United States.

The American Assembly

In October 1950, Eisenhower announced at a Faculty Club luncheon his intention to establish the American Assembly at Columbia. He had been working on the idea for almost two years when W. Averell Harriman and his brother Roland generously deeded Arden House, an estate forty-eight miles from New York City, to Columbia, offering an attractive headquarters for the enterprise.

From 1945 through 1950, Columbia's president was driven by two issues that bedeviled conservative Republicans of his day: concerning foreign affairs, he asked how the United States could best fight the Cold War; and domestically, he worried about how free enterprise could be effectively protected against encroachments of the federal government. Eisenhower did not envision rolling back either Communism or the New Deal. But he fervently believed that the overreaching growth of both needed to be contained. In concert with his brother Milton, he believed that American universities such as Columbia should play a leading role in "studying, explaining and perpetrating our American system."

Consequently, in his prospectus to would-be donors to the American Assembly, Eisenhower emphasized America's domestic challenges. In a thinly veiled critique of the New Deal, he warned ominously, "We have always known that democracy could be destroyed by creeping paralysis from within." He conceded that strong central government, deficit spending, agricultural and tax subsidies, and social welfare might be required during emergencies, but their cumulative effect could discourage initiative and responsibility, stifle production, depress the economy, commandeer property, and, in the end, create dictatorship.

The American Assembly, of course, could not, in and of itself, protect the United States from such catastrophe, but by hosting the nation's top business, labor, agricultural, medical, scientific, academic, and political leaders along with economists, engineers, social scientists, and other top experts, Columbia

University could assume a leadership role in developing factual, nonpartisan study papers on the most pressing domestic and international problems facing the United States and the free world. For example, Eisenhower proposed that one of the vital questions to be addressed by the American Assembly might be: "In the modern, complex economy, with its acute interdependencies among great groups of specialists, what is the proper dividing line between the responsibilities and rights of the individual on the one hand, and the necessary controls of the central government on the other?"

This was one of Eisenhower's recurrent themes. To all those asked to contribute to the establishment of the American Assembly, it was evident that they were being invited to participate in an Eisenhower crusade that might extend beyond the campus of Columbia University.

Briefly, Eisenhower used his American Assembly initiative as a stage on which to express openly his political views. As a civilian, Eisenhower could now share his criticism of FDR's economic policies. At the Saint Andrews Society in New York City, and later in Texas, he continued to hammer on anti–New Deal themes that sounded like pure politics. Intemperately, he told the Texans, "If all that Americans want is security, they can go to prison," where they would be fed and housed. Otherwise, to preserve human dignity and liberty, one must not bow one's head to "any dictatorial government." The reference to the Soviet Union was clear, but lest his allusion to the New Deal escape anyone, Eisenhower added that Americans must not be tempted by governmental paternalism at the risk of losing their priceless birthright of freedom. In his heart, of course, he knew that certain sacred New Deal programs, namely, Social Security, were untouchable.

His blunt conservative rhetoric even upset some of his Republican friends. As long as Eisenhower confined his public comments to generalities about national security and fighting Communism, he escaped most criticism. But when he began to talk like an ambitious politician, he opened himself to counterattack. Among others, Milton advised that he back off his political assaults and limit himself to less controversial subjects. Otherwise he would create the impression that he was actually running for president. "You don't need my advice," Milton wrote his brother, "but I'd quit making speeches on everything but education."

Surprisingly, perhaps, while soliciting funds from his well-heeled friends, Eisenhower did not ask them to enroll in a campaign to combat America's spiritual crisis. But for Eisenhower, the spiritual question was never distant. The vital question of how to balance individual (or corporate) economic liberty with increasing regulations from the federal government mirrored analogous dialectics involving civil rights and religious freedoms. Turned another way, the question might be framed: How can individual autonomy be preserved in an age of creeping heteronomous authority? Or, more religiously, how does the free man dignified by God maintain his integrity before the unconditional demands of duty?

The problem, as Eisenhower well understood, is that this Augustinian dilemma probes our ultimate concern—that is, why are we alive and for what are we willing to die? During the war, soldiers under his command in Europe repeatedly asked him why they were fighting and dying. From Eisenhower's perspective, they were, of course, fighting to protect and save the American way of life—democracy, liberty, freedom, justice—founded on God's affirmation of the dignity of all humankind. At Columbia University, it became his duty to teach this life-and-death lesson about the responsibilities of citizenship to American youth. The American Assembly, however, reflected the realities of Eisenhower's tenure at Columbia. His vision for Columbia did not mesh well with the aspirations of the academic faculty, nor would national security requirements enable him to focus time and energy on his Columbia crusade.

Eisenhower's brief stint at Columbia, and especially the American Assembly, provided him a superb venue for meeting the nation's top businessmen, industrialists, bankers, financiers, oilmen, and attorneys. Through its trustees and alumni, Columbia provided him entrée to many of the most influential publishers, scientists, doctors, educators, and religious and political leaders in the country. Foundations, the Association of University Presidents, and the Council on Foreign Relations, among others, opened additional doors for the Columbia president.

Accordingly, Columbia proved an important springboard for Eisenhower into the White House. Under the cover of promoting Columbia's American Assembly, in 1950 Eisenhower was able to launch an effective, albeit unofficial, presidential campaign before taking leave from the university to head NATO in January 1951. The fact that important Democrats and leading contributors to Democratic candidates, such as Averell Harriman, Tom Watson, and Texas oilman Sid Richardson, enthusiastically supported the American Assembly lent a bipartisan dimension as well as corporate resources to Eisenhower's favorite project. With over four thousand supporters and organizations on the official mailing list, the American Assembly easily provided a core constituency for the Friends for Eisenhower.

CHAPTER SIX

Supreme Allied Commander Europe

Following the Soviet blockade of Berlin in June 1948, Russian testing of an atomic device in August 1949, and the Communist invasion of South Korea in June 1950, Eisenhower felt increasing pressure to return to active military duty. During the Berlin Airlift, efforts were begun by the United States and Great Britain to resurrect some version of the victorious World War II Atlantic alliance. In April 1949, nine Western European nations plus the United States, Canada, and Iceland signed the agreement creating the North Atlantic Treaty Organization (NATO). Consequently, the Korean War actually stimulated efforts among the United States and its allies to strengthen European security. During the Korean War, not only did the United States offer European allies increased military assistance, but Eisenhower also became the obvious choice to command the joint NATO forces. After preliminary discussions, in late October 1950, President Truman ordered Eisenhower back to active service—and on December 19, 1950, the North Atlantic Council announced that General Eisenhower had been appointed the first Supreme Allied Commander Europe (SACEUR).

Just before Christmas, he visited Capitol Hill, where he faced one of his greatest immediate challenges in forging the new alliance. His hero, former president Herbert Hoover, who wanted to reduce, not expand, America's military commitment to Europe, had already sharply criticized Truman's defense initiatives. Eisenhower, upset over Republican opposition to collective security, tried to convince congressional isolationists to support NATO. In one of the most fateful meetings in American political history, Eisenhower met with Ohio senator Robert A. Taft about the NATO project. Taft had voted against the NATO treaty in the Senate and was even more adamant than Hoover that the president had no authority to commit troops to the defense of Europe without congressional approval. Eisenhower, who had no quarrel with Taft's domestic agenda, wanted the senator to pledge his support for American contributions to the NATO command. Perhaps with his eye on the 1952 presidential campaign, Taft refused to support Eisenhower's mission to forge a strong NATO aided by American troops.

Had Taft supported NATO at this juncture, perhaps Eisenhower would have shelved his own presidential ambitions, but instead Taft inadvertently increased the likelihood that he would face a formidable challenge for the GOP nomination in 1952. The possibility that a fervent right-wing isolationist might run for president in 1952 increased the certainty that Eisenhower would hear another call to duty in the foreseeable future.

Road to the White House

The story of Eisenhower's road from NATO to the White House has been well told by William B. Pickett in *Eisenhower Decides to Run* (2000). While in Europe organizing NATO, he received no end of cards and letters urging him to run for president in 1952. In addition, a constant stream of wealthy visitors crossed the Atlantic to offer advice and encouragement to the general. However much he was tempted by the lure of the presidency, Eisenhower, who had consistently expressed his loathing for politics, was not about to campaign openly for the Republican nomination. It would be different if he were called by the people, or drafted by the Republican nominating convention, but short of that, he would not personally insert himself into the race for the White House.

At home, without his expressed consent, Senator Frank Carlson of Kansas quietly lined up political support. Meanwhile, in September 1951, former New York governor Thomas Dewey; attorney Herbert Brownell, Dewey's campaign manager; and Eisenhower's good friend General Lucius Clay organized the Citizens for Eisenhower Committee to raise money for an Eisenhower campaign and to place Eisenhower's name on state primary ballots. After Taft took the Senate floor to criticize Eisenhower's appointment to command NATO, Senator Henry Cabot Lodge of Massachusetts flew to Paris to urge Eisenhower to declare himself as a candidate for president.

Again, Eisenhower demurred, but he later admitted that Lodge's visit had caused him to think anew about the need to stop Taft's threat to international security. Taft was not exactly the antichrist, but he did represent a demonic challenge to all that Eisenhower had stood for during the previous decade. On his sixty-first birthday, October 14, he wrote confidentially to a few trusted supporters that he was a Republican and that if called to duty by nomination, he would resign from the army to campaign for the presidency.

Still, with crucial work yet to be completed at NATO, Eisenhower wanted to postpone his resignation from the army for as long as possible. Being true to his duty was not a fiction for the general, and increasingly he could not ignore the feeling that he was inexorably pulled in two directions. Although Taft could continue to hold his seat in the Senate while campaigning for president, by army regulation, Eisenhower could not declare himself a candidate for political office and continue as SACEUR of NATO. Thanking his friends for their support, he explained that his course was simple because he did not intend to deviate from his duty. He realized that he might seem to be "pontifical," but he repeated again that he could "only abide by my hope of doing my *duty.*" If his political future were isolated from his duty, it would collapse into the realm of personal ambition, where it would become corrupted. This intensely religious man lamented to Bill Robinson of the *New York Herald Tribune,* "I do not know why it is so difficult for so many to believe this!"

His plan, he revealed to his closest friends, was to remain in France until June 1952 to focus on the establishment of SHAPE (Supreme Headquarters Allied Powers in Europe), NATO's headquarters whose mission included establishing a European army and assisting in the foundation of European political and economic unity. The burgeoning "Ike for President" clubs in the United States would have to move forward without him until his job with NATO was completed.

Eisenhower's overall plan hit a snag when he learned in December 1951 that Governor Sherman Adams intended to enter his name in New Hampshire's March primary. Army regulations made it impossible for Eisenhower to engage in any political activity, but he supposed that a genuine "draft" by New Hampshire Republicans would be acceptable. Accordingly, he informed key supporters that he would not campaign for the nomination in New Hampshire, but he wrote them that he considered himself a Republican. In effect, from this point on, there would be no turning back for Eisenhower.

Unbelievably, he still wanted to think of himself as a noncandidate. His dilemma was embedded deeply in his own psyche, where he was torn between his belief that he was the only man who could lead the West through the Cold War and his reluctance to allow his ambition to capture his soul. He was pushed forward by his devotion to duty while repelled by his perception that politics was largely self-serving and corrupt. But he was also a shrewd leader, who did not want to appear vainglorious like MacArthur but instead wanted to be regarded as one who humbly, but not too reluctantly, allowed himself to be carried forward on the shoulders of his enthusiastic supporters. He would not drive his own chariot through the streets of the city, but he could follow the groundswell of the cheering crowd to meet his destiny.

Deciding to Run

To help Eisenhower feel that duty called him to the White House, millionaire Jock Whitney helped to organize a midnight Eisenhower rally at Madison Square Garden in February. New York's famous arena normally held about sixteen thousand but that night packed in a surging crowd of thirty-three thousand boisterous Eisenhower enthusiasts who partied and cheered for Eisenhower until dawn. There were, of course, customary speeches, and the crowd joined in singing Irving Berlin's "I Like Ike," adapted from *Call Me Madam*. Three days later, Jacqueline Cochran, the famous aviator, flew to Paris via commercial airliner with a film of the gigantic rally. As political theater, the rally/film was unprecedented. Whitney judged his man correctly. Watching the enthusiasm for his candidacy, bathed in the obvious love of ecstatic Americans, experiencing the unbridled emotion of his fans, Eisenhower could not resist the power of this existential moment. Relaxing over cocktails after the film, Cochran toasted the next president of the United States.

With tears welling in his eyes and sensing that he had reached a turning point in his life, a mellow Eisenhower reminisced about his boyhood in Abilene, his brothers and father, but mostly about his indomitable mother, who continued to serve him as a guiding influence. Cochran listened patiently but did not shirk her mission. It did not matter how much fervor the people demonstrated for Eisenhower; unless he declared himself a candidate for president, Taft would seize the nomination. He knew she was right and promised he would return to the United States soon. It was a fateful decision. Not only would he leave NATO with the work uncompleted, but also he would need to resign his commission in the army. As he teetered on the boundary between military and civilian service, he was a warrior, not a politician, whose identity would be shaken to its foundation by this new calling. In effect, his friends were asking him to make a gigantic leap of faith into the political world with consequences that would surely be both divine and demonic.

Senator Taft was among politicians who accused Eisenhower of being vague and shallow. Indeed, during the New Hampshire primary campaign, almost no one knew where Eisenhower stood on major political issues. Occasionally, Eisenhower sounded as if he were anti–New Deal, but he obviously belonged to the internationalist wing of the Republican Party. But other than that, Taft contended, he had taken no discernible position on issues that deeply concerned conservative Republicans.

To counter Taft's criticism and to promote Eisenhower's candidacy, with Cliff Roberts's and Bill Robinson's support, the *Herald Tribune* printed excerpts from Kevin McCann's campaign book, *Eisenhower's Creed*. The irony that Eisenhower had spent a lifetime avoiding association with all creedal organizations other than the US Army apparently bothered no one.

Compared to the Silver Lecture, *Eisenhower's Creed* was superficial but folksy and anecdotal. McCann was skilled in the art of writing political cliché. He faithfully summarized Eisenhower's key beliefs, but his discussion of the candidate's views often lacked specificity and context. For example,

Eisenhower's Creed was long on anti–New Deal rhetoric but short on what Eisenhower would do to limit growth of the federal government, enhance states' rights, reduce federal spending, lower taxes, balance the budget, cut the deficit, or protect economic freedom against government bureaucracy. Actually, the "Eisenhower creed" endorsed "progressive" measures such as the graduated income tax, the Interstate Commerce Commission, and the Securities and Exchange Commission. Eisenhower believed in the middle of the road, but nothing in *Eisenhower's Creed* offered a clue as to what that meant for national economic or social policy except that he was determined to avoid the gutter into which many politicians had fallen. Only in the defense of NATO and the principle of international cooperation was Eisenhower unmistakably specific. His "creed" was consistently forthright in declaring that the United States should not assume the posture of a modern Rome, that the Russians did not constitute an immediate military threat, and that, when United States national interests were not threatened, the United States should adopt a live-and-let-live approach toward other sovereign states.

Domestically, while the United States should not tolerate subversives dedicated to sabotaging American society, there was no need to require a loyalty oath from all teachers or to institute draconian suppression of civil liberties. The only explicitly religious expression in *Eisenhower's Creed* was tucked away in a paragraph explaining Eisenhower's call to the presidency of Columbia University. Columbia had merely been a change of headquarters from which he waged his American crusade. "I believe fanatically in the American form of democracy," he had written his friend Swede Hazlett, "a system that recognizes and protects the rights of the individual and that ascribes to the individual a dignity accruing to him because of his creation in the image of a Supreme Being and which rests upon his conviction that only through a system of free enterprise can this type of democracy be preserved." There it was—in fewer than sixty-five words—the heart of Eisenhower's civil religion faith that inextricably bound together belief in the Supreme Being, American democracy, and modern capitalism.

In truth, Eisenhower's middle-of-the-road stance on domestic issues was not programmatic; rather, it reflected his temperament regarding contemporary politics. In a long, hastily written dissertation, Eisenhower responded to Bill Robinson's request that he outline his basic political beliefs. The essay was not polished, but it strikingly revealed Eisenhower's dialectical philosophy of history that began with ancient Rome and continued to the present. In general, his understanding of history was a conventional amalgam of Gibbon, Condorcet, John Locke, the Founding Fathers, Auguste Comte, Whiggery, and moderate classical liberalism. He believed that civilizations tended to rise and fall according to an organic cycle of youth, maturity, and venerable age, but that historical progress itself was linear.

By the mid-twentieth century, the United States had achieved middle-aged maturity. Gone were the days of "youthful lustiness, freedom and growth" characterized by "rapid increases of wealth" and opportunity and "impatience with any kind of control or authority." As wealth was amassed and concentrated in a maturing society, so risks were increasingly avoided, and opportunity and growth declined. In a maturing society, "caution and respect for custom" increasingly replaced venture and confidence. Like the timid steward in the biblical parable, Eisenhower reminded Robinson, in a mature society the wealthy wanted to protect their gains by metaphorically hiding their talents in the ground.

Progressivism, in Eisenhower's opinion, was the natural manifestation of a mature economy. Historically, progressives were dedicated to the preservation of the greatest possible opportunities for individual "self-development and advancement, spiritually, intellectually, and economically." This meant, of course, promoting public education, social service, and community welfare. But most importantly, in the spirit of Eisenhower's youthful hero Theodore Roosevelt, the progressive's task was "to combat and break down concentrations of power, of whatever kind or location, whenever these unjustifiably or unnecessarily exercise authority over the lives and fortunes of men."

Eisenhower realized that his manifesto could be corrupted to endorse either radical or reactionary political agendas. Historical experience taught that social organization has been established to ensure orderliness and stability within society: that is, political and business organizations, churches, schools, labor unions, and families all restrict human behavior for the greater good of the common interest. Eisenhower believed that the greatest social sin was selfishness and greed, while initiative and self-reliance were among the highest American virtues. He was not unmindful of the delicate balance between rule of law and human liberty, and he confessed to Robinson that it was "difficult to define the exact line of demarcation between necessary control and rules of conduct on the one hand, and unjustifiable seizure of power on the other." In his mind, the middle of the road was not only a broad highway of political consensus but also a fine line that separated progressive government from political regimentation.

Theodore Roosevelt was a progressive because he made it his mission to curb the power of concentrated wealth and industrial monopoly that was inimical to the happiness and livelihood of the nation's citizens. In a mature industrial economy, Eisenhower conceded that regulatory and redistributive policies could be justified as a necessary means to an orderly and measurably free life. He confessed that he was willing to look beyond the graduated income tax, the Interstate Commerce Commission, and the Securities and Exchange Commission to endorse antitrust laws, social security, minimum-wage scales, and other regulatory measures used by the New Deal to stave off economic distress and natural catastrophe. Despite the bitter complaints of doctrinaire laissez-faire advocates, Eisenhower believed that none of these progressive programs violated "our basic concepts of freedom, justice and right." But as a conservative, he remained wary that government extravagance might itself create a concentration of self-interested power as dangerous to human freedom as the rapaciousness of the robber barons of the nineteenth century. Between extremes of laissez-faire and governmental regimentation, Eisenhower envisioned occupying a middle ground at midcentury that best satisfied America's spiritual, intellectual, and material needs. To stay balanced in the middle of the road was not easy, he confided to Robinson, but "*it is the ever-continuing problem of free men.*"

Despite his absence, Eisenhower handily won the New Hampshire primary over Taft and, as a write-in candidate, ran a strong second to Harold Stassen, the favorite son, in Minnesota. The American people, he now believed, were calling him to accept a "transcendent duty" to lead the nation through the perils of the Cold War. Yet, at this decisive moment, he felt curiously alone. The letters and cards that came pouring into his NATO office, many expressing the urgency that he return home to become actively involved in the presidential campaign, only served to increase his sense of isolation and vulnerability. In March he wrote wistfully to Bill Robinson, "I am here (at SHAPE) absolutely alone as far as any assistance in the political area is concerned." In part, he was increasingly frustrated by the pressures of his NATO assignment while walking the tightrope of welcoming visitors and answering correspondence yet not appearing obviously political. To help calm his nerves, Harry Bullis sent him a prayer: "Oh God, give me sympathy and sense to keep my courage high, God give me calmness and confidence, and please a twinkle in my eye." Bullis knew his man—it was Eisenhower's kind of prayer to the Supreme Being.

What to Do about Church?

During this gray period, the Reverend Billy Graham traveled to Paris to encourage Eisenhower to run for president. Eisenhower's good friend, the

Texas oilman Sid Richardson, encouraged Graham to write the general expressing the evangelist's hope that Eisenhower would lead Americans in a moral crusade to establish good government. Eisenhower, who remarked, "that was the damnedest letter I ever got," later asked Richardson, "who is this young fellow?" With Richardson's help, Graham visited Eisenhower in Paris, where they were mutually impressed. Although Eisenhower had not yet announced his candidacy, it is doubtful that at this late date, February, Graham had much influence on the general's decision to run except to bring assurance of the enthusiastic support of Texas oil millionaires. No doubt, Graham effectively preached the Gospel of Texas Oil as well as the Word of Jesus Christ. Graham also encouraged Eisenhower to join a church, but Eisenhower said he would not join a church for political reasons. Were he to join a church after the election, he confided to Graham, it would probably be a Presbyterian church.

When Cliff Roberts raised the same question about church membership, Eisenhower explained that although he and his brothers were "very earnestly and seriously religious," they were also "a little bit 'non-conformist'" regarding church membership. Given their upbringing, they had no choice but to be intensely religious. Among others, Clare Boothe Luce, a converted Catholic, also told him he had to join a church because the youth of the nation looked to him as a role model. Although he claimed no objection to attending church, he continued to treasure his religious independence. It might be advantageous to join a church, but from Eisenhower's perspective, the only reason for doing so was political, not religious. But he conceded that it would be easier to say he was a Presbyterian than to confess that he was a Christian of some sort.

Church or no church, Eisenhower knew he was heading into a maelstrom of politically inspired criticism once he declared for the presidency. To Republican political strategist Howard Chase, he expressed his worry about how hardscrabble politics might affect Mamie. There would be innuendo concerning his alleged affair with Kay Summersby. Mamie had been dismayed by the allegations during the war, and the opening of this wound would be painful. Mamie herself might become the subject of scurrilous gossip that she had a drinking problem when in fact she suffered from inner-ear problems. From the political right, Eisenhower was accused of being a Communist sympathizer who had shirked capturing Berlin to appease Stalin. On the political left, he was accused of being anti-Semitic and racist. Among America's hatemongers, including Gerald L. K. Smith, he was labeled "the terrible Swedish-Jew," the "Kike's Ike," and the "Jew's Front."

Ike Had Been a Democrat!

One of the truest allegations, and perhaps one of the most unnerving to right-wing Republicans and left-wing Democrats alike, was that Eisenhower had once been a Democrat. At a press conference on January 10, 1952, President Truman announced that, as a youth in Abilene, Eisenhower had once been a precinct worker for a Democratic candidate for governor. The story hit the front pages of the morning *Kansas City Times* but was corrected to deny that Eisenhower had ever campaigned for a Democrat, but rather reported that nineteen-year-old Ike had been a speaker at a "small" Democratic dinner/rally in Abilene in November 1909. This was his stem-winding "Student in Politics" speech, in which he denounced the antiprogressive, gold-bug eastern Republican establishment. Shading the truth, the *Times* reported that his talk was more a student report than a political speech. He had not intended "to arouse any great Democratic fervor," the paper asserted. "Eisenhower's talk was on the theme of the importance of education in politics. . . . It appears that his talk was strictly non-partisan." Whether or not Eisenhower had ever campaigned for Democratic candidates has never been established. The *Times* editor was absolutely on target by emphasizing Eisenhower's belief in the importance of education to developing citizenship, but he completely missed the origins of the progressive Republican that Eisenhower was to become. What is stunning to the historian is the similarity between the "Student in Politics" speech, written in 1909, and Eisenhower's dissertation on governance composed for Bill Robinson in 1952, forty-three years later, just a month after Truman's press conference.

Candidate Eisenhower

Eisenhower resigned from the army on April 11 and returned to the United States on June 1, 1952. On June 4, he formally announced his candidacy for the presidency before a rain-drenched crowd in Abilene. On the same day, he dedicated the cornerstone of the Eisenhower Museum and Library. His rhetoric concerning excessive taxation, bloated government, and burgeoning inflation safely covered conservative ground. But, as some observers noted, his remarks were delivered with a fervently religious tone that underscored Eisenhower's hometown nostalgia for simple virtues and an uncomplicated life. He did not hide that his was a troubled soul, living on the boundary:

Those days were essentially simple ones [he shared with his fellow Kansans]. We did not feel intimately any relationship to Iran. We did not think about needing the tin and tungsten of Malay, or the uranium of the Belgian Congo, or the tin of Bolivia. We felt rather independent and alone, and life was simple enough that we didn't have to trouble our heads too much with those things that bother us today. But now we realize the world is a great interdependent complex entity that will allow no one to enjoy the luxuries that we had then . . . the luxury of living alone and caring little for the outside. We have learned no part of us can prosper; no nation can really in the long run be at peace and have security unless others enjoy the same.

What he told the crowd in Abilene, and announced to the world, that June day was that his presidency would be a crusade to lift America's isolationist mind-set out of the nineteenth century, to confirm her post–World War II commitment to world peace, and to carry that resolve forward to confront the atomic age.

Eisenhower became a formal candidate for president barely one month before the Republican National Convention convened in Chicago on July 7. Of course, Eisenhower-for-president clubs, loosely coordinated by Henry Cabot Lodge, had sprung up all over the nation. With the support of contributors such as Sid Richardson, the campaign was not short of cash. Herbert Brownell, Dewey's campaign manager, who had learned hard lessons in former campaigns, worked diligently and effectively to secure delegates for Eisenhower. As in 1912, the Republican Party was split down the middle between the Old Guard party establishment, mostly from the Midwest and the South, who supported Robert A. Taft, and the insurgent, progressive, internationalist wing of the party, generally from the West and East Coasts, who rallied behind Eisenhower. Brownell and Lodge shrewdly outmaneuvered the Republican National Committee so that, by the convention's first ballot, Eisenhower had secured 595 delegate votes to Taft's 500. When Stassen threw Minnesota's 20 delegates to Ike, a second ballot was not necessary.

Eisenhower's election in November was not exactly a foregone conclusion, given that in 1952 the Republicans were a minority party. But he campaigned effectively, and to the Democrats' outrage, he refused to exacerbate raw tensions within the GOP. As best he could, he supported his conservative running mate Richard Nixon, made peace with Taft, refused to openly denounce smarmy senator Joseph McCarthy, and campaigned with arch-isolationist Indiana senator William Jenner. In truth, the greatest threat to

Eisenhower's victory came not from Adlai Stevenson but from the unrepentant, militant right wing of the Republican Party. Nevertheless, Eisenhower paid a fearsome price for his victorious compromise with the Republican right wing. Academic historians, especially those at Columbia University, most of whom preferred Stevenson, could never forgive him for his alleged moral hypocrisy.

On October 24, less than two weeks before the election, Eisenhower promised to "go to Korea" to find a way to end the war. That promise probably sealed the election for the general. On November 4, he won 55 percent of the vote (an Electoral College landslide of 442–89). It was a solid win for the Republicans, who also won a narrow majority in both the Senate and the House of Representatives. For the first time in two decades, the Republicans would occupy the White House and be the majority party in both houses of Congress.

Ike's Ultimate Concern

Discover a person's ultimate concern, Paul Tillich wrote in a 1957 article entitled "What Faith Is: Faith as Ultimate Concern," and you will find the foundation of a person's faith. Faith as ultimate concern, according to Tillich, "is an act of the total personality . . . the most centered act of the human mind." That is, faith as ultimate concern is faith concerned about the unconditional. Humans are unique, Tillich believed, because in addition to physical needs they have spiritual concerns, be they cognitive, aesthetic, social, or political. These spiritual concerns have the potential of becoming ultimate concerns if they are perceived as unconditional. Should citizens make national security their unconditional concern, then all other claims of faith such as benevolence, economic prosperity, family, justice, humanity, and aesthetic concerns will be sacrificed. For Tillich, faith as ultimate concern was not an abstraction. "There is no faith without a content toward which it is directed," he stated simply.

Duty was Eisenhower's ultimate concern, and his unconditional commitment to duty, as Mamie understood, defined his centered, personal self. Although he did not share Tillich's theological vocabulary, he knew that his devotion to duty occupied the center of his religious faith. It was a faith that had grown incrementally since his childhood in terms of both object and intensity. First came his devotion to family, friends, school, and community. Thereafter followed his pledge to duty to West Point, the army, the nation, and the Western alliance. Finally, he was called to the presidency to serve a transcendent duty involving governance of the United States and leadership of the free world. His call to duty was not merely a civil calling; it was also a consuming religious calling. In 1947, when he described himself as "the most intensely religious man I know," he was making both a political statement and a religious confession. In confessing the intensity of his religious faith, Eisenhower, in effect, affirmed that his unconditional duty to God and country was his ultimate religious concern.

In God We Trust, 1952–1955

M ake no mistake, the tidal wave that swept Eisenhower into the presidency in 1953 was energized by wealthy, influential men from a sector of America's power elite whose party had not occupied the White House for twenty years. Ike rode to victory with the money and broad support of corporate and business Americans who wanted peace, stability, and unity both at home and abroad. They also wanted lower personal and corporate taxes, freedom from government regulation, reduction of the "welfare state," and a government sympathetic to the financial and commercial needs of American businessmen. By and large, they were men of the same social and economic standing as those who contributed generous gifts to the American Assembly in Arden House at Columbia University and enthusiastically applauded Eisenhower's Silver Lecture. Among the political and religious beliefs they shared with the general was a common commitment to the "American way."

Prior to World War II, slightly less than 50 percent of Americans were church members. Following World War II and into the 1950s, Americans rushed to join churches in unprecedented numbers, until church membership reached almost 70 percent. For thousands of citizens who joined or rejoined congregations in the 1950s, the Eisenhowers' decision to become members of a Presbyterian church hardly seemed hypocritical or opportunistic. Norman Vincent Peale, Bishop Fulton Sheen, and Billy Graham, among others, provided the public face of this remarkable religious revival. In addition to religious publications, TV shows, and "tent" revival meetings, American religious renewal was also stoked by numerous public interest groups, including Eisenhower's favorites, the American Legion's "Back to God" movement and the Freedoms Foundation's promotion of the "American Way."

Apprehension hung over America as the 1952 presidential election approached: there was palpable tension concerning the Cold War, impatience with the deadlocked Korean War, anxiety over the threat of nuclear holocaust, and uncertainty over assuming leadership of the "free world." Just under the surface seeped uneasiness about race and ethnicity, worry about the economy, and angst that somehow Americans had lost touch with God. At the dawning of the Eisenhower era, those who voted for Ike seemed to want more than a change of political parties; many voters were searching for spiritual rebirth for their country, which they believed was losing its unity and identity.

As Kevin M. Kruse wrote in his 2015 book *One Nation under God*, "For Eisenhower, the most important thing about religion was its power to unite Americans around a common understanding of their past and to dedicate them to a common plan for their future." In the Freedoms Foundation, Eisenhower found an organization sponsored by businessmen that promoted both God and free enterprise, that is, the American way of life. With Herbert Hoover, Eisenhower helped the Freedoms Foundation write its charter. Again, with Hoover's assistance, he designed the Freedoms Foundation's *Credo of the American Way of Life*, a monument that the *Reader's Digest* generously illustrated (see p. 186, below). The foundation stones were labeled "Fundamental Belief in God," which supported a block that read "Constitutional Government Designed to *Serve* the People." Resting on this pedestal were two large tablets, shaped very much like the Ten Commandments, that listed the "Political and Economic Rights, which protect the dignity and freedom of the individual," seventeen basic rights of Americans, including the Bill of Rights and the Rights of Free Enterprise. Eisenhower hoped that this monument depicting God and the Constitution and supporting basic American rights might be displayed in Washington, DC. That did not happen, but its message did become central to his campaign.

Soon after his election, Eisenhower spoke off-the-cuff to the Freedoms Foundation board: "Our form of government has no sense, unless it is grounded in a deeply felt religious faith, and I don't care what it is," to which he quickly added, "With us, of course, it is the Jud[e]o-Christian concept but it must be a religion that all men are created equal." Of all of Eisenhower's religious comments, this ad lib became the most famous. Not surprisingly, Republican politicians, clergymen, and laity praised Eisenhower's piety and fervent spirituality, while Democrats and liberal commentators laughed at Eisenhower's apparently "bland" and "shallow" religious beliefs. Perceptively, Will Herberg, author of *Protestant-Catholic-Jew* (1955), caught the importance of the president's offhand remark.

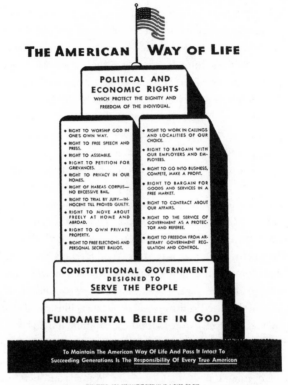

THE AMERICAN WAY OF LIFE

POLITICAL AND ECONOMIC RIGHTS
WHICH PROTECT THE DIGNITY AND FREEDOM OF THE INDIVIDUAL.

- RIGHT TO WORSHIP GOD IN ONE'S OWN WAY.
- RIGHT TO FREE SPEECH AND PRESS.
- RIGHT TO ASSEMBLE.
- RIGHT TO PETITION FOR GRIEVANCES.
- RIGHT TO PRIVACY IN OUR HOMES.
- RIGHT OF HABEAS CORPUS— NO EXCESSIVE BAIL.
- RIGHT TO TRIAL BY JURY—IN- NOCENT TILL PROVED GUILTY.
- RIGHT TO MOVE ABOUT FREELY AT HOME AND ABROAD.
- RIGHT TO OWN PRIVATE PROPERTY.
- RIGHT TO FREE ELECTIONS AND PERSONAL SECRET BALLOT.

- RIGHT TO WORK IN CALLINGS AND LOCALITIES OF OUR CHOICE.
- RIGHT TO BARGAIN WITH OUR EMPLOYERS AND EM- PLOYEES.
- RIGHT TO GO INTO BUSINESS, COMPETE, MAKE A PROFIT.
- RIGHT TO BARGAIN FOR GOODS AND SERVICES IN A FREE MARKET.
- RIGHT TO CONTRACT ABOUT OUR AFFAIRS.
- RIGHT TO THE SERVICE OF GOVERNMENT AS A PROTEC- TOR AND REFEREE.
- RIGHT TO FREEDOM FROM AR- BITRARY GOVERNMENT REG- ULATION AND CONTROL.

CONSTITUTIONAL GOVERNMENT
DESIGNED TO
SERVE THE PEOPLE

FUNDAMENTAL BELIEF IN GOD

To Maintain The American Way Of Life And Pass It Intact To Succeeding Generations Is The Responsibility Of Every True American

THIS CREDO, FOR PERMANENT DISPLAY, IS A PART OF THE BOY SCOUTS OF AMERICA-FREEDOMS FOUNDATION 1956 "GET OUT THE VOTE" AWARDS PROGRAM

*GENERAL
1956
POSTER-68*

Herberg recognized Eisenhower's expansive faith for what it was: affirmation of a tri-faith America that Eisenhower probably inherited from his years in the army. The letter *P, C,* or *J* (later *H*) was stamped on most GIs' dog tags so that chaplains of all faiths and religious persuasions could minister appropriately to stricken and dying soldiers. The chaplaincy's common and cooperative ministry to men of all faiths served as an important unifier of soldiers in combat. This lesson was not lost on Eisenhower, as he affirmed America's Judeo-Christian tradition as a unifying premise for the American way of life. As Ronit Y. Stahl has observed in her 2017 work *Enlisting Faith: How the Military Chaplaincy Shaped Religion and State in Modern America*, "As a product of the army, Eisenhower's utterance reflected the success of the modern military chaplaincy's effort to build, teach, and promote moral monotheism as the defining feature of American religion. . . . And as in the military, this American religion rested on what Eisenhower called 'the Judeo-Christian concept.'"

Because he was profoundly indifferent to denominational traditions and dogma, superficially Eisenhower became the personification of American popular piety and vague religiosity. He possessed a radiant smile and conventional virtue. But to some critics he seemed hypocritical. Radio commentator Elmer Davis observed how unbecoming it was for the president to declare July 4, 1953, a day of prayer and then go fishing in the morning, play golf in the afternoon, and play bridge with cronies into the night. Perhaps most damning for nervous detractors was the praise Eisenhower received from evangelist Billy Graham, who anointed Eisenhower the nation's spiritual leader, or the president of Republic Steel, who proclaimed that Eisenhower was "the only man since Christ who [could] bring peace to the world."

CBS commentator Eric Sevareid did not trust Eisenhower's religious sincerity. For Sevareid, Eisenhower's religious concerns were too political, too secular, and too opportunistic to be taken seriously. (Sevareid did not believe that Kennedy and Nixon were religious men either.) Thus, while conservatives embraced Eisenhower's religious rhetoric, liberals suspected that the president had found it expedient to appear religious. In general, liberals believed that Eisenhower's religion was shallow, both theologically and scripturally. But then, liberals rarely explored the nonpolitical religious culture of the American heartland.

Eisenhower had been raised in a religiously conservative and pacifist household that held politics at arm's length. His religious heritage fostered a nonpolitical approach to government—an attitude that tended to be individualistic, utopian, moralistic, and populist. In the army, he embraced the inclusivity of the Protestant-Catholic-Jewish religion, the tri-faith tradition invented in the twentieth century. (See Kevin M. Schultz, *Tri-Faith America: How Catholics and Jews Held Postwar America to Its Protestant Promise* [2011].) Until his nomination for president in 1952, Eisenhower had been so conspicuously nonpolitical—as well as nondenominational—that Democrats had actually considered nominating him for president because the tri-faith ideology shared the same theological and philosophical roots of many other Midwestern Protestants. First, there was a major strain of secular humanism that could be traced to the eighteenth-century Enlightenment philosophers. This tradition, described in Carl Becker's 1932 work *The Heavenly City of the Eighteenth-Century Philosophers*, emphasized progress, liberty, equality, brotherhood, reason, and education, the building blocks of Eisenhower's social philosophy, which he learned at home, Abilene High School, and West Point. A second strain contributing to nonpolitical Protestantism contained the strong influence of nineteenth-century pietism that blessed "private virtues such as thrift, honesty, purity, sobriety and hard work"—so-called Midwestern small-town values associated with Eisenhower's boyhood.

In the 1950s, many liberal Protestants still yearned for the heavenly city of the eighteenth-century philosophers, but their faith in the progressive perfectibility of man was shattered by the Great Depression, World War II, and the Cold War. Conservatives like Eisenhower, who had been deeply influenced by biblical pietism, on the other hand, clung to the old American civil faith in reason, progress, and basic human goodness.

There is, of course, the problem of analyzing the intellectual and religious history of Dwight Eisenhower even if one is aware of the origins and complexity of his religious journey. Supposing one dismisses the stereotype of an empty-headed Ike whose most serious reading was Zane Grey westerns, there remains difficulty in reconstructing Eisenhower's religious beliefs because he did not think systematically about religious issues. Like most Midwesterners, Eisenhower was private about his religious faith; he believed it was nobody's business but his own. Nonetheless, after 1948, while keeping his personal faith to himself, he spoke out frequently and fervently about his civil religion based on the "American way."

Americans have frequently confused the constitutional requirement for separating church and state with the national habit of conflating religion and politics. While the Constitution prohibits the establishment of a national church, it does not prevent Americans from adopting a public, civil religion. Although the American civil religion has no official priests, the public faith links national mission and destiny with the belief that America, "one nation under God," enjoys an exceptionally ordained history.

Eisenhower's civil religion was supported by three assumptions: that God warranted the dignity of every individual; that this faith established the cornerstone of American democracy (see his Freedoms Foundation monolith); and that each generation was called to defend American democracy against godless destroyers of liberty. In 1947, Eisenhower offered a confession of his growing public faith to the Daughters of the American Revolution: "Insistence upon individual freedom springs from unshakable conviction in the dignity of man, a belief—a religious belief—that through the possession of a soul he is endowed with certain rights that are his not by the sufferance of others, but by reason of his very existence."

Five years later, at the dedication of the Eisenhower Museum in Abilene, in a reprise of his inaugural address, Eisenhower rededicated himself to the civil faith of the Founding Fathers:

Faith in a Provident God whose hand supported and guided them; faith in themselves as the children of God, endowed with purposes beyond the mere struggle for survival; faith in their country and its principles that proclaimed man's right to freedom and justice, rights derived from his divine origin. Today, the nation they built stands as the world's mightiest temporal power, with its position still rooted in faith and in spiritual values.

In the first year of his presidency, Eisenhower greeted the governing board of the National Council of Churches. Speaking to them, Eisenhower compared a soldier's civic duty with a pastor's religious calling. This descendant of pacifist River Brethren and Jehovah's Witnesses acknowledged that his military profession might seem the antithesis of the religious vocation of the assembled clergy. But even before he became president, Eisenhower believed "with very great vehemence" that military duty called him to an identical purpose of the ordained clergy. While chaplains, pastors, and religious leaders served primarily under God's right hand—the hand of forgiveness and grace—the soldier served as an agent of God's left hand—the hand of law and justice. Both soldier and pastor were dedicated to the preservation of free government, which meant affirming the equality and dignity of man and, therefore, the glory of God.

Eisenhower's civil faith was simply stated. The United States government was "merely a translation in the political field" of America's deeply felt civil religion. The sacred texts of the American civil religion, he explained to the National Council of Churches, were, among others, the Magna Carta, the American Declaration of Independence, and the French Declaration of the Rights of Man. Together, these historic documents had established the principle that government recognized the equality and dignity of man. But this premise, Eisenhower stated repeatedly and consistently, would be completely baseless without the belief in a supreme being, "in front of whom we are all equal."

What one notices concerning Eisenhower's public statements about civil religion is that they are not strictly Christian and actually stretch beyond tri-faith America. There are good political reasons for this, of course, but on its face, Eisenhower's public faith harmonized smoothly with the faith of the Founding Fathers and contemporary America. Eisenhower believed that American democracy had deep Judeo-Christian roots, but not all the roots were necessarily Christian, let alone Judaic. Without belief in God, democracy was meaningless for Eisenhower. But the successful working of the democratic system did not depend upon believing the gospel message of Christian redemption through Jesus's death and resurrection. Atonement theology was not germane to American governance. In that sense, Eisenhower's America was not a Judaic-Christian nation. When Eisenhower said he did not care about the origins of "deeply felt religious faith," he meant that he did not care about the theological origin of faith, as long as it affirmed a beneficent supreme being. He was expressing a far more inclusive, but increasingly popular, sentiment than any of his critics suspected.

While he spoke often of America's Judeo-Christian heritage, this modern tri-faith tradition mostly bound together America's white population—northern, southern, and eastern European Christians and Jews. But it did not easily embrace black churches and excluded Muslim, Hindu, and Buddhist believers, among others. Ever seeking the middle of the road, Eisenhower was cautious in pushing forward and, no doubt, was politically fortunate that his religious inclinations that leaned beyond tri-faith America toward universalism were not detected and exposed by his political and religious opponents.

Prayer, Eisenhower believed, was the central religious act of his civil religion. In contrast to liturgies, sacramental systems, worship customs, and conflicting religious doctrines, prayer unites everyone who believes in one supreme being. Although so-called nonsectarian prayers may not satisfy doctrinaire believers, when couched in the rhetoric of the civil religion, prayers can both galvanize political will and mask ideological differences. It was prayer, Eisenhower believed, that most distinctly differentiated the Communist system from the American way of life. "More precisely than in any other way, prayer places freedom and Communism in opposition, one to the other," Eisenhower remarked at the 1953 lighting of the national Christmas tree. Communism could find no purpose in prayer, Eisenhower observed, because Marxist materialism denied the existence of God, the foundation of America's belief in the dignity of man. The United States, on the other hand, drew hope, strength, and, most importantly, unity from prayer. "As religious faith is the foundation of free government," he believed, "so is prayer an indispensable part of that faith."

Although prayer was central to Eisenhower's personal faith and his civil religion, he did not believe that God eternally meddled in history or acted as a transcendent "fixer-upper." He paid lip service to Americans' belief in a providential God, as have almost all presidents, but he was elusive about what impact God actually had on national or personal history. To the prayer breakfast of International Christian Leadership in February 1953, Eisenhower remarked:

> Today I think that prayer is just simply a necessity, because by prayer I believe we mean an effort to get in touch with the Infinite. We know that

even our prayers are imperfect. Even our supplications are imperfect. Of course, they are. We are imperfect human beings. But if we can back off those problems and make the effort, then there is something that ties us all together. We have begun in our grasp of the basis of understanding, which is that all free government is firmly founded in a deeply felt religious faith.

Later, at Christmas 1953, Eisenhower remembered George Washington at Valley Forge 176 years earlier. During that bitter and critical winter when the patriots' cause was near defeat, Washington's best reserve was sincere and earnest prayer, from which he and the Continental troops received new hope and new strength of purpose in the cause of freedom. According to Eisenhower's credo, God responded to community prayers petitioning for wisdom, strength, and understanding. God also received thanksgiving. Again, God helped not as a divine manager of human affairs but rather as a transcendent reminder of America's common heritage bequeathed by the founders, who cherished divinely ordained freedom. In time of crisis, prayer provided collective instruction, discernment, renewal, resolve, and unity. Public prayer fostered community wisdom and humility, courage and integrity, perspective and patience. Prayer should teach Americans "to shun the counsel of defeat and of despair, of self-pride and self-deceit." While prayer taught trust and hope, more importantly, prayer taught the security of faith. For Eisenhower, prayer, like peace, was essentially a verb, a verb that pointed toward action.

These religious sentiments were not simply the president's pious meanderings. Eisenhower gave considerable thought to the meaning and function of prayer and had concluded that prayer was the central religious act of his civil faith. Given that he was lukewarm toward liturgical religion, it is evident that prayer provided Eisenhower the spiritual equivalent of the Word and sacrament offered by the mainline churches. His was a communal faith, less focused on worship and praise of the Almighty or on securing God's blessing for the United States than on seeking through prayer community understanding of and motivation to pursue America's historic mission "under God." Consequently, Eisenhower's religious concerns could not be adequately expressed within the context of personal, denominational, or sectarian faith. His God was not as personal as that of evangelicals, nor was the Supreme Being as distant as that of the rationalists. Like his mother, Ida, Eisenhower possessed strong universalist inclinations, as his famous London Guildhall Address revealed.

Whether he celebrated American national unity, extolled the commonality of the English-speaking peoples, or promoted his vision for a United States of Europe, Eisenhower's elastic civil religion included all who shared his belief in God, who helped mankind to walk in dignity, "without fear" and "beyond the yoke of tyranny." First and foremost, then, this man from Abilene prayed to strengthen America's universal commitment to human brotherhood.

In part, his religious perspective was misunderstood in an age of neoorthodoxy and revivalism because he had no interest in the promotion of religious denominations, doctrines, theology, or "born-again" Christianity. His faith was more in line with the emerging pluralism springing from the military and business communities. As he stated in his inaugural address and repeated at Christmas, he prayed for the strength of conviction that "whatever America hopes to bring to pass in the world must first come to pass in the heart of America." Even imperfect prayer was a civic necessity, Eisenhower stated, because national shortcomings notwithstanding, prayer bound all Americans, from every walk of life, together in their efforts to reach out toward the Infinite.

Eisenhower's inaugural prayer, the first ever written by a president, faithfully reflected his civil religion. As befitting public prayer, the president's prayer was universalist in tone and content. Not surprisingly, he prayed for God's help, teaching, and strength; that is, Eisenhower prayed for the power of discernment so that his administration might govern in the interests of all the people, "regardless of station, race, or calling." And what was his authority? Eisenhower believed that the American Revolution marked a turning point, the defining moment in American history when, "to establish a government for free men and a Declaration and Constitution to make it last," the founders had professed that "We hold that all men are endowed by their Creator" with certain rights. This one sentence confirmed that American government was rooted in a deeply felt religious faith. To think otherwise, Eisenhower stated, simply made no sense.

Eisenhower's ultraserious, unconditional dedication to duty, however, could have its humorous side as well. Eisenhower's inaugural prayer had surprised almost everyone, but it also emboldened his Christian supporters. Secretary of Agriculture Ezra Taft Benson, an elder in the Mormon Church who firmly believed that the United States was a "Christian nation," suggested that each cabinet meeting begin with a prayer. Piously, Benson wrote the president, "I know that without God's help we cannot succeed. With His help we cannot fail." Liking the idea, Eisenhower agreed to begin each cabinet meeting with silent prayer—except for one Friday morning when he impetuously plunged immediately into the first agenda item. Cabinet secretary Max Robb discreetly passed Ike a note about his slipup. "Oh, goddamnit," Eisenhower exploded. "We forgot the silent prayer!"

Death—an Ultimate Concern

Obviously, there were significant political incentives for Eisenhower's religious confirmation, baptism, and membership in the Presbyterian church. Were there more traditionally religious concerns also motivating Eisenhower at this time?

Theologian Paul Tillich, in three books in the 1950s, *Systematic Theology* (1951), *The New Being* (1955), and *Dynamics of Faith* (1957), defined religion as the object of our "ultimate concern," usually centering on issues concerning being and nonbeing or death. Discern a person's "ultimate concern," Tillich argued, and you discover the person's religion: "The concern about our work often succeeds in becoming our god, as does the concern about another human being, or about pleasure. The concern about science has succeeded in becoming the god of a whole era in history; the concern about money has become an even more important god, and the concern about the nation the most important god of all."

Death, or anxiety about death, plays a central role in most world religions. Richard Marius, in *Martin Luther* (1999), wrote that Luther's Reformation theology cannot be understood apart from the great reformer's obsession with death and his fear of annihilation. Eisenhower was not obsessed with death in 1953 when he was baptized, but he had agonized over more than his share of personal loss and human carnage on World War II battlefields, the Nazi death camps, and the Korean peninsula.

For a sixty-two-year-old, his personal losses may not have been unusual, but they had been devastating. His beloved son Icky had now been dead over thirty years, but the pain never lessened. His father had been gone a decade; his dear mother, about half as long. "Gee" Gerow had been a marshal in the inaugural parade, but his wife, Katie, Mamie's best friend, had died of a mysterious illness just before Eisenhower was ordered to the Philippines. While serving with MacArthur, Ike's best friend, Jimmy Ord, had needlessly died in a freak airplane accident. And Kay Summersby's fiancé had been killed in North Africa just weeks before their wedding. Most recently, Mamie's father, John (Pupah) Doud, his surrogate father, had died in June 1951, after years of precarious health. Still, as always, the finality of death came as a shock. Characteristically, when young, Mamie tried to minimize death and push it away. For her husband, death became a daily companion.

Eisenhower's first personal experience with mass death—of the death of scores of men under his command—happened in 1918 at Camp Colt, Gettysburg, when 175 soldiers died in the 1918 flu epidemic. He was shaken, in part because he did not even have enough coffins for decent burial of the deceased. In the 1920s, he served on Pershing's American Battle Monuments Commission surveying and reporting on American European battlefields of World War I. Although it was a decade since the armistice, study of the battlefields taught him an unforgettable lesson in the terrible carnage of World War I. Later, as theater commander of American forces in World War II, Eisenhower felt personal responsibility for the well-being of his men in North Africa, Sicily, Italy, Normandy, the Ardennes forest, and beyond. More than 180,000 American officers and enlisted personnel, directly or indirectly under Eisenhower's command in the European/Atlantic theater, were killed in battle. And then there were hundreds of thousands of others killed in the war: in the London Blitz, the Falaise Pocket, the firebombing of Dresden, the destruction of Cologne and Berlin, the Nazi ovens, the Russian winters, and horrors too numerous to enumerate.

Death in World War II could be abstract but also brutally personal. With the Battle of the Bulge raging, Eisenhower learned that a close friend, Admiral Sir William Ramsay, died when his airplane crashed after takeoff from a Paris airfield. Distraught, Eisenhower wrote Mamie that war was a brutal business. "It is hard just to sit and pray," he sighed. "But be of good courage—we must hang on to the faith, and hope—and we must believe in the ultimate purpose of a merciful God."

Although not alone among United States military leaders, he had opposed the mass killing of Japanese with the atomic bomb. "It was not necessary to hit them with that awful thing," he later reflected. On a postwar low-level flight on his way to Moscow, Eisenhower was appalled as he surveyed an almost empty wasteland from the Polish border to the Russian capital. Conditions in Germany differed in scale, but not in kind, with those in the Soviet Union. Millions were dead, missing, or destitute. Cities were ash heaps and industry reduced to rubble. The concentration camps had veiled atrocities of horrific scale. It was in this World War II context of unimaginable destruction and incomprehensible inhumanity that Eisenhower had experienced an intensified stirring of religious revival.

In October 1953, Eisenhower prophetically described the deadly horrors of nuclear warfare to the United Church Women. Although Americans had escaped the physical ravages of World War II, the United States' security had disappeared with the threat of surprise nuclear attack by long-range bombers. In an atomic war, he graphically predicted, "Death and terror are symbolized by a mushroom cloud floating upward from the release of the mightiest natural power yet uncovered by those who search the physical universe. . . . In its wake we see only sudden and mass destruction, erasure of cities, the possible doom of every nation and society."

Death—and fear of death—often raises questions of human purpose and destiny, especially when death carries away the young and innocent. Traditional Christian theology has proclaimed that the "wages of sin" is death, which if true, can alone lead to anxiety and despair over the meaninglessness of life. Ida's River Brethren friends tried to soften this harsh judgment by reassuring Eisenhower's mother that, in his love and mercy, God had called the unbaptized baby Paul to his heavenly home. Ida would not accept the theology that God had killed her baby in order to "call him home," nor would Eisenhower accept such consolation twenty-five years later when Icky died of scarlet fever. His faith was shattered by Icky's death, Eisenhower later confessed to Billy Graham. Thereafter, having lost confidence in orthodox Christianity, he drifted religiously for more than thirty years. He and Mamie rarely attended church or army chapel because he could not find a minister—a soul mate—to help him spiritually.

Paul Tillich has written that one way to deal with the anxiety of death is to exclude it from "daily life to the highest possible degree." For a time, Eisenhower's ultimate concern was the army, his career, his family and friends, in roughly that order. But the anxiety over performance, promotions, status, and recognition ultimately gave way during the war to an anxiety of a higher order. He fretted to his friend Swede Hazlett that too many Americans thought that victory was a "God-given right and theirs without cost."

Eisenhower was never wracked by doubts about the Allies' eventual victory over the Nazis. He fussed with planning, to be sure, but he harbored few doubts that the Germans would be crushed ultimately if he could hold the Allied coalition together on the western front while the Soviets thrashed the Wehrmacht on the eastern front. Still, the cost in men and material was horrific, while the collateral deaths among noncombatants were almost incalculable. And it was not just death but the massive killing, not only by the Germans but also by his own men and allies, that drove Eisenhower to seek transcendental answers to why nations war against one another, answers that were beyond the call of duty to the army, the Constitution, and his country. Deep in his soul he asked what purpose was served by all the bloodshed and threat of bloodshed in the twentieth century?

His questions about the purpose of the war in particular, and life in general, were not unique. Any divinity student could have penned a similar list. "Where did we come from? Why are we here? What is the true nature of our existence? And where are we going? In time of test or trial, we instinctively turn to God for new courage and peace of mind." But while common during

The wages of sin is death, but the gift of God is eternal life through Jesus Christ our Lord. Romans 6:23

one of history's most brutal wars, Eisenhower's questions about national purpose were not naïve, bland, or simpleminded; they echoed Paul Tillich's contemporaneous *The Courage to Be* (1952). Wherein does the soldier find courage to do his duty in the face of almost certain death? Tillich wrote:

> Courage is the affirmation of one's essential nature, one's inner aim or entelechy, but it is an affirmation which has in itself the character of "in spite of." It includes the possible and, in some cases, the unavoidable sacrifice of elements which also belong to one's being which, if not sacrificed, would prevent us from reaching our actual fulfillment. This sacrifice may include pleasure, happiness, even one's own existence. In any case it is praiseworthy, because in the act of courage the most essential part of our being prevails against the less essential. It is the beauty and goodness of courage that the good and the beautiful are actualized in it. Therefore, it is noble.

Eisenhower knew well the "band of brothers" hypothesis that explained why soldiers fight and die for their buddies on the battlefield. In March of 1944 at Sandhurst, Britain's equivalent to West Point, he encouraged newly commissioned officers to become a father, as well as a leader and mentor, to their men. He knew from firsthand experience that a disciplined, principled father could mold a strongly bonded brotherhood.

But he also noted that men in foxholes, or at the moment of their death, often "turn to some higher Power for comfort and courage." The duty of officers, Eisenhower believed, was defined by a higher purpose that included support of the Allied cause. In rhetoric similar to that of Franklin D. Roosevelt, he asked the Sandhurst graduates to rally around the crusade against Hitler's hordes to defend freedom as cherished by all those of Anglo-American heritage. "We had to proclaim our faith," he explained later. "It was our faith in the deathless dignity of man."

With this confession of faith, Eisenhower again revealed the core belief, the foundation, of his civil religion. "The deathless dignity of man," as understood by Eisenhower, was the eternal truth for which soldiers could die and nations should battle evil. In Tillichian terms, this transcendent principle could demand unconditional, "unavoidable sacrifice" in defense of one's own being. No dictator, no earthly power, could ultimately crush human dignity. But although guaranteed by Providence, each generation of God's children was called to affirm that human dignity sanctified and ennobled life. The courage to be faithful even unto death sprung from his confidence that no battle monument raised on his grave could be more beautiful than one inscribed "He served his country in selfless obedience to his duty."

Eisenhower's favorite biblical passage was from Psalm 127:

Except the LORD build the house, they labor in vain that build it; except the LORD keep the city, the watchman waketh but in vain.

The psalm not only affirms the sovereignty of God but also emphasizes that humans have a divine responsibility to discern and implement God's will on earth. Ida had taught Eisenhower similarly. The New Testament, of course, also highlights the importance of human endeavor ("For we are . . . created in Christ Jesus unto good works" [Eph. 2:10]), but Eisenhower characteristically favored the more inclusive, Old Testament, version of this religious call to prayerful action.

One Nation under God

Eisenhower responded positively to two initiatives advocating public recognition of God's Lordship over the United States. The first involved adding two words, "under God," to the Pledge of Allegiance to the American flag. Originally written in 1892 by Francis Bellamy, a Baptist preacher and socialist, the pledge was not officially endorsed by Congress until 1942. Reflecting America's reconciliation after a bitter Civil War, Bellamy's original pledge promised fealty to "one nation indivisible." At the onset of the Cold War, however, patriots suggested that God be recognized in the pledge as an affirmation that a higher power blesses and guides American government and society. The Knights of Columbus were especially active in promoting the change, but nothing came of the idea until Eisenhower entered the White House.

On July 4, 1950, at the Boy Scouts of America Jamboree at Valley Forge, Eisenhower lectured the boys on the meaning of the Pledge of Allegiance. Its simple words summarized the core of the "American code," he told the Scouts. And it was imperative during the Cold War "that every American be proud to proclaim his loyalty." Eisenhower pulled no punches in describing the Communist threat to the assembled boys: "Those who seek to destroy free government use every means to gain their ends—the brute force of weapons; the sneak attack; the brazen lie of propaganda; the infiltration of traitors; the false promises that conceal black designs. They plot to confuse, weaken, divide or cripple those who support the principles so clearly and sharply defined on this day in 1776."

Celebrating Abraham Lincoln's birthday in February 1954, Eisenhower attended services at the New York Avenue Presbyterian Church and sat in the Lincoln pew. The Reverend George MacPherson Dockerty's sermon, "A New

Birth of Freedom," featured Lincoln's Gettysburg Address, from which he concluded that America's strength lay not in its military might but in its "spirit
and higher purpose." Unfortunately, Dockerty observed, there was nothing
unique in America's Pledge of Allegiance—it could be the pledge of almost
any nation. What was missing in the pledge was the affirmation of uniquely
American values. Promoting Lincoln's civil religion, Dockerty asserted that
Lincoln's phrase "under God" was the defining religious concept that characterized America's historical destiny.

Not surprisingly, Dockerty's sermon resonated deeply in Eisenhower's
thoughts. He enthusiastically endorsed Dockerty's proposal, and the following Monday arranged for a bill to be introduced in Congress to amend the
pledge to incorporate Lincoln's words. On June 14, 1954, Eisenhower proudly
signed a joint resolution of Congress amending the United States Flag Code
to include the words "under God" in the Pledge of Allegiance.

"From this day forward," Eisenhower remarked at the signing, "the millions of our school children will daily proclaim in every city and town, every
village and rural school house, the dedication of our nation and our people
to the Almighty."

"In God We Trust"

Similarly, about a year later, Congressman Charles E. Bennett (D-FL) introduced a bill to add "In God We Trust" to all United States' coins and currency. Bennett had been an isolationist as a college student at the University
of Florida but fought valiantly against the Japanese in a guerilla force on
New Guinea. Nelson Rockefeller, a special assistant to the president, alerted
Eisenhower about Bennett's proposal. Rockefeller advised that legislation
might not even be necessary if Eisenhower decided to approve the motto
on his own. At first, Eisenhower was interested in Bennett's idea but not
enthusiastic.

The motto "In God We Trust" had a long history. It first appeared in an
obscure stanza of "The Star-Spangled Banner," written by Francis Scott Key—
"And this be our motto: In God is our Trust." During the Civil War, Northern
pastors urged Secretary of the Treasury Salmon Chase to inscribe "In God We
Trust" on US greenbacks and coins as a declaration that the Almighty favored
the Union cause in the Civil War. In 1864 (expanded in 1865) Congress authorized Treasury to inscribe the motto on various coins, a practice that lapsed

after the war. Theodore Roosevelt wanted to abandon the motto altogether because he thought the inscription on American coins was sacrilegious. But the motto gradually returned so that, by 1938, it appeared on all US coins but not on paper currency.

When it became apparent that there was strong support in Congress for Bennett's bill, Eisenhower warmed to the idea. Bennett reflected widely shared beliefs, including those of the president. "Nothing could be more certain," Bennett proclaimed to the House, "than that our country was founded . . . with a firm trust in God." The motto "In God We Trust" was indigenous to the United States, Bennett believed. So that no one could misunderstand his motive, Bennett invoked the Cold War to counter the Soviet threat to American values. "In these days when imperialistic and materialistic communism seeks to attack and destroy freedom, we should continually look for ways to strengthen the foundations of our freedom." Adding the motto to all United States money would serve as a public confession and a "constant reminder" that Americans believed that their economic and political fortunes received the blessing of Providence.

Bennett's bill sailed through the Democratic Eighty-Fourth Congress, with the House giving the coinage and currency proposal an enthusiastic voice vote. As a follow-up, in July 1956 Congress sent a companion measure to the White House declaring "In God We Trust" the national motto, replacing the unofficial motto *E Pluribus Unum* (One Out of Many) that appeared on the Great Seal of the United States.

Unintentionally, but ironically, in their Cold War scramble to affirm that God was on America's side, both the president and Congress undercut two of the nation's most important proclamations that the United States stood as one people in opposition to international Communism. By downplaying that the United States was "one nation indivisible" in the pledge and by shoving aside "One Out of Many" as a national motto, Eisenhower inadvertently affirmed the primacy of a higher authority at the expense of the Union.

Eisenhower would have been dismayed had he thought these measures fostered divisive religiosity in American partisan politics. "In God We Trust" and "under God" were, after all, embedded in America's historical heritage. From the beginning, Americans had been an intensely religious people. In the Declaration of Independence, references had been made to "Nature's God," the "Creator," "Supreme Judge," and "Divine Providence." In his Gettysburg Address, Lincoln echoed the faith of most Americans, north and south, that they were a chosen people, a nation under God, whose destiny was blessed by Providence. But fundamental to Eisenhower's civil religion was the belief that God not only blessed the nation but also conferred human dignity on each of its citizens. If that idea were lost, such as occurred in Nazi Germany, the nation would be doomed. In Eisenhower's mind, affirmation of God and country was not a violation of the separation of church and state but the central concept of American democracy.

Importantly, Eisenhower echoed his predecessor, Harry Truman, who also believed that "religion and democracy in this country have risen side by side. They have mutually strengthened each other." Both Truman and Eisenhower supported the Advertising Council's "Religion in American Life" program. In his radio address in October 1949 promoting "Religion in American Life," Truman confirmed that Americans were strong enough to meet the challenge of the Cold War. "We are strong enough," the president reported, "because we have a profound religious faith. The basic source of our strength as a nation is spiritual. We believe in the dignity of man. We believe that he is created in the image of God, who is the Father of all."

Truman's civil religion sentiments, of course, were almost identical to Eisenhower's, which only underscored just how much Eisenhower's civil faith was in the American mainstream. Speaking at the New York Avenue Presbyterian Church in April 1951, Truman observed, "Divine Providence has played a great part in our history. I have the feeling that God has created us and brought us to our present position of power and strength for some great reason."

In concert with his predecessor, Eisenhower believed Truman's "great reason" was the containment of materialistic, nonbelieving Communism. The amendments to the pledge and the motto sailed through Congress and were overwhelmingly supported by the American public, their political leaders, and the clergy. Understandably, Eisenhower believed he had positioned himself in the middle of the road in terms of the proper relationship between religion and the state.

For the most part, Americans strongly support the constitutional principle that mandates the separation of church and state. They normally expect their presidents to be religious, however, and believe they should be Christian. Concurrently, they also expect the federal government to be neutral by not favoring one denomination over another. A neutral but tolerant government should not only protect freedom of worship but also foster religious liberty. All presidents are expected to maintain liaison with mainstream religious bodies, and from time to time may address religious conferences and corre-

spond with religious leaders. Observing traditional Christian holidays, deco-
rating the White House for Christmas, and issuing annual proclamations for
Thanksgiving Day are traditional presidential functions. Eisenhower observed
all these roles as well as answering thousands of religious letters from Americans accustomed to swamping presidents with questions about their favorite
Bible verse or favorite hymn.

Eisenhower and Dulles

As early as December 1949, Eisenhower and John Foster Dulles shared personal views about American politics, the religious foundation of government,
and the possibility of Eisenhower running for president. Both believed American politics were undignified and degrading. While running for office, one's
beliefs were inevitably distorted and one's character was almost certainly
smeared. Yet Dulles, a Presbyterian, also believed that democracy as practiced
in America was the political expression of religious conviction. Eisenhower
agreed that "government is some kind of religious belief . . . [but] it doesn't
necessarily have to be Christian." In effect, they confessed to one another
that preservation of American democracy was their ultimate concern. For
each, politics embodied the demonic reality of human governance, while democracy was a divine gift of salvation for all humankind. When Dulles gently
encouraged Eisenhower to run for president, the conflicted general sighed
that he was anxious to do his duty. During the subsequent 1952 presidential
campaign, Dulles served as Eisenhower's foreign policy advisor. Although
Dulles's foreign policy views differed somewhat from Eisenhower's, religiously
they complemented one another, and Dulles also provided a religious bridge
between the Roosevelt/Truman and Eisenhower administrations.

Eisenhower, Dulles, Roosevelt, and Truman shared similar views about
a providential God, human dignity, and the religious beliefs and intentions of the Founding Fathers. Most importantly, they agreed that World
War II and the Cold War were, for the West, a life-and-death religious
struggle of Western (a.k.a. Christian) civilization against a materialistic
atheistic ideology. Dulles, like Eisenhower and Truman, believed that in
time the Soviet Union would collapse from its internal contradictions.
In the meantime, however, he favored a militant policy of containment
to counter Soviet expansionism. Eisenhower's appointment of Dulles as
secretary of state came as no surprise because Dulles was widely regarded

as the Republicans' most knowledgeable expert on foreign affairs. Given Eisenhower's temperament and dialectical religious worldview, Dulles proved an excellent choice. During Eisenhower's White House years, the president and Dulles were both members of the Reverend Elson's National Presbyterian Church.

Special Assistant for Religious Affairs

At the onset of his administration in 1953, the president's staff handled religious matters on an ad hoc basis similar to how previous administrations had dealt with them. There was no White House office of religious affairs. Presidential Chief of Staff Sherman Adams and Press Secretary James Hagerty, both Episcopalians, coordinated the administration's religious policy, usually in consultation with the president. Hagerty, of course, orchestrated Eisenhower's public relations with the press. The White House staff coordinated speech writing, appointments, and meetings of a religious nature while presidential assistant Kevin McCann (United Church of Christ) was responsible for writing several religious speeches and proclamations. Columnist Emmet Hughes and Bernard Stanley, who were Roman Catholics, and Maxwell Rabb, of the Jewish faith, usually handled matters pertaining to their respective religious persuasions.

One of the first manifestations of the new administration's interest in religion was the appointment of historian Edward P. Lilly to the National Security Council's Operations Coordinating Board (OCB). An academic, Lilly earned his PhD in American colonial history at Catholic University of America. Among his assignments on the OCB, Lilly explored how religion might be used as a tool in psychological warfare against Communism. Lilly proposed that the administration support the Orthodox Church both within the Soviet Union and on its fringes. In this way, religion might be used not only to help contain Communism but also to undermine its hold on captive peoples.

At the suggestion of Minnesota congressman Walter Judd, in 1954 the United States Information Agency (USIA) appointed Earlham College professor of religion Elton Trueblood chief of religious policy. Rev. Elson of the National Presbyterian Church was so enthused by this that he invited the anti-Communist professor to be the guest preacher at a service attended by the president. A Quaker, Trueblood had worshiped often with Eisenhower's Republican predecessor Herbert Hoover. Much to the administration's surprise, opposition to Trueblood's appointment came not from the religious left but from the fundamentalist right. Upset that Trueblood, a former chaplain at Stanford, was not sufficiently conservative, the fundamentalist American Council of Christian Churches accused Trueblood of advancing the ecumenical policies of the National Council of Churches. The fundamentalists demanded that Trueblood be fired and his office abolished in keeping with the separation of church and state.

Taken aback, the administration assured its religious critics that the USIA had no domestic agenda but instead was dedicated to opposing Communism by rallying believers of all faiths, Protestant, Catholic, and Jewish, along with sincere believers in Buddhism and Islam, against a common foe who would attack religion everywhere in the name of atheistic materialism. The goal of the Eisenhower administration religious office was to forge a Cold War united front against Communism analogous to the Allied effort that had defeated Nazism. They were surprised but undeterred by this unexpected opposition. With the cooperation of the CIA, the State Department, and the USIA, undisclosed funds were distributed behind and along the fringes of the Iron Curtain to bolster religious opposition to the Soviet regime, including support for the Lutheran bishop Otto Dibelius of Berlin; Bishop Athenagoras, patriarch of Istanbul; Cardinal Mindszenty of Hungary; and South Vietnam's Ngo Dinh Diem, the Roman Catholic leader of his Buddhist country.

The ad hoc management of White House religious matters ended in July 1956 when Eisenhower appointed Frederick E. Fox to be his special assistant for religious affairs. Fox was the first ordained minister appointed to the White House staff since Presbyterian Rev. Edward D. Neill served as Lincoln's correspondence secretary. Rev. Fox, who served as pastor at the Williamstown (Massachusetts) Congregational Church, had earned a bachelor's degree from Princeton and a divinity degree from Union Theological Seminary in New York City. In addition, he had studied sociology and rural economics at Cornell, served four years in the US Army Signal Corps, and served as a pastor in Zambia and for congregations in Arizona, New York, and Ohio. In the Signal Corps he rose from private to captain while serving from Normandy until VE-Day.

Perhaps Eisenhower was attracted to Fox because he was an Old Testament scholar. Fox was recruited to the White House staff during the 1956 presidential campaign by speechwriter Kevin McCann, whom he had met in Ohio when McCann was president of Defiance College. Initially, Fox believed he was hired for his writing skills and not because he was a clergyman. But Fox quickly gained Eisenhower's confidence because of his friendship and connections with the liberal religious establishment, and thus his ability and willingness to communicate with and, if needed, challenge it.

At Union Theological Seminary, Fox had not only closely studied the theology of Reinhold Niebuhr but also counted among his friends Ernest W. Lefever, who was just beginning his teaching career at the University of Maryland after earning a PhD from Yale. Lefever, who would become a prominent foreign affairs expert and founder of the Ethics and Public Policy Center in Washington, wrote a biting and, in Fox's opinion, gratuitous essay, "The Candidates' Religious Views," for *Christian Century* comparing the religious beliefs of Adlai Stevenson with those of Dwight Eisenhower, much to Eisenhower's disadvantage.

Adlai Stevenson, Eisenhower's Democratic opponent in 1952 and 1956, was a Unitarian (as was his mother) who joined the Presbyterian church (his father's) just prior to the 1956 election. No one seemed to notice that Stevenson maintained membership in two congregations and did not become a Presbyterian until after Eisenhower had. According to Lefever, membership in the mainline Presbyterian church was about all Stevenson and Eisenhower had in common religiously. Lefever believed that Stevenson's religious heritage was more intellectual and sophisticated than Eisenhower's. Educated at Princeton and Harvard, Stevenson reportedly admired the breadth, perception, and social morality of Reinhold Niebuhr. To his credit, Lefever does not claim that Stevenson was converted to Niebuhr's worldview by reading *The Nature and Destiny of Man* or other works by the theologian: "Rather, like George F. Kennan and other men in public life, he has found in Niebuhr an eloquent and convincing spokesman for an understanding of man and history which grew out of his own experience in practical politics. Niebuhr has often been able to articulate, clarify and enrich ideas which these men held only vaguely and tentatively."

Although Niebuhr had not directly influenced Stevenson's religious thought, Lefever argued that Niebuhr provided a penetrating and accurate lens through which to examine Stevenson's religious beliefs. According to Lefever, if Eisenhower's faith was "simple, vague, fervent and crusading," Stevenson's religious beliefs, as illuminated by Niebuhr's lens, were both "more complex and more specific." Like Niebuhr, Stevenson reflected on the paradox and irony of American history. While Stevenson acknowledged the sovereignty and transcendence of God, he also stressed the limits of human wisdom and power. Stevenson's God prompted examination of human finiteness and self-interest. Because evil was pervasive in the world, morally simplistic solutions to social problems were ineffective. Lefever concluded that "Stevenson's Niebuhrian view of man and history [was] coupled with an equally Niebuhrian sense of responsibility for justice and peace."

Stevenson's "Niebuhr" versus Eisenhower's "Billy Graham"

Predictably, in Lefever's uneven comparison of Stevenson's alleged Niebuhri-anism with Eisenhower's friendship with Billy Graham, the supposed naïveté of the president's religious faith was accentuated. Rather than an-alyzed as textured and subtle, Eisenhower's thought was parodied as the antithesis of Stevenson's sensitive and ironic understanding of the human existential condition. Who could miss the contrast between the religion of the urbane, Ivy League–educated Stevenson and that of the rustic, West Point–educated Eisenhower?

At the White House, Fox was infuriated by the *Christian Century*'s partisan mixture of politics and religion at the president's expense. Fox was especially dismayed by the tendency of his intellectual friends to attribute more sub-stance to Stevenson's religious views than was warranted while denigrating Eisenhower's allegedly unexamined faith. Had Lefever compared Eisenhow-er's faith to anyone's, he should have compared it to the faith of his mother, Ida, rather than that of Billy Graham, with whom he had little in common religiously. But it never occurred to Lefever to explore Eisenhower's River Brethren heritage or the influences of the Jehovah's Witnesses during his youth, which were, in their own way, intellectual and sophisticated, but not in the way Lefever could have understood rationally or could have taken se-riously theologically.

Despite Fox's angst, however, Lefever was not entirely off base in his anal-ysis of Eisenhower's and Stevenson's views about God, man, and history. Both believed that God had created "man" in his own image and that the Supreme Being had granted all humans certain rights, freedoms, and responsibilities. They differed, Lefever argued, in their belief concerning God's relationship to mankind and on human ability to achieve social and material progress. Ei-senhower, according to Lefever, believed that God was immanent and helpful to free men, while Stevenson believed in God's transcendence and human dependency before a sovereign Judge.

These differences created important contrasts in their worldviews. Ei-senhower was more optimistic that a human had a "God-given ability to be master of his own destiny." Peace, happiness, justice, and prosperity were all within human grasp—science was a vital engine to universal progress. Human progress was thwarted by evil, selfish persons—atheists, material-ists, and Communists—who did not affirm that man was a spiritual being. In this regard, God was the source of strength who indeed was on the side of the righteous. Although God blessed American efforts to combat Communism, Eisenhower seldom asked whether he was an instrument of God's will or purpose.

In contrast, Stevenson emphasized both God's distant sovereignty and human limitations. Lefever explained that Stevenson's God was not a source of strength for "our side" but rather a source of wisdom and righteousness that not only inspired but also judged all men and nations. Perhaps nations could ultimately achieve peace by working for justice in the human community, but most likely America could only secure an imperfect peace fraught with hard problems that might never be solved. For Stevenson, America's appropriate stance before God and history was Niebuhrian, that is, filled with awe, humility, and self-examination. America's faith in the quick fix was not only tinged with arrogance and pride but was also unchristian because it ignored the need for atonement in a world drowning in sin.

Their differences were striking. Eisenhower could turn a jaundiced eye toward institutions—government, domestic and foreign; the church; labor unions; even occasionally the army and big business. But he tended to make a moral distinction between evil leaders of oppressive institutions and the people who served them in lower levels or who were victims of their misdeeds. Generally, what was needed was to "throw the bums out," whether they were thugs in Nazi Germany or corrupt politicians in Washington, DC. Stevenson was more prophetic. He believed that human institutions, especially democratic governments, largely reflected the values, morals, and aspirations of the people who supported them. "You, the people," he told his fellow Americans, were directly responsible for the corruption and incompetence of the government. In fact, government officials often served the people far better than the apathetic electorate deserved.

Fox was outraged by Lefever's depiction of Eisenhower as a religiously shallow, naïve, and simpleminded president. On White House stationery, he fired off an indignant letter to Harold E. Fey, editor of the *Christian Century*, publisher of Lefever's screed, complaining that Lefever "tries to make Mr. Stevenson look like a modest, yet profound follower of Reinhold Niebuhr and he tries to make President Eisenhower look like a boastful, superficial follower of Billy Graham." Nothing could be further from the truth, Fox asserted. The Old Testament scholar countered that the "simplicity" of Eisenhower's faith was more akin to that of King David than to that of Billy Graham. He reminded Fey that King David had also been accused of exploiting religion. Eisenhower and King David were similar, Fox continued, in that during complex times both were decisive leaders who, nevertheless, held the overwhelming affection of their people. What did Fox think was the most apt comparison? "I would say the President's religion, like David's, is about as simple as the 23rd Psalm."

Fox's deep biblical knowledge, his spiritual sincerity, his religious compatibility with Eisenhower's Judeo-Christian emphasis, his contacts among the mainline churches and the National Council of Churches, his contacts at prominent seminaries, and his vigorous willingness to promote and defend Eisenhower's civil religion were welcomed by the president. But mostly, Eisenhower prized Fox's professional confidentiality and studied avoidance of self-promotion while at the White House. Eisenhower was delighted that Fox fit perfectly into the quasi-military White House staff where the president could relate to him as if he were an army chaplain assigned to the general's staff. Soon, Fox was officially appointed as the first White House special assistant for religious affairs, whose duties included drafting the president's speeches on religious subjects, serving as a biblical resource for the president and the White House staff, answering letters about religious matters, and being a liaison between the White House and religious organizations. Fox took great care to help channel Eisenhower's religious enthusiasm in directions that did not violate the sacred principle of the separation of church and state. Perhaps more than any of the president's religious advisors, Fox helped temper Eisenhower's religious rhetoric during the president's second term.

National Prayer Breakfasts

The chief weapon against Communism in the believer's arsenal was prayer. Prayer, especially community prayer that reached out to all Americans, was the central religious act of Eisenhower's civil religion. Although his civil religion was not sacramental, it might be said that for Eisenhower, prayer itself was a sacrament—a holy act. Traditionally, Christian sacraments are religious rites instituted by Christ himself as a means of grace. As such, sacraments require an earthy substance—water in baptism and wine and bread in the Eucharist—so that invisible grace can be received and distributed through tangible elements among the congregation. For Eisenhower, the tangible elements in the sacrament of prayer were the gathering of the faithful, the posture of prayer, and the words of praise for the Supreme Being and comfort for the worshipers. Prayer, Eisenhower believed, was the most powerful means of uniting the American people spiritually and could be sung as well as spoken.

His inaugural prayer and prayers before cabinet meetings were Eisenhower's best-known innovations concerning public prayer. But he was also instrumental in establishing the Presidential Prayer Breakfast and in institutionalizing the National Day of Prayer.

Prior to Eisenhower's inauguration, Senator Frank Carlson of Kansas, a Republican, meeting with the president-elect at the Commodore Hotel in New York City, invited his fellow Kansan to attend one of the Senate's Wednesday morning prayer breakfasts. According to Carlson, Eisenhower could not have been more enthusiastic. Without hesitation, Ike replied that he would be delighted. Presumably, Eisenhower knew that the Senate prayer breakfasts were affiliated with International Christian Leadership (ICL), also known as the Fellowship, which sponsored prayer breakfasts across the United States and Canada.

Abraham Vereide founded the ICL in 1935. Vereide, a Norwegian immigrant and Methodist minister, also originated Goodwill Industries in Seattle in 1916 to help fellow immigrants. Alarmed by the militancy of the Industrial Workers of the World (the IWW, also known as the "Wobblies") union on the Seattle waterfront and the influence of socialists in municipal government, Vereide invited Christian business leaders to breakfast to pray and discuss what to do about the pernicious influence of radicals and the New Deal in the Pacific Northwest. The idea grew rapidly—in two years' time, over two hundred breakfast prayer groups were organized in Seattle. The agenda was simple. Christian businessmen and male civic leaders met for breakfast on a nondenominational basis, prayed and read the Bible together, and built trust and camaraderie to promote Christian ideals in their communities and government. Vereide's visionary principle fit neatly into Eisenhower's worldview and philosophy of prayer.

After founding breakfast prayer groups in the Pacific Northwest and elsewhere, in 1942 Vereide helped organize the first prayer breakfast in the US House of Representatives. The next year a breakfast prayer group was started in the Senate. When Frank Carlson invited Eisenhower to the Senate prayer breakfast in 1953, key members included Carlson, Karl Mundt (R-SD), Everett Dirkson (R-IL), and Strom Thurmond (D-SC).

The Senate prayer breakfast group met in the Vandenberg Room, which had a capacity of thirty-five. When the House of Representatives breakfast prayer group learned about the president's intentions to pray with the senators, they asked to be included. When word snowballed around Washington that Eisenhower was going up to Capitol Hill to pray at the ICL breakfast, requests to attend poured into Carlson's office. Quickly, Carlson realized that

the Senate's limited dining facilities could not accommodate the crowd pressing for prayer breakfast invitations. In addition, the Secret Service and the
FBI let Carlson know that bringing the president to the Capitol for breakfast
was no routine matter. Dismayed, Carlson feared he would have to cancel
the event.

Ultimately, Carlson recalled that hotel executive Conrad Hilton owed him a
favor. In May 1952, in Denver, Hilton had met with Eisenhower. The following
appointment for Ike was with Billy Graham. Carlson, who was assisting with
Eisenhower's meetings, told Hilton he could meet with Graham after the evangelist's appointment with the general. Hilton, a devout Catholic, was delighted
with his thirty-minute visit with Graham and promised Carlson he would return the favor if he could ever be of help in a Christian or religious cause. Now
Carlson collected his debt. Calling Hilton personally from his Senate office,
Carlson explained his logistical problems. Would it be possible, Carlson asked,
to use the ballroom at Hilton's Mayflower Hotel for the ICL prayer breakfast?
Oh, and by the way, could Hilton pick up the tab for the breakfast? "How many
will you have?" Hilton asked cautiously. "About 250," Carlson replied, not anticipating that the actual number would turn out to be 400.

The Presidential Prayer Breakfasts, later to become the National Prayer
Breakfasts, were among Eisenhower's major religious legacies, although the
organization and sponsorship of the breakfasts were an integral part of the
program of Vereide's International Christian Leadership. National Prayer
Breakfasts have been held in Washington, DC, every year since 1953, with the
president usually in attendance. Every president since Eisenhower has prayed
with the assembled lawmakers and dignitaries. During the first fifteen years or
so, Billy Graham often gave the opening address, exhorting the congregation
to follow Jesus Christ. From 400 attendees in 1953, the annual event has grown
to roughly 3,500 guests from over one hundred countries.

Although sensitive to having his name exploited by special interests,
Eisenhower took no umbrage at Vereide's making him a headliner in the
prayer breakfast movement. Superficially, at least, Vereide's religious movement appealed to Eisenhower because it reflected his own civil religion
values. Besides attracting men whom he admired such as Senator Frank
Carlson and evangelist Billy Graham, the Presidential Prayer Breakfasts
were both nondenominational and nonpartisan. The movement emphasized prayer, study, and discussion while sidestepping theological and doc-
trinal issues. The main religious rite was the breakfast and prayer that, above
all else, fostered fellowship among mostly conservative businessmen and
politicians.

Vereide's principal social/political agenda, besides promoting Christian values in the marketplace and government, was to energize Christians in the fight against Communism at home and abroad. All this fit neatly into Eisenhower's civil religion faith. If there were other agendas in the prayer breakfast movement besides building Christian relationships, Eisenhower turned a benign eye toward them.

National Day of Prayer

Not as successful as the Presidential Prayer Breakfast, and also of great disappointment to Eisenhower, was the president's initiative to institutionalize the modern National Day of Prayer.

Days of prayer were among the most historic traditions of the American civil religion and were begun in the British colonies by New England Puritans who proclaimed days of prayer and fasting. In the American civil religion, days of prayer and fasting, although sometimes observed in the spring, were related to proclamations of thanksgiving normally celebrated in the fall. The Second Continental Congress and Congress under the Articles of Confederation regularly proclaimed days of prayer and fasting, as have presidents of the United States from time to time.

In 1863, following the pivotal Union victory at Gettysburg, President Abraham Lincoln proclaimed a day of thanksgiving for the last Thursday of November. Sarah Hale, editor of *Godey's Lady's Book*, urged the establishment of a national holiday of thanksgiving, and Lincoln believed such a day might help bind the wounds that the North had suffered in the Civil War. Lincoln's proclamation, written by Secretary of State William Seward, not only offered thanksgiving for the nation's "deliverance and blessings" but also offered "humble penitence for our national perverseness and disobedience."

Thereafter, prayer days for fasting, reflection, and repentance generally fell into disuse until 1952, in the midst of the Korean War, when Billy Graham called for American leaders everywhere to fall on their knees in prayer before almighty God. "What a thrill would sweep through this country," Graham prophesied, as hope and courage were rekindled by a day of prayer. Eager to show the world, and their constituents, how the United States differed from the Soviet Union, Congress quickly passed by unanimous consent a joint resolution establishing a National Day of Prayer, other than Sunday, on which Americans could turn to God in prayer and meditation in their churches or as individuals. Congressman John F. Kennedy and Senators Lyndon Baines Johnson and Richard Nixon were among the supporters of the measure. Thereafter, befitting the civil religion observance that it was, President Truman proclaimed July 4, 1952, as the first National Day of Prayer under the mandate of Congress. In his proclamation, Truman encouraged Americans in their churches, homes, and hearts to "beseech" God for wisdom, strength, and patience, prayer themes that accorded nicely with Eisenhower's beliefs.

The following year, 1953, the newly inaugurated Eisenhower chose the same day, July 4, to observe the second annual National Day of Prayer. Like Truman, his proclamation cited the text of the Declaration of Independence, in which the signers had invoked "the protection of divine Providence" with faith and humility.

Unlike Truman, or any other president, for that matter, Eisenhower referenced Abraham Lincoln's 1863 proclamation appointing a day for national prayer, humiliation, and fasting. Quoting Lincoln's "Proclamation Appointing a National Fast Day" in April 1863, Eisenhower's 1953 "Proclamation Appointing a National Day of Prayer" observed that "it is the duty of nations as well as of men to own their dependence upon the overruling power of God, to confess their sins and transgressions in humble sorrow, yet with assured hope that genuine repentance will lead to mercy and pardon."

It was uncharacteristic for Eisenhower as a disciple of American civil religion to call for a collective confession of sins and repentance. In fact, no modern American commander in chief could ask proud Americans to fall on their knees to ask forgiveness for national sins, domestic or foreign. Following World War II, perceiving themselves as the saviors of Western civilization, Americans generally believed the United States was not only the most powerful nation but also the most successful democracy in history. How incongruous it would have been to expect triumphant Americans to wear sackcloth and ashes to confess their sins during the National Day of Prayer.

Sitting next to the president in church one Sunday, Fox almost shuddered when he heard Eisenhower confess the very sins that he was accused of committing by political opponents and media critics: "We have left undone those things which we ought to have done, and we have done those things which we ought not to have done. And there is no health in us." What if a religiously zealous and ethically unprincipled congressional committee took the president's confession of sin seriously and literally? Fox could not "imagine a modern President beating his breast on behalf of the Nation and praying 'God be merciful to us sinners.'"

Lukewarm citizen turnout for the National Day of Prayer deeply disappointed Eisenhower. It was unrealistic to expect Americans to flock to their churches in droves on the Fourth of July. Because Independence Day fell on Sunday in 1954, Eisenhower was free to pick another date for the day of prayer, so he chose a day in late September. In 1955, the National Day of Prayer, celebrated on October 26, was overshadowed by the fact that Eisenhower was still recuperating at the Fitzsimons Army Hospital in Denver from his September heart attack. The 1956 national prayer day, on September 12, was dominated by the presidential election campaign.

On October 2, 1957, no longer distracted by his health or partisan politics, Eisenhower and Mamie attended a special prayer service at National Presbyterian Church. Attendance was sparse, and the president felt as though he were praying alone. Back at the White House, he demanded that Fox explain why the National Day of Prayer had been a dud. Fox checked with the State Department. Had the president's proclamation been circulated? Had there been press coverage or other publicity? Fox's report back to the president was not encouraging.

Indeed, the State Department, discouraged by the dismal press coverage of the 1956 National Day of Prayer, had on its own initiative mailed out over fifty proclamations to religious publications and press services. While some religious journals had published the proclamation, it received scant notice in the popular press. (The *New York Times*, for example, buried the notice at the bottom of the society page.) The publicity had been so poor in 1957 that Presbyterian churches generally had given no notice to the National Day of Prayer in their Sunday bulletins. Franklin Clark Fry, president of the United Lutheran Church in America, admitted that he had not even received a copy of the proclamation. Embarrassed, Fry admitted that he knew little about the day of prayer. Fox concluded his report to the president that the National Day of Prayer simply had zero grassroots appeal.

Fox identified three shortcomings of the National Day of Prayer. The first, lack of publicity, he had already discussed with Eisenhower and the State Department. The problem was not a failure to get the word out, but rather that the president's proclamations had fallen upon barren ground. Fox knew well that parish ministers planned their church calendars more than a year in advance, but because the National Day of Prayer had no fixed day, or even month, it was impossible for ministers to anticipate from year to year when the event would take place.

More serious than the lack of publicity or wandering dates was the fact that many ministers thought the National Day of Prayer lacked focus. Rev. Morgan

Noyes, Fox's former professor at Union Theological Seminary and author of his favorite book on prayer, noted that most of his colleagues were very uncertain about the purpose of the National Day of Prayer. There were numerous prayer days during the church year, Noyes reminded Fox, all dedicated to a clear purpose such as missions or hunger. Eisenhower's proclamation, on the other hand, seemed to be a vague call for Americans to pray on a special day for those things that Christians should be praying for daily. Noyes stated his criticism succinctly: "The Proclamation for a 'Day of Prayer' seems to lack an occasion and any definite aim, any special objective."

The problem was that when Congress mandated the National Day of Prayer in 1952, it provided no specific reason why Americans should gather for a government-sponsored prayer day in their churches and homes. The mandate itself seemed manifestly reason enough. The latent purpose of the National Day of Prayer, of course, was to announce to the world that Christian America stood as a mighty bulwark against international Communism, but that motive was too theologically problematic to trumpet openly in a nation that avowed separation of church and state. And, of course, even Eisenhower did not believe the United States was a "Christian nation." Fox advised Eisenhower to use the national prayer day as a vehicle by which to focus on America's spiritual heritage and strength. Just as Thanksgiving was set aside as a day of thankful prayer for America's *material* blessings, so the National Day of Prayer could be a day of prayer for America's *spiritual* blessings, and if scheduled in October, it might dovetail with United Nations Day, Bible Week, and Worldwide Communion Sunday, among others. In other words, the president should find a good date and inclusive purpose for the National Day of Prayer and stick with it.

Eisenhower liked Fox's idea of focusing on America's spiritual heritage and strengths as a purpose for the National Day of Prayer. To his friend Emmet Hughes at *Time-Life*, he confessed that he wanted greater attention placed on America's spiritual values. He knew that such an effort should not be couched as a struggle between freedom and Communism. But at the same time, he believed that Americans were too focused on their material blessings, especially "bombs and machines and gadgets as the arsenal of our national and cultural strength." What was missing in America's pride about being the most powerful nation on earth was the fact that democracies, indeed all civilizations, were founded on religious faith and values. What he had learned in World War II was that America's most potent force was spiritual. The Founding Fathers affirmed that God was the author of individual rights—and it followed that the declared purpose of government (and World War II) was to secure those God-given rights. As he had stated before: "Without God, there could be no American form of government, nor an American way of life. . . . Recognition of the Supreme Being is the first—the most basic—expression of Americanism. Thus, the Founding Fathers saw it; and thus, with God's help, it will continue to be."

Eisenhower could not have been clearer about the foundation of his civil religion faith: although democracy may not be God's preferred form of human government, nonetheless, without God, democracy, as Americans knew it, was impossible. In some way, he believed, this is what the government-sponsored National Day of Prayer should be about.

Civil Religion and Eisenhower's "Simple" Faith

There is no doubt that Eisenhower's civil religion was "simple," if simple is defined as uncluttered by dogma and uncomplicated in worship. But however simple, his faith was not vague. One of his public critics, William Lee Miller, a professor of theology at Yale University, complained that Eisenhower's religious rhetoric was dominated by pious generalizations about the need to believe in and have faith in ideals greater than ourselves—ideals like honesty, integrity, decency, fair play, service, and duty. Like many of his fellow Americans, Miller quipped, in his 1964 *Piety along the Potomac*, Eisenhower was a "very fervent believer in a very vague religion."

Miller was correct that Eisenhower's civil religion was not supported by a theologically impenetrable deity, nor infused with mysticism and supernaturalism or informed by studies at a prestigious theology seminar. But his civil faith was consistent with the religious beliefs of Thomas Jefferson and the eighteenth-century philosophes who embraced the idea of progress, guided by Providence, that had historically advanced Western civilization. Free government guaranteed by the Constitution of the United States, Eisenhower believed, was the embodiment of the founders' collective religious faith that God had imbued all citizens with basic human rights. In turn, the principal duty of constitutional government was to preserve man's God-given rights. He had repeatedly stated these basic precepts since 1945.

Anyone who missed his message simply had a deaf ear regarding Eisenhower's religious beliefs. He stated repeatedly that every person was born with a soul endowed with inalienable rights that no one had the right to take away. At the Jewish Theological Seminary of America, he emphasized that both Jews and Christians believed that "although man is made of the dust of the earth, having had the breath of life breathed into him, he is a living soul." That doctrine, learned "at our mothers' knees," he explained, was the fundamental religious belief that Americans would fight to defend against fascist paganism to the right and communistic atheism on the left. Again, at Franklin and Marshall College, he outlined his civil faith carefully, albeit inelegantly: "Our concept of government is based upon human dignity, a belief that man has a soul, and our system, I think, springs out of this. We believe in the man as a dignified entity, the possessor of certain rights, mainly because he is born. We can never forget that men have fought, bled, died, and suffered to establish that truth and hand it down to us."

Eisenhower's spiritual emphasis was never intended to foster religion for its own sake. It was his brother Milton who had convinced him that the fundamental differences among cultures were not political or economic but religious. The universal spirit of religion could bring unity to the nation and peace to the world. But promoting the universal spirit of religion alone would not suffice. Eisenhower reminded Stanley High, senior editor of *Reader's Digest*, that in addition to spiritual renewal, efforts to promote world peace must focus on fulfilling the personal needs of spiritually longing individuals, including offering them basic education while reducing poverty, homelessness, and hunger—all impediments to human dignity and freedom.

In his 1959 book *The New Shape of American Religion*, theologian/historian Martin Marty succinctly summarized Eisenhower's religious creed:

I believe in democracy.
A democracy cannot exist without a religious base.
Free government is the expression of a deeply felt religious faith.
You cannot simply explain free government in any other terms than religious.
This is the faith that teaches us all that we are children of God.
This faith teaches us that our ideals of democracy and freedom . . . are eternal laws of the human spirit.
The founding fathers wrote this religious faith into our founding documents . . . they put it squarely at the base of our institutions.
Happily, our people have always reserved their first allegiance to the kingdom of the spirit.
America is the mightiest power which God has yet seen fit to put upon his footstool.
America is great because she is good.

Marty noted that Eisenhower was president of all the people. His private faith, if it did not impact public policy in any way, would be of little historical interest. His public faith, on the other hand, was highly consequential and problematical in that it created confusion among people of traditional faith. Because he used religious rhetoric that sounded Christian, churchgoers often failed to realize that Eisenhower's civil creed was "not a witness to God who is the Father of Jesus Christ, but a witness to God who is the Father of Demos— the democratic spirit of the nation." Marty noted correctly that Eisenhower did not conflate his civil faith with the tri-faith Judeo-Christian tradition.

By the time he ran for president in 1952, Eisenhower had honed his public confession of civil faith. In his last campaign speech in Boston on November 3, Eisenhower proclaimed that the American creed teaches us that we are all children of God. "It teaches us the divine origin of each man's dignity. It teaches us the sublime meaning of our brotherhood under His Fatherhood. This faith teaches us that our ideals of democracy and freedom . . . are eternal laws of the human spirit." Fighting to defend these eternal laws of God against ruthless, aggressive despotism in North Africa in 1942 and beyond into the Cold War is what made war against tyranny a holy war, a *crusade*, as Eisenhower was wont to call it.

His father's mantra, "religion, placed in man by God, is most natural to him," resonated in Eisenhower's soul. His belief that God endowed the human spirit gave Eisenhower courage to believe that the United States continued to be a beacon of hope for all mankind. America was great because America was good, Eisenhower trusted, and, in turn, if America ever ceased to be good, it would cease to be great.

CHAPTER EIGHT

One Nation, Indivisible, 1954–1958

E isenhower believed himself to be the leader of the modern Republican Party, by which he meant moderate Republicanism situated politically midway between the New Deal and right-wing isolationism. He
embraced conservative political and economic principles, as he understood
them, coupled with a strong commitment to international security alliances.
"The middle of the road is all of the usable surface," he asserted. "Both extremes—right and left—are in the gutters." Eisenhower's seemingly bland
conservatism masked a thoughtful and troubled Cold War president.

Liberal journalists frequently criticized Eisenhower for his failure to use
the president's bully pulpit to denounce McCarthyism or to champion civil
rights, two favorite causes among liberals. On the other hand, Eisenhower
revisionists have noted that Eisenhower was a "hidden-hand" president who
preferred to work behind the scenes to achieve controversial objectives.
Whether he was confronting Senator Joseph McCarthy or confirming civil
rights, political liberals contended that Eisenhower's so-called hidden hand
often had to be forced open by events not of the president's making—that is,
the army-McCarthy hearings or the integration crisis at Central High School
in Little Rock. Eisenhower's true colors about these matters seem revealed in
his oft-quoted quip, "I made two [mistakes while president], and they're both
sitting on the Supreme Court."

Was President Eisenhower a myopic president insensitive to great moral
issues, or was he a savvy political leader managing his administration with
the politics of indirection? While both interpretations of Eisenhower's presidency have enjoyed historical currency, they frame their analysis of the Eisenhower administration in terms unsympathetic to Eisenhower's own moral
imperatives.

217

No amount of revisionism, however, can transform Eisenhower's manifest conservatism into latent liberalism. Although modern Republicans might brand him a RINO (Republican in name only), politically, economically, socially, and ethically Dwight D. Eisenhower was what he seemed to be—a conservative progressive with internationalist leanings. He was not insensitive to the excesses of McCarthyism, however, or indifferent to racial prejudice. Antagonistic to extremism of all stripes, Eisenhower in 1953 believed that the United States faced greater physical, economic, and spiritual threats in the Cold War than it had during the Great Depression or from foreign enemies during World War II.

Dark Clouds of Cynicism

Eisenhower's office as pastor in chief of the civil religion did not inspire everyone. A sour note echoed through the Appalachian Mountains. Speaking to the United Auto Workers, Senator Matthew M. Neeley, Democrat from West Virginia, scornfully denounced Eisenhower as a religious hypocrite for his weekly posturing with Pastor Edward Elson on the church steps following Sunday services. Reminding the automakers that Eisenhower had not joined a church until after becoming president, Neeley complained, "Next Monday I don't want to have to see in the papers a picture of the President and a story that he attended . . . church. Away with hypocrisy."

Neeley was obviously miffed that Eisenhower gained priceless publicity by his weekly church attendance. Not excusing Neeley's boorishness, his discomfort regarding Eisenhower's religious photo ops is understandable. In contrast to the wartime news photographs that conveyed a narrative of leadership when Eisenhower visited airborne troops before the invasion of Normandy or compassion when he toured the liberated concentration camps at war's end, the church-door pictures of a grinning Ike shaking hands with his admiring pastor only portrayed religious piety without depth or substance.

Nonetheless, the Christian community and press rallied to the president's defense. Dr. Eugene Carson Blake, president of the National Council of Churches, vigorously defended the president, stating that in matters of faith no one has the right to sit in judgment of another's religious sincerity. Even in West Virginia, Neeley was criticized. The Right Reverend Wilburn C. Campbell, Episcopal coadjutor bishop for West Virginia, remarked that it was Neeley "who was revealed," not the president. "It is best to treat such statements with contempt and silence," Campbell recommended. Labeling

Neeley's speech as a "scurrilous attack," the *Lutheran Companion* indirectly affirmed Eisenhower's role as pastor in chief of the civil religion by speculating that the president's inaugural prayer, his baptism, and the Christian tone of his speeches had had a greater impact on American religiosity than most people realized. At any rate, "Neeley's tempest" subsided quickly after Ike's heart attack on September 24, 1955.

The Sacred and Profane

Neeley's attack on Eisenhower did not exactly stir up his famous temper, but it did not help quiet it either. During the spring of 1955, as pressure built before the forthcoming summit conference with the Soviet Union in Geneva, Eisenhower's fearsome temper exploded with increasing frequency and fury. Speechwriter Bryce Harlow, who witnessed some of Eisenhower's most intense outbursts, recalled that it was like "looking into a Bessemer furnace," a human Bessemer furnace that turned pink, red, and purple while belching out a stream of barracks profanity fermented through years of army life and warfare. That year he repeatedly reduced his dutiful secretary Ann Whitman to tears.

Years before, his mother, Ida, counseled her son to control his temper. He had taken her Bible lessons to heart, understood them, but never completely mastered his demonic self. So intense was his devotion to his sacred duty that when his inner self revolted against its unconditional demands, profane energy spewed forth like an exploding volcano.

The conflict between the sacred and the profane in Eisenhower, perhaps similar to that within his friend George Patton, does not imply that this intensely religious man was also a religious hypocrite. Some religious traditions believe that the sacred and the profane occupy different realms of being; others believe that the manifestation of sacred and profane within one body (an individual, institution, or nation) reflects the existential tension between the divine and demonic principles of human living.

In Eisenhower's world, there were no persons or institutions that were either, in and of themselves, sacred or profane (except, perhaps, the Nazis). That was one of the reasons he resisted religious ritual that wore a holy mask hiding the profane reality of the human temperament. His job taxed him heavily. Like a migraine headache, his temper continued to storm even as the press praised the new peaceful "spirit of Geneva" and his approval rating soared to 79 percent. Everyone agreed that Eisenhower needed a vacation.

Ironically, Eisenhower suffered his first heart attack when he was in "heaven," close by the Colorado Rocky Mountains. Visiting and painting at Byers Peak Ranch, owned by his friend Aksel Nielson, were a religious experience for Eisenhower, according to his grandson David. Certainly, the ranch and the Colorado mountains were a sanctuary for him. In August, the president and Mamie flew to the "Western White House," the Denver residence of his mother-in-law and Mamie's girlhood home, where Eisenhower was able to pursue his favorite pastimes. The visit included fishing and painting at Byers Peak Ranch and golf in Denver, where the president kept in touch with Washington, DC, through communications at Lowry Air Force Base.

Eisenhower's idyllic vacation ended on a hectic autumn day. His morning round of golf was dogged by missed phone calls from Dulles. Perturbed that his morning game had suffered, after eating a hamburger smothered in onions, he decided to play nine more holes in the afternoon. This round too was interrupted when Dulles finally made connection with a call Eisenhower thought totally unnecessary. As his temper rose, he fumed at being harried by the secretary of state; his phone calls had undermined his concentration on his game. By the eighth hole, complaining of indigestion from the onions, he quit. Calmer when he returned home, he painted, ate a light dinner, played billiards, and, tired, retired early.

Heart Attack!

Around 2:00 a.m. the president awoke with chest pain that he thought was acute indigestion—the onions again. Mamie thought he looked sick, however, and called Dr. Howard Snyder, the president's physician, who accompanied them to Denver. Arriving at 3:00 a.m., Snyder confirmed Eisenhower's acute indigestion and treated the president accordingly. It was not until noon, September 24, that Snyder suspected that Eisenhower may have suffered a heart attack. He was whisked to Fitzsimons Army Hospital, where tests confirmed that troublesome onions were the least of the president's problems. He was seriously ill with a heart condition for which, in 1955, there were few effective medical remedies other than rest, diet, exercise, and reduction of stress.

Eisenhower's heart attack raised the major question of whether he would be fit to run for reelection in 1956. Not surprisingly, he answered that question not in terms of his personal health or mortality, or the wishes of Mamie or his family, but rather in terms of his duty to his country. On September 17, he had exchanged personal and confidential correspondence with Milton concerning the 1956 elections. Regarding the inevitable speculation concerning the president's intentions, Eisenhower revealed himself to Milton, "Of course you know exactly what that decision would be unless extraordinary circumstances would convince me to the contrary." But he was perturbed to be taken so much for granted by regular Republican politicians.

His most fervent hope had been that under his leadership fresh ideas and new leadership would emerge within the Republican Party, thus cementing his political legacy. But, in his opinion, that had not happened. "Of all the defeats I have suffered," he lamented to Milton, "the one that disturbs me the most is the apparent inability to get the leadership of the Republican Party to think constructively and dynamically about the problems of the day." He could not have made a clearer statement about his dilemma, which was created by the divine and demonic principle in political history. The tendency of the political system to "lean on one frail mortal" was a manifestation of this existential tension. One week before his heart attack, he complained to Milton that everything good that he had worked for was now held hostage by the necessity that he "remain alive, healthy, strong, and accept the nomination." He had never been more prophetic in his life. Fortunately, he assured his brother, he felt better during his Colorado vacation than he had for a long time.

Running Again in 1956

As his letter to Milton revealed, Eisenhower was not only fully aware of his own mortality but also resigned to pursue a second term in order to fulfill his incomplete political agenda. But, like the good soldier he was, once an objective was within his sights, he could wait patiently—that is, he could "retain as long as possible a position of flexibility"—until pulling the trigger "at the last possible moment." Two dominant principles would determine his decision to run. The first, of course, was his concept of duty; the second, a corollary that he learned in high school and at West Point, was never to "let down" a close friend.

All the drama in the 1956 presidential race focused on Eisenhower's health and Nixon's renomination as vice president. The Reverend Billy Graham, who had urgently encouraged him to run again for president, now wrote that it was God's will that Eisenhower should retire. Because no one understands the mysterious ways of God, Graham counseled, it was best that we faithfully accept his evident decision on what was best for Eisenhower and the nation. It was not apparent, however, that this serious illness had any impact on Eisenhower's religious beliefs.

Ida's son was aghast at Graham's premonition that God had struck him down in order to forestall a second Eisenhower term. Rather, gambler that he was, he accepted the hand he had been dealt, more determined than ever to fulfill his duty if possible. Once the political issues were resolved and Eisenhower appeared fit enough to meet the rigors of the campaign, and once the Democrats nominated Adlai Stevenson to run again against the popular president, the results seemed predictable. In terms of presidential elections, Eisenhower won a landslide victory in 1956, carrying forty-one out of forty-eight states, winning the Electoral College 457 to 73, and amassing 57.4 percent of the popular vote. As Clarence Lasby has noted, to this day scholars have been loath to speculate on whether the president's health had any impact on Eisenhower's political agenda.

The Suez Crisis

Eisenhower's dictum of "never letting his friends down" was severely tested during the 1957 Suez crisis. In the spring of 1956, Rabbi Hillel Silver, a prominent American Zionist, met with Eisenhower and Dulles to encourage the United States to sell armaments to the State of Israel. Suspecting that Rabbi Silver was in fact acting on behalf of the Israeli government, Dulles, desiring to protect Eisenhower's policy of "friendly impartiality" in the Middle East, declined the rabbi's request. Later, New York's Cardinal Spellman complained that American Jews were making excessive demands on behalf of Israel. At this point, it was easier for the administration to placate Catholic apprehensions concerning American policy toward Israel than to appear to be driven by Zionist lobbyists.

Following the overthrow of Egypt's King Farouk in 1952, Colonel Gamal Abdul Nasser became leader of the Egyptian Republic. Nasser, a strong pan-Arab nationalist, sought Western support for building the High Aswan Dam on the upper Nile River. Through the aegis of the World Bank, the United States and Great Britain pledged $1.5 billion toward the huge project. The deal began to unravel, however, when Nasser purchased weapons from Communist Czechoslovakia. Perturbed that Nasser played the West against the Communists, Eisenhower angrily directed Dulles to warn Nasser that Egypt's behavior could result in the United States suspending Egypt's "most-favored-nation" status. Ignoring Dulles, Nasser promptly extended diplomatic recognition to Communist China. Consequently, the British pulled out and Congress refused appropriations for the project, thus negating the Aswan Dam deal.

In retaliation, Nasser nationalized the Suez Canal, which the British had built and, at the time, owned and maintained. As if to rub salt into wounded British pride, he also negotiated with the Soviets to save financing for the high dam project. Seizure of the Suez Canal was not only a severe blow to British pride but it also threatened to sever the vital artery that carried oil from the Middle East to the British Isles. The Israelis and the French also had deep national grievances against Nasser's regime. The Israelis regarded the Egyptians as their most dangerous Arab foe, while the French believed that Nasser was secretly assisting the Algerian rebels' fight for independence. Ignoring Eisenhower's warnings to not overreact to the nationalization of the Suez Canal, the British, French, and Israelis secretly plotted to invade Egypt, reclaim the canal, destroy Egypt's army, and oust Nasser in favor of a more friendly government. Although American intelligence verified something was afoot, America's NATO allies assured Eisenhower that no major military action was planned.

Israel launched the first attack on Egypt across the Sinai desert a little more than a week before the presidential elections. The following day, Britain and France joined the assault. Eisenhower was outraged. Tactically, he thought the war might be successful, but strategically he believed it could prove disastrous by driving an alienated Arab world into the arms of the Soviet Union. As the ostensible "leader of the free world," he was mortified that he had been kept in the dark about the invasion plans. His good friends had betrayed him. He saw no alternative but to demand the cease-fire supported by the Soviet Union at the United Nations. All around, the Suez war proved a fiasco, especially for the British and the French, whose influence in the Middle East all but evaporated.

Eisenhower hoped to seize the moral high ground by demonstrating that moral principle was of greater importance than national self-interest. But few were impressed by American altruism in this high-stakes power game over oil and regional dominance. For a time, Eisenhower won considerable good will from the Arab world, especially after he spoke at the dedication of the new Washington, DC, Islamic Center. This moment of good feeling between Americans and the Arab world proved a hollow friendship that steadily eroded in the turmoil created by continuing Israeli/Arab strife.

As a soldier, Eisenhower had developed a cynical skepticism about the rough-and-tumble American political process. He was acutely conscious that the army could be as demanding and insatiable as any special interest group. Consequently, he viewed with a jaundiced eye other militantly organized groups, such as the American Zionists, who were outraged by his appeal at the United Nations to stop the fighting.

Perhaps the most hurtful criticism came from Reinhold Niebuhr, on the Christian left, who attacked Eisenhower for ignoring European dependence on Middle Eastern oil, abandoning Israel in its struggle for national survival, turning a blind eye to the Soviet threat in the Arab world, and undermining the Atlantic alliance. Worst of all, Niebuhr likened Eisenhower's "pacifism" in the face of Nasser's belligerence to the moral blindness of American isolationists who had denied the seriousness of the Nazi threat prior to World War II.

Civil Rights

Of all the issues that darkened Eisenhower's reputation among liberals, the most cutting was his alleged indifference to civil rights. Eisenhower, a Midwesterner with close friends and financial supporters throughout the segregated South, was said to be apathetic and slow-footed when it came to promoting racial equality following World War II. Few accused Eisenhower of actually being racially bigoted, but his middle-of-the-road positions on tough political, economic, and social issues often seemed to tilt in favor of hidebound southern and rural conservatives instead of northern and urban social progressives.

The mythology concerning Eisenhower's supposed civil rights lethargy is deep and persistent. According to liberal legend, what little he accomplished was at the prodding of his attorney general, Herbert Brownell. Furthermore, he was said to have later regretted his appointment of Earl Warren as chief justice, calling it the "biggest damn fool mistake" he made as president. Lastly, because liberals persist in believing that he opposed the Supreme Court's decision in *Brown v. Board of Education of Topeka*, he allegedly missed the opportunity to play a major leadership role in racial desegregation at this important turning point in American history.

Regarding Eisenhower's record on civil rights, historian David Nichols believes it is important to evaluate what the president actually did to implement civil rights rather than to lament what he preached (or failed to say) from his bully pulpit. For the 1950s, Eisenhower's actions regarding civil rights implementation were impressive. The prevailing myth is that almost nothing was done to advance civil rights during his administration except for the *Brown* decision, and that Eisenhower ruefully implemented that Supreme Court decision.

According to Nichols, the reality "can be summarized in two sentences":

> In the 1950s, Dwight Eisenhower was more progressive on civil rights than Harry Truman, John F. Kennedy or Lyndon Johnson. Eisenhower, in partnership with Attorney General Herbert Brownell, desegregated White House events, completed desegregation of the armed forces, desegregated the District of Columbia, combated employment discrimination in the government and in businesses with government contracts, appointed pro–civil rights judges to the Supreme Court and the lower federal courts, engineered the passage of the first civil rights legislation since Reconstruction, and dispatched troops to Little Rock, Arkansas, to enforce a federal court order for school desegregation.

Additionally, Eisenhower encouraged his cabinet members to appoint blacks to important posts. In the White House, he hired a black secretary, the first African American in history to serve in the White House professionally in a position other than servant. A year into his presidency, he appointed J. Ernest Wilkins, a Chicago lawyer, to be an assistant secretary of labor, the highest subcabinet appointment ever for a black American. In the fall of 1954, while sitting in for Secretary of Labor Mitchell, Wilkins became the first black in American history to attend a cabinet meeting as an officer. Eventually Wilkins would sit on the president's equal employment committee and be appointed to the Civil Rights Commission.

Eisenhower also moved E. Frederick Morrow from the Commerce Department to the White House executive staff to serve with Maxwell Robb as a special assistant on African American affairs. While a black newspaper, the *Pittsburgh Courier*, announced that Eisenhower had appointed sixty-five blacks to professional positions in the administration, others sniffed that it was only "tokenism." But tokenism or not, Eisenhower was steadfastly following in the steps of Branch Rickey, who had elevated Jackie Robinson to the Brooklyn Dodgers in 1947. Like Rickey, Eisenhower had torn out a page in all-white history that would never again be written the same.

When Eisenhower saluted his inaugural parade marching down Pennsylvania Avenue in February 1953, it would be the last time the president of the

United States would review this triumphal procession through the heart of a segregated American capital. By 1957 and his second inaugural, the District's public schools, public accommodations, government offices, and military bases were largely free of the legal shame of Jim Crow.

When he asked Herbert Brownell to be his attorney general and when he appointed Earl Warren chief justice of the Supreme Court, Eisenhower knew that he had selected men who were committed to overturning *Plessy v. Ferguson*, the 1896 Supreme Court ruling that protected racial segregation with the principle of "separate but equal" public facilities and services. Eisenhower had already ordered the desegregation of children in the armed services' schools. The day following the *Brown* decision, he asked the commissioners of the District of Columbia to make the nation's capital a model for school desegregation throughout the United States.

A man of his times and culture, Eisenhower felt great trepidation about the looming struggle for civil rights launched by the *Brown* decision. While he did not disapprove of the *Brown* decision, if he could have managed history, he would have proceeded moderately and cautiously to implement the Court's decision. He knew segregationists in the South would fervently resist integration, perhaps violently. He knew from his days playing high school football that some resisted competing with blacks, let alone siting with them in school, riding next to them on a bus, eating in the same restaurant with them, or sharing public restrooms. Perhaps he remembered his own fisticuffs with Dirk Tyler. Most of all, he was fearful that, in reaction to forced integration, southern segregationists would close their public schools, to the educational detriment of both blacks and poor whites.

Fatefully for his reputation, in the discussions with Brownell he decided to justify his enforcement of the Supreme Court's decree as a matter of duty under the law rather than as an issue of moral imperative and social justice. In doing so, he left himself open to accusations that he was unenthusiastic about implementing *Brown*. Ultimately, there would be no middle-of-the-road position he could stake out on this explosive issue.

Eisenhower favored states' rights, but not when states' rights were in conflict with the United States Constitution as interpreted by the Supreme Court. In addition, because he believed strongly in the separation of powers among the three branches of the federal government, he refused to comment on Supreme Court decisions because he did not want to set an awkward precedent—if he expressed his opinion on one Supreme Court case, he would be pressed to comment on all controversial court decisions.

Consequently, he disappointed all those who demanded that he provide moral leadership for the burgeoning civil rights movement from the president's bully pulpit. Eisenhower did not appear to understand that the efficacy of his good works was overshadowed in the minds of his critics by his reluctance to embrace the objectives of this religiously led political and social movement. His failure to endorse *Brown* unequivocally, critics charged, not only delayed its implementation but also emboldened segregationists to resist integration to the bitter end.

Overlooked in this interpretation is that die-hard segregationists needed no encouragement from the president to resist the Court by all means possible. Eisenhower's dilemma was that the Supreme Court in its *Brown* decision had provided no guidelines for desegregating the nation's public schools. While he could exercise presidential power to integrate the military, integrate federal facilities, and enforce nondiscrimination clauses in federal contracts, he had no authority to interfere directly in the administration of local public-school districts.

Herbert Brownell knew that Eisenhower did not want to become a crusader for civil rights while president of the United States. But he also understood that Eisenhower had "strong views on the necessity of enforcing the law and . . . deep respect for the Constitution, its separation of powers, and the duties it placed upon the President." Initially, to avoid executive interference in matters before the Court, Eisenhower tried to maintain his distance from the justices. Brownell convinced him, however, that the attorney general, as an "officer of the court," had a duty to advise the justices as best he could regarding the constitutionality of racial segregation, including promoting lawful means of correcting *Plessy v. Ferguson*. Brownell knew that Eisenhower would resonate positively to the attorney general's call to duty.

Accordingly, through Brownell, Eisenhower urged the Court to adopt enforceable desegregation guidelines for the lower federal courts. Delay for the sake of delay was intolerable. Eisenhower and Brownell proposed that the courts give school districts ninety days to present acceptable desegregation plans or become subject to court-ordered integration.

In issuing its directives on implementation a year later in *Brown v. Board of Education II*, the Warren Court ignored the administration's aggressive approach by directing segregated school districts to integrate "with all deliberate speed." Without a ninety-day deadline, however, segregationists manufactured a myriad of reasons for delay, ultimately placing the burden for enforcement on the victims and their families. Incredibly, Warren publicly criticized Eisenhower for not urging compliance with the Court's orders, disregarding the fact that the Court itself had created major problems for enforcement by the Justice Department. Eisenhower did not sour on the *Brown* decision; he soured on the Court's, and especially Warren's, failure to provide workable, enforceable desegregation guidelines.

For Eisenhower, the middle of the road on civil rights dramatically narrowed. Although Eisenhower continued to affirm his belief in the equal dignity of all Americans and the rights of all American citizens to enjoy freedom and opportunity, he stopped short of endorsing the goals of civil rights organizations or of offering ringing endorsement of the *Brown* decision. Unlike John F. Kennedy and Lyndon Johnson, Eisenhower refused to make common cause with the National Association for the Advancement of Colored People (NAACP) because he regarded it primarily as a political interest group. He desperately wanted to keep to the middle ground in what was fast becoming the nation's most contentious domestic political issue.

Then, in August 1955, outraged whites lynched fourteen-year-old Emmett Till, who they alleged disrespected a white woman in Mississippi. Blacks were horrified at Till's murder, and his mother demanded that Eisenhower do something. J. Edgar Hoover, director of the FBI, cynically reported that Communists were exploiting the uproar over Till's lynching. With no jurisdiction over a murder committed in rural Mississippi, the Justice Department advised Eisenhower not to get involved. When Eisenhower remained silent, Fred Morrow, Eisenhower's black advisor, was at his wit's end that no one in the administration felt called upon to denounce the Mississippi murder. The day after an all-white jury found the defendants innocent of Till's murder, Eisenhower suffered his heart attack in Denver.

On December 1, 1955, while Eisenhower was recuperating at his home in Gettysburg, Rosa Parks, having finished work, boarded a segregated bus in Montgomery, Alabama, for her ride home. When the front section reserved for whites filled, the bus driver ordered four black passengers seated in the back of the bus, in the "colored" section, to relinquish their seats to whites. For Parks, who had recently attended a memorial for Emmett Till and two other murdered blacks, this indignity proved to be the last straw. She refused to move because she was "tired of giving in," she later reported.

Although Rosa Parks was not the first to resist bus segregation, when she was thrown off the bus, arrested, and convicted four days later of violating Montgomery bus ordinances, her case became a cause célèbre sparking the successful 381-day Montgomery bus boycott, from which Martin Luther King Jr. emerged a major civil rights leader.

At the height of the Montgomery bus boycott, nineteen Southern senators and seventy-seven representatives signed the so-called Southern Manifesto calling for resistance to court-ordered racial integration of schools by "all lawful means." Of course, the discriminatory principle of "separate but equal" defended by the Southern Manifesto also applied to public transportation, restaurants, and public accommodations. Encouraged by the Southern Manifesto, White Citizens' Councils organized throughout the South with the express purpose of challenging all integration initiatives in the Old Confederacy and its border states.

Alarmed by the strident rhetoric of the White Citizens' Councils and growing militancy of the civil rights movement, Eisenhower futilely tried to find political footing on the middle ground of this nasty national debate. First, he called for "moderation and patience." He would not dignify the Southern Manifesto as "nullification" of the Constitution, but he also warned the congressmen that he was sworn to defend and uphold the Constitution—and that they should not mistake his resolve to do his duty. Nevertheless, while affirming that steady progress had been achieved—by March 1956, more than a quarter-million black children in border and southern states were enrolled in integrated schools—he advised the need for patience, moderation, and mutual understanding. In keeping with his political temperament, he cautioned that "extremists on neither side [were not] going to help this situation."

The Southern Manifesto intensified Eisenhower's fear that, if pressed too hard, southerners would abandon the public-school system, a consequence that was simply unthinkable given its impact on rich and poor, black and white alike. He appealed personally to Billy Graham for assistance in dealing with integration issues throughout America's Bible Belt. In 1953, Graham had integrated his revival in Jackson, Mississippi, and thereafter had met Martin Luther King during the Montgomery bus boycott. With the encouragement of Representative Frank Boykin (D-AL), Graham advised Eisenhower at the White House on March 20, 1956.

Eisenhower fumed about the political cost of the *Brown* decision, because Democrats throughout the South politicized desegregation as a Republican initiative. Graham sympathized with the president's dilemma. Graham believed that the *Brown* decision had actually set back integration efforts but expected that in the end segregation was unsustainable. Graham noted that the moral values were clear, but that the social issues, compounded by fear and resentment, were much more intractable. Nonetheless, he already had scheduled meetings with southern religious leaders and was willing to carry the president's message to them.

Eisenhower followed up his meeting with Graham with a carefully composed "Dear Billy" personal letter in which he endorsed Graham's strategy of enlisting southern Christian ministers in the civil rights movement. "Ministers know that peacemakers are blessed," Eisenhower assumed, and they should also know that the most effective peacemaker is one that prevents a fight rather than someone who has to patch up a bloody quarrel. This sentiment, of course, perfectly summarized his approach to civil rights.

Religious moderates such as Eisenhower and Graham often supported social progress, in general, but then drew the line at progress bought at the cost of social strife, violence, and death. As envisioned by Eisenhower, the most explosive social issue was the integration of elementary children in the public schools. Eisenhower suggested certain themes southern pastors could emphasize that focused on the integration of adults rather than juveniles. Perhaps Graham's colleagues could champion the election of a few qualified blacks to local school boards, or to city and county commissions. And southern graduate schools could easily begin to admit black students on merit under color-blind selection procedures. Sermons promoting racial reconciliation would come to the attention of federal judges, "who themselves would be inclined to operate moderately and with complete regard to the sensibilities of the population."

Eisenhower's fantastic epistle recruiting Billy Graham to be his apostle for racial peace not only reflected the president's gradualism but also revealed his deep ambivalence regarding overreach of the federal government into local government. When he initiated integration in the army in 1946–1947, there had been stubborn resistance from many officers under his command. But at that time he did not care. Orders were orders—he could knock heads together when necessary, and, because he would be moving on, he could afford the fight.

His letter to Graham revealed how isolated he had become in the White House, an isolation amplified by the inherent difficulty of the president's receiving and giving confidential advice. When Graham could not resist sharing the president's letter with his associates, Eisenhower reminded his friend that he should keep correspondence from the president confidential, saying, "otherwise I could not have written as I did." Nonetheless, that same day Eisenhower wrote the president of the Southern Baptist Convention expressing his commitment to the twin principles of moderation and progress.

What he did not articulate well, even to Billy Graham, was his belief that America's racial issues were deeply rooted in politics, economics, and sociology. In addition, profoundly different cultures divided the races in America—a cultural divide so deep that people who called themselves Americans did not share the same memories, values, or ultimate concerns about the destiny of their country. For Eisenhower, equality of the races was actually much more than a great moral issue. Race in America roused fundamentally different religious assumptions about God's creative purpose in how the races should best live together. Eisenhower hoped that the civil religion could ameliorate America's racial divisions by uniting citizens around a common civil creed of freedom and justice based upon universal human dignity. In this regard, the segregation problem transcended American law and even the Constitution.

His confessions to his dear friend Swede Hazlett were especially revealing of how Eisenhower's civil faith shaped his understanding of America's racial crisis. First, he shared a widely held belief that laws were rarely effective if they did not represent the will of the majority of citizens. He cited the prohibition experiment of the 1920s, when he and Hazlett were young officers. Prohibition failed, he believed, because Americans were unwilling to support enforcement of the law. When emotions and religious beliefs are deeply engrained, logic and reason must ease forward carefully, mindful of human feelings, or risk tragedy rather than progress.

For almost sixty years, *Plessy v. Ferguson* had encouraged constitutionally sanctioned racial separation, including school segregation. Consequently, southern political, economic, social, and religious culture was regarded not only as fully respectable and legal by most whites, but also as thoroughly American and morally sanctified in the eyes of God. Eisenhower believed that the *Brown* decision alone could not quickly overturn threescore years of history, racism, and custom. The law, of course, was not self-enforcing. But until racial integration was accepted in the hearts and minds of white southerners, law enforcement itself was also limiting. The civil rights dilemma allowed Eisenhower no broad middle-of-the-road policy. Although he preferred to proceed with moderate enforcement and stepped-up education, in the last analysis he never dithered about what his duty required.

"But I hold to the basic purpose," he concluded to Swede Hazlett. "There must be respect for the Constitution . . . or we shall have chaos." He could not imagine a successful democracy in which every citizen "had the right to interpret the Constitution according to his own convictions, beliefs, or prejudices." This was not merely Eisenhower's political opinion but revealed the depth of the unconditional demand of his civil religion. "Chaos would develop," he repeated. "This I believe with all my heart—and shall always act accordingly."

Eisenhower's expressed hope to Billy Graham that blacks would become more politically active on southern school boards and on city and county commissions was not pious rhetoric. Since the end of World War II, civil rights legislation had regularly been introduced in Congress, but a coalition of southern Democrats and conservative Republicans had just as routinely defeated every civil rights bill. Nevertheless, in his 1956 State of the Union address, Eisenhower outlined what he thought was encouraging progress in securing civil rights, especially in Washington, DC, and federal facilities. He not only asked Congress to establish a bipartisan civil rights commission that would recommend actions for removing voting and economic roadblocks for minorities but also, for the first time, announced his readiness to sponsor civil rights legislation. For his efforts, southern Democrats accused Eisenhower of "cheap politics" for currying the favor of black voters, while civil rights leaders reproached him for sidestepping antilynching legislation or not cutting off federal funds to segregated schools.

At last, with black expectations and frustrations mounting and with violence in the South intensifying, Eisenhower turned to the Democratic-controlled Congress for help. At Brownell's urging, he endorsed the Justice Department's draft civil rights act that would strengthen black voting rights in the South. Eisenhower personally lobbied Republican senators to support his voting rights legislation. The bill would create a Civil Rights Commission, a civil rights division in the Department of Justice, but most importantly, Eisenhower's legislation would have granted power to the attorney general to seek injunctions against the violation of any civil right, especially voting. For southern Democrats, Eisenhower's civil rights bill was dead on arrival; liberal Hubert Humphrey groused that the Republicans had hijacked his legislation while the NAACP complained that the bill did not go far enough to combat vicious racial violence.

In 1957, the civil rights debate centered on the expansion of federal power to enforce court orders in the South. Southern Democrats bitterly denounced Eisenhower's bill, and especially the granting of new powers to the attorney general, as a return to the nightmare of Reconstruction, when federal troops forced southern compliance to the will of the Radical Republicans. Scrambling history, segregationists argued that Eisenhower would create a "Soviet-type gestapo" that could tyrannize the South. Most alarming was the prospect of losing the right to a trial by jury in criminal cases involving civil rights. In the Deep South, where civil rights violations were tried as criminal cases before all-white juries, convictions were rare.

The administration's bill would replace most criminal proceedings concerning civil and voting rights with civil injunctions that could be decided solely by a judge. Although seemingly less draconian, critics howled that southerners were being denied their sacred right of trial by jury. Eisenhower, who was quite aware of the various means that had denied blacks the right to register and vote, replied that the right to vote was America's most sacred birthright.

Lyndon Baines Johnson (D-TX), the Senate's majority leader, found himself not in the middle of the political highway but on a wobbly tightrope strung between southern Democrats and his own presidential ambitions. If there were to be civil rights legislation at all, he had to mollify southern segregationists, yet not alienate liberal Democrats; take credit for whatever was accomplished; and blame Eisenhower and the Republicans for any shortcomings in the civil rights legislation.

A legislative genius, Lyndon Johnson managed to accomplish all his goals while receiving the lion's share of the credit for passage of the Civil Rights Act of 1957. Before voting on the civil rights bill, however, Johnson maneuvered to remove the main enforcement provision from the act—the authority for the attorney general to obtain court-ordered civil injunctions on a broad range of civil rights infractions, including violations of voting rights. Johnson also wanted to guarantee a jury trial in all civil rights cases, including voting, which, in effect, left the fate of civil rights enforcement in the hands of all-white (and mostly male) southern juries. Eisenhower, willing to risk defeat of the entire bill, dug in his heels. At the president's insistence, a weakened compromise voting rights provision was inserted into the bill—federal prosecutors and judges would have the discretion of determining whether or not contempt of court citations required a jury trial or merely a hearing before the judge.

Although seriously weakened by Johnson with the complicity of liberal Democrats, the Eisenhower/Brownell–sponsored Civil Rights Act of 1957 became the first civil rights law adopted since Reconstruction. To be sure, Johnson and the liberal Democrats deserved their fair share of credit for joining the Eisenhower Republicans in passing this landmark legislation. Yet, these same liberal Democrats, who looked aside while Johnson eviscerated the voting rights provisions, had the temerity to blame Eisenhower for the law's shortcomings.

While some civil rights leaders thought that no civil rights law was better than a flawed law, Martin Luther King endorsed the 1957 Civil Rights Act as a foundation for more comprehensive legislation. King proved prescient. Though the act was disappointing, there would be no turning back from the eighty-year drought in civil rights legislation. The power of southern Democrats to beat back civil rights legislation had been defeated. Overlooked in most histories is the fact that the majority of votes in the Senate for the 1957

Civil Rights Act were Republicans (thirty-seven of the sixty yes votes; the Democrats split 23–15).

Despite its limitations, the 1960 Civil Rights Act, also sponsored by the Eisenhower administration, strengthened voting rights for blacks. The so-called landmark Civil Rights Act of 1964 had its own weaknesses, but together, the Civil Rights Acts of 1957, 1960, and 1964 laid the foundation for subsequent civil rights legislation. Eisenhower took great satisfaction in his historic accomplishment.

Little Rock

The Little Rock crisis confronted Eisenhower with his ultimate challenge to civil rights and school desegregation enforcement. Following the murder of Emmett Till, the Montgomery bus boycott, and the Southern Manifesto, the tempo of southern resistance to racial integration, including violence, steadily increased. In Alabama, Autherine Lucy was expelled from the University of Alabama. In Tennessee, a mob blocked black children from entering a high school, and in Texas, the governor used the Texas Rangers to keep children out of school. In Washington, DC, crosses were burned on the lawns of some Supreme Court justices and Attorney General Brownell discovered that someone had poured kerosene under the bedroom windows where his children slept.

It seemed almost inevitable that at some point federal authorities would be forced to intervene at the local level to enforce the *Brown* decision. After the director of the FBI, J. Edgar Hoover, reported to the president's cabinet mounting resistance to desegregation in the South, Eisenhower, Brownell, and others began to map out contingency plans for dealing with violent defiance of court-ordered integration. As Eisenhower noted in his memoir *Waging Peace*, Governor Orval Faubus of Arkansas gave him no time to "rejoice" over passage of the Civil Rights Act of 1957.

Even as the civil rights legislation was wending its way toward Eisenhower's desk, Faubus ordered Arkansas National Guard troops to Little Rock to prevent black students from enrolling in Central High School. The Little Rock school board had devised a moderate plan for integrating the city's schools gradually, beginning with limited black enrollment in the high school. On September 2, Faubus, acting on the pretense that he was protecting students and property and maintaining peace, ordered the National Guard to stop black students from entering Central High when the school opened the next day. In the ensuing stalemate, while the Guard and state police stood firm, a mob of angry whites descended on Central High School, where black children were denied entrance to their classrooms. In the midst of this turmoil, the school board petitioned the federal judge for relief from Faubus's orders. The judge refused to be intimidated by Faubus's tactics, setting the governor on a collision course with the federal government and the president of the United States.

Eisenhower and Brownell had already discussed the use of troops to break a stalemate in Little Rock. While troops of the 101st Airborne at Fort Campbell, Kentucky, were put on alert, Brownell dispatched FBI reconnaissance to Arkansas. Mindful of the political repercussions of dispatching federal troops to a state capital of the Old Confederacy, Eisenhower waited until all recourse was exhausted in the federal courts. He even entertained Arkansas congressman Brooks Hays's plea that he meet personally with Governor Faubus at the president's vacation retreat to work out a peaceful resolution of the conflict. When Hays assured Eisenhower that Faubus was not a doctrinaire segregationist, the president, who knew the value of providing one's adversaries face-saving submissions, agreed to talk with Faubus privately. At the conclusion of their private meeting, Eisenhower believed that Faubus had not only agreed to respect "the supreme law of the land" but also had consented to keep the peace in Little Rock. Brownell was skeptical that anything good would come from the governor's apparent concession.

Politically, Eisenhower paid a high price for his attempts to find a peaceful solution to the Little Rock crisis. The Democrats seemed unrestrained in their attempts to politicize the crisis. Hubert Humphrey chided Eisenhower for not rushing to Little Rock personally to lead the black students by the hand into their schoolrooms. The governor of Wisconsin accused him of dithering, while the governor of Massachusetts called for a bipartisan committee of governors to resolve the issue. Martin Luther King warned that the president's indecisiveness could set the cause of integration back a half century. After Eisenhower's fruitless meeting with Faubus, the Democratic Advisory Council, which included Truman and Stevenson, believed that Eisenhower had failed to do his duty by not convincing Faubus to uphold the Constitution. Humphrey again chimed in, saying that everyone was looking to Eisenhower for leadership, but "he hesitates and does nothing." Not to be outdone, the Communist press in Moscow trumpeted that the "anti-Negro violence" in Little Rock was actually condoned by the federal government.

From the beginning, however, for all who would listen, Eisenhower was crystal clear about how the standoff between the governor and the president had to be resolved. In March 1956, Eisenhower observed that no responsible person had talked about "nullification" by states of Supreme Court edicts, but if they had, there would be a serious crisis, because he was sworn to uphold the Constitution of the United States.

Subsequently, at his news conference of September 11, 1956, Eisenhower outlined the broad scenario by which he would become involved in local school desegregation disputes, including sending in federal marshals or troops if necessary. His scenario was hypothetical, and he did not mention boots and bayonets, but his interpretation of his authority was clear. He had no authority to intervene in matters under the jurisdiction of local officials or the governor until the federal court adjudicated the issue at hand. Should local authorities defy the federal court, Eisenhower explained, he would have no choice but to intervene, with force if necessary. This is precisely what had happened at Little Rock.

Following his meeting with Eisenhower, Faubus withdrew the National Guard but did not provide security for the school or safety for its students. Unfortunately, Faubus also advised the black students to stay away from school, allowing a cooling-off period. When school resumed on Monday morning September 23, the Little Rock police force was overwhelmed by an angry white mob determined to prevent the nine black students from entering the building. In the confusion, somehow eight of the black students managed to slip in a side door. Enraged, the crowd threatened to storm the high school to drag the students out. After the mob breached the barricades surrounding the school, the police decided to remove the students for their safety. With the local situation approaching chaos, both Superintendent of Schools Virgil Blossom and Mayor Woodrow Wilson Mann appealed to Washington for help. With efforts to negotiate a peaceful end to the impasse with Faubus in tatters, those who wanted Eisenhower to lead a moral crusade against the evils of racial discrimination were deeply disappointed in what they characterized as his utter mismanagement of the crisis.

It was Mayor Mann's telegram to the president that convinced Eisenhower it was time to act. Eisenhower was infuriated by what he considered Faubus's double-dealing betrayal. He lamented: "Cruel mob force had frustrated the execution of an order of a United States court, and the Governor of the State was sitting by, refusing to lift a finger to support the local authorities." According to the contingency plan he had developed with Brownell, Eisenhower issued a proclamation, "Obstruction of Justice in the State of Arkansas," commanding all persons engaged in unlawful activity to cease and disperse. As Eisenhower would soon discover, however, he was damned when he did not act and then damned when he did.

The following morning, September 24, the situation in Little Rock worsened. Any hope that the protestors in Little Rock might respect the president's proclamation was soon dashed when the situation spun out of control. The need for troops in Little Rock was urgent. In the name of "humanity, law and order and . . . democracy," the mayor pled, send the army quickly. There was only one justification for using federal troops against civilians—and that was to uphold the law. At 12:15 p.m., Eisenhower ordered Chief of Staff General Maxwell Taylor to deploy the 101st Airborne to Little Rock while he prepared to address the nation.

Speaking from the house of TR, Wilson, and FDR, and flanked by portraits of his most admired Americans—Franklin, Washington, Lincoln, and Lee—Eisenhower explained to the nation why he sent the paratroopers to Little Rock. Disorderly mobs led by demagogic extremists had deliberately prevented the implementation of orders from the federal court. Whether one agreed or disagreed with the *Brown* decision, the issue was clear, Eisenhower stated. Mob rule could not be allowed to override Supreme Court decisions; if it was so allowed, anarchy would result. The rule of law and the sanctity of individual rights rested upon the certainty that the president would perform his constitutional duty. The rioting in Little Rock had left him with no choice. Finally, bowing to the need to affirm human rights as well as to maintain law and order, he boldly invoked not only the Constitution of the United States but also the Charter of the United Nations, which affirmed "faith in fundamental human rights" and "in the dignity and worth of the human person . . . without distinction as to race, sex, language, or religion." These were fundamental precepts of Eisenhower's civil religion as well. With the reestablishment of law and order in Little Rock, so too would be restored "the image of America and all of its parts as one nation indivisible, with liberty and justice for all."

"One nation, indivisible." Had Eisenhower forgotten about God? Not at all. By citing both the United States Constitution and the United Nations' charter, Eisenhower had not meant to imply that the United Nations had jurisdiction in America's domestic affairs, but rather that both documents, and also the French Declaration of the Rights of Man (1789), affirmed the universal dignity of mankind, a civic doctrine that made no sense, in Eisenhower's opinion, without a belief in God. But as a youth at Lincoln School in Abilene and, later, as a cadet at West Point, he had pledged his national allegiance, his duty, to "one nation, indivisible." It was this historic meaning of the Pledge of

Allegiance that was most fitting for the state of Arkansas on that September evening in 1957.

For all of his southern sympathies—and they were real—like Lincoln, he believed race relations bedeviled America with an almost intractable moral dilemma. And also, like Lincoln, he withheld judgment of the people of the South as a whole. Above all, Eisenhower was a unionist and an internationalist whose civil agenda was not dictated by local or sectional politics.

Eisenhower had been loath to dispatch federal troops as police to enforce the law at the point of a gun against American civilians. He also knew that his actions were not unprecedented. Brownell and the Justice Department had traced the legal history back to 1792 when Washington signed legislation authorizing the use of militia to quell social unrest. Subsequently, Washington had personally led militia to suppress the Whiskey Rebellion. Eisenhower counted thirteen previous occasions on which the commander in chief had dispatched troops to pacify domestic civil disorder. Historically, presidents had most often used federal troops to compel tax collection, to enforce the fugitive slave laws, or to break labor strikes on behalf of American corporations. Never had federal troops been used to guarantee that black teenagers had the right to a decent public education.

Indeed, Eisenhower was especially sensitive to the symbolic significance of sending federal troops into the South to reaffirm the constitutional supremacy of federal law. Twenty-five years earlier he had accompanied General Douglas MacArthur on the thankless task of clearing the Bonus Army out of their Anacostia encampment. He had learned a number of lessons in that encounter, not the least of which was the need to suppress civil disorder with overwhelming force. "Adequate force minimized casualties," he had written in his Bonus Army study. "Suspected weakness on the side of law and order encourages riotous elements to resist, usually resulting in open conflict, while obvious strength gains a *moral* authority that is normally all-sufficient." In asymmetrical conflict between the army and civilian demonstrators at Little Rock, victory would go to the side that established and maintained moral legitimacy.

While their numbers were about equal, the 101st Airborne enjoyed a vastly superior advantage over the mob in leadership, training, and arms, all of which were conspicuously displayed. To maintain moral legitimacy, however, it was important that the 101st Airborne not become overly aggressive, but instead, if violence ensued, to assume a defensive posture so that the mob always appeared the irrational, illegitimate aggressors. In that regard, Eisenhower won a decisive victory at Little Rock with little property damage and no loss of life while upholding the rule of law.

Reactions to Little Rock

The public response to Eisenhower's sending the troops to Little Rock was encouraging but not overwhelming. While approximately three-quarters of Americans outside the South approved of his action, overall the national split was about 64 percent in favor to 36 percent against, a healthy electoral margin but not strongly impressive regarding a matter with fundamental constitutional implications with deep racial consequences. Some journalists still criticized him for his allegedly lukewarm enforcement of *Brown*. There were complaints that he had failed to condemn Faubus personally and was too empathetic with southerners. He was accused of dithering and mismanagement, of being too legalistic and timid. Lyndon Johnson moaned that there should not be troops from either side "patrolling our school campuses." John F. Kennedy openly censured the president for sending federal troops to Little Rock, implying that the army would not have been needed had the old soldier managed the situation effectively. Even former president Harry S. Truman criticized Eisenhower's deployment of troops to Little Rock rather than supporting it.

Not surprisingly, the most caustic criticism came from southern journalists and politicians. A reporter accused Eisenhower of stirring the embers of southern resentment over their defeat in the Civil War. One southern governor remarked that Eisenhower's action was tantamount to the United States waging war on Arkansas. A senator accused Eisenhower of trying to destroy the "social order of the South," and another promised that if Eisenhower sent troops into his state, he would "give him a fight such he has never seen before." An Alabama congressman complained that not only had Eisenhower acted illegally but also that the 101st Airborne was an unwarranted occupying force. There were not enough troops to occupy every school in the South, he commented wryly.

By far the most bitter and insulting reaction came from Richard Russell (D-GA), chair of the Senate's Armed Services Committee. The president had already been accused of establishing a "military dictatorship" in Little Rock. Russell, who had lost his stranglehold on civil rights legislation, now blasted Eisenhower with a devastating broadside. In a statement he also released to the public, Russell compared Eisenhower's orders to the 101st Airborne with Adolf Hitler's personal command of the Nazi SS. Asserting that American paratroopers "must have copied" from a manual that Hitler issued his storm troopers, Russell alleged that the army had used "highhanded and illegal methods" to control the mob in Little Rock while "disregarding and overriding the elementary rights of American citizens."

In truth, Eisenhower responded, the army had bopped one man on the head with a billy club while sticking a second man in the arm with a bayonet—both suffering only superficial wounds. Russell was cagey in that he did not challenge the constitutionality of the commander in chief's deployment of the troops to Little Rock, only their alleged brutal behavior while confronting peaceful citizens. He also promised a thorough investigation of the allegations by the Senate Armed Services Committee.

Eisenhower was blistered by this attack from Senator Russell. To be criticized publicly by the chairman of the Armed Services Committee was one thing; to be accused of using gestapo tactics on citizens of the United States was quite another. As calmly as possible for the infuriated president, Eisenhower lectured Russell that deploying the 101st Airborne should not have been necessary. If the governor had not obstructed the court, the Arkansas National Guard could have handled any lawlessness. But actually, he believed the National Guard would have been unnecessary since other Arkansas communities had integrated their schools peaceably. But when the governor stirred up "mobs of extremists" to flaunt the Supreme Court, the president had no choice but to act. To the senator who had inspired the Southern Manifesto, Eisenhower laid out the stark alternative: "Failure to act . . . would have been tantamount to acquiescence in anarchy and the dissolution of the union."

And he was dumbfounded how a patriot such as Russell, who had served faithfully in the United States Navy during World War I, could conflate American servicemen with Hitler's hated storm troopers. "In one case military power was used to further the purposes and ambitions of a ruthless dictator, in the other to preserve the institutions of free government." And then, always the dutiful soldier, he promised that the secretary of the army would investigate all alleged wrongdoing by the soldiers and report directly to the senator.

By no means were all the reactions to Little Rock negative. Eisenhower received a welcome thank you from the parents of the Little Rock nine, who affirmed that their faith in democracy had been strengthened. A former mayor of Little Rock confirmed that Eisenhower's action was necessary, and a member of the Little Rock school board wrote that Eisenhower's actions had been "most appropriate." Harold Engstrom explained that the school board could not openly oppose the governor without further agitating the mobs that already had badly damaged Little Rock's and America's reputation. Nevertheless, Engstrom believed that Eisenhower had saved Central High School from serious academic damage, and he assured the president that he, the school board, and other conscientious citizens of Little Rock would continue to support the American ideals that Eisenhower exemplified. In thanking Engstrom, Eisenhower briefly summarized his long-term strategy for dealing with school integration—a strategy not shared by militants of either side: "I believe that if all of us are patient and considerate in our dealings with others, but firm in support of principle, we shall proceed toward a solution to this problem much faster than if we allow emotion and ignorance and demagogic appeals to characterize our words and actions."

The intractable problem with Eisenhower's civil philosophy was that those who glowered at one another across America's racial divide were not prepared to extend either patience or respect to one another—nor did they trust or respect Eisenhower when he said that they should.

Perhaps most gratifying was the support of numerous religious leaders in Little Rock. Bishop Robert Brown, the Episcopal bishop for Arkansas, telephoned that church leaders in Little Rock supported the president and offered their help, which included holding prayer vigils for peace and justice. To the Little Rock ministers, Eisenhower justified his deployment of the paratroopers with what he considered two interlocking principles. First was the domestic need to affirm the American union with respect for self-governing institutions and unswerving loyalty to free government; second was the requirement to defend American freedom against the relentless attack of atheistic Communism. Little Rock was not merely a local squabble, in Eisenhower's worldview, but also a Cold War challenge in which a successful regional challenge of the Constitution would terrifyingly increase America's vulnerability to attacks from abroad. The contest in Arkansas was, ultimately, a transcendent religious problem, he wrote the Little Rock clergy: "The liberties we so much love, that we practice among ourselves because of the basic belief that we constitute one brotherhood under the fatherhood of God, demand that we stand together steadfastly against the relentless assaults of international communism."

Moving on Civil Rights

Again, Eisenhower affirmed his belief that legislation, litigation, and troops alone would not solve the deep-seated racial problems of America, created by history, culture, sectional identity, racial prejudice, and hatred. As James McPherson has reminded us, what was at stake was nothing less than the survival of legal and social institutions that supported white supremacy in the

South. From Eisenhower's perspective, leadership, including religious leadership, must also play a patient role in pulling the nation together.

During the emergency, Eisenhower thought often about the historical lessons he had learned from the Bonus March, the Civil War, and his youth in Abilene. Similar to Lincoln prior to Fort Sumter, Eisenhower decided not to attack white supremacy head-on, but rather to justify his actions in terms of constitutional law, skirting the more divisive debates about the merits of school desegregation. To Walter T. Forbes, a Tennessee manufacturer of knitting and weaving yarns, Eisenhower parried the businessman's criticism of the agitators, the NAACP, and the biased press by encouraging Forbes to foster positive race relations in his own company. Again, not directly confronting the issues, Eisenhower wrote, "Time and again I have personally and publicly urged patience, education, and understanding as the real cure to this problem and have pointed out the difficulties that arise from extremism on any question."

Although Eisenhower had been tarred as timid and naïve, Ralph McGill, editor and publisher of the *Atlanta Constitution*, praised him for his great patience, good will, and moderation shown toward the people of the South during the Little Rock standoff with Faubus. According to McGill, only Eisenhower's leadership in the crisis had prevented events from falling into the hands of extremist mobs. Eisenhower found McGill "highly sensitive" to his emotions and convictions. Someday, he told McGill, he would like to tell him a story about how he had learned, "the hard way," to practice patience and conciliation.

Similarly, when his old friend and assistant C. D. Jackson praised his "patience, human insight and generosity" in the *New York Herald Tribune*, Eisenhower, recalling the time he had battered his fists raw on the apple tree, confessed that for a man of his temperament, it had not been easy to master the virtues of "patience and moderation" that some of his critics had found so objectionable. This included his public practice of not mentioning the names of persons with whom he had an angry, acrimonious dispute.

Despite the fact that southern segregationists discovered that Eisenhower could not be bullied into turning his back on the Supreme Court, his reputation for promoting racial justice was not widely enhanced among black civil rights leaders. In some respects, his sponsorship of the Civil Rights Act of 1957 and his face-off with Orval Faubus at Little Rock actually disenchanted key civil rights leaders who thought him, at best, lukewarm toward civil rights issues. They longed for a leader in the White House who shared their unconditional moral imperative about combating the evils of American racism.

Eisenhower's sympathies seemed distant, his emphasis legalist, his attention forced, and his evident empathy for southerners troubling. But worst of all, he apparently did not share their sense of urgency. With virtually no personal connections in the black community and with limited understanding of black history and culture, Eisenhower was at a great disadvantage in communicating with black leaders. His black White House advisor, Fred Morrow, tried his best to be a liaison between the president and the black community, but Morrow himself felt awkward in this role.

Before he met with the Negro Publishers Association on May 12, 1958, Eisenhower was advised by Morrow to avoid using phrases such as "you people." In his homily to the black publishers, Eisenhower reviewed his own evolving experience with civil rights, noting progress in both law and practice. He reiterated his mantra that laws themselves would not solve social problems buried deep in the human heart. Predictably, the president then offered the same advice he had been recommending to white southerners, to White House aides, and especially to himself. Morrow gasped as Eisenhower counseled that his black audience must adopt "patience and forbearance," virtues he prayed for regularly. It was as if Eisenhower had a tin ear in urging patience and understanding to black Americans who had suffered through hundreds of years of slavery, decades of Jim Crow discrimination, intimidation from the KKK, and the horrors of white lynch mobs.

His attempt to be forthcoming and honest had misfired. Black leaders as disparate as Roy Wilkins of the NAACP, Thurgood Marshall, and Jackie Robinson were appalled by Eisenhower's failure to understand that black Americans were ensnared by a web of malicious law spun since the end of Reconstruction by determined white supremacists. Congressman Adam Clayton Powell Jr. complained aloud that although Eisenhower had time to consult personally with white southerners concerning the racial crisis (that is, Orval Faubus, Richard Russell, and Billy Graham), he had no time to meet with black civil rights leaders.

Initially, Martin Luther King, who had been trying for a year to meet with the president, was unhappy with Eisenhower's civil rights leadership, but ultimately King strongly endorsed Eisenhower's deploying troops to Little Rock. Justice must be rooted in a "new moral climate," King wrote. Sending in the troops was not only the right thing to do, King said, it was also the Christian thing to do. With Richard Nixon and Max Rabb encouraging the president, a month and a half after meeting with black publishers Eisenhower finally agreed to meet with King and other black civil rights leaders.

Eisenhower's reluctance to meet with black civil rights leaders was a consequence of his conservative political philosophy. He perceived the political scene much as he viewed the religious domain; it was dialectally divided by extremes of principle, belief, and practice. Just as he steered toward the middle ground of religious faith, so he was determined to bestride the middle of the political road between extremes of left and right ideology. As always, he was suspicious of what he regarded as special interest groups. Given his predilections and his lack of familiarity with black leadership and history, unfortunately Eisenhower tended to view black militants as part of the problem rather than as part of the solution. Throughout the Little Rock crisis, he had heard recurrent accusations from white southerners and even some northerners that outside agitators were responsible for stirring up extremist mobs in otherwise peaceable communities. Consequently, he had been overly cautious about meeting with black leaders, in part because he did not want to inflame further white extremists in Little Rock, but also because he had not wanted to jeopardize passage of the Civil Rights Act of 1957. Ironically, Eisenhower's moderate but steady pace implementing civil rights reform had been overrun by rapidly rising black expectations.

Eisenhower's greatest handicap concerning his relationship with black leaders, however, stemmed from his unfamiliarity with the black community. Fred Morrow and his valet notwithstanding, he had not developed a cadre of black friends or associates outside his official circle. Although he had deep empathy for even the poorest of white southerners, he had little personal understanding of the depths of black suffering and humiliation imposed by generations of whites through slavery and Jim Crow. And although he was an intensely religious man, he had almost no insight into the evangelical influence of the black church and its clergy. He repeatedly stated that law alone could not resolve America's racial problems. Yet his call for religious leadership to assist in moral revival included his friend Billy Graham but did not enlist black churches or clergy like Martin Luther King. He did not seem to understand that the burgeoning civil rights crusade would become one of the most important religious movements in American history. In all probability, Eisenhower viewed King as a civil rights agitator but perhaps minimized the fact that King was also a Christian pastor.

Their meeting on June 23, 1958, was cordial but tense. The meeting included Martin Luther King, A. Philip Randolph of the Leadership Conference on Civil Rights, Roy Wilkins from the NAACP, and Lester Granger, chair of the Urban League. Randolph praised the president for his courage, integrity, and leadership in handling the Little Rock crisis. Wilkins applauded the administration's progress on integrating the armed forces and passing the civil rights bill. But, led by King, they also pled for Eisenhower to campaign against the use of federal tax dollars to fund racial segregation in any way. King believed that Eisenhower's outspoken moral support for desegregation would lift the spirit of America. Then Granger turned up the heat by reporting rising black expectations. Conceding that there had been some progress toward civil rights, Granger observed that the black community had become angry because, suddenly, the progress appeared to have stopped. Bitterness among blacks had been exacerbated by Eisenhower's call for patience on May 12.

Surely his visitors could sense the volcanic anger rising in Eisenhower's gorge. As calmly as possible, the president shrugged his shoulders in dismay. How was it possible, he asked rhetorically, that "five and a half years of effort and action" in the field of civil rights had yielded heightened bitterness among the Negro people? Trying not to drip with sarcasm, he asked if redoubled efforts would only sow deeper bitterness among blacks. Recognizing his gaffe, Granger quickly tried to reassure Eisenhower that the black community was not bitter about him personally, but rather, they were angry at whites who continued to resist integration efforts.

Unintentionally, Granger had let the cat out of the bag. Eisenhower was already frustrated that Democrats were successfully reaping political credit for what had been accomplished while he was being held politically accountable for all that had fallen short. And election returns gave no indication that Republicans had significantly benefited from the black vote, despite the administration's politically costly civil rights initiatives. Everyone pretended that the meeting with the black leaders had been successful, while the president's aides assured him that all was well. Eisenhower may have been naïve about the realities faced by black America, but he was not beguiled by the wishful optimism of his staff.

In contrast to the Kennedys, who literally embraced Martin Luther King, Eisenhower maintained respectful distance from the charismatic black preacher. During the Civil War, Lincoln had also limited his rationale for the conflict to upholding the Constitution, defending the Union, and enforcing federal law in the secessionist states. Because he remained publicly uncommitted to the emancipation of slaves, Lincoln was denounced by resentful abolitionists as "stumbling, halting . . . and irresolute." The famous black abolitionist Frederick Douglass went so far as to assert that Lincoln had allowed himself to become a "miserable tool of traitors and rebels." That Eisenhower suffered similar invectives almost a hundred years later should not be surprising. The difference is that Eisenhower missed the historical turning point while Lincoln did not. Restrained by political considerations, both presidents moved cautiously, lest they alienate white voters needed to maintain their parties in power. But by September 1862, following the bloody battle at Antietam, Lincoln told his cabinet that he had made a covenant with God. When the rebel armies were driven out of Maryland, he would issue his Emancipation Proclamation. By morally embracing the abolition of slavery as well as defending the Constitution, Lincoln became the Great Emancipator. A century later, it was John F. Kennedy who ultimately became the martyr for civil rights, not Dwight D. Eisenhower.

Other than Little Rock, Eisenhower found dramatic opportunity to affirm his moral support of desegregation in the South. At his press conference of October 7, 1957, he was asked directly if he thought that the crisis in Little Rock reflected "the failure of religious leadership, faith and principle in the South." And if so, what should the churches be doing to stitch together the torn social fabric in Arkansas? Eisenhower confessed that he had been in correspondence with southern religious leaders about this very question. As clearly as possible, he restated the fundamental tenets of his civil religion as they pertained to Little Rock specifically and to race relations and civil government generally. He repeated his central belief that free government rests upon the "deeply held religious conviction" in "the equality of man" by the fact that all citizens are children of God. It is our common "Creator," God, who validates democratic government—and if Americans did not believe that, then *the people* ought to reevaluate their rationale for self-government. He did not stop there but took a bold leap, defining "a very peculiar, very specific, and very important" role that ministers of all denominations should play in affirming the government of the United States: "All religious leaders have a special responsibility for supporting the institutions of free government because, conversely, it is only free government where there is freedom of worship, as there is freedom of the press and freedom of speech and thought and so on."

In short, Eisenhower believed that civic rights, like Franklin Roosevelt's Four Freedoms, bound church and state together but did not violate the Constitution's prohibition of an established religion. Just as he had a duty to support the Constitution of the United States, so America's religious leaders had a calling to support the freedom of religion. Consequently, the clergy, in defense of the Constitution and the Union, should rally to support *Brown*, Little Rock, and the desegregation of American society. This was the just, Christian thing to do. But there was nothing ambiguous or tentative about how his civil rights policy was linked inextricably to his civil religion.

When queried about the success of his June 23 meeting with the civil rights leaders, Eisenhower acknowledged its usefulness but reaffirmed his basic principle that the president's duty, and that of the attorney general, must focus on enforcement of law under the Constitution. Again, he conceded that "punitive law," as he characterized it, could not succeed unless it enjoyed the moral support of the nation's citizens. The "cure" for America's racial problems lay with each citizen in the land. Like their president and their pastors, all citizens were called to do their duty to uphold the basic Constitution and legal procedures rather than exercise their parochial prejudices and emotions.

Eisenhower had faced this American dilemma repeatedly: with the fascist French admiral Jean-François Darlan, whom he had allowed to remain military governor of North Africa in return for a French cease-fire; with Russian marshal Georgy Zukov, with whom he had cultivated a warm friendship in pursuit of postwar cooperation with the Soviets; with demagogue senator Joseph McCarthy, whom he had ignored as best he could for the sake of Republican Party unity; with obstreperous governor Orval Faubus, with whom he had tried to negotiate a peaceful solution to the Little Rock crisis; and with segregationist senator Richard Russell, with whom he still had to work regardless of the senator's outrageous insults. These and a lesser host of dictators, autocrats, oligarchs, plutocrats, monopolists, militarists, pettifoggers, and bigots continually tested Eisenhower's patience and charity.

Ethical trade-offs are common in domestic politics as well as in foreign affairs, and the ethical problems were much the same. In this regard, Little Rock was a mere tactical skirmish in the long-range struggle to secure civil rights for all Americans. Professional soldier that he was, Eisenhower devised a strategic approach to implementing civil rights initiatives. As he stated again and again, laws, even tough laws, were necessary but not sufficient to secure civil rights for blacks, the poor, and women. Characteristically, he favored moving forward on a broad front that included enlarging educational opportunity and expanding voting participation (in the same 1957 budget message to Congress in which he became the first president to endorse the Equal Rights Amendment for Women, he also advocated lowering the federal voting age from twenty-one to eighteen, and making qualified appointments to the federal judicial bench). Specifically concerning black civil rights, he was committed to enfranchising black voters throughout the South and appointing federal judges who would uphold *Brown* and additional federal civil rights legislation.

Although after Little Rock Eisenhower's attention was increasingly occupied by foreign affairs, nonetheless civil rights remained a high priority on his domestic agenda. As he had feared, a wave of school closings swept across the South as segregationists decided to abandon their public-school systems rather than integrate them. Then in April 1959, a white mob in Mississippi lynched a young black man accused of raping a white woman. The FBI found Mack Parker's bullet-ridden body floating in a river. Unlike the Emmett Till lynching in 1955, Eisenhower publicly condemned the lawlessness of the killing. When the local Mississippi grand jury would not review the case, the Justice Department convened a federal grand jury to determine whether Parker's civil rights had been violated. When the federal grand jury failed to return an indictment against Parker's killers, there was nothing more that the federal government could do.

Not as morally shocking, but profoundly upsetting of racial peace, in February 1960 four black students began their nonviolent sit-in at a Woolworth's lunch counter in Greensboro, North Carolina. While Harry Truman said he would have thrown these protestors out of his store, Eisenhower believed that this sort of peaceful assembly in a public place was not only constitutional but had been regarded as proper by Americans since the founding of the country.

While Eisenhower, like Lincoln, was cool about the social integration of the races, he was also clear in his own mind that legal, political, and economic discrimination based on race, religion, or national origin was morally wrong. From Eisenhower's perspective, everyone from all races, nationalities, and religions enjoyed God's grace and dignity. Although the Eisenhower administration sent civil rights legislation to the Congress in 1958 and 1959, in each session Majority Leader Lyndon Johnson failed to support the administration's bills that would have enhanced the attorney general's authority to enforce civil rights legislation, provided federal grants-in-aid to states to assist in desegregation efforts, and strengthened voting rights. Southern senators dug in their heels to oppose all efforts to implement school integration, but by 1960, under continued pressure from the White House, Lyndon Johnson brokered a deal between the southern wing of his party and northern liberal Democrats to support a bill limited to voting rights. Stripped of federal financial support for school integration, the Civil Rights Act of 1960 passed the Senate with only eighteen hard-core southern segregationists voting against it. The law contained a key proposal by Attorney General William Rogers authorizing federal judges to appoint referees to oversee registration and voting in precincts where the court determined there existed a "pattern of discrimination."

Although Eisenhower did not get all he wanted in the Civil Rights Act of 1960, he was well pleased with voting rights provisions that were essential to any long-term progress toward dismantling Jim Crow culture in America. While Senator Lyndon Johnson continued to receive the lion's share of credit for passage of the Eisenhower administration's civil rights program, the president took pride in his accomplishments in this area. In his last State of the Union message to Congress on January 12, 1961, he summarized the progress in his two terms, which included the Civil Rights Acts of 1957 and 1960, the first civil rights legislation since the end of Reconstruction. In addition to abolishing segregation in the armed services, veterans hospitals, the civil service, and the District of Columbia, much the same had been accomplished in federal offices and military facilities in and around the country. Through the president's Commission on Government Contracts and Government Employment Practices, discrimination had been attacked not only in federal employment but also among federal contractors. The Civil Rights Commission had collected essential data on housing, voting, and education practices, while the Civil Rights Division of the Department of Justice had taken steps to enforce voting rights and the elimination of Jim Crow laws. Eisenhower conceded that much work in civil rights needed to be done to follow up on these "pioneering" labors, but continued effort was imperative not only because it was the moral thing to do but also because the impact of crushing Jim Crow was more than national—it was worldwide.

Guaranteeing the vote for blacks was essential strategically, but the most important, and unnoticed, long-range strategic civil rights legacy of President Eisenhower was his judicial appointments to the federal courts. Without protection from the federal courts, the civil rights scaffolding built by federal law and regulation would come tumbling down. Eisenhower repeatedly cautioned that law alone could not purge shameful Jim Crow from the land, but without law buttressed by the Constitution as interpreted by the federal courts, there could be little progress toward a racially free and peaceful America. Historian David Nichols has convincingly documented that Eisenhower's appointments to the federal bench were his most significant contribution to civil rights progress.

All doubt concerning Eisenhower's commitment to *Brown* should have been erased by his next appointment to the Supreme Court, following Warren. With Brownell's strong support, Eisenhower nominated John Marshall Harlan II to be an associate justice. Emblematically, Harlan was the grandson of Justice John Harlan, who had cast the sole dissenting vote in *Plessy v. Ferguson*. Both grandfather and grandson believed that the Constitution ought to be color-blind. Eisenhower did not back away from what he knew would be a bruising battle to gain Senate confirmation for Harlan. Led by Senator

James Eastland of Mississippi, eleven Southern senators voted against Harlan after an unsuccessful, four-month-long attempt to derail the nomination.

Eisenhower's third appointment to the Supreme Court was no less audacious or important for strengthening the Warren Supreme Court. He told Brownell that, if possible, he would like to appoint a Democrat to the Court, to exemplify his nonpartisan commitment to constitutional government. Then, to his surprise, Cardinal Spellman brought to his attention a draft resolution from Catholic bishops meeting in Washington, asking the president to appoint a Catholic to the Court at the first opportunity. Spellman reassured the president that the bishops were not unhappy with his administration, but Eisenhower got the point, commenting to Ann Whitman: "At the same time, this paper [from the bishops] does show the acute sensitiveness of particular groups in the United States . . . of what they consider to be proper and equitable representation on all important governmental bodies, especially the Supreme Court."

Concurrently, he was being intensely pressured to demonstrate that he had no bias against the South by appointing a qualified southerner to the Court. But because Eisenhower could find no southern jurist he believed would uphold *Brown*, at Brownell's urging, he chose William Brennan, a distinguished judge on the New Jersey Supreme Court. Brennan was not only a Catholic and a Democrat, but in Eisenhower's opinion, he also strengthened the Court because of his experience on a state court. To the continuing unhappiness of Southern senators, Eisenhower never appointed a southerner to the Warren Court.

Following his second inauguration, in July 1957 he shared with his old Abilene friend Swede Hazlett his conflicted views of the emerging civil rights movement. No other event in the post–World War II era had upset domestic tranquility more than the 1954 Supreme Court decision on racial segregation in schools. The Court's judgment profoundly altered the constitutional relationship among the federal government, the states, and American citizens, in that the responsibility for assuring each citizen his or her constitutional rights now fell most heavily on the federal government rather than on the states. This sudden shift altered threescore years of relative autonomy among the states for establishing and enforcing laws and customs governing interracial relationships in almost all aspects of daily life.

Eisenhower confided to Hazlett that he did not believe such a revolution could be quickly realized without severe social disruption, possibly violence. The Court in 1896 had legitimized racial segregation so that white supremacy became viewed as not only respectable but also legal and moral. The Supreme

Court's decision alone was not going to reform these ingrained social values. On this, Eisenhower was undoubtedly correct. Conservatively, he believed that only "moderation in legal compulsions" accompanied by universal education could ultimately achieve the goals of integrationists. That was why he was so deeply concerned about the survival of the public school system in the South. And here Congress could provide vital assistance in public school funding. Massive, violent, deadly resistance to civil rights had not yet disgraced America. On this issue, for peace and progress, Eisenhower self-consciously decided not to use the bully pulpit of the presidency to champion civil rights for blacks. He chose rather to lead by indirection and his "hidden hand," and thereby he forfeited his civil rights legacy to John F. Kennedy and Lyndon Johnson.

Civil Rights and Nuclear Weapons

In 1957, Eisenhower believed the United States faced two major threats: political chaos at home if every citizen became a law unto himself, and atomic Armageddon from abroad if the pell-mell nuclear arms race was not controlled.

Both Cold War era challenges created public policy dilemmas for the Eisenhower administration, because each offered no clear-cut moral choice for this conservative government. Despite being urged to enlist in the crusade for civil rights, Eisenhower felt the wisdom or timing of the *Brown* decision was irrelevant. Regardless of the complicated dynamics of the standoff at Little Rock, his duty as president was clear-cut. Right or wrong, the decision of the Supreme Court had to be upheld. But it doesn't follow that Eisenhower was lukewarm about the *Brown* decision. He wrote Hazlett, "If the day comes when we can obey the orders of our Courts only when we personally approve of them, the end of the American system, as we know it, will not be far off." Chaos would rule, not democratic government.

What was not widely understood by Eisenhower's critics was that he governed by a sense of duty—a religious sense—that he was called into service of his country to fight for justice and righteousness. His biggest worry was the constant question of doing the right thing. Whether it was civil rights or atomic energy, he acknowledged that certain problems were so complex and difficult that there were no satisfactory answers. Sometimes, he lamented, it was a matter of choosing whether you wanted a broken arm or a broken leg. But he had the satisfaction of knowing that he had done the best he could— that was all Ida ever asked for, and all he ever asked of himself.

When Eisenhower was under fire for being indecisive on civil rights, Robert Frost consoled him with a simple, eight-word poem: "The strong are saying nothing until they see." Grateful, Eisenhower confessed that he appreciated and needed Frost's comfort. And he liked the poet's maxim "perhaps best of all."

The Iron Cross, 1953–1961

N uclear weapons, both fission and thermonuclear, dominated American foreign relations after World War II. Throughout the Cold War, the threat of nuclear holocaust stalked every American president, including Dwight D. Eisenhower. Among the challenges America faced at the end of World War II, none was more intractable than the imperative to manage and control nuclear science and technology.

In 1945, the United States enjoyed dominance in nuclear science. Within four years, however, the Soviet Union had tested its first atomic device. Within three years, the atomic age itself was superseded by the thermonuclear age when an H-bomb thundered across the Pacific from the Bikini Atoll. In 1953, few Americans were prepared to surrender the United States' nuclear monopoly or understood the significance of the thermonuclear (hydrogen) bomb.

Eisenhower was not the architect of the atomic energy establishment he inherited in 1953, but by the time he left the White House in 1961, he had profoundly altered the course of nuclear history by amending the structure and mission of the US Atomic Energy Commission. Concurrently, the Eisenhower administration also established the country's nuclear defense triad—strategic bombers, nuclear submarines, and intercontinental missiles armed with thermonuclear warheads. In his presidential memoir, *Mandate for Change* (1963), Eisenhower observed:

> I have pondered, on occasion, the evolution of the military art during the mid-fifties. The Army in which I was commissioned a second lieutenant in 1915 underwent phenomenal changes in the thirty years from then until the Germans surrendered in 1945. . . . But those changes, startling as they were, faded into insignificance when compared to those of the postwar period.

Often overlooked in Eisenhower biographies is the fact that on one issue—the danger of nuclear holocaust—Eisenhower not only was outspoken but also used every available pulpit, including the United Nations, to promote nuclear restraint. Although he delegated responsibility for developing nuclear policy to Lewis Strauss, chairman of the Atomic Energy Commission, and to John Foster Dulles, secretary of state, Eisenhower dedicated himself politically, morally, and religiously to promoting international peace and disarmament in the nuclear age.

As an exegetical president, Eisenhower wrestled publicly with the problem of evil associated with managing a horrific but potentially beneficial nuclear technology. As the nation's president/pastor, he played a seminal role in interpreting the West's nuclear dilemma within the context of American civil religion. Eisenhower's vision was prophetic to the extent that he perceived grave danger to America's governmental and economic institutions should the United States fail in the management and control of the international atom. He was outspoken in applying the precepts of American civil religion to the Cold War's nuclear challenge. His role was exegetical—defining, explaining, and encouraging. Among challenging postwar problems Eisenhower faced as president, none was more perplexing than the need to manage and control nuclear science and technology for both peace and war.

The Nuclear Dilemma and the New Look

More than most presidents, Eisenhower understood the horrors of nuclear war and took steps to control the military atom while fostering peaceful atomic uses. No American politician in the 1950s wrestled more with the nuclear dilemma than did Eisenhower. Nuclear disarmament was a central but allusive objective of his administration, and failure to achieve a nuclear test ban was his largest disappointment as president.

When Eisenhower became president in 1953, the Cold War race for thermonuclear weapons was in full tilt. While president, he presided over the transition from the atomic to the thermonuclear age—a change as foreboding as the birth of the atomic age itself. While Americans and Soviets hurried to build their nuclear stockpiles, the National Security Council adopted NSC 162/2, a document that outlined a "new look" for NATO, substituting thermonuclear weapons for costly American armies in Europe. John Foster Dulles summarized the strategic reliance on consequences of the New Look, as the national security policy of the United States was called, in his "massive retaliation" speech to the Council on Foreign Relations. Revised in the spring issue of *Foreign Affairs*, the speech outlined the defense policy that promised overwhelming nuclear retaliation in response to a Communist attack on the Western allies. The New Look presumed that strategic nuclear weapons would deter Soviet aggression without seriously damaging the American economy.

But the New Look was not simply an aggressive nuclear doctrine. Dulles's "massive retaliation" speech marked the high-water mark of American nuclear bellicosity. From 1953 through 1964, "atomic diplomacy," practiced by the Truman administration, steadily gave way to the "nuclear diplomacy" of Eisenhower and Kennedy. Truman's atomic diplomacy had used the bomb as an intimidating threat to the Soviet Union and other Communist nations. Although Truman gave lip service to pursuing the peaceful atom, he entertained little hope for international control of nuclear science or for nuclear disarmament. Instead, Truman charted a course that accelerated the nuclear arms race by plunging the world into the thermonuclear age.

The nuclear diplomacy practiced by Eisenhower and Kennedy, on the other hand, not only exploited the military atom but also fostered peaceful uses of atomic energy to advance American foreign policy objectives. Their nuclear diplomacy was not simply Cold War brinkmanship and nuclear saber rattling. Rather, it not only included arms-control, nuclear-testing, and disarmament negotiations but also embraced the international pursuit of the peaceful atom, nuclear power, and mutual security.

Consequently, Eisenhower's Atoms for Peace initiative provided counterpoint to the nuclear arms race. The interplay between atoms for war and atoms for peace, which characterized Eisenhower's nuclear diplomacy, was revealed most clearly in his "Chance for Peace" speech (April 16, 1953), followed by his "Atoms for Peace" speech (December 8, 1953), when he warned of devastating consequences of nuclear war while calling for Soviet cooperation in developing peaceful uses. Throughout, cooperation as well as confrontation with the Soviets were at the heart of Eisenhower's nuclear diplomacy. While focusing on the nuclear arms race and the difficult negotiations for arms control with the Soviets, historians have often missed the linkage between Eisenhower's Atoms for Peace initiative and his dedication to limiting nuclear weapon proliferation. There would be continuity between Eisenhower's and Kennedy's nuclear diplomacy that culminated in the Limited Nuclear Test Ban Treaty of 1963.

Eisenhower endorsed nuclear deterrence and supported the development, testing, and deployment of tactical and strategic nuclear weapons. But he also believed that atomic secrets could not be long kept. He advocated candor about the dangers of nuclear warfare and consistently favored international cooperation and sharing nuclear technology when appropriate. Importantly, and central to understanding his commitment to atoms for peace, Eisenhower felt a moral repugnance for the nuclear bomb, which he repeatedly characterized as "that hellish contrivance" or "that awful thing."

The Bomb and World War II

It is not certain when Eisenhower first learned about the Manhattan Project. Like Vice President Truman, Eisenhower seems to have had little knowledge about the secret atomic bomb project. Omar Bradley learned about the Manhattan Project from President Roosevelt in 1943, but apparently Bradley did not discuss the matter with his boss. On May 11, Eisenhower received warnings about the possibility of German radiological warfare, but because the threat was remote, he told few among his staff of the problem. Eisenhower did not have explicit knowledge of the atomic bomb project until the Potsdam Conference, where he learned about the successful Trinity test near Alamogordo, New Mexico.

Although he accompanied President Truman to Potsdam, the president did not seek Eisenhower's advice about the atomic bomb. At Potsdam, Eisenhower lunched with Truman and reviewed strategy for ending the Pacific war but played no role in the decision to drop the atomic bomb. The War Department had already decided to use America's atomic weapons against Japan, and Eisenhower's opinion about the matter was irrelevant. In discussions with Secretary of War Henry Stimson, however, Eisenhower forcefully expressed his opposition to atom-bombing Japan. Recalling Stimson's reasoning for employing the atomic bombs, Eisenhower later wrote: "I had been conscious of a feeling of depression and so I voiced to him my grave misgivings, first on the basis of my belief that Japan was already defeated and that dropping the bomb was completely unnecessary, and secondly because I thought our country should avoid shocking world opinion by the use of a weapon whose employment was, I thought, no longer mandatory as a measure to save American lives."

"It was not necessary to hit them with that awful thing," he later wrote in *Crusade in Europe* (1948). John Eisenhower remembered his father's distress at Stimson's description of "a bomb so powerful that it exceeds the imagination of man." Over the years, Eisenhower's moral revulsion over the atomic bomb never lessened; instead, the specter of nuclear war helped shape his worldview and military policies.

Within weeks of the Potsdam Conference, Eisenhower visited the Soviet Union and was in Moscow when the Japanese surrendered following the bombing of Hiroshima and Nagasaki. Apparently, he did not talk about the bomb while in Moscow. Rather, Eisenhower expressed optimism about the future of American-Soviet relations. "I see nothing in the future that would prevent Russia and the United States from being the closest possible friends," he told reporters in Moscow. What he hoped for, at this juncture, was a postwar peace guaranteed by the British fleet, the American air force, and the Soviet army.

Privately, Eisenhower worried about the effect the atomic bomb would have on American-Soviet relations. While in Moscow, he observed firsthand the Soviets' reaction to the news from Hiroshima and Nagasaki. Before the atom bombing of Japan, he was sure the Allies and the Russians could keep the postwar peace. Afterward, he was not certain. "I had hoped the bomb wouldn't figure in this war," he lamented. But the world had changed. "Now I don't know," Eisenhower reflected. "People are frightened and disturbed all over. Everyone feels insecure again." For the next fifteen years of his public life, neither the bomb nor the Soviets would ever be far from his thoughts.

The New World

Eisenhower returned from Moscow to a new world. Although he knew little about atomic weapons, he admitted that the bomb had complicated his doctrines of warfare. In September 1946, when a reporter asked about his views concerning atomic warfare, he said it was too soon to know the importance of atomic weaponry, but it was bound to be considerable. Nevertheless, he believed the government should be forthcoming about the effects of atomic bombing. "What the world needs is truth," he stated. Atomic bombs mounted on missiles threatened cities in all parts of the world. It was possible, he thought, that science had produced a weapon so terribly destructive that war had become impossible. The bomb might "blackmail" the world into peace, Eisenhower offered with guarded optimism.

The atomic bomb was only one factor that contributed to Eisenhower's depression in the fall of 1945; the destruction he surveyed across the Soviet Union and Poland was appalling. Conditions in Germany differed in scale, but not in kind, with those in eastern Europe. Millions were dead or missing. Millions more were homeless. Cities were in ashes, and industry reduced to rubble. It was in this context of unimaginable destruction and incomprehensible inhumanity that Eisenhower's early postwar views of the Soviet Union and atomic weapons were germinated.

Although he was depressed over the prospects of nuclear war, Dwight Eisenhower was an incurable optimist. There are those who have characterized his religious faith as naïve, but Eisenhower tenaciously believed that even the worst of trials might be turned toward good. Whether it was the unspeakable sacrifices of the Allies in World War II or the awful portent of the atomic bomb, Eisenhower not only believed but also virtually willed that these events work toward the ultimate benefit of mankind.

The contrast between Eisenhower's optimistic internationalism and Truman's pessimistic atomic diplomacy was stark. Perhaps Eisenhower was distressingly naïve and Truman refreshingly realistic in 1945. Shortly, as the nuclear arms race heated up and the Red Scare tightened its grip on Americans' nerves, Eisenhower too would get caught up in Cold War xenophobia. Notably, when he ran for president in 1952, he was defensive about his earlier pro-Russian views and later even tried to claim that he had warned President Roosevelt of the postwar Russian threat as early as 1941. But although Eisenhower ultimately became a Cold Warrior, as president his nuclear diplomacy also reflected his earlier optimistic faith concerning cooperation with the Russians and the potential peaceful uses of atomic energy.

The Influence of Clausewitz

In the terrible aftermath of World War II, Eisenhower remained a disciple of Carl von Clausewitz, the author of *On War*, in his understanding of the interrelatedness of political and military affairs. According to Clausewitz, the political objectives of warfare not only defined military strategy but also determined tactics and weapons, including their deployment and intensity of use. For Clausewitz, war was quintessentially a political act. War and diplomacy, violence and peace, or perhaps one could just say war and peace were not independent historical skeins but rather were intertwined threads in a tapestry of international relationships that defined the political/power relationships among states.

The complex international tableau, of course, was neither bipolar nor static. Eisenhower, who had read Clausewitz three times under the tutelage of Fox Conner, internalized the Clausewitzian principle that "war is merely the continuation of [foreign] policy by other means," a maxim that became the foundation for Eisenhower's nuclear diplomacy.

In November 1945, when Truman named Eisenhower army chief of staff, three atomic energy policy issues, all related, immediately confronted Eisenhower. The first concerned domestic management of nuclear energy programs, including the future of the Manhattan Engineer District, the agency under the leadership of General Leslie Groves that developed and tested America's first atomic bombs. The other two issues, international control of atomic energy and the development and testing of atomic weapons, were also closely related to the fate of the Manhattan Project and its research laboratories and industrial facilities.

Eisenhower returned from Europe with no detailed knowledge of America's nuclear strength or its programs. He began regular meetings with General Groves and received a detailed technical briefing about present and future nuclear capability from Colonel K. D. Nichols, Groves's deputy. He viewed War Department films of the Hiroshima and Nagasaki bombings and, with Groves and Secretary of War Stimson, discussed the looming nuclear arms race. The central question, of course, was who would determine atomic energy policy in the postwar world, the military or civilians.

The Atomic Energy Commission

Truman had already proposed to Congress the establishment of a civilian-controlled Atomic Energy Commission (AEC). Immediately, the army countered with the May-Johnson bill, which would have retained military control of atomic energy. In this struggle over the control of atomic energy, Eisenhower offered the army no help, and indeed, could not remember being in Washington during congressional hearings on the May-Johnson bill. Ultimately, he cautiously supported the McMahon bill, which established the civilian Atomic Energy Commission. Eisenhower decided that the McMahon bill was acceptable to the general staff and that security interests of the United States could be adequately protected under civilian management of atomic energy. If Eisenhower was not enthusiastic about the McMahon bill, he never expressed opposition to civilian control of atomic energy.

He was less ambiguous in support of international control of atomic energy, provided adequate safeguards could be guaranteed. On November 15, while Secretary of State James Byrnes developed a proposal to create a United Nations Atomic Energy Commission, Eisenhower testified before the House Military

Affairs Committee to promote one of his favorite causes, universal military training. Stating that he believed the Soviet Union wanted nothing more "than to keep friendship with the United States," Eisenhower also speculated that if all nations would promise a complete exchange of nuclear science and technology through the United Nations, "you would at least inspire confidence, and thereby you could give such secrets to all nations and it would make no difference."

When challenged by Congressman J. Parnell Thomas (R-NJ) that the United States should attempt to maintain its nuclear monopoly through secrecy, Eisenhower replied, "Let's be realistic. The scientists say other nations will get the secret anyway. There is some point in making a virtue out of necessity." Eisenhower not only believed that the nuclear monopoly of the United States would be short-lived (two to five years), but he also wanted the United States to exploit its lead in nuclear technology both diplomatically and economically. Even if one questions that Eisenhower's November 1945 call for United Nations control of atomic energy with safeguards was disingenuous, the fact remains that this same combination of manifest idealism and realism highlighted President Eisenhower's later nuclear diplomacy.

Eisenhower was not unmindful of the national security implications of maintaining tight control over atomic secrets. As reflected in his decisions concerning the cases of the Rosenbergs and Oppenheimer in 1953—the former, Julius and Ethel Rosenberg, convicted Soviet spies; the latter, suspected of disloyalty and stripped of his security clearances—he displayed the old soldier's instinctive reaction to atomic espionage. Personally, he had neither patience nor sympathy for spies, disloyal Americans, or suspected security risks, even if they were parents of small children. Nevertheless, Eisenhower advised the Joint Chiefs of Staff in December 1945 that, while the highest possible degree of atomic secrecy would best serve United States military interests, diplomatic and political considerations required reassessment of the ban on sharing nuclear technology. Again, noting the nation's transitory nuclear monopoly, Eisenhower urged his colleagues to evaluate proposals for sharing nuclear technology, including for peaceful uses, both with allies and with the United Nations, to promote practical industrial applications of atomic energy coupled with effective enforceable safeguards to prevent possible military use.

Bernard Brodie and the Absolute Weapon

Although Eisenhower pondered alternative peaceful uses of atomic energy, atoms for war, not atoms for peace, dominated the postwar thinking of military strategists, including Eisenhower. At Yale University, Bernard Brodie, a brilliant young academic who joined the faculty of the Institute of International Studies in August 1945, worked feverishly with colleagues to assess the impact of the atomic bomb on military doctrine. Brodie pored over all available bombing evaluations and intensely studied the *Smyth Report*, the War Department's official report of the Manhattan Project, and concluded that the atomic bomb not only magnified the destructiveness of aerial bombing but also revolutionized the nature of war itself. According to Lawrence Freedman, Brodie identified four "axioms of the nuclear age": "the impossibility of defense against nuclear attack; the hopeless vulnerability of the world's major cities; the attraction of a surprise pre-emptive attack; and the necessity of a strong capability for retaliation."

Brodie also believed that if one accepted Clausewitz's precept that political objectives determined both war-making doctrine and military strategy, then it followed that fighting a major nuclear war was inappropriate for achieving any rational war aim. Brodie believed that Clausewitz's *On War* was more pertinent to understanding America's nuclear dilemma than "most of the literature specifically written about nuclear war." Specifically, Brodie wrote:

> Among books [on war] we pick up a good deal of useful technological and other lore, but we usually sense also the absence of that depth and scope which are particularly the hallmark of Clausewitz. We miss especially his tough-minded pursuit of the idea that war in all its phases must be rationally guided by meaningful political purposes. That insight is quite lost in most contemporary books including one which bears a title that boldly invites comparison with the earlier classic, Herman Kahn's *On Thermonuclear War*.

In February 1946, Brodie sent to Eisenhower a draft of "The Absolute Weapon: Atomic Power and World Order." No doubt, Eisenhower recognized the Clausewitzian rhetoric in Brodie's title. Eisenhower, in turn, circulated Brodie's draft to Generals J. Lawton Collins, Hoyt Vandenberg, and Curtis LeMay. Eisenhower's reflections on Brodie's draft, written in notes and marginalia, provide unique insight into his views about nuclear weapons. While Brodie argued that atomic bombs had "altered the basic character of war itself," Eisenhower, who had personally surveyed World War II's devastation across central Europe, was not sure. Conventional firebombing of European and Japanese cities often had been just as destructive as the atomic bomb.

Brodie estimated that as few as ten A-bombs could destroy any city. "It is now possible," Brodie wrote, "to wipe out all cities of a great nation in a single day." Eisenhower demurred, not yet convinced that the atomic bomb had revolutionized all warfare. Firebombing could also wipe out entire cities in a day or two. He was impressed by the devastating power of the atomic bomb, and he knew that it had changed some aspects of how war could be waged. In an atomic war, mass seaborne invasion such as Normandy would be suicide for amphibious forces. In the twinkling of an eye, Eisenhower's historic Operation Overlord was obsolete. But Eisenhower would not concede that the bomb had superseded conventional armies and navies.

While conventional forces were not yet useless, Eisenhower nonetheless agreed with much of Brodie's analysis. For example, when Brodie emphasized the limitations of defense strategies (which, of course, Clausewitz also believed), Eisenhower penned in the margin, "I've always lived by this doctrine." Eisenhower concurred with Brodie that there was no effective defense against atomic bombs, especially atomic warheads delivered by rockets. But a huge atomic arsenal would not guarantee security in the atomic age. Brodie argued that numerical superiority of atomic bombs would not "endow its possessor with the kind of military security which formerly resulted from superiority" in armed forces. If it were true that the atomic bomb would be ineffective for achieving political objectives, Eisenhower wondered if the A-bomb would be relegated "to the position of chemical warfare in World War II."

Eisenhower's analysis of Brodie's "The Absolute Weapon" reflected the mentoring of Fox Conner and his reading of Carl von Clausewitz. Clausewitz could not imagine an ultimate weapon capable of singularly winning a war. According to Clausewitz, no war consisted of a lone, isolated battle won with a single, devastating blow. Indeed, conflict was never final in war, but rather was part of the continuing power relationship among nations or peoples. But, if atomic bombs could threaten a decisive strike, then preparations would tend toward totality, for no omission could be rectified. Even if the atomic bomb were not the winning weapon, the nuclear age pushed nations toward a permanent state of war—continually preparing for total war.

While Eisenhower resisted Brodie's belief that atomic bombs revolutionized war, he agreed with him that the bomb, in and of itself, had not made war more violent. Like Eisenhower, Brodie noted that cities could be effectively destroyed with TNT and incendiaries, such as occurred in the firebombing of Dresden and Tokyo. What made the atomic bomb different from other weapons was that it concentrated violence and death in time, exposing nations to a crippling, preemptive surprise attack. Eisenhower endorsed Brodie's corollary that, because there was no defense against a surprise atomic attack, the "first and most vital step in any American security program . . . [was] to take measures to guarantee . . . retaliation in kind." That is, the United States would have to build a convincingly effective nuclear counterforce as a deterrent. Without endorsing Brodie's thesis about the obsolescence of conventional armies, he underlined Brodie's conclusion that "any system for the international control . . . [of nuclear weapons] should include safeguards promising practically 100% effectiveness."

Eisenhower's belief that safeguards would need to be almost 100 percent effective also underscored the daunting challenge of nuclear arms control. Nuclear weapon safeguards would be futile without comprehensive international inspections of peaceful nuclear research and technology, especially technology related to nuclear power reactions that, if unregulated, could produce weapon-grade plutonium such as that used in the Nagasaki bomb.

As a student of Clausewitz, Eisenhower was not indifferent to the profound ethical questions of waging nuclear warfare. Clausewitz had written specifically on the moral factors of war. Eisenhower's moral repugnance toward nuclear weapons should not be surprising. He had opposed the atomic bombing of Hiroshima, and in 1945 told Secretary of War Stimson that it was "completely unnecessary" to use atomic bombs on an already defeated Japan. He never justified using the bomb to end the war or to save thousands of American lives. He believed the war in the Pacific would end soon, with or without the bomb. In addition, he worried about shocking the world by using a weapon that primarily targeted civilian lives.

The Baruch Plan

In the spring of 1946, the United States offered a blueprint for the international control of nuclear energy to the United Nations Atomic Energy Commission. The American proposal became known as the Baruch Plan, after Bernard Baruch, the international financier who presented the Truman administration's report to the United Nations. Under the Baruch Plan, the United Nations would limit the use of atomic energy to peaceful purposes only. Baruch not only called for international management of peaceful atomic energy but also proposed outlawing atomic weapons once adequate verification systems were established. On June 14, 1946, before the postwar nuclear arms race had begun, Baruch called for a nuclear freeze. In addition, he asked for nuclear disarmament along with outlawing "other weapons—bacteriological, biological, gas, perhaps . . . war itself."

Critics of the Baruch Plan have argued that it was dead on arrival: that the Americans cynically advanced the plan knowing that the Russians would never accept it. Indeed, when Baruch met with Eisenhower and other military leaders in April to discuss the plan, the consensus was that Russian support for it was "almost unthinkable." As it turned out, Eisenhower's views about the international control of atomic energy hardly mattered, because the Truman administration paid little attention to his opinions on these matters.

However, Eisenhower's comments on the plan do reveal his personal views about international management of atomic energy. Without international control of atomic energy, he wrote, nuclear war could not be avoided. Yet even in the unlikely event that the United States and the Soviet Union reached an agreement on inspections, Eisenhower warned that, given nuclear production technology, "no system of inspection can be expected to guarantee completely against the construction of *some* atomic bombs."

Eisenhower's realism regarding the limitations of nuclear safeguards also informed his perception of the nuclear dilemma confronting the United States in 1946 and later. Atomic bombs were not the only weapons of mass destruction threatening American security. Eisenhower believed that biological and chemical weapons could prove no less devastating than the atomic bomb, and even more difficult to control. As he viewed the arms-control dilemma, he did not want the United States to rush into a treaty to abolish nuclear weapons without taking steps to assure that all weapons of mass destruction were brought under control. Otherwise, an aggressor who deliberately eschewed atomic weapons but threatened to lay waste to the United States with biological or chemical weapons might confront the United States. Categorically, Eisenhower declared that the United States should be party to no control treaty that militates against its vital security interests.

And yet, the nuclear dilemma was such that the vital interest and security of the United States could only be guaranteed under the international control of nuclear energy. To achieve nuclear peace, Eisenhower believed that Americans could yield much, including some national sovereignty, to secure a nuclear arms agreement. Years later, Baruch recalled that, in the control of atomic energy, Eisenhower did not demand anything the United States was not willing to give to other nations. But Eisenhower did not regard the Soviet Union as the only impediment to nuclear arms control. He was also skeptical that the American public would support military action against a violator of a nuclear disarmament threat.

The Nuclear Arms Race

Just two weeks after Baruch promoted world peace before the United Nations, atomic thunder rolled across Bikini Atoll when the United States launched its first postwar nuclear weapons test. Reaction from the Soviets was predictable, and *Pravda* charged that the United States was hypocritical, promoting atomic disarmament while enhancing its nuclear weapon stockpile. Whether the American tests were provocative or simply provided the Soviets an excuse to accelerate their own nuclear programs, the Russians had achieved a chain reaction by Christmas Day 1946 and had built a production reactor by fall 1948. On August 29, 1949, the Russians exploded their first atomic bomb in Siberia. In January 1950, President Truman authorized the Atomic Energy Commission to proceed with the development of the hydrogen bomb. Thereafter, the pell-mell nuclear arms race defined the most intense years of the Cold War.

Even as the Cold War intensified, Eisenhower did not mask his skepticism about the strategic dominance of the atomic bomb. When newspaper columnist Dorothy Thompson wrote him denouncing the Baruch Plan as "perfectly fallacious," Eisenhower responded firmly. Building bigger atomic bombs would not promote American security. Some scientists, he noted, predicted that biological warfare might easily surpass nuclear weapons in destructive effects. Who knew what weapons of mass destruction science might develop? And who could say with assurance what nation was ahead in the nuclear arms race? Furthermore, temporary supremacy in atomic weapons provided only uncertain deterrence, he wrote. Perhaps thinking of the pounding the Russians withstood in World War II, he noted, "certain nations and peoples are peculiarly allergic to threat."

Thereafter, Eisenhower got to the heart of the matter. He did not believe the United States could preserve world peace through a Pax Americana guaranteed by nuclear superiority. No American leader, regardless of popularity, could sustain the perpetual readiness required to police the world with nuclear weapons. "National sentiment," Eisenhower reflected, "would be an unyielding factor." In Eisenhower's judgment, diplomacy that relied on threats from the United States to wield atomic weapons to achieve goals was profoundly flawed in its assumptions. Eisenhower would not concede that international control of atomic energy was impossible or that war with the Soviet Union was inevitable. Regardless of Cold War rhetoric, he did not believe that the Soviet Union wanted war and still held on to the fleeting hope of a nuclear rapprochement with the Soviet Union.

His skepticism about the effectiveness of atomic diplomacy, however, went beyond vain optimism concerning the Soviets or misplaced trust in the United Nations. To achieve American hegemony through atomic diplomacy, the United States not only had to possess the ability to deliver a decisive blow, but most importantly, it also had to express the unequivocal willingness to do so. The Russians would not be intimidated by atomic diplomacy unless they were certain America had the moral will to crush them with atomic bombs. Eisenhower shuddered to think about what kind of America that might be.

In contrast to his explanation to Dorothy Thompson, Eisenhower praised Ben Hibbs's June 1946 *Saturday Evening Post* editorial that called for optimism and trust in dealing with the postwar problems. "Hurrah," Eisenhower said, cheering Hibbs's piece entitled "It's Time We Declared Peace." "I cannot escape the conviction," he wrote Hibbs, "that the world has now been living so long in the negative and sterile philosophies of conflict and has gotten so used to thinking in punitive and destructive terms that it is difficult indeed to shift thinking, procedures, and activity back into constructive channels."

When president, Eisenhower would launch Operation Candor not only to instruct Americans about the dangers of the nuclear age but also to raise their hopes concerning prospects for peaceful uses of atomic energy. In 1946, he urged Hibbs and his colleagues to press forward, educating the public about theory and doctrine but also with concrete examples and problems. Prefiguring Operation Candor in 1953, Eisenhower praised Hibbs for constructively keeping matters of war and peace before the public.

A Hand of Friendship

When the Russians turned a deaf ear to America's reasonable disarmament proposals, Eisenhower asked himself *why*? In his mind, the United States should adopt only one fixed condition for a disarmament agreement: that adequate inspections and verifications be guaranteed. When the United Nations General Assembly asked the Security Council to consider general as well as nuclear disarmament, Eisenhower was unperturbed. To his colleagues on the Joint Chiefs of Staff, Eisenhower advised, "neither publicly nor in our own thinking must we ever fail to support every *honest* proposal toward world disarmament."

But the issue went beyond merely supporting acceptable disarmament proposals. According to Eisenhower, the United States had been on the defensive in disarmament negotiations. At the United Nations, where the Soviet Union pressed for general disarmament, the United States continued to advocate step-by-step negotiations in keeping with Eisenhower's own cautious and gradualist temperament. The American approach, however, not only gave the Soviets a propaganda advantage, but as Eisenhower noted, it also frustrated Americans "who are honestly concerned with the importance of this great problem."

Eisenhower was ready to move to a more positive and aggressive approach to the disarmament talks as well as other diplomatic initiatives. Expressing an opinion he would maintain as president, he concluded "that if every kind of armament were abolished in the world, the United States would be by far relatively the strongest." The United States had nothing to fear from complete, total, and universal disarmament, provided effective inspections were ensured. Furthermore, educational exchanges among leaders in the arts, sciences, and religion would not only unlock gates through the Iron Curtain but would also help advance American interests. Typically, Eisenhower had mixed idealism and realism in his proposal to the Congress. Years later, these same sentiments informed the Eisenhower administration's motives for sponsoring the Geneva Atoms for Peace Conference in 1955 and in promoting Eisenhower's People to People program after 1956.

Increasing talk about preemptive atomic bombing of the Soviet Union also distressed Eisenhower. "I decry loose and sometimes gloating talk about the high degree of security implicit in a weapon that might destroy millions overnight," he told a gathering in St. Louis. His moral indignation was evident, but so was his cool reasoning. National security could not be measured solely in terms of offensive strength. As he reminded his audience, no modern nation had ever built a mightier war machine than Nazi Germany in 1939, and none was more broken and smashed than Germany six years later.

On February 7, 1948, Eisenhower ended his term as army chief of staff and retired from active duty so that he could accept the presidency of Columbia University. When he left the army after more than thirty years of service, he offered a final report on American military preparedness. Eisenhower denounced the hysterical pressure and demagoguery of political naysayers. Despite scaremongers, he believed that the United States was first in wealth, industrial production, technical achievement, and citizen skill. Americans should neither despair of the peace nor be swept into panic by the threats of the day.

Because the Soviet Union did not possess nuclear capability in 1948, Eisenhower projected that the United States would not lose an atomic war if

Americans were prepared to retaliate against attack. He was not blasé about the destructiveness and horror of nuclear war and confessed that substantial preparedness against attack would be difficult but not impossible. "[The enemy's] means can be no greater than our means," he wrote. "His [strategic] task can be made a hopeless one." Optimistically, Eisenhower concluded that the nation's "readiness can nullify in advance any aggression [an enemy] may plan." In 1948, Eisenhower had not yet begun to calculate the strategic or moral consequences of thermonuclear warfare, thus his assessment of the effects of nuclear war was limited to the destructiveness of fission weapons.

Eisenhower's understanding of nuclear issues was not static, however. While commander of the Allied forces in Europe during World War II, he had opposed the atomic bombing of Japan, and yet as commander in chief of NATO forces, he prepared to use atomic weapons in the defense of Europe. From 1945 to 1952, he was one of the few American military leaders who worried always about the morality of nuclear arms, and yet, when elected president, he had limited knowledge of the United States' nuclear program, including production and stockpiles of weapons. And he had only a vague idea of the potential of peaceful applications of atomic energy. Indeed, the new president could appear remarkably ambivalent concerning nuclear energy. He had frightened Winston Churchill with his opinion that atomic bombs should be considered conventional weapons; on the other hand, he seemed to understand the dangers of placing so much power in the hands of government, where risks of human failure, miscalculation, espionage, and ambition could lead to nuclear holocaust.

Eisenhower's views remained constant as to the best means to secure lasting peace. He believed there was no alternative to a strong United Nations. He urged Americans to make every honest effort through the United Nations to reduce armaments, and even suggested that Americans act with patience and forbearance, making it clear to all that they intended to live and let live.

Eisenhower's "live and let live" philosophy was severely challenged in 1948 when he was caught up in the Red Scare sweeping the American political landscape. Despite his moderate final report as chief of staff, he was becoming militantly anti-Communist. Eisenhower's disillusionment with the Russians was all the greater, because his hopes for postwar partnership had been so high following his triumphal visit to Moscow. When Stalin denied Zhukov's visit to the United States and instead banished him to Odessa, Eisenhower was upset that Zhukov's downfall, in part, was a consequence of their mutual friendship. He placed great stock in personal diplomacy, and Zhukov's disgrace was a clear signal to Eisenhower that the Soviets were indifferent to whatever role the generals might play in preserving postwar peace.

As the Cold War deepened and Eisenhower's political ambitions grew, his anti-Communism intensified. The Communist takeover of Czechoslovakia and the Berlin crisis of 1948 marked the end of Eisenhower's dreams of immediate cooperation with the Soviet Union. When talks collapsed and the Berlin blockade lengthened, Eisenhower shared his bitter disappointment with Secretary of War James Forrestal. "Until now," he wrote Forrestal in September 1948, "I had believed that . . . the Russians . . . would find some skillful way to retreat sufficiently far to ease the tension." But they seemed so overconfident that Eisenhower feared the Russians might push everyone beyond endurance. The time had come, he reluctantly advised, for the allies to make war plans and "to be ready to act on a week-to-week basis."

By 1951, Eisenhower was a quintessential Cold Warrior, outwardly suspicious of the Russians on all issues, determined to contain Communist expansion, and committed to maintaining America's nuclear dominance. While serving as president of Columbia University and supreme commander of NATO, Eisenhower denounced the Soviet threat frequently and plainly. Nevertheless, he remained wary of strident anti-Communist hysteria.

Nuclear Cooperation with the British

Two issues, nuclear cooperation with the British and the development of the hydrogen bomb, provide additional insight into the foundation of Eisenhower's nuclear diplomacy. Partners with the United States in the race for the atomic bomb, the British had looked forward to postwar cooperation with the United States. Although the Quebec Agreement of August 1943, supplemented by the Roosevelt-Churchill Hyde Park Aide-Mémoire, seemed to guarantee Anglo-American nuclear partnership after the war, the United States Atomic Energy Act of 1946 established security restrictions that precluded the United States sharing technical information with foreign governments.

Eisenhower was caught unawares by the restrictive requirements of the McMahon Act, as the Atomic Energy Act of 1946 was called. He favored sharing some nuclear weapon test data with the British. He assumed the British would continue to be American allies and could not understand why the United States denied its friends technical nuclear information that, on their own, they could develop anyway. He was certain that any war with the Soviet

Union would be a nuclear war, and that America's allies would become fully engaged. Atomic secrets, Eisenhower believed, should be shared with the British on the same basis that the Allies had shared the Ultra code-breaking program during World War II.

The issue, of course, transcended sharing nuclear weapon secrets. The British also wanted to share technical information concerning peaceful uses, including nuclear power: information, to be sure, that was equally useful in building weapon facilities and power plants. While Eisenhower understood this nuclear dilemma, he also feared that the United Kingdom would be a weaker ally if the United States refused to share atomic technology. The stringent provisions of the Atomic Energy Act not only hampered joint military preparedness but also proved inimical to promotion of peaceful uses.

The H-bomb Debate

In August 1949, the Soviet Union tested their first atomic bomb, just about on time in the five-year schedule that Eisenhower, among others, predicted. There followed an acrimonious but secret debate on whether Americans should accelerate development of the thermonuclear bomb, a fusion device much more powerful than the fission bomb. The H-bomb debate involved not only nuclear scientists raising questions about the feasibility of obtaining suitable fusion reactions but also politicians inquiring about the motives and loyalties of certain leading American scientists. Truman's decision to build the H-bomb ended the policy debate but did not dispel suspicion that somehow the Russians had obtained the atomic bomb through espionage. This legacy of recrimination would also have a profound influence on shaping Eisenhower's nuclear diplomacy.

Eisenhower did not participate in the H-bomb debate and avoided getting entangled in the thermonuclear controversy. Instead, he worked tirelessly to win support for NATO, which was to play a key role in his nuclear diplomacy as president. Concurrently, he reflected on the implications of Truman's H-bomb decision. He was especially skeptical of pessimists who characterized the H-bomb as a doomsday weapon. No matter how powerful the hydrogen bomb, Eisenhower believed, it could be used for good or evil.

He thought the press had an obligation to educate the American public about the dangers and limitations of nuclear warfare. The press performed no service by emphasizing that the United States was vulnerable to national extinction, a mantra that hampered clear thinking and reasonable action. He was also aware that strict secrecy about American nuclear capabilities distorted public understanding of atomic energy and fueled nuclear fears. "If we are all to be destroyed in the twinkling of an eye," Eisenhower asked rhetorically, "what is there to do about it?" Eisenhower resisted such moral defeatism throughout his public life.

As supreme commander of NATO, Eisenhower planned to use atomic weapons to defend Western Europe. As president, he also threatened to use them to end the Korean War. The New Look, his critics charged, only escalated atomic diplomacy into brinkmanship. In this respect he was an atomic diplomat prepared to brandish nuclear weapons to achieve diplomatic objectives. He was outspokenly anti-Communist, highly suspicious of the Soviet Union, and vocally opposed to Reds in the university and government. As he took the oath of office as president of the United States, Eisenhower appeared to be a quintessential Cold Warrior.

In his first inaugural address, however, he mentioned neither nuclear energy nor the nuclear arms race. But in a veiled reference to the thermonuclear bomb whose development was still classified top secret, he asked darkly: "Are we nearing the light—a day of freedom and peace for all mankind? Or are the shadows of another night closing in on us? . . . Science seems ready to confer upon us, as the final gift, the power to erase human life from this planet."

Thermonuclear Realities

While his audience may have missed the point, we can sense Eisenhower's uneasiness and his changing views about nuclear warfare. After he was briefed by the Atomic Energy Commission regarding the H-bomb, Eisenhower struggled to comprehend the effect of this strategic weapon that might destroy civilization itself. He realized instantly that the hydrogen bomb was to the atomic bomb what the atomic bomb was to TNT bombs. A thermonuclear weapon not only reduced the ratio of cost to destructive capability but also increased the desperate problem of arms control in an uncertain world.

As president, however, he would pursue a policy of nuclear diplomacy as we have defined it, not atomic diplomacy. Eisenhower's nuclear diplomacy occasionally threatened use of nuclear weapons to achieve foreign policy objectives, but it also included initiatives to secure international management and control of the military and peaceful uses of nuclear science. The seeds for Eisenhower's nuclear diplomacy were all planted in the postwar years, 1945–1952, as was revealed in his Gabriel Silver Lecture on Peace at Columbia University, March 23, 1950. Operation Candor, the "Chance for Peace" speech, the "Atoms for Peace" speech, the Geneva peaceful uses conferences, his Open-Skies Proposal, American sponsorship of the International Atomic Energy Agency, the European Atomic Energy Community (EURATOM), and finally, his futile pursuit of nuclear-test-ban and disarmament negotiations—all had their roots in these formative years.

Eisenhower was both a moralist and a realist about the management and control of nuclear energy. He was one of the few American leaders who worried about the morality of nuclear arms but also advocated the development of peaceful uses. He knew there were no atomic secrets, but he wanted to protect as long as possible those secrets that could damage the security interests of the United States. He did not want to panic the American public, but he believed they needed to know about the risks they faced in the nuclear age.

Finally, his nuclear worldview was not bipolar. As is evidenced in his Atoms for Peace and disarmament initiatives, Eisenhower never gave up hope of reaching an accommodation with the Soviets based upon reliable safeguards and inspections. Nevertheless, as indicated by United States sponsorship of the International Atomic Energy Agency and EURATOM, Eisenhower also negotiated a nuclear diplomacy independent of Soviet involvement. One of the most significant accomplishments of Eisenhower's nuclear diplomacy was the negotiation of over forty bilateral treaties for peaceful uses that provided for the exchange of nuclear science and technology.

When he was elected president in 1952, most Americans did not know that Eisenhower opposed the atomic bombing of Japan in 1945. He had returned from war-ravaged Moscow in 1945 depressed about the atomic bombing of Hiroshima. As his nuclear worldview developed and matured between 1945 and 1952, he resolved to pursue peaceful applications of atomic energy. Had critics known about David Eisenhower's pyramid wall chart that predicted the imminent, catastrophic end of the world, they might have understood the origins of Eisenhower's moral compass concerning the use of nuclear weapons. Eisenhower had pondered fiery Armageddon as a child and had rejected his father's apocalyptic religion. While president, Eisenhower's moral revulsion over use of the atomic bomb never lessened, but rather became a major force shaping his worldview, domestic politics, and civil religion.

Derailed Disarmament and Peace Talks

Disarmament talks among the United States, the Soviet Union, and the United Kingdom were derailed by the advent of the thermonuclear age, as each nuclear power assessed the strategic implications of the hydrogen bomb.

Although the talks were not officially abandoned, the positions of the great powers became dramatically solidified. The United States, anxious to reduce the military threat of the Red Army in Europe, linked the abolition of nuclear weapons with *immediate* general disarmament under enforceable verification. On the other hand, the Soviet Union, behind in the nuclear arms race but dominant in conventional forces, called for outlawing nuclear weapons as a first step, to be *followed* by negotiations to reduce conventional arms and the establishment of verification systems. For their part, the British were not interested in any international agreement to outlaw development of nuclear weapons until *after* they had joined the exclusive nuclear club as a full partner.

After his inauguration, Eisenhower's immediate priority became ending the Korean War. In secret National Security Council (NSC) meetings, he explored the possibility of using atomic bombs in Korea. With Eisenhower's knowledge and the NSC's approval, the Joint Chiefs of Staff developed a contingency plan for the use of tactical atomic bombs on the Korean battlefield. Through diplomatic channels, Eisenhower hinted that the United States might unilaterally scrap limited warfare in Korea.

A consummate poker player, Eisenhower knew that an effective bluff must be absolutely credible. As long as use of tactical atomic weapons was taboo in the West, an effective nuclear deterrent could not be built. By transferring the control of atomic bombs from the civilian Atomic Energy Commission to the air force, Eisenhower hoped to convince friends and foes alike that he might authorize use of nuclear weapons. Earlier, as supreme commander in World War II, he had demonstrated his willingness to employ the strategic bombing of German cities to hasten the end of the war. While Eisenhower would have liked to believe that his nuclear bluff worked, the death of Stalin in March 1953, as much as anything, may have brought the Communists to the peace table at Panmunjom.

Death of Stalin

At the death of Soviet premier Joseph Stalin in March 1953, according to diplomatic historian Walter LaFeber in *America, Russia, and the Cold War* (1997), the Cold War "assumed new and puzzling traits." Georgy Malenkov, and then Nikita S. Khrushchev, assumed leadership of the Soviet Union, offering new possibilities for easing the Cold War. As Stalin had lain dying in Moscow, Eisenhower sent prayerful consolation to anxious citizens in the Soviet Union while reminding Americans everywhere who were tempted to celebrate the

Soviet dictator's death that Russians, too, were "children of the same God who is the Father of all peoples everywhere." While trying to comfort the Russians, Eisenhower optimistically affirmed to people everywhere that "Russia's millions share our longing for a friendly and peaceful world."

At the height of the Cold War, his was a remarkable presidential prayer that asked Americans to petition God to watch over the vast and officially godless Soviet Union. Stalin died the following day, March 5. At his news conference that day, reporters wanted to know if Stalin's passing would alter America's Cold War foreign policy. Reporters' questions about American policy regarding the new Soviet leaders in the Kremlin were understandable; puzzling, however, was their studied silence concerning the religious implications raised by the president. Even the reporter from the *Christian Science Monitor* had no interest in commenting on Eisenhower's use of the bully pulpit at the time of Stalin's death—the president's religious sentiments concerning Stalin's demise simply did not seem newsworthy.

When Stalin died in March 1953, Eisenhower believed the United States stood at a time of unique danger and opportunity. His father, David, had predicted such moments of historical judgment. Eisenhower was neither a millenarian nor a Manichaean, but his religious worldview was informed by dialectical interplay between divine and demonic forces in history, an understanding not dissimilar to that of his father or of the contemporary theologian Paul Tillich. Typically, Eisenhower had described his struggles against the dark forces of history in the rhetoric of crusades. His use of crusade rhetoric, however, was not intended to pit followers of Jesus against nonbelievers but rather to highlight the epic nature of history in dramatic language understood by ordinary Americans.

Eisenhower's crusades were metaphorical in the same vein as Lyndon Johnson's War on Poverty. But Eisenhower understood the complexity of history. His religious beliefs affirmed that the Russians were children of God. Despite his transformation into a Cold War president, Eisenhower still believed, as he had in 1945, that the Russian people genuinely longed for peace and friendship. With Stalin's death, Eisenhower saw a chance for peace.

A Chance for Peace

His father, David Eisenhower, believed in three ages, or dispensations, in history, the last of which would be preceded by a fiery holocaust that foretold the second coming of Christ. His son's vision of the middle way, in contrast,

If true, DDE was not a biblical christian.

rejected belief in a divine apocalyptic end to history. Eisenhower preferred to seek human salvation within nature and history and entertained no capitulation to the forces of evil or death in this world.

For Dwight Eisenhower, the spring of 1953 was a time of hopeful transition, a moment of *kairos*, Paul Tillich would say, when the world was summoned to choose between peace and peril. It is mystifying how scholars can read Eisenhower's "Chance for Peace" speech, which he presented to the American Society of Newspaper Editors on April 16, 1953, and still conclude that he was vague, uninformed, and disinterested. Like his 1909 talk "The Student in Politics," "A Chance for Peace" marked a watershed in Eisenhower's thinking that manifestly echoed a Cold War political agenda while latently revealing Eisenhower's religious transformation.

"A Chance for Peace" described the historical turning point literally:

> This is one of those times in the affairs of nations when the gravest choices must be made, if there is to be a turning toward a just and lasting peace. It is a moment that calls upon the governments of the world to speak their intentions with simplicity and honesty. It calls upon them to answer the question that stirs the hearts of all sane men: *is there no other way the world may live?*

Shortly after World War II, when hopes for peace were highest, the Iron Curtain descended over Europe, dividing the West from the Soviet-dominated East. As tensions mounted, the world panicked into a terrible atomic armaments race. What could the world hope for if there were no exit from the dreadful dance of nuclear threat and counterthreat? Eisenhower asked rhetorically. The *worst* was nuclear Armageddon that could destroy civilization, as we knew it. The best that could be hoped for was a life of perpetual fear; a life in which wealth and labor were dissipated in an endless nuclear arms race; and a life in which governments were discredited because they could not achieve prosperity and happiness for humankind. The costs of the Cold War were staggering and debilitating. To emphasize his point, Eisenhower composed a hymn, a lamentation:

> Every gun that is made,
> Every warship launched,
> Every rocket fired
> Signifies, in the final sense,
> A theft

From those who hunger and are not fed,
From those who are cold and not clothed.

These great costs were not paid in cash alone. The Cold War consumed the daily work of laborers, the creativity of scientists, and the future of children. In social priorities, a bomber cost thirty schools, two electrical power plants, two hospitals, or fifty miles of highway. A single destroyer would buy eight thousand new homes for a small Kansas town. Paraphrasing the 1908 Democratic presidential nominee, William Jennings Bryan, Eisenhower solemnly observed, "Under the cloud of threatening war, it is humanity hanging from a Cross of Iron."

As pessimistic as Eisenhower's remarks may have seemed, he outlined a way to liberate America from the Cold War. Ultimately, "A Chance for Peace" was not a jeremiad; it instead offered redemption from the nuclear arms race. Despite increasing stockpiles of nuclear weapons, Eisenhower continued to search for rapprochement with the Soviet Union, on American terms, of course. He recalled that brief moment of joyous victory in the spring of 1945 when Americans, British, and Russians embraced as comrades in arms looking forward to a world at peace as a tribute to the millions who had died in the crusade to defeat fascist tyranny.

In the aftermath of Hiroshima and Nagasaki, the United States and the Soviet Union had taken different paths, each seeking to buy security through international alliances and nuclear arms. The results were ironic and tragic. Enormous investment in weapons of mass destruction had lessened everyone's security. Although some of Eisenhower's prerequisites for peace included standard Cold War demands for a free Germany and a free Eastern Europe, he also offered to explore modest, incremental steps toward arms control and disarmament. To be sure, suggestions for international control of atomic energy for peaceful purposes were not new with Eisenhower. But, if adopted, they exemplified confidence-building initiatives certain to lessen Cold War animosities.

"A Chance for Peace" was one of Eisenhower's finest speeches. It was not free of raw Cold War propaganda in its condemnation of Soviet tyranny. Eisenhower hated Stalin's heteronomy as intensely as he had hated Hitler's despotism. But, in contrast to the Nazis, with whom no moral compromise was possible, Eisenhower hoped that the new Communist leaders in the Kremlin might be amenable to making small, verifiable steps toward peace. Eisenhower was not naïve about the difficulty of his proposals, but he hoped that a "Chance for Peace" outlined a workable path toward peace.

Trust and goodwill would be difficult to establish with the Soviets in the Cold War atmosphere, especially because Americans insisted that it was the Russians who were responsible for creating Cold War tensions. Inside the Kremlin, "A Chance for Peace," which was long on rhetoric but short on concrete proposals, could be easily dismissed as American psychological warfare. In addition, Eisenhower's peace overtures would be challenged by die-hard Cold Warriors at home. If his arms-control proposals were modest, in part it was because he had to mollify Cold Warriors in Congress, his administration, and NATO allies as well as the new leaders of the Soviet Union. The "details of disarmament programs were necessarily critical and complex . . . and no nation possessed a perfect, immutable formula." But, he concluded, "the formula mattered less than the faith."

Nightmares of nuclear Armageddon haunted Eisenhower. In his role as president/pastor, he wanted to educate the American people about the realities of nuclear warfare while offering hope to the world. He grew up in a religious tradition that viewed history as the battleground between the forces of good and evil—an eternal struggle between the divine and demonic principles in creation. But if there were no middle ground between good and evil, how could Eisenhower move to the middle of the road in this diabolical cosmic drama?

He had refused to meet with General Alfred Jodl, the apotheosis of Nazi evil, when the German officer came to Rheims to sign surrender documents on May 7, 1945. Later, shoving brittle Cold War rhetoric aside, he viewed the Russians differently. Perhaps there was a warrior's bond—certainly there had been a warm friendship and genuine respect between Eisenhower and Zhukov. Although they were avowed atheists, Eisenhower did not condemn the Soviets as hopelessly evil, as he had the Nazis. The reality of atomic weaponry may have dictated no other choice. But Eisenhower's dilemma was palpable: How could he lead his "Crusade for Peace" against Communism from the middle of the road?

Not completely paralyzed by his concerns about nuclear annihilation, Eisenhower drew on his faith that God intended for humans, including Russians, to employ atomic energy for peaceful purposes. "A Chance for Peace" was a public prayer offering a middle way in public policy by instructing Americans about the realities of the nuclear arms race while pointing toward new paths to peace. Characteristically, Eisenhower tried to seize a historical opportunity in 1953 rather than drift passively with the Cold War tide. "A Chance for Peace" outlined a call for nuclear arms control and disarmament from which

Eisenhower would not deviate. At the United Nations in December 1953, at the Geneva conferences in 1955 and 1958, and during the seemingly fruitless negotiations to limit atmospheric nuclear testing, Eisenhower would never lose sight of the historical objectives envisioned in "A Chance for Peace."

Also in April 1953, Eisenhower graphically described the horrors of nuclear warfare to the United Church Women. Although America had escaped physical destruction in World War II, the United States' oceanic security had disappeared with the threat of nuclear attack by intercontinental bombers. America had few choices.

> The choice that spells terror and death is symbolized by a mushroom cloud floating upward from the release of the mightiest natural power yet uncovered by those who search the physical universe. The energy that it typifies is, at this stage of human knowledge, the unharnessed blast. In its wake we see only sudden and mass destruction, erasure of cities, the possible doom of every nation and society. [He had softened this imagery by striking reference to "windrows of unidentifiable dead" from the final version of his text.]

He edged away, slightly, from his focus on Soviet intransigence toward identifying atomic energy itself as the problem. But Eisenhower did not abandon hope that the titanic force of nuclear energy could be directed to the useful service of mankind.

Atoms for Peace

Eisenhower's "Atoms for Peace" speech to the United Nations in December 1953 was a companion to his "Chance for Peace" speech in April 1953, both of which had been anticipated by the Gabriel Silver Lecture on Peace at Columbia University in 1950. While the National Security Council drafted NSC 162/2, "The New Look," for strategic nuclear deterrence, Eisenhower and his closest White House advisors labored over how to inform the American public about the realities of the thermonuclear world.

A State Department disarmament study group headed by J. Robert Oppenheimer advised that Americans did not understand the danger of the nuclear arms race or the awful threat of the hydrogen bomb. In the opinion of Oppenheimer's committee, the United States had adopted an excessively rigid policy of massive retaliation that left the nation without flexibility to

Dwight Eisenhower as a West Point cadet, 1911–1915

Mamie, Icky, and Ike ca. 1920

COURTESY OF THE DWIGHT D. EISENHOWER PRESIDENTIAL LIBRARY, ABILENE, KS

General Fox Conner, the "Grey Eminence," Eisenhower's mentor in Panama from 1922 to 1924

Eisenhower family reunion following Dwight's graduation from the Command and General Staff School, 1926; *left to right:* **Roy, Arthur, Earl, Edgar, David, Milton, Ida. Dwight is sitting on the steps.**

John, Ike, and Mamie in 1933

General Eisenhower and 101st Airborne Division paratroopers before D-Day, June 6, 1944

COURTESY OF THE DWIGHT D. EISENHOWER PRESIDENTIAL LIBRARY, ABILENE, KS

Ohrdruf concentration camp gallows, 1945
COURTESY OF THE DWIGHT D. EISENHOWER PRESIDENTIAL LIBRARY, ABILENE, KS

Dwight, Mamie, and Reverend Edward Elson after church on Inauguration Day, January 20, 1953

NATIONAL ARCHIVES AND RECORDS ADMINISTRATION

Eisenhower addressing the United Nations regarding "Atoms for Peace,"
December 8, 1953

The Eisenhower and Nixon families leaving the National Presbyterian Church on inaugural morning, January 20, 1957. The Reverend Edward Elson stands next to Richard Nixon.

Mamie, Field Marshall Montgomery, Ike, and Gettysburg pastor Robert MacAskill, May 12, 1957. Mother's Day, May 12, was Rev. Robert Mac-Askill's second Sunday preaching at the Gettysburg Presbyterian Church. Field Marshall Bernard Montgomery attended the service with Mamie and Dwight Eisenhower. PHOTO ENHS 2439, GETTYSBURG TIMES.

Frederic Fox (on the right) served as the White House Special
Assistant for Religion, 1957–1961. Prior to his White House appointment, in addition to serving as pastor to various American
churches, Fox also served as a missionary in Africa.

Troopers from the 101st Airborne Division escort Little Rock Nine students at Little Rock's Central High School, September 1957

Eisenhower meeting with civil rights leaders, June 23, 1958; *left to right:*
Lester Granger, Martin Luther King Jr., E. Frederic Morrow, Eisenhower,
A. Philip Randolph, William Rogers, Rosco Siciliano, and Roy Wilkins

The Place of Meditation in Abilene, KS, the burial place of
Dwight, Mamie, and Icky

COURTESY OF THE DWIGHT D. EISENHOWER PRESIDENTIAL LIBRARY, ABILENE, KS

Eisenhower crypt inside the Place of Meditation

respond to the Soviet nuclear threat. The terrible fury of the Castle Bravo thermonuclear test in the spring of 1954 underscored the bankruptcy of the "massive retaliation" doctrine even before the ink was dry on Dulles's *Foreign Affairs* article.

Eisenhower was moved by the disarmament panel's insistence that the government should be candid with itself and the American people about the realities of the nuclear arms race. Through the summer and into the fall of 1953, Eisenhower and his advisors, principally C. D. Jackson, an Eisenhower speechwriter and advisor on psychological warfare, planned Operation Candor, through which the administration would alert Americans about the destructiveness of nuclear war. "A Chance for Peace" had previewed his "Atoms for Peace" speech to the United Nations on December 8, 1953.

The United Nations' dais proved to be Eisenhower's ultimate bully pulpit in his quest for a nuclear peace. Again, the president described in graphic language the ghastly threat of nuclear warfare. But, determined not to be overwhelmed by the prospect of nuclear Armageddon, he offered hope of developing peaceful alternatives to the atomic bomb. In his address to the United Nations, he pledged that the United States would devote its entire heart and mind to finding "a way by which science shall not be dedicated to death but consecrated to life."

He underscored the importance of negotiating peace with the Russians by patiently implementing small steps toward international understanding. Drawing from his personal religious perspective, he averred that "salvation cannot be attained by one dramatic act," a stunning confession for a Christian to make. Then, using ancient religious imagery contrasting darkness and light, he called for the United Nations "to move out of the dark chamber of horrors into the light" in its search for peace. Waves of applause temporarily cleansed the hall of acrimony when even the Russians joined the acclamation. His "Atoms for Peace" speech at the United Nations was a highlight of his public life, matched only by his London Guildhall Address.

Eisenhower's "Atoms for Peace" speech is central for understanding his nuclear diplomacy. In the shadow of Castle Bravo and the Soviet's thermonuclear test, Eisenhower hoped that his Atoms for Peace initiative would break the deadlocked arms-control talks with the Soviet Union. While pursuing peaceful alternatives to nuclear weapons, he envisioned establishing an International Atomic Energy Agency, a forum through which nations could promote international management and control of atomic energy.

Additionally, Eisenhower's nuclear diplomacy envisioned creating regional nuclear cooperatives such as EURATOM, negotiating bilateral agreements of cooperation on peaceful uses, establishing international exchange programs, and sponsoring conferences on the peaceful uses of atomic energy in Geneva in 1955 and 1958. The president's proposals also required a major rewriting of the 1946 Atomic Energy Act to allow the United States to share nuclear technology with friendly nations. The Atomic Energy Act of 1954 provided the basis for both the development of nuclear power and the fostering of international cooperation. "Massive retaliation" was not a guarantor of nuclear peace. What had changed was the advent of the thermonuclear age that gave gravitas to Atoms for Peace. The greatest danger was no longer Communism but the thermonuclear bomb that threatened the annihilation of friend and foe alike.

There Are No Atomic Secrets

Although Eisenhower promoted peaceful uses of nuclear energy while charting alternatives to stalled arms-control negotiations, he was aware of the difficulty of controlling nuclear proliferation while advancing the peaceful uses of atomic energy. As clearly as any political leader, he also knew that it would not be long before scientists around the world found the secrets that the Manhattan Project had wrung from the atom. The British and the Soviets already knew basic atomic secrets, and the French were not far behind. In this respect, Eisenhower was a hardheaded realist who regarded American nuclear technology, both military and peaceful, as a "wasting asset." That is, Eisenhower knew that technology guarded by the US Atomic Energy Commission would soon be acquired by other nations through their own efforts.

In 1953, the United States still enjoyed dominance in nuclear science, but that advantage could not last indefinitely. Although Eisenhower was in no rush to share America's atomic secrets, neither did he want to lose the opportunity to further the United States' commercial and military interests around the world. As one State Department official explained to Nelson Rockefeller, the development of international atomic energy under American leadership would provide an "Atomic Marshall Plan" for the world in general, and Europe in particular.

Eisenhower regarded nuclear science as a "wasting asset" in two respects. Militarily, he believed that the United States could gain no long-range advantage in the nuclear arms race. Consequently, he was willing to outlaw nuclear weapons without a companion agreement on conventional weapons. Although the bomb might serve as a deterrent to war, it was also the only weapon that seriously threatened American security because it could cripple industry—crippling industry was the winning factor in all American conflicts since the Civil War. If nuclear weapons were successfully banned, the Russians would be left with superior conventional forces, but American industry could readily cope with any conventional military assault on North America. Eisenhower predicted that the United States and the Soviet Union would eventually reach a nuclear standoff.

By the summer of 1954, there seemed to be little or no progress made on Eisenhower's Atoms for Peace initiative. C. D. Jackson complained to the president that "foreign policy by Presidential speeches, without follow-through, just doesn't work." What was absent, Jackson thought, was that no one was responsible for promoting Atoms for Peace. Taken aback by Jackson's allegations that he had failed to provide dynamic nuclear leadership, Eisenhower tried to calm his trusted advisor. He agreed that dramatic speeches had limited impact, but he insisted that the follow-up be taken with small, confidence-building steps. For those who grew impatient with the slow pace of diplomacy, Eisenhower loved to quote the poet Arthur Clough:

> For while the tired waves, vainly breaking,
> Seem here no painful inch to gain,
> Far back, through creeks and inlets making,
> Comes silent, flooding in, the main.

The old warrior thought it senseless to assault Cold War barricades with sword lifted high, waving to his allies to follow. He wanted NATO and EURATOM to march abreast in a broad diplomatic front with no Yankee Doodle heroic horseman leading the charge. The United States claimed too much regarding its leadership of the free world, he believed. "This business of saying we are out in front, we know all the answers, you boys come along, we will help you with this and that," he said, was counterproductive. As he had stated in his Silver Lecture, there was no need to remake the world into the likeness of the United States; that would not work.

Surprisingly, in September 1954 the Soviet Union announced its willingness to discuss protocols for the international management of peaceful atomic energy. The Soviets also wanted to negotiate a ban on all nuclear weapons. The Soviet offer to help sponsor the International Atomic Energy Agency (IAEA) caught the Eisenhower administration off guard. Given their United Nations behavior, Soviet presence at the conference table did not bode well for the success of the negotiations. But Eisenhower refused to be pessimistic about

Soviet obstructionism. He simply refused to limit his nuclear diplomacy to the establishment of the IAEA. Whatever the Soviets' intentions, it would not be possible for them to block all his peaceful-uses initiatives.

The Soviets read the handwriting on the wall when the United Nations endorsed Eisenhower's proposal for an international peaceful-uses conference in Geneva for the summer of 1955. Yet, while the United Nations organized the first international nuclear science fair, the United States pressed ahead with its own initiatives for global development of atomic energy. By the time the peaceful-uses conference convened in August 1955, the US State Department had negotiated two-dozen bilateral treaties on cooperative development of the peaceful atom, an unprecedented initiative in nuclear diplomacy. Although the United States supported creation of an international atomic energy agency, Americans actually preferred to promote peaceful uses with nuclear power and research agreements because these bilateral treaties provided the United States greater economic and military leverage than working through the United Nations.

The first peaceful bilateral treaty, signed in June 1955 with Turkey, authorized American firms to sell research reactors to Turkey and to provide help in developing nuclear medicine and biological, agricultural, and industrial research using radioactive isotopes. Concurrently, the United States secured a military agreement that included a secret provision to provide the United States with bases for U-2 spy planes and ballistic missiles. Many of the peaceful bilateral treaties were accompanied by similar secret military agreements for overseas bases, purchase of uranium, or promise of protection under the American nuclear umbrella.

Eisenhower knew that Turkey could build a modest nuclear stockpile within six years if it felt threatened by nuclear-armed neighbors. He believed that the best way to deter nuclear proliferation (there was no way to stop it completely) was to help friendly nations benefit from nuclear technology without having to pay enormous costs creating a nuclear weapons arsenal. Atoms for Peace programs, especially nuclear power programs, would not dampen the fear of nuclear war, but by lessening the likelihood that small nations would build nuclear forces, Eisenhower believed that his peaceful initiative would strengthen American alliances while refuting Russian propaganda that the United States only dealt in nuclear war. As became abundantly clear, Eisenhower's nuclear diplomacy was not simply an extension of Truman's confrontational atomic diplomacy with the Soviet Union.

Primarily, Eisenhower's Atoms for Peace initiative was oriented toward Europe in that the United States placed its greatest diplomatic effort behind

EURATOM, the European nuclear cooperative embracing France, West Germany, Italy, the Netherlands, Belgium, and Luxembourg. Modeled after the European Coal and Steel Community, EURATOM not only would generate electrical power for industrial uses but would also finance and coordinate nuclear research and development in Europe. Eisenhower had first advocated a United States of Europe at the English-Speaking Union in 1951. Now he believed that European unification through NATO, the Brussels Pact, and the Coal and Steel Community was necessary for a stable Western alliance and world peace.

By the elections of 1956, Eisenhower's nuclear diplomacy was fully mature. On the peaceful side, nuclear initiatives emphasized international development through EURATOM, the IAEA, and bilateral treaties providing research and power reactors as well as nuclear technology relating to biology, medicine, agriculture, and other peaceful uses. On the military side, the Eisenhower administration shored up NATO defenses with a vigorous program of developing weapons, obtaining new bases, and adopting the New Look in strategic planning. The Atoms for Peace initiative provided linkage between military-use and peaceful-use bilateral treaties, thereby promoting nuclear nonproliferation by encouraging participating countries not to pursue an independent nuclear weapons program. Although progress in nuclear arms-control negotiations seemed impossible, the Eisenhower administration continued to seek a way for slowing the nuclear arms race. The problem was not so much in devising disarmament proposals as in securing reliable verification through inspections.

Overlooking opposition from the Pentagon and the Atomic Energy Commission, Dulles encouraged flexibility in arms-control negotiations because he believed that the United States would lose military bases if it did not engage in bona fide disarmament diplomacy. Agreement was possible with the Russians, Dulles thought, because the Soviet Union, the United States, and NATO genuinely wanted to end the expensive and dangerous nuclear arms race. Inspection remained the crux of the problem, which is where Dulles thought the State Department should focus its efforts. Eisenhower agreed. Noting that on-site inspection was the most politically sensitive issue, the president concluded the obvious: the disarmament plan that prevailed would be determined by which inspection scheme would be acceptable to all the superpowers.

Eisenhower envisioned that his "Open Skies" proposal offered at the 1955 Geneva conference might provide the blueprint for an acceptable plan. To the relief of the Atomic Energy Commission and the British, the Soviets dismissed Open Skies out of hand. Although he doubted that the Russians

would accept his proposal, Eisenhower believed that it would not hurt to offer a confidence-building step to workable inspection procedures. Instead,
the Soviets saw through his ploy and ridiculed the idea for its simplicity. To
implement Open Skies, Eisenhower had suggested that the Americans and
Russians allow aerial photography of nuclear facilities after both sides had
exchanged blueprints of their plants. Would the United States allow ground
observation and inspection posts? Soviet delegates asked. And, to be workable, the Russians insisted, Open Skies had to include surveillance of all allies,
East and West. Even if the United States talked NATO allies into going along,
there remained Communist China, whom the United States steadfastly refused diplomatic recognition. From this perspective, the Russians thought
Open Skies was a dead letter.

Another avenue for negotiations was the reduction of atmospheric weapon
tests. The disaster of the Castle Bravo test, the 15-megaton thermonuclear device that had dropped radioactive fallout on Japanese fishermen, Marshall
Islanders, and the US Navy, heightened worldwide demand to halt nuclear
testing. The United States successfully deflected a 1955 United Nations resolution calling for the end of testing but could not counter Pope Pius XII's
Christmas prayer to outlaw nuclear weapons and their testing. As fear of radioactive fallout increased, British prime minister Anthony Eden asked whether
the United States and the United Kingdom might limit atmospheric testing.
Dulles was pessimistic. Verification, as always, was key to any international
agreement. If the nuclear test ban could not be policed, cheating could not
be prevented.

On the eve of his triumphal 1956 reelection, Eisenhower was frustrated at
the lack of progress toward disarmament. With elaborate planning on Operation Candor, an address to the United Nations, and high-level negotiations
with the Russians and American allies, the administration seemed to be using
a sledgehammer to drive a tack. Profoundly discouraged, his faith in progress and humanity seriously tested, Eisenhower foresaw only the steady drift
toward nuclear war. In February 1956, he urgently asked the National Security Council for ideas on how to break the diplomatic impasse on channeling
nuclear science and technology into peaceful uses. If the H-bomb could be
banned, he mused, the world and humanity would be better off.

Although Eisenhower won by a landslide in 1956, his nuclear diplomacy
was not strengthened by his electoral mandate. Positively, his Atoms for
Peace initiative had achieved notable success. In addition to the creation of
EURATOM and the International Atomic Energy Agency, by 1961 the United
States had negotiated thirty-nine bilateral treaties, including both research and

nuclear power agreements. Associated with the peaceful bilateral treaties were eleven additional mutual defense agreements. This remarkable productivity in New Look nuclear diplomacy not only reflected the vitality of Eisenhower's Atoms for Peace initiative but also demonstrated the interrelationship between peaceful uses of nuclear energy and mutual security systems.

Test Ban and Disarmament Negotiations

On the other hand, the Eisenhower administration had not made corresponding progress in disarmament and nuclear test ban negotiations with the Soviet Union. In addition to the 1956 elections, Eisenhower's heart attack, the Suez crisis, the Hungarian Revolution of 1956, *Sputnik*, and the U-2 crisis all deflected energy and eroded the confidence needed to achieve agreement. Nevertheless, prospects for a nuclear test ban brightened in the spring of 1957. In March, the United Nations disarmament subcommittee gathered in London for its last, and most fruitful, meeting. Despite stubborn opposition from the Atomic Energy Commission, Eisenhower and Dulles provided unconditional support for a nuclear weapons test ban. Soviet negotiator Valerian Zorin also arrived in London communicating the Kremlin's willingness to implement a nuclear test ban with effective supervision. He suggested a temporary moratorium until the nuclear powers could work out verification details.

Most significantly, Zorin proposed that an international inspection commission establish inspection posts in the United States, the United Kingdom, the Soviet Union, and the Pacific test site. The Russians had offered a major concession, and Eisenhower immediately recognized it. For the first time, the Soviets expressed willingness to establish inspection posts within the Russian heartland.

Nevertheless, it took five more years and another president before a partial nuclear weapons test ban treaty was signed. Unfortunately for Eisenhower's legacy, the Soviets' timing was bad, and once again disarmament talks stalled. In the summer of 1957, none of the nuclear powers wanted an immediate end to testing nuclear weapon designs. The French still did not have a nuclear weapon, while the other nuclear powers had major tests planned. In the United States, the Atomic Energy Commission wanted to develop "clean" weapons (that is, nuclear weapons with minimal radioactive fallout). After the shock of *Sputnik* in October 1957, Eisenhower's greatest obstacle to moving forward was achieving consensus in his own administration on acceptable technical plans for ending atmospheric testing.

Meanwhile, the nuclear weapons race picked up speed. Not only had nuclear weapon stockpiles ballooned by obscene numbers, but weapons testing had also escalated. According to one count, the nuclear powers detonated forty-two devices in 1957, compared to nineteen the year before. Both the Soviets and the Americans planned major test series in 1958. Yet, as testing increased, the superpowers knew that eventually they would have to cope with the alarming buildup of atmospheric radioactive fallout. Given the increasing danger of atmospheric thermonuclear tests, some limitation on nuclear testing became imperative. On March 31, 1958, following the largest test series in nuclear history, the Soviet Union announced a unilateral suspension of tests. The Russian move, of course, forced the United States to suspend its tests following the Hardtack series in September. The unpoliced nuclear weapons test moratorium would hold until September 1961, when the Russians unilaterally resumed testing again.

U-2 Spy Plane

So crucial was the inspection issue that Eisenhower could not resist authorizing another high-altitude reconnaissance flight over the Soviet Union in May 1960. Unfortunately, the U-2 spy plane was shot down, and its pilot, Francis Gary Powers, captured, by the Soviets only weeks prior to the scheduled Paris summit conference. With both the Democrats and Soviet premier Khrushchev demanding accountability from Eisenhower after the U-2 was shot down, hopes for progress at the Paris summit collapsed. The U-2 fiasco and the subsequent cancellation of the Paris peace conference marked the end of Eisenhower's disarmament initiatives. Instead, Khrushchev mocked Eisenhower, and, at home, Democrats denounced him for mismanaging national security while the Russians gained superiority in satellites and missiles. The so-called missile gap would prove to be nonexistent, but Eisenhower was despondent. His hopes of securing a nuclear test ban collapsed with the crash of the U-2 in the Russian heartland.

He had always been very lucky, even during the darkest days of World War II. He knew that arms control was a high-stakes, high-risk game. Given the intransigent domestic opposition to arms control, it is remarkable that Eisenhower accomplished as much as he did. Even limited measures were perceived as a threat to entrenched Cold War budgets and industrial interests. From his high school days, he had always been a risk-taker, a cagey card player, but since *Sputnik* and the U-2 crisis, his luck had run out, and Eisenhower lost his opportunity to become a historic nuclear peacemaker.

Disappointment

Eisenhower's greatest disappointment as president was his failure to end the nuclear arms race. Following Stalin's death in 1953, he hoped that Kremlin leadership might be receptive to nuclear peace proposals. The alternative, he predicted, was an endless arms race along a road that led to nuclear war and/ or national bankruptcy. All the hopes for Atoms for Peace were overshadowed by the imperative to test, stockpile, and deploy nuclear weapons. "We should stop while we are ahead," he advised the Atomic Energy Commission. Unfortunately, he did not follow his own advice when it came to authorizing U-2 spy flights. As a result, Eisenhower not only lost his chance to secure a nuclear test ban treaty but he also fumbled away his historical legacy as a nuclear peacemaker. After the August 1963 signing of the Partial Nuclear Test Ban Treaty prohibiting the testing of nuclear weapons in the atmosphere, underwater, and outer space, President John F. Kennedy received the historical credit for this arms-control breakthrough. Largely forgotten was the foundation laid by Eisenhower's nuclear diplomacy beginning with his "Atoms for Peace" speech in 1953. After 1963, neither Democrats nor Republicans, working from differing partisan agendas, found Eisenhower's nuclear diplomacy a useful historical legacy.

The Military-Industrial Complex

Ironically, this exegetical president would be remembered for his prophetic "Military-Industrial Complex" farewell address, which he gave just three days before the inauguration of the New Frontier. Even before the U-2 fiasco and the diplomatic debacle in Paris, Eisenhower had been thinking about presenting a farewell address. In May 1959, somewhat offhandedly, he mentioned to speechwriter Malcolm Moos that he hoped Congress might invite him to make a farewell address. In April 1960, Fred Fox, Eisenhower's advisor on religious affairs, reread Washington's farewell address and thought a similar address from Eisenhower would be appropriate.

In addition to the persistent nuclear dilemma, two issues nagged Eisenhower as he approached retirement. He continued to ask why Germany's Wei-mar Republic had collapsed so utterly, first into financial anarchy and then into military despotism. More generally, he pondered the worldwide tendency for orderly societies to break down into mob-ridden anarchy.

Within his worldview, this could only be understood as the wages of sin—that is, the consequences of the unbridled pursuit of self-interest by those who put selfish gain before the best interests of the nation. He saw the same tendencies in the United States and worried that class, regional, economic, and political selfishness might seriously undermine American democracy.

Perhaps Eisenhower's greatest fear was of an excessively militarized "garri-son state." When he first ran for president in 1952, he believed that it would be disastrous for world peace and American global interests if isolationist senator Robert Taft were elected president. Now, eight years later, with the election of an inexperienced John F. Kennedy to the presidency, he did not worry whether Kennedy would be sufficiently internationalist but rather whether he would be soft meat for the ravenous military industry and its aggressive lobby. From firsthand experience, he had dealt with the ever-increasing demands of the modern military.

Not only did World War II end America's isolation from the international community, it also revolutionized the role of the military in American life. For the first time in American history, the United States did not demobilize following a war because the Cold War and the Korean War suddenly halted military downsizing. Instead, the United States maintained large professional armed services. In 1960, the expenditure on military security in the United States exceeded the combined net income of all American corporations. Yet, the military services, seeking increased strength, were never satisfied with gen-erous budgets. Americans experienced the emergence of a permanent defense industry vital to regional economies and protected by senators and congress-men who reaped political profit by becoming Cold War hawks. Moreover, a host of retiring officers created a small army of powerful lobbyists forever advocating greater military spending. Collectively, Eisenhower labeled them the "military-industrial complex."

He played a major role in the revolutionary transformation of the military in American life. It was ironic that the most famous son of Abilene, this off-spring of pacifist parents, helped engineer transforming political, social, and cultural changes in American armed forces. He served under, commanded, united with, or opposed many of the great warriors of the twentieth century, including Pershing, Fox Conner, MacArthur, Marshall, Patton, Bradley, Clark, Montgomery, Broke, Alexander, Tedder, de Gaulle, Rommel, Model, van

Rundstedt, and Zhukov. Yet, after leaving the White House, to Kennedy's bewilderment, he requested that he be restored to his former rank of General of the Armies.

As a professional soldier who understood military culture intimately, Eisenhower feared that American democracy was unprepared to deal effectively with a permanent military establishment. While the idea of the "military-industrial complex" was not his alone, in his 1950 Silver Lecture, Eisenhower obliquely warned that nations that maintained a military establishment in excess of their defensive needs were tempted to serve as "judge, jury and sheriff" in settling international disputes. Such muscle-bound states would be tempted to put their own interests first and to go it alone, enforcing their idea of world peace without assistance from allies or the United Nations.

Eisenhower envisioned himself as the first post–World War II president to guide an America radically transformed by the nuclear age. As in "Chance for Peace," in his farewell address he offered a warning about the atheistic, ruthless Soviet Union. Surprisingly, however, he made no direct reference to the bomb. Instead, Eisenhower warned about two new threats, vastly different from any the United States had ever faced. Observing that the continuing economic partnership between the huge military establishment and burgeoning defense industry was new in American history, he affirmed that this development was essential for national security. But Americans should understand that the structure of American society would be shaped by the new military-industrial class. Its impact on American culture, values, and identity, "its total influence—economic, political, even spiritual—would be felt throughout the nation." "In the councils of government, we must guard against the acquisition of unwarranted influence, whether sought or unsought, by the military-industrial complex. The potential for the disastrous rise of misplaced power exists and will persist."

What was he talking about? It turns out that he was more disillusioned by domestic political schism than he was by the failure of the Paris peace talks. Rather, economic bankruptcy and political gridlock could disillusion Americans who did not heed Eisenhower's warning that a military-industrial complex of vested self-interest threatened to corrupt the nation's cherished democratic values. Greed and selfishness, which stood opposite the pole of duty in Eisenhower's theology, sapped the spiritual foundations of American democracy by fostering "dreadful fear and hate," the nemesis of "a proud confederation of mutual trust and respect."

Unlike John F. Kennedy's inaugural address a few days later, Eisenhower's farewell was slightly off-key and largely fell on deaf ears. In contrast to

"A Chance for Peace" and "Atoms for Peace," which targeted the Soviets and the bomb as America's chief external threats, the "Military-Industrial Complex" speech looked inward at America's contradictory and vulnerable national soul. A decade hence, Walt Kelly's Pogo famously observed, "We have met the enemy and he is us," funny for readers of the comic pages but not humorous in the public debate. Americans have never welcomed soul-searching by their presidents. They resonated more positively to Kennedy's pledge that Americans would "pay any price, bear any burden, meet any hardship, support any friend, oppose any foe, in order to assure the survival and the success of liberty."

Eisenhower's "Military-Industrial Complex" speech was his valedictory. And as occasionally happens on such occasions, Eisenhower used his bully pulpit to settle some political scores. The Democrats had won the presidency but not Eisenhower's respect. In Eisenhower's opinion, the fact that Stevenson in 1956 and Kennedy in 1960 had played fast and loose with the national security issues was deplorable enough; that they publicly accused Eisenhower of knowingly neglecting security was unforgivable to the old soldier. They might as well have accused him of shirking his unconditional duty to his country. Consequently, in addition to its high-minded rhetoric promoting balance between the needs of security and the imperatives of liberty, the farewell address also contained a political scolding of the new president and the defense lobby.

Eisenhower lived in a world of dialectical tension between forces of light and forces of darkness. In part, his religious worldview was a variation of the world portrayed on his father's wall chart. It was the Cold War world that pitted atheistic Communism against American democracy; it was the atomic world that discovered new divine and demonic uses of science and technology; it was the world of the military-industrial complex that balanced national security imperatives and special interests with human freedom and dignity; it was a democratic world in which citizens balanced self-interest with social duty. Pastors have the advantage of employing a *deus ex machina* to resolve such intractable dilemmas. Eisenhower's civil religion provided no such luxury, which exposed him to charges that, at best, his faith was piously superficial and, at worst, cynically manipulative.

From a cynical perspective, one might conclude that Eisenhower's religious rhetoric actually discouraged debate and subverted democracy because it presumed that the American way of life would ultimately prevail. It should be emphasized, however, that Eisenhower used the president's bully pulpit to shape the twentieth century's great nuclear debate. Through Operation

Candor, "A Chance for Peace," "Atoms for Peace," and his farewell address, the president used his office to join in the great debate over humankind's nuclear dilemma. Cynicism aside, in the final analysis Eisenhower believed in civil progress through democratic dialogue but not in the ultimate expiation of human sinfulness. While American democracy made no sense without a sincere belief in God, he never prophesied supernatural salvation from the sins of civil history.

Abilene, End of the Trail, 1961–1969

A bilene is mentioned once in the Bible, in Luke, to date the beginning of the ministry of John the Baptist when Lysanias was tetrarch of Abilene. Meaning the "place of the meadows," Abilene was an apt name for this Kansas town located just north of the Smoky Hill River, whose Mud Creek tributary bisected the community. For Texans after the Civil War, however, Abilene meant the "end of the trail," a wild railhead town where the Kansas Pacific Railroad waited for Texas longhorns driven northward on the arduous Chisholm Trail. Between 1867 and 1871, when railheads reached farther south, an estimated three million longhorns, accompanied by tens of thousands of cowboys, were driven to, and sometimes through, Abilene, Kansas.

By 1960, Dwight Eisenhower had changed the identity of the old cattle town considerably. As president, in 1956 he signed the Interstate Highway Act that launched one of the engineering marvels of the twentieth century. By the end of Eisenhower's second term, much of Interstate 70 through central Kansas had been completed. In the long run, the economic and social impacts of the new superhighway system on the town were as great as those of the Chisholm Trail and the railroads.

The Dwight D. Eisenhower Presidential Library and Museum

But more than the interstate highway system, Eisenhower's decision to locate his presidential library and museum in Abilene indelibly fixed Abilene's identity as the boyhood home of the thirty-fourth president. Fittingly, the Eisenhower Center lies just two miles from I-70 on Buckeye, Abilene's main north-south street. Following World War II, the Eisenhower Foundation established a memorial honoring Eisenhower, veterans, and their World War II accomplishments. In November 1946, just two months after Ida's death, the brothers turned over the deed to their boyhood home to the Foundation, with the intention of establishing a "national shrine."

Eisenhower's home sits abstracted in space and time beside the Eisenhower Presidential Museum and Library in Abilene. Uncle Abraham's large barn is gone; so are the family garden, the outbuildings, the iris bed that filled the parking strip along Southeast Fourth Street, the sidewalks, and even the town streets. The Eisenhower house floats on a green lawn removed from its historical roots. There is little family history inside the house, either. Ida's precious piano remains along with a few other family relics. But except for the family Bible, the religious heart of the home is gone. David's wall chart depicting the millennium is lost. Ida's large collection of *Watchtower* magazines was given away—not even a token issue or two is displayed. Almost nothing remains to suggest the substance of their intense religious faith.

Fittingly, the final plans for the Eisenhower Center included a small nonsectarian chapel, named a Place of Meditation, where visitors could prayerfully reflect upon the meaning of American democracy. Eisenhower decided a chapel near his boyhood home would make a fitting grave site for his family, including Icky, who was buried in Denver. By June of 1966, construction of the privately financed chapel was completed.

Eisenhower made no provisions for the symbols of his religious heritage at the Place of Meditation; only the grave sites of Eisenhower, Mamie, and their son Icky, who died of scarlet fever at three years of age in 1921. While Icky's death became the greatest disappointment and disaster of Eisenhower's life, for Ike and Mamie, the Place of Meditation offered no evident solace rooted in their Presbyterian faith, his River Brethren heritage, or any other religious tradition, including that of his parents, David and Ida. Even here in Abilene, Eisenhower kept his grief and God's spiritual comfort to himself. Yet, sitting quietly in the Place of Meditation reflecting on the transcendent meaning of the Eisenhower Center, one can begin to perceive the depth of Eisenhower's affection for his family, his hometown, America, and beyond.

At Ease

Upon leaving Washington, with John's help, Eisenhower immediately began work on his presidential memoirs, *The White House Years: Mandate for Change, 1953–1956,* and *The White House Years: Waging Peace, 1956–1961.* They were solid history, and their sales were good but disappointing when compared to those of *Crusade in Europe*. *Crusade* told the gripping saga of American and Allied forces in their grand triumph over demonic Nazism. *The White House Years* sung no victorious theme and seemed turgid in comparison.

Consequently, the editors of Doubleday asked for a softer, more humane Eisenhower autobiography that revealed the warmth, the humor, and even the pathos of the great hero. He rewarded Doubleday with an enthralling and revealing memoir that was quintessential Eisenhower, filled with great stories of growing up and coming of age in Abilene and West Point, the trials of life in the interwar army, and the drama of World War II. George Patton, Douglas MacArthur, Winston Churchill, Franklin Roosevelt, John Pershing, and Fox Conner played starring roles, while appropriate bit parts from Knute Rockne, Jim Thorpe, Lou Little, Harry Truman, and Erwin Rommel, among others, enriched the stories. The memoir is brilliantly titled *At Ease: Stories I Tell to Friends* and was designed so that the relaxed reader could graze through the collected chapters in just about any order, excepting that one should begin with chapter 1, in which Eisenhower entered West Point to embrace his life's calling.

At Ease also established beyond doubt that Eisenhower's mother, Ida, had the most significant religious impact on his life. Ida provided core fundamentals of Eisenhower's mature faith, including her belief in a providential God who dealt life's cards, to be played by autonomous persons blessed with human dignity and called to solemn duty. From Ida, he received affirmation of his personal worth before God and his personal responsibility for his own destiny. She planted the seed of duty that would firmly take root at West Point.

Furthermore, he was forthcoming about Ida's Jehovah's Witnesses beliefs, information that many writers had either not known, or ignored, or discounted as having any important bearing on Eisenhower's private or public life. Mother and son differed, of course, on matters pertaining to a citizen's responsibilities to the state, but they shared a profound faith that all persons were children of God imbued with freedom to make their own decisions on matters of conscience.

David also left his mark, if not as profoundly. David had been attracted to the Jehovah's Witnesses by their mystical belief in the eternal struggle between divine and demonic forces in history. His son Dwight was no mystic, but he adapted his father's beliefs into a secular version of the historical dialectic between good and evil—that is, between the principles of duty and altruism on the one hand, and selfishness and greed on the other. In addition, his father taught him to respect the Word, but not as a fundamentalist who believes in the literal reading of the Bible. According to family lore, whatever David's proficiency, his father kept his Greek dictionary handy to explore shades of meaning in Greek of the King James Bible translation that served as their major scriptural text.

Aftermath of the Election of 1960

While *At Ease* reinforced middle America's image of Ike as a genuine, wholesome national hero, Dwight himself, like many septuagenarians, was losing touch with the cultural and social currents in American life. He largely withdrew from politics during his retirement years while he immersed himself in the past by writing his memoirs.

To some extent, Eisenhower's writing projects allowed him partial escape from his sense of failure as president. Eisenhower's domestic political legacy was essentially snuffed out when Nixon lost the presidential election of 1960. The morning after the November elections, John Eisenhower found his father in the Oval Office "slumped in his swivel chair staring at nothing through the window to the South Grounds." John wrote in his memoir that he had rarely seen his father so depressed. "All I've been trying to do for eight years [to move the Republican Party into the mainstream of American politics] has gone down the drain," he lamented to his son. "I might just as well have been having fun." He had not sought political revolution, but instead failed to move the Republican old guard toward the center of America's political spectrum.

From Eisenhower's perspective, the 1964 presidential election was even worse. When Republicans nominated conservative senator Barry Goldwater of Arizona for president, Eisenhower reluctantly endorsed his party's candidate despite predictions of political disaster. Disaster struck, of course, but not so much for right-wing Republicans, who elected eight "Goldwater Republicans" to House of Representative seats in the South. The big losers were moderate Republicans, after Democrats captured thirty-six additional seats in the House. Poignantly, in the afterword of *Waging Peace*, Eisenhower confessed his failure to increase the GOP's appeal among the American electorate by moving the party to the political center.

Following Lyndon Johnson's landslide presidential victory in 1964, Eisenhower largely withdrew from partisan politics. As American involvement in Vietnam deepened, so did Eisenhower's commitment to the war. In general, Eisenhower, who had more or less kept the peace during his presidency, did not favor armed incursion that was halfhearted. His criticism of America's role in the Bay of Pigs fiasco was not so much that the Cuban invasion was ill-advised but that the United States had not supported the insurgents with overwhelming force. Correspondingly, when Johnson sought his advice about the conduct of the Vietnam War, Eisenhower was more hawkish than he had been as president. Once American armed forces were committed in Southeast Asia, Eisenhower believed, there was no choice but to prosecute the war with utmost vigor. The United States should coordinate with its NATO allies, make it clear to the enemy that it would employ whatever military force was necessary to defend South Vietnam, adopt as its principal war aim the destruction of the Communists' will to fight, and stand ready to negotiate, but only from a position of strength.

Turmoil of the 1960s

Although he lived isolated and protected at the Gettysburg farm and in Palm Desert, California, he was only partially shielded from the turmoil of the 1960s. As president, he had opposed extremism in all forms, but in the early 1960s Americans more and more rejected the centrism—political, social, and cultural—that he cherished. The assassination of President John F. Kennedy sent shock waves through the country. Violent suppression of civil rights fed militant demands for justice and equality. As the tempo of the war in Vietnam escalated, so did the frenzy of antiwar demonstrations at home. To the left of center, recurring demonstrations, marches, sit-ins, and teach-ins were transforming American university and college campuses. On the right, 1964 Republican presidential candidate Barry Goldwater proclaimed, "Extremism in the defense of liberty is no vice. And moderation in the pursuit of justice is no virtue."

Eisenhower was both appalled and discouraged by the strident discourse that characterized American society in the 1960s. Well before the political violence and chaos of 1968, he lamented that the media daily reported "sickening and depressing" accounts of lawlessness, selfishness, disloyalty, and all kinds of wickedness, to the extent that many Americans had lost their capacity for honesty and righteous indignation. In his most impassioned jeremiad to date, in August 1967, Eisenhower lectured the nation via *Reader's Digest* in an article entitled "We Should Be Ashamed!" How was it, he asked rhetorically, that one of the most prosperous and free nations in history could descend into "an era of lawlessness"? Perhaps picking up from Barry Goldwater's 1964 campaign, Eisenhower concluded that Americans had lost respect for "law and order." The 1965 riots-revolution in Watts, provoked by police brutality, stoked terrors of social anarchy. He could not understand how both whites and blacks could participate in riots that destroyed the neighborhoods and cities in which they lived.

He believed that the national crisis was essentially a religious crisis in which citizens had lost self-discipline, respect for duty, and affection for their country and their neighbors. The biggest losers in the rioting were the nation's youth, who for some reason did not live by the American creed. Still, while he advocated a hard line in Vietnam, he cautioned about overreacting to fearmongering at home.

The 1960s: Too Close to Home

Unfortunately, in the midst of the social and political upheaval of the 1960s, his grandson David bore some of the brunt of Eisenhower's worry about the character and moral stamina of modern American youth. Eisenhower was disappointed when David chose the "little ivy" Amherst College instead of West Point, where grandfather and father had attended. He would rather that his grandson was cloistered at the military academy on the Hudson River than be exposed to antiwar, draft-resisting radicals on one of the nation's most prestigious liberal arts campuses.

Because he had turned eighteen his senior year, David was obliged to register for the draft before he graduated from high school. At this juncture, his grandfather sent David $25, encouraging him to have a little fun but also enjoining him to accept his duty "cheerfully" should he be called to active service in the armed services. The old soldier also gave David gratuitous advice about moral living and the need to focus on his education goals rather than be distracted while dating Nixon's daughter Julie. In turn, David gave his granddad a recording of his Amherst College singing group, the Zumbyes, which included "Climb Every Mountain," to augment his large record collection.

When Julie Nixon and David Eisenhower scheduled their wedding for December 22, 1968, the general, not pleased with David's mop of curly hair, offered his grandson $100 if he would get a short, military-style haircut for his wedding. David reported that he got a light trim that was not short enough to satisfy his grandfather—so no $100. Although David later made light of the incident, his grandfather's refusal to affirm in a small way David's personal values must have hurt.

Civil Religion after the White House

Although bedeviled by domestic turmoil and the deepening opposition to the Vietnam War, religiously Eisenhower was most upset by the Supreme Court's decision on school prayer. In June 1962, the Court ruled in *Engle v. Vitale* that it was unconstitutional for the State of New York to authorize an official school prayer to be used, albeit voluntarily, in the state's public schools. To many Americans the prayer seemed blandly innocuous: "Almighty God, we acknowledge our dependence upon Thee, and we beg Thy blessings upon us, our parents, our teachers and our country. Amen." The prayer was scarcely more religious than the morning Pledge of Allegiance to the flag, in which students daily pledged their allegiance to "one nation under God." In the *Engle* case, however, the Court ruled that New York's authorized state prayer violated the establishment clause of the First Amendment mandating the separation of church and state. *, ,, no establishment . . .*

A year later, in *Abington Township School District v. Schempp* (June 1963), the Supreme Court broadened its previous decision by ruling that teachers and school officials could not organize or lead prayers or devotional readings from the Bible. Students were still free to pray privately or in groups and to bring their Bibles to school and to discuss religion with friends as long as their religious activities did not disrupt school routine.

Following the *Engle* decision, Eisenhower released a statement lamenting the Supreme Court's decision on prayers in school: "I always thought that this nation was essentially a religious one. I realize, of course, that the Declaration of Independence antedates the Constitution, but the fact remains that the Declaration was our certificate of national birth. It specifically asserts that we, as individuals, possess certain rights as an endorsement from our common Creator—a religious concept."

Although he believed the decision was technically correct, he thought the Court was doing the nation a disservice (and unintentionally aiding the Communists) by prohibiting public schools from teaching that citizens are fundamentally spiritual beings and that the United States was founded on religious principles. He was not arguing that the United States was a Protestant nation or a Christian nation; he simply could not understand why the Court could not affirm that the United States was a religious nation.

Shortly after the school prayer decisions, his Gettysburg pastor asked Eisenhower to participate in the consecration of their new church building. On the program with Eugene Carson Blake and Dr. Donald McCloud from Princeton Theological Seminary, in June 1963, Eisenhower agreed to give a public talk on the role of the church in contemporary America.

Thoughts of the Battle of Gettysburg, of Lincoln, Meade, and Lee, were not far from his mind when he reminisced about Camp Colt, where he and Mamie had brought their son Icky during the First World War. It was one hundred years since the Army of the Potomac turned the tide of the war at Gettysburg, saving the Union and American principles of the equality of man. It had been almost a half a century since Eisenhower had trained men at Camp Colt to make the world "safe for democracy" and lost 175 men to the 1918 flu pandemic. Understandably, for Eisenhower, Gettysburg was almost sacred ground.

It was appropriate, he thought, to share his religious thoughts with fellow believers. Eisenhower understood the intent of the establishment clause in the First Amendment, but he also knew that no one objected to reading in classrooms the Declaration of Independence, which included these words: "We hold these truths to be self-evident, that all men are created equal, that they are endowed by their Creator with certain unalienable Rights, that among these are Life, Liberty and the pursuit of Happiness."

Furthermore, Lincoln had believed that the Declaration of Independence established the moral foundation for American democracy. Although there was no mention of the Deity in the Constitution, Eisenhower asserted that the American form of government was "the political expression of a deeply felt religious faith," as proclaimed in the Declaration. The belief in the equality of all men was a political belief rooted in religious faith. He did not understand how the Supreme Court could ban the teaching of beliefs and values fundamental to the democratic governance of the nation. Nor could he envision an alternative rationale for justifying the American system. In order to teach fundamental civic values, he asked plaintively, was it possible for the public schools to "give our children the basic kind of religious instruction without bringing religion [meaning sectarian belief] into the curriculum"?

Eisenhower pressed on. What he meant, he explained, was that dedicated teachers, children of God all, could witness to their faith while not literally proclaiming the gospel of Jesus Christ. He believed that all conscientious teachers give "expression" to their faith regardless of whether they're teaching music, economics, science, or philosophy, or coaching athletics. It was not essential for teachers to lead prayer or to read the Bible in class to be a spiritual presence for their students. The Supreme Court could not suppress that reality. He assumed that it was essential for the long-term functioning of American government that the nation's schoolchildren be taught in a moral atmosphere that recognized the existence of a Supreme Overlord.

Listening to the tape years later, grandson David did not miss the significance of Eisenhower's term "Supreme Overlord," which played off the code name of the Allies 1944 invasion of western Europe—Operation Overlord.

David knew that Eisenhower's use of "Overlord" at Gettysburg was purpose-ful—he wanted to link the Allies' "crusade" against Nazi tyranny with the Union's victory at Gettysburg in 1863. At the end of both wars, Americans had confirmed their moral leadership in the world.

He believed that only Western values could ultimately satisfy the "material, intellectual, aesthetic, and spiritual desires" of liberated peoples. Eventually, he predicted, Western principles—including the belief in the dignity of all men, free enterprise, and human liberty as reflected in Roman law, the Magna Carta, the American Declaration of Independence, and the Bill of Rights—would surge around the globe, sweeping aside Communism and totalitarianism ev-erywhere. Unspoken was the corresponding belief that such a triumph would need to be accompanied by a global religious revival affirming the sovereignty of a beneficent supreme being.

His 1963 church talk summarized the core beliefs of his civil religion—beliefs he had outlined before. To the American Legion in 1955 he had insisted: "Without God, there could be no American form of Government, nor an American way of life. Recognition of the Supreme Being is the first—the most basic—expression of Americanism. Thus, the Founding Fathers saw it, and thus, with God's help, it will continue to be."

Personal Faith

In 1965, Sherwood E. Wirt, a Presbyterian minister, interviewed Eisenhower in Indio, California, for an article in *Decision*, published by the Billy Graham Evangelistic Association. Graham hoped to create a revealing narrative of Ei-senhower's faith journey that linked him to Graham's ministries. Before the interview, Graham warned Wirt how "Eisenhower was inclined to be rather inarticulate on spiritual matters." Undoubtedly, what Graham meant was that Eisenhower was not inclined to confess that Jesus was his personal Savior. Nor did he claim to have been "born again" as a Christian or offer conversion testimony common to American evangelicals.

Although Eisenhower's religious rhetoric often echoed eighteenth-century rationalism, by conventional definition, Eisenhower was a Christian—his bap-tism and confirmation in the Presbyterian church alone attest to that basic fact. But was it duty alone that drove him into the church? He rarely referenced Jesus in public, and although he confessed his sins during the Presbyterian liturgy, he did not highlight atonement theology. His appreciation of Jesus

not a biblical definition [handwritten marginal note]

was largely historical and secular; he was an obscure teacher who tramped Palestine's rough and barren hills for three and a half years and remarkably left his imprint on Western government and its codes of jurisprudence—a man "who has meant more to civilization—western civilization certainly—than any other individual in history."

Eisenhower knew about the controversy regarding the historical Jesus but had utterly no respect for atheists. At times he expressed stronger feelings about atheists than he did about Jesus. "It takes no brains to be an atheist," he snorted. They were not true to themselves as human beings, he believed. For the most part, he thought atheists were ignorant and prejudiced, and perhaps suffered from an inferiority complex. There was nothing subtle or vague about these beliefs.

Wirt confirmed Graham's assessment to a point, but he also discovered that Eisenhower could be very clear about his fervent belief in God. Had he known Eisenhower better and been experienced in interviewing public officials, Wirt might have appreciated more the dynamics of interviewing this cagey politician who was well practiced in obfuscation when asked difficult, sensitive questions—in this case, about the development of his very private beliefs in God and his Christology.

Initially, Eisenhower patronized Graham's agent by observing that "some ministers nowadays" were "getting too intellectual for their own good." But he quickly added that he did not believe everything in the Scriptures literally. It was a classic Eisenhower smoke screen, introducing his personal analysis of Holy Scripture. Getting to the point, he thought that the creation stories had to be understood allegorically. He dismissed Bishop Ussher's seventeenth-century calculations that the earth was approximately six thousand years old. But the age of the earth, as such, did not particularly interest Eisenhower. Nor did he care how long the Supreme Being had taken to create the universe: a week, six thousand years (one day equaling one thousand years), or whatever. Such details did not interest him as matters of religious faith.

Although there is no evidence that Eisenhower knew about Georges Lamaître's big bang theory, he apparently embraced a version of Kant's and Laplace's nebular hypothesis that the earth was once a molten ball. And he was comfortable with evolutionary theory about the development of *Homo sapiens*. Over time, humans evolved to the point where they could "communicate intelligently and bargain and negotiate" to form the foundations of economics and civilization. Yet, he did not view creation itself as homocentric. Earth, he noted, was a very small planet in a solar system that itself was but a tiny speck in the universe. What overpowered human comprehension, in his opinion, was the visible order—the intricacy and mathematical precision of creation that hosted human consciousness, intelligence, and ingenuity. He was hardly alone in wondering about the purpose of it all.

Eisenhower was much more reflective regarding his belief in God. First and foremost, his was a creator God. The countless stars in the heavens were perhaps the greatest manifestation of God's presence in the universe. Just as he believed that democratic government "made no sense" without a deeply held belief in God, so his cosmology presumed the existence of a creative "power . . . far greater than our own." The orderliness of the universe, the mathematical precision of the natural world, testified to God's transcendent wisdom.

Although Eisenhower owed much to his mother's religiosity and spirituality, in terms of cosmology and his understanding of human history, his father was the predominant influence. David, with his mechanical bent and his mystical visions of the end of time, bestowed on his son a belief in a rational creation tottering on the edge of cataclysmic destruction caused by human folly and selfishness. But Eisenhower's belief in God saved him from despair. His calling as a soldier rested on his trust that a beneficent, rational God monitored creation.

In his study of military history, Eisenhower believed that he detected the hand of God in great battles, from ancient history to modern times. On the other hand, he did not believe that a providential God determined the outcome of battle any more than he believed the Almighty had taken sides with either George Meade or Robert E. Lee at Gettysburg. He recalled that Abraham Lincoln was not sure that God was on his side but had prayed that he was on God's side. That was Eisenhower's hope. Right or wrong, he prayed that God would respect his decisions. The judgments were his to make, the challenges were his to solve—not God's.

Although Eisenhower professed to believe in a providential God, he rarely, if ever, felt God's push or pull either toward this goal or that. His favorite metaphor concerning God's involvement in history originated with his mother, Ida. Solitaire was one of Ida's recreational indulgences, and she advised her sons, "The Lord deals the cards—you play them."

Eisenhower, an avid, skillful card player, especially at poker and bridge, took his mother's advice to heart. He assumed that the cards dealt by the Lord included the twentieth-century card, the Kansas card, and the parent card. The moral of the lesson was that it was up to him to play his cards as best he could. More importantly, having been created in the image of God, he was free to play his cards as he chose. Ida's metaphor was apt for her son because Eisenhower knew that in life's game of cards, the Dealer dealt several hands, some better than others. There were losers, but on balance, he had been blessed with winning hands.

As a youth in Abilene, he had been taught by Bob Davis not to rely on luck alone but to count his cards and to calculate the odds. In cards, patience was all-important; knowing one's opponent was critical; self-confidence coupled with bluff, essential. Eisenhower especially loved bridge because the game mirrored war and diplomacy, with emphasis on building long-term partnerships, developing clear communications, adopting winning strategies, and employing successful tactics.

What can be missed in Ida's card-game metaphor, however, is that Eisenhower's providential Dealer did not pick the winners and losers. Like chess, whether at Gettysburg in 1863 or on the Normandy beaches in 1944, it was the players themselves that determined the outcome of the battle. Eisenhower's providential God was not a transactional deity who ran the world for a price, but rather was an existential God who established the material and spiritual conditions for his creation. Like any organism on earth, Ida believed her sons would have to adapt to their circumstances or change them as well as they could, but because they were human, they also had an obligation to God not simply to react to what was happening but to help shape their world according to what they believed was right.

When Eisenhower decided to attend West Point, Ida did not believe her son was called by God to be a soldier. He was an autonomous young man, and although his decision broke her heart, neither she nor David stood in the way of his God-given freedom to chart his own destiny. Eisenhower's belief in God was characterized less by dogmatic faith than by hopeful trust that at the end of the day—when all the praying and planning were done and the decisions to act had been made and the discharge of his duty was complete— one could only trust that God was good. That trust was all the certainty one could have.

While Eisenhower loved his mother's bold imagery of God as the Great Card Dealer, he was wary of anthropomorphizing the deity. Eisenhower believed that God was beyond human comprehension and that man's relationship with God was essentially indefinable. He had little patience with theology or religious rites that tried to circumscribe his encounter with the Almighty. For example, he had submitted to baptism because it was a requirement to become a member of the Presbyterian church. But he thought that squabbles over sprinkling or immersion, frontward or backward, children or adults were not only silly but that they also lost the essence of Christianity. Personally, like David and Ida, he favored adult baptism, when a person could make a conscious, free choice in the matter. But Mamie insisted that they attend all the infant christenings of their grandchildren, so he did. God was generous and understanding. What difference did it make—even symbolically, he asked himself. He couldn't be "bothered" with such petty details, he confessed to Billy Graham's associate. Mostly, he believed that religious ritual and obtuse theology got in the way of simple prayer and the old hymns his mother played on her piano.

He also admitted that he did not believe it was his duty to attend church, which was a revealing confession from the general who believed that remaining faithful to his duty was his highest sacred obligation. He felt little or no loyalty to denominationalism and no need at all to affiliate with a specific religious persuasion. He joined the Presbyterians simply because it was Mamie's church and he felt that as president he needed to set a good example. Had she been Lutheran, Methodist, or something else, he would have been just as happy to join those churches. Perhaps competition among denominations increased church attendance; he did not know. Eisenhower was a silent ecumenist who believed that virtually all Christian churches should congregate under the same tent. But he did not attend a church because it professed "true" doctrine, or to receive the sacraments, or to listen to the choir, or to sing the hymns (although he enjoyed the latter, his singing was often boisterous but not on pitch).

Mostly he had attended church to pray and to hear the pastor's sermon as an interlude in an otherwise hectic week in the White House. He hungered for a spiritual sermon that explored the power of the "inner soul" and related matters that were generally ignored during the hurly-burly of daily Washington living. And it was essential that the preacher be optimistic, because he was fighting the age-old battle against human self-centeredness. During the war, Eisenhower had learned that no pessimist had ever won a battle. From this perspective, attending church became an extension of his adult search for a place of prayer and peace.

Although pressed to accept Jesus as his personal Savior, Eisenhower remained uncertain about what was meant by "salvation" and "heaven." There was no doubt in his mind that there existed a very merciful God. And he was not unnerved that the Almighty could not be detected through normal human senses. On the other hand, he had profound questions about the nature of the human soul and the permanence of human consciousness. God was Spirit who occupied no place in particular and all creation in general. For that reason, he had difficulty with the concept of a heaven as habitation where God and believers would dwell in everlasting life and love. God as Holy Spirit had no need for a home called heaven when he already occupied all creation.

He recalled that his father, David, had believed that "religion, placed in man by God, is most natural to him." Eisenhower may not have been a pantheist, but because he believed that God's Spirit infused everything, he had a Franciscan understanding of the incarnation. This was most radically expressed in his belief that God, in his grace, had bestowed dignity (or "religion") on all people. Not only were all people equal as the religious children of God, but also, by their grace-filled dignity, all were incarnate with the Holy Spirit.

Eisenhower was perplexed about how heaven could be a sanctuary where souls enjoyed everlasting life in worship and communion with God. In earlier conversations with Billy Graham, he had tried to grasp this idea, central to atonement theology and salvation history. Patiently, Graham had explained this mystery through the quotation of Bible verses, but Eisenhower became hung up on the materialist issues involved in believing the doctrine of the resurrection of the body. For the idea of everlasting life to have any meaning, Eisenhower thought that the soul had to have consciousness that would include a historical awareness essential for self-identity. Although he did not conflate consciousness with the human brain, Eisenhower could not fathom how consciousness was possible after the brain was dead. Once the soul left the seat of reason, Eisenhower asked rhetorically, what was left? At that he surrendered. Just as Ida deeply grieved the loss of her infant son Paul, so Ike longed to see his little boy Icky again. But whether there would be a joyous reunion in heaven, he just did not know. And with that, Eisenhower's thoughts had drifted off.

Not surprisingly, Wirt failed in his mission to obtain Eisenhower's confession that he accepted Jesus as his personal Savior. As a compromise, when he had finished the rough draft of his article for *Decision* magazine, Wirt asked Eisenhower for a brief paragraph on what Jesus meant to him personally. Eisenhower replied in his own hand.

It takes no brains to be an atheist. Any stupid person can deny the existence of a supernatural power because man's physical senses cannot detect it. But there cannot be ignored the influence of conscience, the respect we feel for moral law, the mystery of first life on what once must have been a molten mass, or the marvelous order in which the universe moves about us on this earth. All of these [are] evidence of the handiwork of a beneficent Deity. For my part, that Deity is the God of the Bible and of Christ, His Son.

Billy Graham wanted, and Wirt dutifully sought but failed to get, robust affirmation from Eisenhower that he had been born again by embracing Jesus Christ as his Savior. This was the best they would get. But in truth, late in life, this statement was a fair summary of what Jesus meant to the old warrior.

It is commonly believed that Billy Graham had a profound impact on Eisenhower's faith. There is no doubt that they were good friends and that Eisenhower enjoyed Graham's company, especially in prayer. Graham visited Eisenhower eight times in the White House and prayed at the dying president's bedside at Walter Reed Hospital. By Graham's account, they discussed heaven and the afterlife twice, each time Graham answering Eisenhower's questions with Bible passages. Eisenhower told Sid Richardson that he found Graham a delightful, unusual personality, and he valued Graham's connection with independent Texas oilmen and his standing with white southern preachers. Historically, with liberals pushing and conservatives pulling, there have even been efforts to move Eisenhower into the religious right wing, using his friendship with Graham as a pry to move him off center. But, as the Wirt interview revealed, Eisenhower's religious beliefs were little influenced by Graham's evangelicalism.

On the other hand, almost unnoticed was the influence of Fred Fox in shaping Eisenhower's mature beliefs. The Reverend Frederick Fox, the Congregational pastor from Williamstown, Massachusetts, became the special assistant for religious affairs in the White House in Eisenhower's second term. Fox was responsible for drafting many of Eisenhower's religious speeches and for providing the president with biblical citations as appropriate. After Fox joined the White House staff, rhetorically it became difficult to disentangle Eisenhower from Fox.

Fox's deep biblical knowledge, his spiritual sincerity, his religious compatibility with Eisenhower's Judeo-Christian universalism, his contacts among the mainline churches and seminaries, and his vigorous willingness to promote and defend Eisenhower's civil religion delighted the president. But mostly, Eisenhower prized his professional confidentiality and studied avoidance of self-promotion while in the White House. Eisenhower relaxed when he discovered that Fox fit perfectly into the quasi-military White House staff where the president could relate to him as if he were an army chaplain assigned to the general's staff. Soon, Fox was answering personal letters about religious matters and providing liaison between the White House and religious press and organizations, especially the National Council of Churches. Fox also took great care to help channel Eisenhower's religious enthusiasm in directions that did not violate the sacred principle of the separation of church and state.

Perhaps more than any of the president's religious advisors, Fox had helped temper Eisenhower's religious rhetoric during the president's second term.

Most importantly, Fox played a role in the development of the "Military-Industrial Complex" speech. When Eisenhower became discouraged because Americans defined "greatness" in terms of production of bombs, machines, and gadgets, Fox reminded him that democracies, indeed all civilizations, were founded on religious faith and values. Americans could take pride in being the most powerful nation on earth only if their spiritual resources matched their military arsenal. The Founding Fathers affirmed that God was the author of individual rights, and it followed that the declared purpose of a great America was to secure those God-given rights.

Salvation in Eisenhower's scheme of values was never individual—it was always collective. If he was reticent about accepting Jesus as his *personal* Savior, it was because he did not think that way. Neither Abilene football, nor West Point, nor the war, nor the presidency encouraged him to think about himself as anything other than the leader of his team. There was no "salvation" for Eisenhower apart from the performance of the team, the work of the community.

Getting Ready

After Eisenhower suffered another heart attack in November 1965, he began to put his affairs in order. The Gettysburg farm and house had been blessed in a small ceremony led by the Reverend Elson after Thanksgiving 1955, following his first heart attack. Now it was time to start letting go. He liquidated his precious herd of prized Angus cattle and sold or otherwise gave away the horses that had been kept for his grandchildren. When his son John expressed no interest in inheriting the Gettysburg farm, he offered it to the Department of the Interior to be used as a memorial and museum. Now it was time to move Icky's body to Kansas.

In June 1966, alone except for the Secret Service, Eisenhower flew to Denver to supervise the transfer of Icky's remains to Abilene, where his lost son was reburied in Eisenhower's Place of Meditation. As granddaughter Susan Eisenhower observed, "In the most profound way, he was preparing for his own death." A year later, with Mamie at his side, Eisenhower visited the chapel to dedicate the small plaque that marked Icky's grave. He was overcome by grief that had never left him, for Icky's death more than four decades before remained Eisenhower's deepest personal loss.

Coincidentally, in 1968, as political and public crises increased, Eisenhower's damaged heart weakened. Faced with sinking popular support for the war, a divided Democratic Party over Vietnam, and the prospects of political defeat, President Lyndon Johnson not only suspended the bombing of North Vietnam but also announced his decision not to run for reelection in 1968. Just four days later, on April 4, Martin Luther King was assassinated in Memphis, Tennessee. The nation simultaneously convulsed with disorderly celebrations on American college campuses of Johnson's ignominious withdrawal and urban rioting ignited in over a hundred cities sparked by King's death. Along with everyone else, Eisenhower was stunned by Johnson's weakness under fire and by the widespread conflagration in American cities. Also at the end of April, Eisenhower, now seventy-seven years old, suffered another heart attack while playing golf with friends in California.

He never fully recovered. He recuperated for a few weeks in California, and then, instead of returning to his Gettysburg farm, he flew to Walter Reed Army Medical Center in Washington, DC, for additional rest and care from the army's medical staff. He knew that the end was near, but according to David, he remained remarkably cheerful. He moved into Ward Eight at Walter Reed, the VIP ward that served presidents, generals, senators and congressmen, and high-ranking officials such as John Foster Dulles. The large and comfortable presidential suite became Ike and Mamie's last home together. David Eisenhower remembered that visiting his grandfather at this time "was wonderful and bewildering. He radiated joy and warmth, a hugging, clasping, happy appreciation of every visit."

His portrait of Winston Churchill hung over the fireplace in his suite's living room, a poignant reminder of his greatest triumphs. Yet when he reminisced with old friends, he usually talked about memories of West Point. Although he would soon be going home to Abilene, it was the army that instilled the core of his personal values and sense of duty.

His grandchildren David and Julie tell a tender story of Eisenhower's last months in Ward Eight. Walter Reed became his last sanctuary, an army home where he was cared for and pampered. For the most part, he was shielded from the turmoil of antiwar protests and toxic politics that characterized his last years. Because both his doctors and Mamie did their best to keep bad news at bay, he did not learn about the assassination of Senator Robert Kennedy until two weeks after the event. But facing death can be lonely and terrifying. Grandson David reports that he memorized the prayer of Saint Francis of Assisi to calm his spirit as darkness approached.

Lord, make me an instrument of your peace.
Where there is hatred, let me sow love;
    where there is injury, pardon;
    where there is doubt, faith;
    where there is darkness, light;
    where there is sadness, joy.

O Divine Master, grant that I may not seek to be consoled as to
    console;
    to be understood as to understand;
    to be loved as to love.

For it is in giving that we receive;
    it is in pardoning that we are pardoned;
    and it is in dying that we are born to eternal life.

He lived long enough to endorse Richard Nixon for president in 1968 and to celebrate Nixon's electoral victory in November. Between Nixon's election and inauguration, he was able to listen to a live audio of David and Julie's wedding. Bedridden during Nixon's inauguration, he noted the January 20, 1969, event in his hospital diary. He had become very fond of Julie Nixon, David's bride, and thus had come to feel closer to Nixon's family. Nixon's election in 1968 seemed to vindicate his presidency somewhat after eight years of Democratic occupation of the White House.

Following emergency abdominal surgery on February 21, he failed noticeably. All hope of returning to the Gettysburg farm was abandoned. He was able to say his last good-bye to Mamie, assuring his wife that he had always loved her. He requested his son John to ask the doctors to let him go. Eventually, he himself asked his doctors to turn off the life-support system (the "bulldozer," he called it) that sustained him for several months. Brother Milton paid his last visit to his brother. The immediate family gathered just outside his room. Apparently, his final words were to ask his doctors to close the shades and to put pillows behind his back to lift him up a bit. At the foot of the bed, his doctor, Leonard Heaton, with John and David Eisenhower, kept the final vigil. Mamie paced in and out of the room and whispered to her comatose husband. He died without heroics just after noon on March 28, 1969.

As was right and proper, General Eisenhower was buried with full military honors. To this day, an honor guard of veterans pays homage to Eisenhower on the anniversary of his birth. Appropriately, a statue of the general gazes across the mall of the Eisenhower Center in Abilene, its bronze eyes resting on the Place of Meditation. Not comfortable being addressed as "Mr. President" for the rest of his life, the old warrior asked his close friends to call him Ike, as they had even when he wore five stars. While president, there had been a kind of veneration of his person, and he did not like it. The adoration of the people, and especially the clergy, had been embarrassing to Eisenhower. As Fred Fox observed, Eisenhower knew he had become a national symbol— but he did not want to be a national idol carrying burdens of the American people "in his big, majestic hands." Burial in Abilene was fitting: out of the spotlight, not far from the interstate but far from the pomp and circumstance of American power.

Civil Religion, Church, State, and
the Place of Meditation

W hat can we say theologically about Eisenhower's civil religion? Although Eisenhower professed no public theology, Frederick Fox, his White House assistant for religious affairs, reflected on the theological dimensions of Eisenhower's religious leadership. Eisenhower had once confessed that he believed in democracy. But so had philosopher John Dewey, who, in *A Common Faith*, published in 1934, outlined a public religion supporting democracy very much like that fostered by Eisenhower but without reliance on God. It would be up to Fred Fox to explore the theological underpinnings of Eisenhower's civil faith.

When Fox, keeper of the White House religious library, searched for an apologia for Eisenhower's role as pastor/president, he discovered William H. Lazareth's work "A Theology of Politics." Given Eisenhower's Lutheran heritage through his mother Ida, the choice of Fox was appropriate. Commissioned by the United Lutheran Church in America, Lazareth's treatise was a Cold War study guide on how to resist ruthless tyranny while simultaneously avoiding nuclear annihilation. A professor of systematic theology and ethics at the Lutheran Theological Seminary in Philadelphia, Lazareth theologically explored the central tension inherent in civil religion—how God ruled through both church and state.

Lazareth built his theology of politics on scaffolding provided by Martin Luther during the Protestant Reformation. Luther distinguished between law and gospel in such a way that they ruled separate realms but still interacted with each other. According to Luther, gospel belongs to the new age of Christ as God's saving power to all who have faith. Law, on the other hand, belongs to the old age of Adam as God's holy will that all men enjoy justice and peace.

Thus, Luther perceived that God rules two kingdoms: the first being the kingdom of Christ's gospel and the church that promises salvation from a loving God; the second being the kingdom of the law and the state that promotes peace and justice on behalf of a righteous God. The right hand of God guides the first kingdom, while the left hand of God directs the latter kingdom. In other words, gospel establishes believers' relationship to God in Christ, while law governs human relationships within the social order.

Just as God conveyed dignity on all men, he also ordained government over human society to constrain inevitable ambition and selfishness. Luther's theology provides insight into what Eisenhower meant when he declared that democracy made no sense without a belief in God. Both Luther and Eisenhower believed the government was instituted among men with God's blessing. (They were far from alone in this belief, of course.) But it should be noted that the law promoted neither a specific form of government nor a given legal code. Although God delegated power to the state, no specific governments, not the United States, nor Great Britain, nor the Soviet Union, nor the United Nations, were ordained by God. The Constitution of the United States was America's constitution, not God's.

God ordained the state to foster peace and justice in a wicked world. Thus, governments' limited purpose was to preserve the law but not to provide salvation through the gospel. While Eisenhower could proclaim that democracy made no sense without a belief in God, there was no such thing as a "Christian" nation or "Christian" institutions apart from the church. Leaders such as Eisenhower might become saved as baptized Christians, but law could only reform the secular institutions they guided. Reason and justice are the principal tools of the state, while faith and love are gifts from the gospel. According to Lazareth, the state remains in perpetual "need of prophetic guidance and judgment of the law of God as proclaimed by the Church so that faith may illume reason and love enlighten justice."

Although sin (selfishness) is inevitable in human affairs, Eisenhower did not believe that warfare was inevitable. He was not a utopian, but neither did he believe that nuclear Armageddon was predestined. As a duty-driven soldier serving at God's left hand, his vocation was not to redeem the world but rather to establish and preserve the rule of law under which all men must live to enjoy harmony and commerce.

Thus, his baptism and confirmation just weeks after his inauguration had deeper religious meaning for Eisenhower than is usually understood. Eisenhower's baptism and confirmation were not only personal rites in which he acknowledged Jesus as his Savior, but they were also a public affirmation of the religious motivation behind his acceptance of the secular office to which he had been called. True to his dialectical worldview, thereafter, as a baptized Christian, Eisenhower lived in the two kingdoms described by Lazareth: the kingdom of grace and redemption in which the Sermon on the Mount outlined an ethic of faith in love, and the kingdom of civil righteousness in which the "Golden Rule" or the Ten Commandments demanded adherence to the rule of law and justice that all rational citizens of all religious persuasions could embrace.

At no time, of course, did Eisenhower articulate a theological understanding of civil religion as Lazareth outlined above. Nor did Frederick Fox publish a theological assessment of Eisenhower's civil religion based on Lazareth's insightful analysis of public theology. It was not what he professed, Fox asserted, but rather Eisenhower's behavior as "pastor to the people" that was theologically consistent with Lazareth's paradigm. Furthermore, Fox, through Lazareth, provided insight into why Eisenhower frustrated Billy Graham and others for not repeatedly proclaiming Jesus as his personal Savior, and why he endorsed what, to some, seemed to be a shallow, vapid universalist civil religion.

Eisenhower's civil religion promoted a variation of natural religion that was consistent with Luther's theology of the two kingdoms. In general, Eisenhower did not conflate the two kingdoms. As a student of the Bible, he did not confuse the gospel with the Declaration of Independence, but he understood the important distinction made by Lazareth that "just as men cannot be saved by reason and the law, neither can society be ruled by faith and the gospel."

The Eisenhower Legacy—American Civil Religion

As we have seen, Eisenhower's civil religion was not original. During the crisis years of the 1930s, 1940s, and 1950s, during the Great Depression, World War II, and the origins of the Cold War, Presidents Franklin Roosevelt, Harry Truman, and Dwight Eisenhower elevated and intensified civil religion rhetoric to rally Americans to combat the threats of economic collapse, Nazism, and Communism. Concurrently, business interests, from the Texas oil patch to the Wall Street boardroom, enlisted conservative activists such as Abraham Vereide and clergy such as Billy Graham to help in the fight against the New Deal. In this regard, Eisenhower became the ideal champion of conservative, middle-of-road, and internationalist Republicans to lead a crusade against threats to free enterprise at home and godless Communism abroad. (See, for example, Darren Dochuk, *Anointed with Oil: How Christianity and Crude Made Modern America* [2019].)

While conservatives cheered him on, however, Eisenhower privately complained to his brother Milton that the Judeo-Christian tradition did not embrace the Muslim, Hindu, and Buddhist religions and others that needed to be included in the American story. America mostly embraced only believers with European origins. Eisenhower was unique in conceiving himself a civil pastor to all Americans who believed in God, and he pushed beyond his conservative business friends by envisioning a spiritual America unconstrained by color and creed. In the midfifties, Sidney Mead noted that since the nineteenth century there had developed a "religion of the democratic society and nation" that celebrated the "American Way of Life." In the mid-twentieth century, Eisenhower became one of the chief disciples of that American civil religion universally defined. Thereafter, there would be no turning back.

Of the three midcentury presidents, Eisenhower was the most exegetical, in that he not only called for a national spiritual revival but by example also repeatedly witnessed to his public faith in America's historical destiny. He believed his deep-rooted sense of duty was self-evident. His love of country could not be questioned. Furthermore, he believed he was a living apostle of America's democratic religion and the tenets of its civil faith. His commitment to God and his duty to his country were one and the same. He believed that Americans of all religious creeds could pledge the same allegiance he did.

Although his civil faith tended toward universalism, it did not embrace everyone. Eisenhower's civil religion excluded atheists, for whom he held contempt, and also conscientious objectors like his mother, Ida, who thought it blasphemous to swear oaths either to God or country. In contrast to the Nazis, however, unbelievers who professed belief in universal principles such as reason, equality, or liberty might be welcomed into the civil religion tent. But conscientious objectors who recognized no supreme authority would always stand uncomfortably beyond the pale.

Eisenhower's civil religion worked because participants were allowed to have their own religious tastes. In general, there were a few common ideals, namely, law, justice, liberty; a few icons, that is, the flag, the Constitution; some sacred texts, namely, the Declaration of Independence, the Gettysburg Address, and the Pledge of Allegiance; saints, especially George Washington and Abraham Lincoln; hymns, including the national anthem and "God Bless America"; and numerous sacred places, such as the Washington Mall, Arlington National Cemetery, Mount Rushmore, and Pearl Harbor. But the civil religion was inclusive and required no un-American beliefs—except perhaps for the suspension of history.

He may not have stated it clearly to everyone, but by moving beyond the Judeo-Christian formula, he broke through the color barrier. Now, not only could one be a Trinitarian or Unitarian, pantheist or humanist, agnostic or mystic, one could be black, brown, or white, and still participate in the celebration of the American civil religion. All that was required was a tolerance for a wide range of religious beliefs, a support of law and order (which, admittedly, became problematic for people of color, for whom the phrase became code for racial control), willingness to compromise, and a commitment to the indivisible unity of the nation.

In matters of religion, however, it is almost impossible to serve two masters. The Christian's first commandment leaves little room for compromise: "I am the Lord thy God. . . . Thou shalt have no other gods before me." Rather than trying to compartmentalize the civil religion of the state from the gospel religion of Jesus, most believers seek a reconciling compromise between church and state that often includes bringing the American flag into the church sanctuary, incorporating patriotic hymns in the church hymnal, acknowledging secular holidays, and praying for the nation, its leaders, and members of the military. For most Americans, such practice is not only harmless but also a positive good in that church and God both validate the fundamental ideals of American democracy. With the blessing of their pastor, worshipers can enjoy the larger celebration of civil religion, say, at a local football game, even if it means rubbing shoulders with those whose religious beliefs might otherwise be suspect.

Most tension is removed, of course, if one believes that God has chosen America to be the new Israel. If the American way of life, including its systems of government and free enterprise, is believed to be part of God's plan of salvation, then the problem of dual loyalty toward the God of the gospel and the God of the nation simply melts away. God's blessing includes bountiful land, patriotic citizenry, divinely inspired constitutional government, free enterprise, social mobility, and a vibrant pluralistic culture. In addition, the idea that God has covenanted with America is often coupled with the belief that it is America's special destiny to convey the benefits of democracy and free enterprise to the world.

Since the Cold War, there has been frequent talk of American exceptionalism among Christian leaders and their political friends. Historically, the Puritans' "city upon a hill," the saga of 1776, nineteenth-century Manifest Destiny, Woodrow Wilson's war to make the world safe for democracy, and Eisenhower's crusade in Europe to save the free world from despotism all contributed to the myth that God endowed America with a mission to transform the world both by example and by deeds. Some Christians have even gone so far as to believe that the United States is the forerunner of Christ's millennial kingdom on earth. Because Christians believe that God is Lord of history, exceptionalism also implies that America is exempt from historical consequences that have brought down other great empires. Many have embraced Lincoln's prophecy that America has become "the last, best hope" for humanity.

Idolatry

Dwight Eisenhower's civil religion would not include Christian nationalism. Nevertheless, civil religion based on Judeo-Christian tradition did promote a significant unintended consequence. According to Kevin Kruse in *One Nation under God*, as long as Americans clung to the Judeo-Christian myth, America's prophetic voice was muzzled. Ironically, the ascendancy of the Judeo-Christian myth, for a season, constrained mainline churches and synagogues from questioning the rise of state power. "After Eisenhower," Kruse observed, "religion would no longer be used to tear down the central state but instead to prop it up. Piety and patriotism became one and the same, love of God and love of country conflated to the core."

When civil religion becomes conflated with theistic religion, neither escapes corruption, which is an insight often attributed to Roger Williams. A looming danger is that religious zealots may impose their idiosyncratic virtues on the whole society, thereby robbing citizens of their political rights and freedom of religion, among others. In America, however, as Roger Williams noted in the seventeenth century, this phenomenon is likely to be especially damaging for the Christian church. According to Williams, "The unknowing zeal of Constantine and other (Christian) emperors did more hurt to Christ Jesus, His crown and Kingdom, than the raging fury of the most bloody Neros.... When Christians first began to be choked, it was not ... in cold prisons, but in down-beds of ease."

For Williams, a church that is in partnership with the state loses its way by following the state in matters central to the church's identity, such as membership, pastoral care, and proclamation of the Word. Regarding proclamation of the gospel, the church should be autonomous, answerable only to God. Relating to matters of law, the church should not only be a good citizen along with other members of society but should also raise its prophetic voice regarding justice for the poor, the hungry, and the outcast.

Instead, idolatry is the great pit into which the church and state can fall. Eisenhower was not entirely insensitive to the threat of idolatry. He had witnessed political idolatry in Nazi Germany and, after a fashion, had warned against it in his "Military-Industrial Complex" speech. But he never envisioned that the Declaration of Independence or the Constitution could become problematic idols.

Should the relationship between Christian faith and the state religion become inverted, however, the nation may replace the church as the object of the believer's ultimate concern—that is, the nation becomes the new Israel with which God has made his covenant. The dominion of national ideology supersedes Christian discipleship as the objective of evangelism. National security and justice undermine forgiveness and charity as the principal religious commitments. By becoming the handmaiden of the state, the church is required to bless democratic governance while whitewashing national history. It offers thanks to God for enlightened leadership—or simply remains a silent, passive partner while the state proclaims its holy mission to carry democracy and free enterprise to the four corners of the world.

Even while Eisenhower was president, it would have taken supreme courage to argue that the church serves best from the margins of society rather than from the seats of power. Inevitably, once the priests and pastors pander to political influence, they lose their prophetic voices. Eisenhower understood this political/cultural phenomenon—it had happened in Germany in the 1920s and '30s. Under the pressure of extreme nationalism and economic hardship, it might happen in the United States. The middle of the road, both politically and religiously, was the only safe pathway for modern, mature industrial democracies.

The Place of Meditation

Dwight D. Eisenhower is the only American president buried in his own chapel. The Place of Meditation, adjacent to his boyhood home, is a grave site designed to symbolize the distinctive, almost singular, nature of Eisenhower's religious beliefs. The chapel on the grounds of the Eisenhower Presidential Library and Museum, owned by the federal government, not the Presbyterian church, is intended to reflect Eisenhower's mature faith. Outwardly nondenominational and nonsectarian as planned, this typical prairie chapel is deliberately lacking symbols of any church, synagogue, or other place of religious worship.

The spire of the chapel, almost as high as the steeple of the Roman Catholic church across the street, points unadorned into the Kansas sky. The vibrant chipped-glass windows suggesting the Kansas sky in early morning or evening are carefully designed so as not to suggest any religious affiliation or to give religious offense. Inside, the inspirational inscriptions from Eisenhower's speeches that curve gracefully around the burial crypt offer no references to biblical texts. Visitors will search in vain for references to ubiquitous civil religious mottoes: In God We Trust, One Nation under God, God Bless America. Instead, the quotations are taken from the Guildhall Address of June 1945, his "Chance for Peace" speech of April 1953, and his Abilene homecoming talk of June 1952, when he declared his candidacy for president. The latter again summarizes the core of Eisenhower's civil faith:

> The real fire within the builders of America was faith—faith in a Provident God whose hand supported and guided them; faith in themselves as the children of God . . . faith in their country and its principles that proclaimed man's right to freedom and justice.

In addition to the burial site for Eisenhower, Mamie, and Icky, the Place of Meditation is a country chapel dedicated to prayer, not to worship. Although Eisenhower had said that the American way of life is grounded in America's Judeo-Christian tradition, Eisenhower's faith was broader than that. As he told his brother Milton, in addition to Protestants, Catholics, and Jews, America's civil faith must also embrace Muslims, Hindus, Buddhists, and adherents of all religions in America that profess belief in a beneficent God. It was his intention that all faiths would feel welcome and comfortable praying in his Place of Meditation, perhaps offering prayers of thanksgiving for America and its blessings.

Like Lincoln, after death Eisenhower lost control of his historical legacy. Although he consulted closely with the architect and actually worked with the designer of the stained-glass window, as far as we know, Eisenhower left behind no written directive concerning the decorative appointments within the Place of Meditation. His son John recalled that "Dad did not want any religious symbols" that would detract from the ecumenical nature of his house of prayer. Nonetheless, sometime in the twenty-first century (records are not yet clear exactly when), a Protestant cross was set in the heart of the sanctuary to "affirm historically" that Eisenhower was a Christian. Does the Christian cross appropriately celebrate Eisenhower's memory at the Place of Meditation? Among some who knew him best, the spirit of Eisenhower's civil religion had been violated. The cross not only transforms Eisenhower's Place of Meditation into a Christian shrine but also inserts political passions into the simplicity of Eisenhower's final resting place.

There is no debate that Eisenhower became a good churchman once he joined Elson's congregation and gave his name and resources to projects of the National Presbyterian Church. But he did not conflate his Christian faith with his civil religion; that is, he did not believe that his membership in a church of the Prince of Peace conflicted with his fulfilling his civil religious duties as a citizen and soldier of the United States. Other denominations might have taken a stand antithetical to his duties to God and country. In that regard, he had been careful in his choice of churches, and the Presbyterians did not disappoint, nor would they insist that he raise a cross above his grave. Among American institutions, there can be no doubt that Eisenhower's ultimate concern was directed toward God and country—the United States and the US Army.

Finally, in this epilogue concerning American civil religion, church, state, and the Place of Meditation, let Eisenhower have the final word with his most famous religious statement. Was he authentic? Was he perfectly clear in what he believed? If so, then answer for yourself what he meant when he declared:

> Our form of government has no sense unless it is founded in a deeply felt religious faith; and I don't care what it is.

Bibliographical Note

The Eisenhower bibliography is voluminous. It is not the purpose of this bibliographical note to list all the important or thoughtful contributions to Eisenhower scholarship. These notes are generally limited to those primary and secondary sources that the author found pertinent to his study of Eisenhower's religious journey. All serious histories of Dwight D. Eisenhower begin and end at the Dwight D. Eisenhower Presidential Library and Museum (DDEL) in Abilene, Kansas. The DDEL maintains an up-to-date bibliography of books, dissertations, and theses about Eisenhower. In addition, the library has prepared the invaluable "Eisenhower and Religion" category in the *Guide to Historical Holdings in the Dwight D. Eisenhower Library*, compiled by Herbert Pankratz in July 2001.

For scholars and researchers who may wish to consult my footnotes supporting this study, a draft manuscript of the original version submitted to the William B. Eerdmans Publishing Company can be consulted at the DDEL.

Eisenhower's printed sources are extensive. Most important are *The Papers of Dwight David Eisenhower*, published in twenty-one volumes by the Johns Hopkins University Press (1970–2001) and edited by Alfred D. Chandler Jr., Louis Galambos, and Daun van Ee. See also, *Public Papers of the Presidents of the United States: Dwight D. Eisenhower, 1953–1960*, 21 vols. (Washington, DC: US Government Printing Office, 1970–2001). Eisenhower's diaries are published in two editions: Robert H. Ferrell, ed., *The Eisenhower Diaries* (New York: Norton, 1981), and Daniel D. Holt and James W. Leyerzapf, eds., *Eisenhower: The Prewar Diaries and Selected Papers, 1905–1941* (Baltimore: Johns Hopkins University Press, 1998). Collections of Eisenhower's correspondence are found in John S. D. Eisenhower, ed., *Letters to Mamie by Dwight D. Eisenhower* (Garden City, NY: Doubleday, 1978), and Robert Griffith, *Ike's Letters to a Friend [Swede Hazlett], 1941–1958* (Lawrence: University Press of Kansas, 1984).

Eisenhower's publications include: *Crusade in Europe* (New York: Doubleday, 1948); *The White House Years: Mandate for Change, 1953–1956* (New York: Doubleday, 1963); *The White House Years: Waging Peace, 1956–1961* (New York: Doubleday, 1965).

See also: Dwight D. Eisenhower, "What Jesus Means to Me" (handwritten draft, May 10, 1965, DDEL).

Eisenhower and his family have written insightful memoirs and family histories. Dwight D. Eisenhower, *At Ease: Stories I Tell to Friends* (Blue Ridge Summit, PA: TAB Books, 1967), is both discerning and enjoyable. John S. D. Eisenhower, *Mabuhay: The Coming of Age in the Philippines* (Washington, DC: Ferrous Books, 2012), is an invaluable memoir of the Eisenhower family in the Philippines. See also John S. D. Eisenhower, *Strictly Personal: A Memoir* (Garden City, NY: Doubleday, 1974), and *General Ike: A Personal Reminiscence* (New York: Free Press, 2003). David Eisenhower's *Eisenhower at War, 1943–1945* (New York: Wings Books, 1986) covers a lot more than World War II. Two memoirs by Eisenhower's grandchildren are superbly insightful but warm: David Eisenhower with Julie Nixon Eisenhower, *Going Home to Glory: A Memoir of Life with Dwight David Eisenhower, 1961–1969* (New York: Simon & Schuster, 2010), and Susan Eisenhower, *Mrs. Ike: Memories and Reflections on the Life of Mamie Eisenhower* (New York: Farrar, Straus & Giroux, 1996). Kaye Eisenhower Morgan, *The Eisenhower Legacy: A Tribute to Ida Stover and David Jacob Eisenhower* (Mesa, AZ: Roesler Enterprises Publishing, 2005), and Milton Eisenhower, *The President Is Calling: A Veteran Advisor for the Presidency Suggests Far-Reaching Changes* (Garden City, NY: Doubleday, 1974), share private moments with the president.

Of the numerous Eisenhower biographies, I am listing only those I believe most pertinent for this book: Kenneth S. Davis, *Dwight D. Eisenhower: Soldier of Democracy* (New York: Smithmark, 1945); Herbert Parmet, *Eisenhower and the American Crusades* (New York: Macmillan, 1972); Robert F. Burk, *Dwight D. Eisenhower: Hero and Politician* (Boston: Twayne, 1986); Piers Brendon, *Ike: His Life and Times* (New York: Harper & Row, 1986); Stephen E. Ambrose, *Eisenhower: Soldier and President* (New York: Simon & Schuster, 1990); Chester J. Pach Jr. and Elmo Richardson, *The Presidency of Dwight D. Eisenhower* (Lawrence: University Press of Kansas, 1991); Stephen E. Ambrose, *The Victors: Eisenhower and His Boys; The Men of World War II* (New York: Simon & Schuster, 1998); Geoffrey Perret, *Eisenhower* (New York: Random House,

1999); Carlo D'Este, *Eisenhower: A Soldier's Life* (New York: Holt, 2002); Michael Korda, *Ike: American Hero* (New York: HarperCollins, 2007); Jean Edward Smith, *Eisenhower in War and Peace* (New York: Random House, 2012); Paul Johnson, *Eisenhower: A Life* (New York: Viking, 2014); Louis Galambos, *Eisenhower: Becoming the Leader of the Free World* (Baltimore: Johns Hopkins University Press, 2018); William I. Hitchcock, *The Age of Eisenhower: America and the World in the 1950s* (New York: Simon & Schuster, 2018).

Among monographs and special studies of Eisenhower and his presidency, the most helpful for the book were Harry C. Butcher, *My Three Years with Eisenhower, 1942–1945* (New York: Simon & Schuster, 1946); Kevin McCann, *Man from Abilene: Dwight David Eisenhower; A Story of Leadership* (Garden City, NY: Doubleday, 1952); Steve Neal, *The Eisenhowers* (Lawrence: University Press of Kansas, 1978); Fred I. Greenstein, *The Hidden-Hand Presidency: Eisenhower as a Leader* (New York: Basic Books, 1982); Richard G. Hewlett and Jack M. Holl, *Atoms for Peace and War: Eisenhower and the Atomic Energy Commission, 1953–1961* (Berkeley: University of California Press, 1989); Michael Birkner, ed., featuring Fred Greenstein, "Eisenhower as President: Finding and Defining the 'Hidden Hand'"; George C. Herring, "'In the Lands of the Blind': Eisenhower and Intervention in the Third World"; and Stephen E. Ambrose, "Eisenhower's Legacy," all in *Eisenhower and the Art of Leadership* (Gettysburg, PA: Gettysburg College, 1990); Herbert Brownell with John P. Burke, *Advising Ike: The Memoirs of Attorney General Herbert Brownell* (Lawrence: University Press of Kansas, 1993); Martin J. Medhurst, ed., *Eisenhower's War of Words: Rhetoric and Leadership* (East Lansing: Michigan State University Press, 1994); Clarence G. Lasby, *Eisenhower's Heart Attack: How Ike Beat Heart Disease and Held on to the Presidency* (Lawrence: University Press of Kansas, 1997); Robert R. Bowie and Richard Immerman, *Waging Peace: How Eisenhower Shaped an Enduring Cold War Strategy* (New York: Oxford University Press, 1998); James David Barber, "Eisenhower as a 'Passive-Negative' President," in *The Eisenhower Presidency and the 1950s*, ed. Michael S. Mayer (Boston: Houghton Mifflin, 1998); Erwin C. Hargrove, *The President as Leader: Appealing to the Better Angels of Our Nature* (Lawrence: University Press of Kansas, 1998); William B. Picket, *Eisenhower Decides to Run: Presidential Politics and Cold War Strategy* (Chicago: Ivan R. Dee, 2000); Travis Beal Jacobs, *Eisenhower at Columbia* (New Brunswick, NJ: Transaction Publishers, 2001); Ira Chernus, *General Eisenhower: Ideology and Discourse* (East Lansing: Michigan State University Press, 2002); Travis Beal Jacobs, *Dwight D. Eisenhower and the Founding of the American Assembly* (New York: American Assembly, 2004); David A. Nichols, *A Matter of Justice: Eisenhower and the Beginnings of the Civil Rights Revolution* (New York: Simon & Schuster, 2007); James Ledbetter, *Unwarranted Influence: Dwight D. Eisenhower and the Military Industrial Complex* (New Haven: Yale University Press, 2011); Evan Thomas, *Ike's Bluff: President Eisenhower's Secret Battle to Save the World* (New York: Little, Brown, 2012); Jack M. Holl, "The Second Battle of Gettysburg: Eisenhower's Fight with the 1918 Flu Pandemic," History News Network, May 3, 2020; William B. Pickett, "Ike and Kay in the Second World War" (White Bear Lake, MN, unpublished manuscript, March 20, 2021).

There has been limited scholarship concerning Eisenhower's religion. There is a myth, however, that Ike's religious faith has been ignored by scholars. That is not true. See Gladys Dodd, "The Religious Background of the Eisenhower Family" (bachelor of divinity thesis, Nazarene Theological Seminary, 1959, DDEL); Stephen E. Wirt, "Interview of Dwight D. Eisenhower at Indio, CA" (March 1965, DDEL); Stephen E. Wirt, "The Religion of Dwight D. Eisenhower," 2 parts, *Decision*, 1965; Merlin Gustafson, "The Religion of a President," *Christian Century*, April 30, 1969; Richard V. Pierard and Robert D. Linder, "Dwight D. Eisenhower and the Intensification of Civil Religion," in *Civil Religion & the Presidency* (Grand Rapids: Academie Books, 1988); Jerry Bergman, "Steeped in Religion: President Eisenhower and the Influence of the Jehovah's Witnesses," *Kansas History* 21, no. 3 (Autumn 1998); Jerry Bergman, "Why President Eisenhower Hid His Jehovah's Witnesses Upbringing," *JW Research Journal* 6, no. 2 (July–December 1999); Gary Scott Smith, "Dwight D. Eisenhower, Dynamic Conservatism, and the Religious Revival of the 1950s," in *Faith & the Presidency* (New York: Oxford University Press, 2006); Jack M. Holl, "Dwight D. Eisenhower: Civil Religion and the Cold War," in *Religion and the American Presidency*, ed. Mark Rozell and Gleaves Whitney (New York: Palgrave Macmillan, 2007); Jack M. Holl, "Dwight D. Eisenhower: Religion, Politics and the Evils of Communism," in *The Problem of Evil: Slavery, Freedom, and the Ambiguities of American Reform*, ed. Steven Mintz and John Stauffer (Amherst: University of Massachusetts Press, 2007); David Holmes, "Dwight D. Eisenhower," in *The Faiths of the Postwar Presidents* (Athens: University of Georgia Press, 2012); Nancy Gibbs and Michael Duffy, *The Preacher and the Presidents: Billy Graham in the White House* (New York: Center Street, 2007), chapters 4, 5, and 7; Jerry Bergman, "Religion and the Presidency of Dwight D. Eisenhower," in *Religion and the American Presidency*, ed. Gastón

Espinosa (New York: Columbia University Press, 2009), and Bergman, *God in Eisenhower's Life, Military Career and Presidency* (Eugene, OR: Wipf & Stock, 2019). For a presentation and analysis of Eisenhower's religious faith from a different perspective, see Alan Sears and Craig Osten with Ryan Cole, *The Soul of an American President: The Untold Story of Dwight D. Eisenhower's Faith* (Grand Rapids: Baker Books, 2019).

In addition to Pierard and Linder's book *Civil Religion and the Presidency*, noted above, the following are useful in understanding America's religious revival and civil religion in the 1950s: Will Herberg, *Protestant-Catholic-Jew: An Essay in American Religious Sociology* (New York: Doubleday, 1955); Ernest W. Lefever, "The Protestant Nonpolitical Approach to Politics," *Christian Scholar* 38, no. 2 (1955); Ernest W. Lefever, "The Candidate's Religious Views," *Christian Century*, September 19, 1956; Martin E. Marty, *The New Shape of American Religion* (New York: Harper Brothers, 1958); William H. Lazareth, "A Theology of Politics," Board of Social Missions of the United Lutheran Church in America, October 1, 1960; William Lee Miller, *Piety along the Potomac* (Boston: Houghton Mifflin, 1964); Robert N. Bellah, "Civil Religion in America," *Daedalus* 96 (Winter 1967); Russel E. Richey and Donald G. Jones, eds., *American Civil Religion* (New York: Harper & Row, 1974); Robert N. Bellah, *The Broken Covenant: American Civil Religion in Time of Trial* (Chicago: University of Chicago Press, 1975); Martin E. Marty, *A Nation of Behavers* (Chicago: University of Chicago Press, 1976); John F. Wilson, *Public Religion in American Culture* (Philadelphia: Temple University Press, 1979); Garry Wills, *Under God: Religion and American Politics* (New York: Simon & Schuster, 1990); Martin E. Marty, *Modern American Religion: Under God, Indivisible*, vol. 3 (Chicago: University of Chicago Press, 1996); Robert Lowry Clinton, *God and Man in the Law* (Lawrence: University Press of Kansas, 1997); Keith Bates, "Edward L. R. Elson: 'Spiritual Helper' to Dwight D. Eisenhower" (Seminar on the Eisenhower Era, DDEL, May 2001); Alan Bearman, "Religion as a Tool of Psychological Warfare in the Fight against Communism during the 1950s: The Case of Billy Graham" (Seminar on the Eisenhower Era, DDEL, May 2001); Jon Meacham, *American Gospel: God, the Founding Fathers, and the Making of a Nation* (New York: Random House, 2006); Kevin M. Schultz, *Tri-Faith America: How Catholics and Jews Held Postwar America to Its Protestant Promise* (New York: Oxford University Press, 2011); Philip E. Muehlenbeck, ed., *Religion and the Cold War* (Nashville: Vanderbilt University Press, 2012); Peter Gardella, *American Civil Religion: What Americans Hold Sacred* (New

York: Oxford University Press, 2014); Kevin M. Kruse, *One Nation under God: How Corporate America Invented Christian America* (New York: Basic Books, 2015); Philip Gorski, *American Covenant: A History of Civil Religion from the Puritans to the Present* (Princeton: Princeton University Press, 2017); Ronit Y. Stahl, *Enlisting Faith* (Cambridge, MA: Harvard University Press, 2017); Darren Dochuk, *Anointed with Oil: How Christianity and Crude Oil Made Modern America* (New York: Basic Books, 2019).

In addition to Roger M. Anders, "Essay on Sources," in Hewlett and Holl, *Atoms for Peace and War* (1989), for a superb and exhaustive bibliography see Brian Madison Jones, *Abolishing the Taboo: Dwight D. Eisenhower and American Nuclear Doctrine, 1945–1961* (Solihull, UK: Helion, 2011). For additional referenced books and sources related to peaceful uses of atomic energy, nuclear weapon development and testing, and international arms control and disarmament, see Michael Howard and Peger Paret, eds. and trans., *Carl von Clausewitz on War* (Princeton: Princeton University Press, 1976); Robert A. Devine, *Blowing on the Wind: The Nuclear Test Ban Debate, 1954–1960* (New York: Oxford University Press, 1978); Lawrence Freedman, *The Evolution of Nuclear Strategy* (New York: St. Martin's, 1983); Fred Kaplan, *The Wizards of Armageddon* (New York: Simon & Schuster, 1983); Robert C. Williams and Philip Cantelon, eds., *The American Atom: A Documentary History of Nuclear Policies from the Discovery of Fission to the Present* (Philadelphia: University of Pennsylvania Press, 1984); A. Constandina Titus, *Bombs in the Backyard: Atomic Testing and American Politics* (Reno: University of Nevada Press, 1986); Gar Alperovitz, *Atomic Diplomacy: Hiroshima and Potsdam; The Use of the Atomic Bomb and American Confrontation with Soviet Power* (London: Pluto, 1994); Herbert Frank York, *Making Weapons, Talking Peace: A Physicist's Odyssey from Hiroshima to Geneva* (New York: Basic Books, 1988); Jack M. Holl and Scott Miller, "Ike and the Bomb: Foundation of Eisenhower's Nuclear Diplomacy" (Eisenhower Centennial Symposium, Gettysburg College, October 1990); Barry H. Steiner, *Bernard Brodie and the Foundations of American Nuclear Strategy* (Lawrence: University Press of Kansas, 1991); Walter LaFeber, *America, Russia, and the Cold War* (New York: McGraw-Hill, 1997); Ira Chernus, *Eisenhower's Atoms for Peace* (College Station: Texas A&M University Press, 2002); Charles J. G. Griffin, "Imaging Peace: Rhetorical Antecedents of 'Atoms for Peace' in Dwight D. Eisenhower's Epideictic Speaking" (Kansas State University, October 2003); Ian Kershaw, *To Hell and Back: Europe 1914–1949* (New York: Viking, 2015).

Other referenced books and important studies include Carl Becker, *The Heavenly City of the Eighteenth-Century Philosophers* (New Haven: Yale University Press, 1932); Paul Tillich, *The Protestant Era* (Chicago: University of Chicago Press, 1948); Paul Tillich, *Theology of Culture* (New York: Oxford University Press, 1959); Charles W. Kegley and Robert W. Bretall, *The Theology of Paul Tillich* (New York: Macmillan, 1961); Paul Tillich, *On the Boundary: An Autobiographical Sketch* (New York: Scribner's Sons, 1966); Billy Graham, *Just as I Am: The Autobiography of Billy Graham* (San Francisco: HarperCollins, 1997); Leonard Mosley, *Marshall: Hero for Our Times* (New York: Hearst Books, 1982), James McPherson, *Battle Cry of Freedom* (New York: Oxford University Press, 1988); Stephen J. Whitfield, *The Culture of the Cold War* (Baltimore: Johns Hopkins University Press, 1991); Thomas Branigar, "No Villains—No Heroes: The David Eisenhower–Milton Good Controversy," *Kansas History* 15, no. 3 (Autumn 1992); Martin Luther, *Whether Soldiers, Too, Can Be Saved,* as cited in David J. Lose, "The Ambidextrous God: Luther on Faith and Politics," *Word and World* 19, no. 3 (1999); Glenn Leppert, "Dwight D. Eisenhower and People to People" (PhD diss., Kansas State University, 2003); William Inboden, *Religion and American Foreign Policy* (Cambridge: Cambridge University Press, 2008), Leif Urseth, "Walter Bedell Smith" (PhD diss., Kansas State University, 2010); Martin Marty, *Dietrich Bonhoeffer's "Letters and Papers from Prison"* (Princeton: Princeton University Press, 2011); Edward Cox, *Grey Eminence: Fox Conner and the Art of Mentorship* (Stillwater, OK: New Forums, 2011); Geoffrey Kabaservice, *Rule and Ruin: The Downfall of Moderation and the Destruction of the Republican Party, from Eisenhower to the Tea Party* (New York: Oxford University Press, 2012); Andrew Preston, *Sword of the Spirit, Shield of Faith: Religion in American War and Diplomacy* (New York: Anchor Books, 2012); Malcolm Gladwell, *David and Goliath: Underdogs, Misfits, and the Art of Battling Giants* (New York: Little, Brown, 2013); Freeman Dyson, "How to Be an Underdog and Win," *New York Review of Books,* November 21, 2013.

Sources

Chart of the Ages, on p. 26 above, is from Charles Taze Russell, *Millennial Dawn*, vol. 1, *The Plan of the Ages* (Allegheny, PA: Tower Publishing, 1886).

Credo of the American Way of Life, on p. 186 above, is from the Cornell University Collection of Political Americana, Cornell University Library.

Index

separation of church and state,
15–16, 188, 199–201, 298, 315; and
symbolism in DE's inauguration,
7–8
civil righteousness, 97, 98
civil rights: *Brown* decision, 224–28;
DE's meetings with black civil rights
leaders, 242–46; DE's moderate
approach to, 228–29, 251; DE's reli-
gious approach to, 229–31, 246; DE's
strategic approach to, 247, 249–50;
legislation, 232–34, 248–49; Little
Rock crisis, 234–41
Civil Rights Act (1957), 233–34
Civil Rights Act (1960), 234, 248–49
Civil Rights Act (1964), 234
Civil Rights Commission, 232, 249
Clark, Mark, 118, 120, 125, 126
Clausewitz, Carl von, *On War*, 84,
258–59, 261, 262
Clay, Lucius, 173
Clough, Arthur, 281
Cochran, Jacqueline, 175
Cold War. *See* Communism and Cold
War
Collins, J. Lawton, 261
Columbia University, 151, 154, 163–64
Command and General Staff School,
85, 86–87
Common Faith, A (Dewey), 311
Communism and Cold War: DE's
peace rhetoric during, 255, 275–80;
and international cooperation,
158–59, 162; and preventive war,
157–58; religion as weapon against,
202, 207; and Stalin's death, 273–74;
as struggle of divine and demonic
forces, 10–11, 14, 149, 200, 201, 274,
277, 290; and Suez crisis, 222–24; as

threat to freedom and religion, 162,
190, 197, 199. *See also* atomic war
Communist Manifesto (Marx), 154
concentration camps, 143–44
confirmation, religious, 11–13, 312–13
Connor, Fox, 78, 82–86, 89, 262
Courage to Be, The (Tillich), 196
Crusade in Europe (DE), 89, 113, 115,
134, 151, 256, 294

Darlan, Jean-François, 247
Davis, Bob, 46–47, 59
Davis, Elmer, 187
Davis, Kenneth, 4, 28, 35–36, 40–41,
56–57, 63, 88–89
D-Day, 136, 138–40, 299
death, fear of, 193–95
Debs, Eugene V., 74
Democratic Party: and civil rights,
232–34, 235, 245; DE's support for
as youth, 50–51, 99, 180; and nuclear
diplomacy, 286
desegregation. *See* civil rights
D'Este, Carlo, 58, 66, 131
Dewey, John, *A Common Faith*, 311
Dewey, Thomas E., 166, 173
Dibelius, Otto, 203
dignity of man, 48, 68, 135, 153, 155, 156,
176, 188, 196, 214–15
Dirkson, Everett, 208
disarmament, 163, 263–64, 266–67,
287
discrimination. *See* civil rights
divine/demonic tension: Communism and Cold War, 10–11, 14, 149,
200, 201, 274, 277, 290; Hitler and
World War II, 113–14, 145–46, 160
Dockerty, George MacPherson,
197–98

Titles published in the

LIBRARY OF RELIGIOUS BIOGRAPHY SERIES

*Sworn on the Altar of God: A Religious Biography of **Thomas Jefferson***
by Edwin S. Gaustad

*The Miracle Lady: **Katherine Kuhlman** and the Transformation of Charismatic Christianity* by Amy Collier Artman

Abraham Kuyper: *Modern Calvinist, Christian Democrat*
by James D. Bratt

*The Religious Life of **Robert E. Lee***
by R. David Cox

Abraham Lincoln: *Redeemer President*
by Allen C. Guelzo

Charles Lindbergh: *A Religious Biography of America's Most Infamous Pilot*
by Christopher Gehrz

*The First American Evangelical: A Short Life of **Cotton Mather***
by Rick Kennedy

Aimee Semple McPherson: *Everybody's Sister*
by Edith L. Blumhofer

*Mother of Modern Evangelicalism: The Life and Legacy of **Henrietta Mears***
by Arlin Migliazzo

*Damning Words: The Life and Religious Times of **H. L. Mencken***
by D. G. Hart

Thomas Merton *and the Monastic Vision*
by Lawrence S. Cunningham

*God's Strange Work: **William Miller** and the End of the World*
by David L. Rowe

Blaise Pascal: *Reasons of the Heart*
by Marvin R. O'Connell

*Occupy Until I Come: **A. T. Pierson** and the Evangelization of the World*
by Dana L. Robert

*The Kingdom Is Always but Coming: A Life of **Walter Rauschenbusch***
by Christopher H. Evans

*A Christian and a Democrat: A Religious Life of **Franklin D. Roosevelt***
by John F. Woolverton with James D. Bratt

Francis Schaeffer and the Shaping of Evangelical America
by Barry Hankins

Harriet Beecher Stowe: A Spiritual Life
by Nancy Koester

Billy Sunday and the Redemption of Urban America
by Lyle W. Dorsett

Howard Thurman and the Disinherited: A Religious Biography
by Paul Harvey

Assist Me to Proclaim: The Life and Hymns of Charles Wesley
by John R. Tyson

Prophetess of Health: A Study of Ellen G. White
by Ronald L. Numbers

George Whitefield: Evangelist for God and Empire
by Peter Y. Choi

The Divine Dramatist: George Whitefield and the Rise of Modern Evangelicalism
by Harry S. Stout

Liberty of Conscience: Roger Williams in America
by Edwin S. Gaustad